Crusoe

Crusoe

Crusoe

*Daniel Defoe, Robert Knox
and the Creation of a Myth*

KATHERINE FRANK

PEGASUS BOOKS
NEW YORK

CRUSOE

Pegasus Books LLC
80 Broad Street, 5th Floor
New York, NY 10004

Library of Congress Cataloging-in-Publication Data is available.

ISBN: 978-1-60598-334-9

10 9 8 7 6 5 4 3 2 1

Printed in the United States of America
Distributed by W. W. Norton & Company, Inc.
www.pegasusbooks.us

For Paul

These Remains are like fragments of a shipwreck that after the Revolution of so many Years ... have escaped the Teeth of Time ... so that the retrieving of these forgotten Things from Oblivion in some sort resembles the Art of the Conjurer, who makes those walke and appeare that haven layen in their graves many hundreds of yeares; and to represent as it were to the eie, the places, Customs and Fashions, that were of old Times.

John Aubrey

Contents

A NEW MAP
of the Kingdom of
CANDY UDA.
in the Island of
CEYLON.

North

Trinkimale

COTIARUM
REGNUM.
Cotiarum

TAMM

COYLOT
Meelos wilipatte

NOURE CALAVA.

WANE ES

CONTREY

Sette
coulang

MAUGOL
COURLY

Futelan
Palari

Manaur

Calpentyn

London Printed for Richard Chiswell at ye Rose & Crown in St Pauls Ch

Note, all the Land inclosed in the large pricked line,
is under ye Iurisdiction of the King of Candy Uda.
All without that Line except Coyles Wanea's Country,
mentioned in this Mapp in which the Malabars live,
belong to the Dutch.

● Places where the Watches are kept.
˙ ˙ ˙ ˙ The way of the Authors escape.

PAN OU LA
REGNUM.

LEAWAVA

Batticalow

Niloga

Vellas

Togamo

JAELE

Fali
Magomoni

Paleteopane

PAUNOA

Bondele
Chalancolo
Malcione
Blackhas

PROVIN:

CIA.

Elow
Bannos

Groote
Bassos

Mago

Nelane

VELLAS.

Yotta
kinde

Maunda
kinde

Pettepal
Candrel

Gerremony
of

MATU:

Elephants

RA:

Ettal goa
Henn

Catana

Kardelues
bay

vangh plaets

Gabetta

Dondere

UAD

BINTANA.

OUVAH.

Dombghery

Oude
kinde

Paregom
patt

HABARAGOM

Barlopouratotun

Denmorum

Dollet das
Corla.

Matura

TENEWARA

Tenewara

Massrant
WALLAPOLA
GODDAPE

AMOS
Carrerpatto
MANY

ITALY.

DOM
REAM.

HEVOI
HATTAY

Monteralla

Candy Dego new

COTE:
MUL.

Grind

PRIN: COMITAT.

Agroa

Lackwell

Noure

Billigamme
Corla

Georgamme

Rockwelle

HORSEPOT

YATTANOUR.

TUNTON
ABOUT

EUDANWA.

Merke

Adams
patt

GALE
CIPAT.
COMIJATS.

Walalwittt
Corla

Point de
Galle

OUDA POLLOT.

DOANSADO

Polando
Jeparatetto

Prangal

Nobbe Corla

Handa
Pondoun

HOTTERA COURLE.

Cota

Raygam
Corla

Pragel
Pachon

Udowo
Corla

Paygat

Billgol Courle

TUNCOURLY

Pittigal
Corle

QUATRE
CORLA
Sapita
Corle

Negombo

Madampe

Colombo

English and French miles

Spanish miles

Dutch miles

South

N
W E
S

MONGOLIA

HOKKAIDO

Peking
Tientsin
CHINA
JAPAN
HONSHU
Tokyo
KOREA
Yellow River
Ōsaka
TIBET
Fukuoka
Hirado
Nagasaki
PACIFIC
OCEAN
Yangtze Kiang
KYUSHU
R. Brahmaputra
Lhasa
Delhi
Agra
Lucknow
R. Ganges
Pearl River
Canton
Okinawa
Tropic of Cancer
Benares BENGAL
GHAL EMPIRE
Calcutta
Mandalay
Hong Kong
FORMOSA
Surat
BURMA
R. Mekong
TONKIN
Hainan
Marianas
Islands
bay
Bay of
Bengal
Rangoon
ANNAN
Goa
Masulipatnam
SIAM
Ayuthia
Manila
LUZON
PHILIPPINE
ISLANDS
odive
nds
Calicut
Cochin
Madras
Pondicherry
Mergui
South
China
Sea
Pelew
Islands
CEYLON
Nicobar
Islands
Aceh
Balambangan
MINDANAO
Maldive
Islands
Coromandel
Coast
Malacca
Singapore
BORNEO
Molucca Is.
CELEBES
Ambon
Equator
NEW
GUINEA
Chagos
Islands
SUMATRA
Benkulen
Bantam
Krakatoa
Batavia
JAVA
Makassar
EAST INDIES
TIMOR

Cocos
Islands

INDIAN OCEAN

NEW HOLLAND

Tropic of Capricorn

To assist the reader in the approximate
measurement of distance each border
segment equals two hundred & fifty miles.

CHAPTER ONE

Two Writing Men

London, 1719

He sees a lone man on a beach.

January 1719. A chill, late-winter afternoon, dark closing in. A man sits at a table, writing, in a solid, red-brick house on Church Street, Stoke Newington, three miles north of the City of London.

Unlike the man on the shore, Daniel Defoe is far from alone. His wife Mary is somewhere about the house. Also three adult, unmarried daughters, Hannah, Henrietta and Sophia. Defoe's life, in fact, is crowded with people: one more grown daughter (married and settled), and two grown sons, both cause for heartache. And beyond his family, booksellers and printers waiting for copy, journalist and political enemies, business contacts, informers, merchants and creditors. Deadlines, bills, legal threats.

But for the moment, Defoe is by himself in his book-lined library in his substantial, three-storey Stoke Newington house, with stables and four acres of grounds, an orchard and gardens. A man now in his fifty-ninth or sixtieth year.[1] By eighteenth-century standards, Defoe is on the brink of old age. He has survived 'a violent fit of apoplexy' and is plagued by gout and 'the stone'. He describes himself as bowed down by 'hints of mortality' and 'the infirmities of a life of sorrow and fatigue'.[2]

But sitting at his table in Stoke Newington, Defoe's bare, wigless head is full of a much younger man on a barren shore, vomiting salt water, running about as though crazed, wringing his hands and beating his chest.

The younger man, of course, is Robinson Crusoe. The surname filched from a long-dead school friend named Timothy Cruso* who

* Spelled without an 'e' but spelling was not standardised in the seventeenth and eighteenth centuries, and Defoe's spelling, even of his own name, varied over time.

grew up to be a Presbyterian minister, famous for his piety and published sermons.

Crusoe, the young man on the shore, stares out at a listing ship, stranded on rocks that rear like stony monsters out of the sea. Behind the shipwreck, the burning globe of the sun slowly sinks down below the horizon.

Some minutes pass. Now the younger man is cradled high up in the fork of a tree near the shore. He is asleep. The sea lions have stopped howling. The tide is so far out that you can scarcely hear the waves crash on the shore.

Defoe's house in Stoke Newington

Or so it might have happened. This, conceivably, is how it all began.

What we know for certain is that in early 1719 Defoe's situation, ensconced in his prosperous-looking Stoke Newington residence with stables and orchard, is not all that it appears to be. He lives in a parish described by a contemporary as 'pleasantly situated, and full of fine Country Houses for Citizens, being about 3 or 4 miles from London'.[3] Defoe has been accused of prostituting his pen to the highest bidder in order to 'repair and beautify his habitation at Newington'.[4] But he does not, in fact, own the freehold of the house and its lands. They belong to a widow named Anne Sutton. Defoe has merely taken out a lease on the 'brick messuage, gardens, orchard etc' at a rate he cannot afford – £20 a year. He is also renting the property under an assumed name, probably to evade creditors.[5]

From the outside, it looks like a well-to-do gentleman's residence, but within the house is 'quaint and queer ... built at several different times', with dark wainscoted walls, narrow passageways and floors made of creaking, uneven boards. There is gossip that Defoe keeps ropes and ladders handy in order to make a swift exit out of a second- or third-storey window should an unwelcome visitor call. Heavy bolts and padlocks secure the doors from the inside. The surrounding gardens and grounds are enclosed by dark, menacingly named alleys: Cutthroat Lane, Hussey Lane and Pawnbroker's Lane.

Two miles south of Defoe in Stoke Newington, an even older man named Robert Knox sits in rented lodgings in the parish of St Peter le Poer writing a letter to his cousin, the Reverend John Strype, who is the vicar of Low Leyton in Essex.[6] Knox and Strype are both nearly eighty, the sole family survivors of their generation, as Knox often reminds his cousin. There has been a close bond between them since childhood. Occasionally they meet up, though not often enough for Knox, who knows that Strype, despite his advanced years, still crosses the River Lea to London most weeks to confer with his anti-quarian friends.

Unlike Strype, Knox has no wife or children. Unlike Defoe, he is well off. He could afford to own an establishment as large as Defoe's rented house in Stoke Newington. But in 1700, when Knox retired from his career as a sea captain, he chose to settle 'in a lodging Chamber' in the home of the Bartlett family in St Peter le Poer, a parish that was once, as its name indicates, impoverished, but is now filled with 'many fair Houses, possessed by rich Merchants, and others'.[7] Behind the Bartletts' house Knox has, 'with the Concent [sic] of the Landlord', 'inclosed a corner of the Court with a bricke wall to make me a small garden in the City of London & planted trees therein', which gives him 'great content'.

But it is a lonely life for the old man. 'Idle and droneish' is how Knox describes his days to 'Cosen Strype'. Knox spent much of his life sailing the world in the service of the East India Company. Now he is too infirm even to take the walks to Hackney Marsh that he used to relish. All his friends from his seafaring days and the Royal Society have died. He hasn't seen his adopted daughter for nearly forty years. Even the widows who pursued Knox when he first retired have given up or found solace elsewhere.

In their letters Knox and Strype exchange news of poor and ailing relations and describe the symptoms of their own illnesses. Knox reports on his 'violent frequent fitts of Gravell' and recurrent 'head ake, a disease', he remarks to Strype, 'incident to our family'. Knox has recently received news that Strype has suffered a stroke in the pulpit while preaching his Sunday sermon. Knox explains that he has been unable to visit Strype because of 'an itching disposition', but he promises to call on his afflicted cousin as soon as he is able to make the coach journey to Low Leyton. When Strype receives Knox's letter he neatly endorses it on the back: 'Capt Knox Notice of my sudden illness while I was at divine service. His present distemper An itching. Both our great Ages.'[8]

In their frequent letters to each other, Knox and Strype also discuss the books they are writing. Strype is labouring to complete his long-delayed, updated edition of John Stow's *Survey of London*, first published in 1598. Knox has toiled even longer on what he calls 'my Booke of Ceylon with Maniscripts [sic] of my owne Life'. For the past twenty years, since Knox retired, his 'Booke' has occupied most of his waking hours.

Knox's *An Historical Relation of the Island Ceylon* was originally published nearly forty years earlier, in 1681, by Richard Chiswell, Printer to the Royal Society, at the Rose and Crown in St Paul's Churchyard. The title page distils its extraordinary contents: 'An Historical Relation of the Island Ceylon in the East Indies: Together with an Account of the Detaining in Captivity [of] the Author and divers other Englishmen now Living there and of the Author's Miraculous Escape. By Robert Knox, a Captive there near Twenty Years.'

The story this book relates is amazing and unprecedented. In 1660, at the age of nineteen, Knox was stranded on Ceylon and taken captive by the King of Kandy. His father's ship, an East Indiaman called the *Anne*, had been badly damaged in a 'mighty storm' off the Coromandel Coast of India. Leaking badly, the ship was forced to seek refuge on Ceylon, the tear-shaped island off the south-eastern tip of India.

Captain Robert Knox (after whom his son was named) sailed into the harbour of Trincomalee on the eastern side of the island in order to repair his disabled ship. Much of Ceylon at this time was under the control of the Dutch East India Company – the great rival of the British East India Company in whose service the *Anne* sailed. But the native King of Kandy still ruled over a large territory at the heart of the island, and the Dutch had abandoned their fort at Trincomalee which now had a native governor. Captain Knox hoped that Trincomalee would provide a safe haven in which to repair the ship, and that he and his men would remain unnoticed – or at least undisturbed – by both the Dutch authorities and the natives.

But news of the arrival of the 'outlandish'* men of the *Anne* soon reached the King of Kandy, Raja Sinha II, in the interior of the island, and the King sent an armed contingent to Trincomalee to investigate. At first the King's soldiers tried to entice Captain Knox and his men inland to the King's territory. But when the 'Britishers' refused to be lured, the soldiers ensnared Captain Knox, his young son and fourteen other men from the *Anne* and forcibly took them captive. It would be twenty years before young Robert Knox saw his 'native countrey', England, again.

When Knox's *Historical Relation of Ceylon* was published in September 1681 – within a year of his miraculous escape from the island and return to England – it caused a sensation and was a best-seller. Among its many early buyers and readers was a young London wholesaler of hosiery and cloth in Freeman's Yard named Daniel Foe. Years later, in 1719, the same man – who has by now reinvented himself as Daniel De Foe, Gentleman of Stoke Newington – will still have Knox's *Historical Relation of Ceylon* on his shelves, perhaps even open on the table before him as he writes his own castaway's tale.

By this time, Knox's Ceylon book has long been out of print. But this wasn't meant to be the case, and for Robert Knox the story is not over. The book had proved so popular when first published, that Richard Chiswell planned – and promised Knox – to publish a second edition. To this end, in September 1681, when Knox had been back in England just a year and was about to go to sea again as commander of the East India Company ship, the *Tonqueen Merchant*, Chiswell provided him with a special, enlarged copy of his printed book, into

---

* 'Outlandish' at this time meant literally 'out of the land' or foreign.

which had been bound many blank folio sheets. Chiswell urged Knox during his second voyage to the East Indies to expand even further his account of his long captivity and also to make revisions and corrections to his original text.

Two years later, in 1683, when Knox arrived back in England after a voyage to India, Bantam, Batavia and Tonkin, he duly delivered to Chiswell the special copy of his book with all the inserted blank pages now crammed full with his handwriting with its elaborate upper-case letters and abundant flourishes. But Chiswell, to Knox's great disappointment, did not, as promised, rush out a second edition of the *Historical Relation of Ceylon*. Knox's disorganised mass of new material, revisions and corrections had been written haphazardly – as memories, ideas and facts came into his head – often late at night by candlelight in his ship's cabin or in a cramped, stifling room in a remote company factory* on the coast of India or Java.

The original 1681 published edition of Knox's book had been edited by his cousin John Strype and also by the scientist Robert Hooke, a leading member of the Royal Society. Now Chiswell realised how great their contribution must have been. Knox's revised and expanded manuscript was disjointed and repetitive. Hooke by this time, though still a close friend of Knox's, was preoccupied with other projects. Strype was also too busy to lend more assistance to Knox. Seventeenth-century booksellers and publishers such as Chiswell were really just printers who did little if any editorial work on the books they published and sold.

Knox, meanwhile, was due to sail again as Captain of the *Tonqueen Merchant*. On 4 April 1684, the East India Company commissioned him to make a voyage to buy slaves on Madagascar and transport them to St Helena, the remote island in the South Atlantic where the slaves were to provide labour for the island's plantations. (The irony of the erstwhile captive turning slave trader never, apparently, occurred to Knox or to his contemporaries.) On the eve of Knox's departure, Chiswell told him that his manuscript needed further work. And so when Knox embarked on his next voyage, his book and manuscript sailed with him once again.

---

* East India Company coastal trading posts, where goods were loaded and unloaded onto company ships, were called factories.

But when Knox returned from this slaving voyage in late 1685 and delivered his reworked (and inevitably further enlarged) manuscript to Chiswell, the publisher was still unhappy with it. Perhaps he realised even at this stage that the more Knox worked on his magnum opus the less publishable it became. The book-seller, however, still didn't give up on the idea of a second edition. Over the next fifteen years, he repeatedly demanded more changes. Knox made three further voyages to the East Indies, and both at sea and on land he continued to work on his 'Booke'.

But when he periodically resubmitted it, Chiswell would put him off with an excuse. Chiswell was not just dismayed by Knox's prolix, disorganised manuscript material; there were other reasons for his reluctance to republish the Ceylon book now. In the last quarter of the seventeenth century and first decades of the eighteenth, books of sea voyages and journeys of discovery began to flood the market. Works such as the best-selling *Voyages* of William Dampier, Woodes Rogers's *A Cruising Voyage Round the World* and John Esquemeling's *Buccaneers of America* had all proved enormously popular. In Chiswell's eyes these were stiff competition for Knox's book and perhaps even superseded it.

But Knox himself remained undaunted. In 1700, when he retired from seafaring and settled with the Bartletts in St Peter le Poer, he worked harder than ever on his 'Booke of Ceylon'. He had also embarked on a separate but related project. As he confided to John Strype, in the mid-1690s he had begun to write an autobiographical account of his life covering the years before and after his captivity on Ceylon. Knox asked Chiswell for another copy of his published book with more blank pages bound into it. Into this second, enlarged folio volume – on the clean pages before and after the printed text – he wrote what he called his Memoir and made even more additions, corrections and revisions to his published Ceylon book.*

---

* After 1700, then, Knox had two separate copies of his *Historical Relation of Ceylon*, both of which had been greatly enlarged by blank folio sheets bound into them. These two folio volumes with manuscript material are called the 'interleaved editions' by the small group of Knox scholars and historians of Ceylon who have looked at them over the years. The interleaved 'second edition' of the *Historical Relation* is now held in the Christy Library at the British Museum. The interleaved 'autobiography' *Historical Relation* belongs to the Bodleian Library at Oxford.

In 1708, seven years after he retired, Knox commissioned an oil portrait of himself which he probably intended to be engraved for the frontispiece of his posthumously published autobiography.[9] It is an impressive, three-quarter-length portrait signed by an artist named P. Trampon.[10] Knox is seated, facing forward, gazing directly out at the viewer. He wears a brown silk robe over an embroidered, oriental-looking red waistcoat and white linen shirt. He has a flowing wig of brown curls that makes him appear younger than his sixty-seven years. His right hand holds a quill pen. The little finger on this hand has a gold ring on it – a simple gold band – which may be the ring that his father gave to him just before he died. Knox's left hand rests on an open volume on which is written 'Memoires of my owne life 1708'. On the wall behind him hang all the symbolic paraphernalia of a gentleman and a ship's captain: a sword, a cane, a pair of pistols, a lodestone attached to a little anchor and a quadrant.[11]

When Knox turns seventy in 1711, he is still working on his book and autobiography with undiminished vigour. Retired life for him is empty and monotonous, but his past is vivid and palpable. It floods and fills to bursting his vacant days. He obsessively reads and rereads the printed 1681 Chiswell edition of his Ceylon book, and as he does, he remembers and adds more and more. He is physically confined to his rented lodgings in St Peter le Poer, but mentally he travels far and wide to Ceylon and to other islands – Java, Sumatra, Madagascar, St Helena and Barbados. He lives again with his long-dead father, his lost shipmates, and with his half-caste adopted daughter Lucea whom he 'loved well' and hasn't seen since he left her in Ceylon all those years ago.

Meanwhile, in the midst of Knox's unflagging industry, his publisher Richard Chiswell died. Chiswell's partner in the book-seller's firm, a man named Daniel Midwinter, was even less inclined to republish Knox's Ceylon book. Midwinter, in fact, tells Knox that the cost of paper is 'too deare' at the present rate to do a second printing. It was at some point after Midwinter's judgement that Knox turned to John Strype for help. Strype's ecclesiastical and anti-quarian books were also published by Chiswell and Midwinter, and initially Knox asked Strype to intercede with Midwinter concerning the 'dearness' of paper.

But Knox was soon prodding Strype into enquiring what other reasons Midwinter might have for delaying publication. Strype spoke to the bookseller and diplomatically reported back to his cousin that Midwinter was concerned about the excessive length of the expanded material and said that Knox was repetitive and 'wrot things twice over'. As Knox pointed out in his reply, this 'cannot make ye things to be Lesse true; tho may show ye infirmity of my age'.[12]

Thirty years earlier, when his book was first published in 1681, Knox had been grateful for the 'assistance of my Cousen John Strype ... who composed' his manuscript into 'heads and chapters for my papers were promiscuous and out of forme'.[13]

By 1711 Knox's book was even more disjointed and 'promiscuous' and Knox once again asked 'Cousen Strype' to introduce 'Method' into his chaotic text. For some years the heavy, interleaved volume of the *Historical Relation*, bulging with Knox's manuscript additions, travels back and forth between Knox's lodgings and Strype's parsonage at Low Leyton. At some point Knox probably resubmits this much-revised 'second edition' to Midwinter once more. We don't know if Midwinter even went to the trouble of reading it. After Knox sends it to him, the folio with all of Knox's revisions and additions vanishes and is not heard of again for almost two hundred years when a keeper at the British Museum acquires it for the museum collections.

So much for Knox's second edition of the *Historical Relation*. After he sends it off for the last time to Midwinter, he still has his autobiographical memoir to fill his days. Just a handful of people know of its existence, and as he grows older, Knox realises there is a very real danger that his autobiography will be neglected and forgotten after his death. So he takes steps to prevent this. In his will he bequeaths the memoir, the 'maniscripts of my own Life', to his grand-nephew, Knox Ward, with instructions that it be published after Robert Knox's death.

Knox's plan, then, was to publish a second edition of the *Historical Relation of Ceylon* during his lifetime, while his memoir or autobiography was to be published posthumously. In 1719, there is no way he can foresee that after his death, in the random, uncaring course of things, his 'Booke of Ceylon and Maniscripts of my own Life' will both disappear. They will lie unread, their very existence unknown until they are finally discovered and then published in their entirety almost 270 years later.

What of Defoe's book?

On 23 April 1719, a printer named William Taylor, with premises near the Ship in Paternoster Row, goes to Stationers' Hall, the headquarters of the Liveried Stationers and Newspaper Makers Company. Both Taylor's shop and Stationers' Hall are close to St Paul's Churchyard — the centre of the London book trade. Taylor enters in the Stationers' Register his 'complete share' in a forthcoming book entitled *The Life and Strange Surprising Adventures of Robinson Crusoe, of York, Mariner.*

The next day the book is advertised in the *London Gazette* and other newspapers. On 25 April, it is on sale for the price of five shillings: a small, octavo-sized volume with an engraved frontispiece of a bearded, barefoot Crusoe in goatskin dress, a musket slung over each shoulder, a knife tucked into his waist, a sword handle just visible behind his left hip.

This, then, is how it all begins. In London, in the early months of 1719, two old men sit alone, shipwrecked by age, illness and disappointment. Both find escape in their castaways' tales of captivity on remote islands. By April, however, Robert Knox's 'booke of Ceylon', which he laboured on for nearly forty years, has foundered and sunk. But Defoe's book, *The Life and Strange Surprising Adventures of Robinson Crusoe*, written in less than four months, is about to be launched in the world.

CHAPTER TWO

Crusoe's Secret

London, 1719–20

Survival is the art of staying alive. Mental attitude is as important as physical endurance and knowledge.

SAS Survival Guide

I learn'd to look more upon the bright Side of my Condition,
and less upon the dark Side; and to consider what I enjoy'd
rather than what I wanted; and this gave me sometimes such
secret Comforts, that I cannot express them.

The Life and Strange Surprising Adventures of Robinson Crusoe

When it was first published in April 1719, *The Life and Strange
Surprising Adventures of Robinson Crusoe* was a small, nondescript-
looking book bound in plain calf.[1] The covers of eighteenth-century
books gave nothing away. You had to open them up to find out what
they were about. Hence the novel's long, cumbersome subtitle inside
which tells us that Crusoe 'Lived Eight and Twenty Years all alone
on an uninhabited Island on the Coast of America, near the Mouth
of the Great River Oroonoque; Having been cast on Shore by
Shipwreck, wherein all the Men perished but himself. With an
Account how he was at last strangely delivered by Pyrates.'

The book ran to 364 pages followed by a page of errata and four
pages of advertisements for other works printed by William Taylor
at the Ship in Paternoster Row. It bore all the signs of a hasty, cheap
production: misprints on nearly every page, irregularly set type and
badly spaced lines. The frontispiece depiction of Crusoe in goatskin
dress was the only illustration.

Taylor, who specialised in religious works and books of travels

and voyages, paid Defoe a flat fee of around £50 – the going rate
for the rights to a popular title.[2] These are the days before copy-
right or royalties. Authors sell their books for a fixed sum to a printer
or bookseller, who can go on to profit – sometimes hugely – from
his investment, as William Taylor soon does with *Robinson Crusoe*.
When Taylor dies five years later in 1724 he is described in the press
as 'an eminent Bookseller, reputed to be worth between forty and
fifty thousand pounds'.[3]

Taylor initially printed a thousand copies of *Robinson Crusoe* –
a relatively large number at the time – but the book sold so well
that a reprint had to be rushed out within a fortnight, on 9 May.
Another was printed just a month later on 6 June and then another
on 7 August. This edition also included a folding 'Map of the World'
by the engraver Herman Moll 'on wch [sic] is Delineated the Voyages
of Robinson Crusoe'.[4]

In the space of just over three months Defoe's book caught on
like wildfire. Word of it spread from London coffee houses and
taverns to servants' quarters in prosperous new homes on the western
edge of the city. Cheap, pirated editions began to appear in booksellers' shops. These two-shilling copies were usually abridged so
they were not only cheaper than Taylor's five-shilling edition, they
were also faster and easier to read because most of the novel's long-
winded, moralising passages were cut out.

Defoe and Taylor were incensed by one particular pirated
abridgement printed by a London bookseller named Thomas Cox
at the Amsterdam Coffee House. On 7 August 1719 – the same day
that the fourth impression of *Robinson Crusoe* went on sale – Taylor
denounced Cox in the *St James Post*, claiming that his illicit version
of the book consisted 'only of some scattered Passages, incoherently
tacked together'. Taylor also initiated a lawsuit against Cox in
Chancery.[5]

Defoe joined his publisher on the high ground and branded Cox's
and other abridgements 'scandalous' and 'knavish' acts of vandalism
that robbed his book of 'its brightest Ornaments'. Defoe held that
such editions were not merely disfiguring, they were also criminal
– tantamount, in fact, to 'Robbing on the Highway, or breaking open
a House'.[6]

But Cox had his own ammunition and now he let fire. In the

Flying Post he announced that his cheap edition was completely legitimate because it had been sold to him by none other than 'the author' of *Robinson Crusoe* – or an agent of the author – who offered the book to him after quarrelling with Taylor over payment. Cox then went on to describe Defoe as 'one of the most prostituted pens in the whole world'.[7] There is no way of knowing whether Cox's account of Defoe's dishonesty in selling *Crusoe* to two publishers is true. But as one scholar has observed, 'it is not improbable' that after selling his book to Taylor, Defoe 'opened up clandestine relations with Cox'.[8] As was the case with so many Chancery suits, however, nothing came of Taylor versus Cox. It proved a boon, however, for Defoe's book. Then, as now, all publicity is good publicity.

On 7 October 1719, just a month after Cox's abridgement appeared, Crusoe's story began to be illicitly serialised in a newspaper called the *Original London Post*. Readers of the broadsheet soon got hooked on the tale of the castaway on his desert island, and it continued to run for seventy-eight instalments until late March 1720.[9]

Robinson Crusoe was also soon travelling the world in foreign languages. The first French translation was published just months after Defoe's book came out in 1719. Between 1720 and 1799 fourteen more French translations were published and nine in German. By the end of the eighteenth century, the novel had also been translated into Swedish, Danish, Russian, Bohemian and Serbian. Nineteenth-century translations appeared in Spanish, Portuguese, Finnish, Maltese, Gaelic, Polish, Hungarian, Armenian, Estonian, Arabic, Turkish and Persian. Today *Crusoe* is available in every written language, including Latin, classical Greek, Chinese, Hindi, Coptic, Inuit, Maori and Esperanto.[10]

In addition to translations, books loosely based on Crusoe's story – in English as well as other languages – began to fill the booksellers' shops. There seemed to be an endless appetite for 'strange, surprizing' tales of shipwreck and captivity on desert islands, and there were plenty of impoverished hacks eager to churn them out. The first of these Crusoe-inspired books was a volume published within months of Defoe's own book that contained two castaway tales: *The Adventures and Surprizing Deliverances of James Dubourdieu and His Wife: Who were Taken by Pyrates and*

Carried to an Uninhabited Part of the Isle of Paradise and *The Adventures of Alexander Vendchurch, Whose Ship's Crew Rebelled against Him and Set Him on Shore on an Island in the South-Sea.* Scores of other desert island accounts soon followed, including *A History of the Strange Adventures and Signal Deliverances of Mr Philip Ashton Who... Lived Alone on a Desolate Island, The Voyages, Dangerous Adventures, and Imminent Escapes of Captain Richard Falconer, The English Hermit or the Adventures of Philip Quarll* and, most memorably, *Lemuel Gulliver's Travels Into Several Remote Nations of the World* which more knowing readers recognised as being, among many other things, a parody of *Robinson Crusoe.*

It would be several hundred years, however, before the term Robinsonade was invented for this genre of inspiring survival tales in the Crusoe mould which continued to be produced in the eighteenth, nineteenth and twentieth centuries.[11] Many Robinsonades, including classics such as *The Swiss Family Robinson, Coral Island* and *Treasure Island,* were written for children, but adults eagerly read them as well. Children were also catered for in Mary Godolphin's *Robinson Crusoe in Words of One Syllable.* According to one scholar, more than five hundred Robinsonades were written in English alone between 1788 and 1910.[12] Dozens more were published in French, German and other languages. Nearly every nationality adopted and adapted Defoe's tale for its own purposes. There was a Dutch Crusoe, a German Crusoe, a French Crusoe, an American Crusoe, a Norwegian Crusoe, an Icelandic Crusoe, a Bohemian Crusoe, a Spanish, Swedish and Austrian Crusoe. In time you could find just about every conceivable Crusoe in print including *The Female Crusoe, The Catholic Crusoe* and even *The Dog Crusoe.*[13] In 1898, an industrious German scholar named Hermann Ullrich published the first and still the most exhaustive bibliography of Crusoe-inspired books: *Robinson und Robinsonaden.* Even though Ullrich died before he completed his monumental work, he listed over seven hundred Robinsonade titles.[14]

By the beginning of the twenty-first century, with the appearance of yet more editions, translations, adaptations and imitations of *Crusoe* – including the advent of television programmes such as *Lost* and *Survivors* – even the most avid and meticulous Defoe scholars and cultural critics had lost count of the book's multitude of progeny.[15]

As the critic Ian Watt put it, *Robinson Crusoe* has become 'almost universally known, almost universally thought of as at least half real'; it has attained 'the status of myth'. But exactly what *Crusoe* mythologises isn't clear because as Watt also observes, myths change over time: 'it is not an author but a society that metamorphoses a story into myth'.[16] Each historical era and every culture has appropriated *Crusoe* for its own purposes, to embody its own morals and to promote its own values. Authors die but books like *Robinson Crusoe* live on. But not in their original guise. As the decades and then centuries pass, succeeding generations of readers inevitably refashion and recreate the book as they read it.

In *Robinson Crusoe*, Defoe created a myth that was both durable and remarkably malleable. Readers, scholars, bibliographers and critics come and go but Defoe's hero, Crusoe, remains: stalwart and invincible on his island, a personification of whatever we wish or need him to be: a Protestant pilgrim like Bunyan's, a hero of Romantic individualism, of Victorian Empire or twentieth-century capitalism, an explorer, an inventor, the embodiment of radical or conservative ideologies, an evangelist, a prophet of positive psychology and the gospel of prosperity, even an anti-hero. You name it and someone has probably thought and said Crusoe has been it. That's his secret: Crusoe is Anyone and Everyone. He is you and he is me.

Back in 1719, however, when Defoe first published *Robinson Crusoe* he could never have imagined the cultural phenomenon he had unleashed on the world. And those who read his book then were unconcerned about its future literary reputation and meaning. Instead, in the midst of the success that greeted Defoe's novel when it first came out, people wondered who lay behind it. Who was Crusoe? And who wrote his book? The title page of *Robinson Crusoe* claimed that it was 'Written by Himself'. But unlike Knox's *Historical Relation of Ceylon* or Dampier's *Voyages*, there wasn't a living, breathing human being in London (or anywhere else) whose name matched that of the putative author – Robinson Crusoe – on the title page.

Defoe published nearly everything he wrote anonymously or under a pseudonym. No author's name appears on the title page of his first full-length work, *An Essay Upon Projects*, which appeared in 1697, though the preface ends with the initials 'D F'. Sometimes it was common knowledge that Defoe was 'the Author' of a particular work. This was the case with his verse satire *The True Born Englishman* published in 1701 – an impassioned defence of the Dutch-born King William and a denunciation of British xenophobia. Two years later Defoe published a collection of his writings, *A True Collection of the Writings of the Author of the True Born Englishman*, which included a frontispiece portrait of the author by J. Taverner, engraved by Van der Gucht. But this was as close as Defoe came to 'signing' one of his works until he published his autobiographical *An Appeal to Honour and Justice by Daniel De Foe* in 1715, one of just a handful of his works published in his lifetime that had his name on the title page.

As with so much else in Defoe's life, he didn't necessarily practise what he preached. Nor was he consistent in his preaching. Sometimes he defended an author's right to publish anonymously on the grounds that it is 'best to continue retir'd' in order to dissociate an author's argument from 'the Meanness and Imperfections of the Author' himself.[17] In other words, a writer wants the reader to 'Do as I say, not as I do – or have done'. This was often the case in fact with Defoe's own writing, most famously in *The Complete English Tradesman* where he warned against and denounced so many of the business practices he himself had been guilty of.

But Defoe was never reluctant to contradict himself. In 1704 he wrote a tract entitled *An Essay on the Regulation of the Press* which strenuously argued that 'the Name of the Author . . . be affix'd to every book' that appeared in print.[18] In other words, all anonymous and pseudonymous publications should be banned. Defoe went even further: he called for legislation that would make it compulsory for booksellers 'to place the Author's Name in the Title [on the title page]'. If a bookseller failed to do this, Defoe argued that the bookseller himself should be liable for prosecution. It is perhaps not surprising that he published this trenchant pamphlet calling for a ban on anonymity anonymously.[19]

Whatever he may have *said* – for and against it – anonymity or the use of a pseudonym was Defoe's habitual practice and the legacy of this has been confusion over how much — and what exactly — he actually wrote. As early as 1753 — just twenty-two years after his death — it was lamented that 'it is impossible to arrive at the knowledge of half the tracts and pamphlets which were written by this laborious man, as his name is not prefixed, and many of them being temporary, have perished'.[20]

The consequence of Defoe's addiction to anonymity and pseudonyms caused uncertainty during his lifetime and has continued to provoke debate ever since.[21] He is one of the most prolific writers in English, but the exact number of works attributed to him has varied over the centuries from 101 to a staggering 570.[22] Defoe wrote for different readerships, in different formats and genres, on opposite sides of issues, using different personae. There was no pinning the man down because so many 'authors' seem to have been busily scribbling in what one of his enemies called Defoe's 'Forge of Politicks and Scandal' in Stoke Newington.[23]

The author of *Robinson Crusoe*, however, *was* pinned down on 28 September 1719, just five months after the book appeared, when Defoe's cover was blown in a 48-page, one-shilling pamphlet entitled *The Life and Strange Surprizing Adventures of Mr D—— De F—— of London, Hosier Who Has liv'd above fifty Years by himself, in the Kingdoms of North and South Britain. The Various Shapes he has appear'd in, and the Discoveries he has made for the Benefit of his Country*. Defoe's initials, the telltale De, his profession as a 'hosier',* and the Latin epigraph on the title page — *Qui vult decipi, decipiatur* ['Whoever wishes to be cheated, let him be cheated] — gave away the hoax of *Robinson Crusoe* and its creator. This pamphlet, like *Robinson Crusoe* itself, was published anonymously. But it was no secret that its author was another London scribbler and long-time rival of Defoe, named Charles Gildon.

In 1719, Charles Gildon's situation was even bleaker than Defoe's in Stoke Newington or Knox's in St Peter le Poer. It could scarcely have been more dire in fact. But this hadn't always been the case.

---

* Among Defoe's many attempts to earn a livelihood, he had been a wholesaler of stockings and other haberdashery goods.

Gildon was born in 1665, into a genteel Roman Catholic family in Dorset. He studied in France with the intention of entering the priesthood, but instead of taking vows, he returned to England and made an 'imprudent marriage' at the age of twenty-three. He migrated to London, lost his faith, discovered drink, wrote for the theatre, consorted with actresses, and 'led in fact a very dissolute life' while maintaining a precarious living first as a man of letters of the better sort and then as a lowly Grub Street hack. In his early days Gildon edited Ovid, turned Shakespeare's *Measure for Measure* into an opera for which Daniel Purcell (the younger brother of Henry) wrote the music, edited Aphra Behn's work and Rochester's letters. He also wrote tragedies in blank verse, but none was a success.

Gildon's career and personal fortunes then began a steep decline, and his beliefs, statements and allegiances became wildly erratic. He embraced Deism, then turned to High Church Anglicanism. He wrote for both the Tories and the Whigs, and managed to antagonise just about everyone including Jonathan Swift and Alexander Pope whom Gildon cruelly described as an 'Aesopic sort of Animal in his own cropt hair and dress, agreeable to the forest he came from'.

The enmity between Gildon and Defoe went back to the early 1700s when Gildon had already begun his downward descent. In his 1703 poem 'More Reformation', Defoe says of Gildon, he 'keeps six whores / Sets up for a Reformer of the town / Himself a first Rate Rake below lampoon'. By 1719, however, Gildon's dissolute, rakish days were over and he'd become an impoverished hack. His wife was dead and he was apparently childless. In order to keep body and soul together, he had to write round the clock. Late-night work by dim candlelight ruined his eyesight. Blind and increasingly lame, he moved from one rented London lodging to another. Pope alleged – perhaps correctly – that syphilis was the real cause of Gildon's blindness.

In 1718, Gildon was living in a garret in Chichester Rents, Chancery Lane. The following year he moved to another 'dark and filthy garret in Bull Head Court at the corner of Jewin and Aldersgate Street'. Here Gildon shared his squalid, cramped quarters with his amanuensis, a man named Lloyd, who read to and took dictation from the blind and frail Gildon.[24]

‘ It was Lloyd who read *Robinson Crusoe* out loud to Gildon in the spring of 1719 and then Defoe's sequel, *The Farther Adventures of Robinson Crusoe*, when it was published in August. Gildon was already working on his anti-Defoe pamphlet when *Farther Adventures* came out, adding more fuel to Gildon's ire and revenge. While Lloyd hastily scribbled down his words, Gildon dictated aloud a savage parody and denunciation of Defoe's hero and his adventures.

The first part of Gildon's *The Life and Strange Surprising Adventures of Mr D—— De F——* is a dramatic vignette set near Defoe's house in Stoke Newington. It is one in the morning and Defoe, on his way home (presumably from a night of carousing), is accosted by his two fictional creations, Crusoe and Friday, who upbraid him for all the inconsistencies, improbabilities and absurdities of their characters. They also make pointed allusions to Defoe's various failed business ventures, bankruptcies and time spent in Newgate.

In vain, Defoe protests to Crusoe that he, Crusoe, is 'the true Allegorick Image of thy tender father D——l . . . I have been all my Life that Rambling, Inconsistent Creature which I have made thee.'[25] The scene reaches its climax when Crusoe and Friday force-feed Defoe his own collected works which swiftly act as an emetic laxative. Crusoe and Friday then toss Defoe in a blanket.[26] The scene closes with Defoe thinking his encounter with his two aggrieved characters has merely been a bad dream that has produced malodorous 'Effects in my Breeches'.

Part two of Gildon's vitriolic critique consists of a lengthy plot summary of *Robinson Crusoe* with many digressions on its errors, solecisms and absurdities, including the fact that after Crusoe removes his clothing onshore and swims out to the wreck of the ship, he fills the pockets of his breeches with biscuits that he finds on board. Defoe is also accused of unnecessary padding – 'repeating the same fact afterwards in a Journal which you had told us before in a plain narration', and inserting tedious didactic passages 'to swell the bulk of your treatise up to a five shilling book'. Friday is 'a Blockhead' who can 'speak English tolerably well in a Month or two', after Crusoe rescues him, but not any better or more intelligibly after he's been with him twelve years.[27]

In the course of all this sniping, Gildon also gives away the underlying reason for his rancour against Defoe. Unlike Gildon himself, Defoe has turned things around late in his life. Defoe's book has been a huge success: it is 'fam'd from Tuttle-Street to Limehouse-hole [particularly insalubrious London neighbourhoods]; there is not an old Woman that can go the Price of it, but buys thy Life and Adventures, and leaves it as a Legacy, with the Pilgrim's Progress, the Practice of Piety, and God's Revenge against Murther, to her Posterity'.[28] Gildon, in his filthy garret, could not have sunk lower, and what infuriates him most about *Robinson Crusoe* is the fame and (Gildon wrongly assumed) the prosperity that it brought to its creator.

Crusoe's myth may mutate over time – metamorphosing from one generation to the next – but buried in the bedrock beneath its various manifestations is Defoe's secret message: work hard, persevere, keep faith and not only will you survive, you will be rewarded and succeed beyond your wildest dreams. In his diatribe against Defoe, Gildon did his best to repudiate this comforting message and to expose it as bogus, a sham. Gildon himself was living proof of the far more common fate of mankind in general and eighteenth-century scribblers in particular – not success but just the opposite: poverty, failure, age, illness, decrepitude and death. No one, however, then or now, wants to listen to Gildon's dark lesson that we are born to suffer, toil and die. It is Crusoe's story – and Crusoe's secret – that we all want to hear.

But where exactly did Crusoe come from? How and why did this character and his story take form in Defoe's imagination in the winter of 1719? For us, Defoe is the father of the English novel. If he had died in 1718, before he wrote *Crusoe*, most of us would never have heard of him. But on that cold, dark January day in 1719 when he began his castaway's tale, Defoe had no intention of making literary history.[29] He was, as usual, short of cash and needed to write something that would sell. Fast.

Defoe gave *Robinson Crusoe* all the trappings of a 'true history' and the book was in fact remarkably similar in many respects to a number of already published works, some of which were written by Defoe himself. Far from being an innovator – the inventor of the English novel – Defoe was a congenital plagiarist. Often he plagiarised his own earlier works, but he was never reluctant to borrow from and refashion a variety of other sources. Everything was grist for Defoe's mill.

When Defoe found a rich seam – his own or someone else's – he mined it for all it was worth. Generations of literary sleuths have tracked down every conceivable source and inspiration that may have contributed to *Robinson Crusoe*: Homer's *Odyssey*, Shakespeare's *Tempest*, Hakluyt's *Principal Navigations of the English Nation*, Samuel Purchas's *Purchas his Pilgrimes*, spiritual autobiographies such as Bunyan's *Grace Abounding*, and *Pilgrim's Progress*, and seventeenth- and eighteenth-century books of voyages by William Dampier, Alexander Exquemelin, Edward Cooke and Woodes Rogers.[30]

Defoe also borrowed extensively from a number of published accounts about real castaways and their ordeals – books that are now largely forgotten, but were avidly read in his day. Besides Robert Knox's *Historical Relation of Ceylon* there were scores more of these curious tales. They related such triumphs of human survival as Fernando Lopez's lonely exile on St Helena in the South Atlantic, Pedro Serrano's survival on a tiny island in the West Indies, Henry Pitman stranded on Tortuga, Lionel Wafer taken captive by Indians in Panama and, most sensationally, Alexander Selkirk marooned on Juan Fernandez Island off Chile. Defoe read – and used – all these and more.

In *Robinson Crusoe* Defoe also borrowed from a quite different popular form: the conduct book – the eighteenth-century equivalent of modern self-help guides or manuals. Defoe was always good at telling other people how to live, though he found it difficult to follow his own advice. In the years just before *Crusoe* came out, he published two volumes of a successful conduct book entitled *The Family Instructor* which, among other things, told parents how to manage unruly, rebellious children. In the years following *Crusoe*, Defoe extended his self-help repertoire to cover such areas as business and financial affairs in *The Complete English Tradesman*, courtship, marriage and sexual relations in *Religious Courtship* and *Conjugal Lewdness*, and yet more family relations advice in a third volume of *The Family Instructor*. He was working on yet another conduct book, *The Compleat English Gentleman*, at the time of his death in 1731.

Robinson Crusoe is kin to all of these. E. M. Forster famously complained that the novel reminded him of a Boy Scout manual – and he had a point.[31] Along with so much else, *Robinson Crusoe* is the ultimate how-to book: a step-by-step guide on how to live in a particularly tricky situation: in Crusoe's case, how to survive alone on a desert island.

When Crusoe is washed up on the island at the beginning, he has three options: he can lie down and give up; he can adapt to his situation and his new environment and be radically changed in the process; or he can labour to resurrect some sort of approximation of his old life and impose it on his circumstances. Historically, various real castaways and captives have usually chosen one of the first two routes of surrender or change. Defoe, who always affirmed that Crusoe's story was true, was well aware, for example, that Alexander Selkirk was initially overcome by a lethargy and despair verging on suicide. According to Richard Steele, whose account of Selkirk Defoe read in *The Englishman*, Selkirk was 'scarce able to refrain from doing himself Violence'.[32] Selkirk's rescuer, Captain Woodes Rogers, described how when they found Selkirk, he had regressed to a near-feral state: 'a Man cloth'd in Goat-Skins, who look'd wilder than the first Owners of them', who 'seem'd to speak his words by halves . . . he had so much forgot his Language for want of use'.[33] Defoe also knew that Robert Knox, Lionel Wafer and others had shed their European clothing and learned a new language – 'gone native', in fact – in order to adapt to their predicament.

Linda Colley has explored this second route of adaptation and transformation in *Captives*, her study of more than a hundred real hostage accounts. At the beginning of the book, Colley invokes James Joyce's assessment of Robinson Crusoe as the 'true symbol of . . . British conquest', but her whole argument is that Crusoe's story – and Crusoe's imposition of his own personality and culture on an alien place – is not the norm.[34] Instead, as Colley puts it, in most captives' stories 'overseas venturing brings no conquests, or riches, or easy complacencies: only terror, vulnerability, and . . . an alteration of self and a telling of stories'.[35]

Robinson Crusoe's island

After Crusoe erects a tent and hollows out a cave to serve as his dwelling, he sets to work making a table and chair, both of which he thinks are essential for his survival on the island. Indeed, Crusoe remarks that 'I could not write or eat' without a table and chair. It never occurs to him to squat or sit on the ground, just as it doesn't occur to him to ask Friday what his real name is or to learn Friday's language. Crusoe instead names Friday after the day of the week on which he rescues him and he teaches him English. He does make several enquiries about Friday's religious beliefs and his native God 'Benamuckee' but then proceeds to stamp all these out by converting Friday to Christianity. In his attempt to recreate his old life on the island, there are some things, however, that Crusoe cannot replicate no matter how hard he tries. He cannot, for example, make that most basic item of human technology, the wheel, which he needs for a wheelbarrow, nor can he make a cask to hold liquid, or ink to write with after his ink from the shipwreck runs out. Crusoe also attempts and fails to make beer, though he succeeds – after protracted and heroic effort – to bake bread.

But the process of Crusoe's imposition of himself and his culture on the island is far more wide-ranging than making some furniture and enslaving a native. It is indeed an epic task: slowly, doggedly, by process of trial and error, Crusoe passes through all the stages of human history and recreates a rough approximation of his old British way of life on his island. Like early man, he takes shelter in a cave, and then builds himself a house. He farms and domesticates animals, makes his table and chair and fashions pottery, bakes bread, explores the island, expands the territory of his realm, battles enemies and cannibals. He rescues Friday, clothes him and makes him into a Christian. And finally, with the arrival of a group of Spaniards and a band of English mutineers, he establishes a colony.

Not only does Crusoe recreate and impose civilisation on a hostile environment, he also conquers his inner landscape of despair. He overcomes doubt, misery, illness, hardship and solitude. If 'poor Robin Crusoe', as his parrot Poll calls him, can do this, then surely we, Defoe's readers, in our far more fortunate, comfortable circumstances, can survive too. This is Defoe's potent message and it has remained seductive, even irresistible, for nearly three hundred years.

But there is even more to *Crusoe*'s hold on our imaginations than this. In Defoe's account, Crusoe is protected and saved by God's Providence, but his story continues to ring true in later, secular times. Crusoe's story shows us that survival and salvation lie not as his creator preached, in Christian faith, obedience and piety, but as Defoe actually *shows* us time and again, in how Crusoe chooses to see the world, the way he looks at things and what he decides to do about them. Defoe was, it can be argued, the first — or at least one of the first — to vocalise that perennially appealing gospel of 'the power of positive thinking', of seeing the glass half full, rather than half empty. There is much that Crusoe cannot change about his plight on the island, but he *can* and *does* change how he thinks, perceives and feels about his situation. In his own words, Crusoe begins 'to exercise my self with new Thoughts . . . I learn'd to look more upon the bright Side of my Condition and less upon the dark Side.'[36] He changes both his 'Sorrows and my Joys; my very Desires alter'd; my Affections chang'd their Gusts; and my Delights were perfectly new from what they were at my first Coming' to the island.[37]

*   *   *

As soon as he published it, Defoe knew that he was on to a winner. In the years that followed – when Defoe was in his sixties, at an age when modern men retire and eighteenth-century men commonly died – he churned out, at an astonishing rate, all his great novels: among them *Moll Flanders, Captain Singleton, Colonel Jack, Journal of the Plague Year* and *Roxana.* All of these recycle and repeat the winning formula Defoe immortalised in *Robinson Crusoe.* On desert islands, in the middle of Africa, in thieves' dens and the filthy, dark cells of Newgate, in plague-ridden London, in the great cities of Europe, on the high seas and in far-flung colonies, Defoe's heroes and heroines time and again overcome all the odds and not only survive but thrive, especially monetarily. This happens because they practise positive thinking; they refuse to succumb to despair (or if they do, they soon rouse themselves); they seize the day and make the best of things. Invariably, fate rewards them with success, health, happiness and wealth.[38]

Defoe is remarkably precise regarding how this all comes about – how positive thinking leads his heroes and heroines ever-forward, and if what he says sounds familiar, it's because modern cognitive behaviourists and 'positive psychologists', life and career coaches, authors of self-help manuals and presenters of uplifting reality television programmes preach the same basic message of self-improvement and self-belief today. Even the methods used to reach the desired goal remain remarkably unchanged. Like a modern self-improver – a weight-watcher, say, or a compulsive shopper or like someone who is too terrified to fly in a plane or even leave the house – Crusoe keeps a regular diary (until his ink runs out), he meditates and he analyses his 'cognitions'. In the parlance of psychologist Martin Seligman in his book *Learned Optimism,* Crusoe challenges his negative 'explanatory style'. He learns 'a new set of cognitive skills', and gains 'control over the way' he thinks 'about adversity'. Crusoe intuitively comes to understand that 'what we think determines how we feel'.[39] His thought processes affect his feelings; how he thinks about things – rather than things or situations in themselves – actually determines his emotions and moods.

Stranded on the island, Crusoe famously draws up a list of the pros and cons of his solitary life, aligning, as he puts it, 'like Debtor and Creditor, the Comforts I enjoyed against the Miseries I suffer'd'.

These parallel lists of pros and cons enable Crusoe to challenge negative perceptions with positive ones.* He writes on one side of his list that he is 'cast out upon a horrible, desolate Island', but on the other side he counters that he 'is alive, and not drown'd' like the rest of the ship's company. He is isolated, 'a solitaire . . . banish'd' from society, but he is 'not starv'd and perishing on a barren place, affording no sustenance'. He has 'not Clothes to cover' himself, but he is in a hot Climate where if he did have clothes he 'could hardly wear them'.[40]And so he carries on, tallying pluses against minuses, or, more accurately, cancelling out minuses with pluses.

Reality, Crusoe discovers, is what you make of it in two senses: what you do to change it; and even more importantly, how you change your thinking about it. This is where hard work, determination and perseverance come in. Or as Defoe himself explains Crusoe's metamorphosis on the island: 'here is invincible Patience recommended under the worst Misery; indefatigable Application and undaunted Resolution under the greatest and most discouraging Circumstances . . . these are recommended as the only Way to work through those Miseries, and their Success appears sufficient to support the most dead-hearted Creature in the World'. [41]

For much of the book, though, Crusoe is ambivalent: he veers between periods of calm and peace and renewed terror and despair. After years of steadily evolving contentment, the sight of a lone footprint on the shore plunges him once again into a 'Life of Anxiety, Fear and Care'. For long, desperate periods he feels a 'Prisoner' on the island, 'lock'd up with the Eternal Bars and Bolts of the Oceans in an uninhabited Wilderness'. He refers to 'my captivity or my reign, what you will'. But ultimately it is Crusoe himself who tips the scale from prison to paradise: it is he who proclaims 'I was King and Lord of all this Country'. His situation remains for the most part the same: he is still stuck on a desert island. But by dint of hard work and positive thinking he has transformed his life. This is an amazing and empowering achievement: here is the secret which lies at the heart of the Crusoe Myth and the endurance of Defoe's novel.

*   *   *

* Crusoe's list of 'pros' resembles the current practice of keeping a 'gratitude journal' recommended by various self-help writers.

Of course, Robinson Crusoe escapes physically as well as psychologically from his desert island when an English ship with a mutinous crew turns up and Crusoe and Friday, despite being greatly outnumbered, assist the beleaguered Captain to battle and overwhelm the rebels, regain control of the ship and finally sail off back to Europe and England. But Crusoe's real deliverance happens long before his physical escape when he discovers how to work his psychological liberation through the power of positive thinking, thus creating a near-idyllic life for himself and Friday on the island.

After he returns to England, good fortune – wealth, a wife and children – is Crusoe's reward for all his years of struggle, industry and positive thinking. But Defoe never intended to let his hero retire in peace and plenty. In the closing pages of the book he sketches a tantalising plot summary of a second part to Crusoe's story: 'all these things, with some very surprising incidents in some new Adventures of my own, for ten Years more, I may perhaps give a farther Account of hereafter'.[42]

The promised sequel, *The Farther Adventures of Robinson Crusoe*, was published by William Taylor on 20 August 1719, less than four months after *Robinson Crusoe*. In a preface, Defoe assures the reader that 'contrary to the Usage of Second Parts' or sequels, the farther adventures of his hero would be 'every way as entertaining as the First' and contain 'as strange and surprising Incidents, and as great a Variety of them, nor is the Application less serious'.[43] The book was obviously intended to cash in on the success of its predecessor.

But it departed radically from Defoe's original story. In *The Farther Adventures*, Defoe's hero is no castaway, stuck on a desert island, but instead a relentless world traveller. Crusoe's nephew, a sea captain, suggests to his uncle that he sail with him on a voyage to the East Indies and China via Brazil with a stop en route at Crusoe's island.[44] Their route, in fact, traces almost exactly the voyages that Robert Knox made in his post-Ceylonese days as an East India Company ship captain. Crusoe finds his nephew's offer 'irresistible', and sails with the ever-faithful Friday in January 1695. They do indeed revisit Crusoe's island and find out how the colonists – Spanish, British and Indian – are faring, but after twenty-five days, Crusoe sails away. Shortly thereafter, on the way to Brazil, Friday is killed, when they are pursued by a canoe full of hostile Indians, one of whom shoots him.

Once Crusoe has 'done with my island' and Friday has died, the vital connection with the first *Robinson Crusoe* is severed. The rest of Crusoe's *Farther Adventures* is devoted to his 'wild goose chase' round the world. From Brazil he sails to South Africa and on to Madagascar, the Persian Gulf, Bengal in India, Siam, Sumatra, Formosa, Tonquin Bay and finally China. Here he embarks on a long overland caravan journey from Peking to Moscow. He passes through the Great Wall of China, battles hordes of wild Tartars, sweeps through Siberia and blows up wooden idols in 'brutish' pagan villages. Finally he reaches Archangel from which he sails to Elbe, proceeds to Hamburg and The Hague, and at last to London, arriving back home, he tells us with his usual precision, with a tidy fortune of £3475 17s 3d on 10 January 1705 'having been gone from England ten years and nine months'.

For nearly all of his *Farther Adventures* Crusoe is pointlessly roaming the world, and to a modern reader, at least, it seems as though Defoe has lost the plot. What is the meaning of all this? To cash in on the original novel is the only convincing answer. In a closing paragraph we are relieved when Crusoe assures us that he has at long last resolved 'to harrass my self no more', and that his rambling days are over. Now seventy-two, he has finally learned the 'Value of Retirement, and the Blessing of ending our Days in Peace' after his 'Life of Infinite Variety'.

Though seldom read today, when it was first published, *The Farther Adventures of Robinson Crusoe* was almost as successful as its predecessor. Two impressions sold out by the end of 1719 and eventually six impressions, the later ones including illustrations, were published. Given this success, Defoe began to have second thoughts about letting his hero retire in peace.

But he also had a great deal of other work on his hands. Despite the fact that he was now sixty, he showed no signs of slowing down. In 1719 and 1720, he was churning out a stream of pamphlets, including ones on stockjobbers (the South Sea Bubble was about to burst), and tracts championing the Spitalfields weavers and condemning the imported East India Company calicos that were threatening the British woollen trade. He was also busy writing two more pseudo-autobiographies: *Memoirs of a Cavalier*, about the experiences of a royalist colonel under Charles I who fought at the battles of Edgehill and Naseby and *The Life, Adventures, and Pyracies of the Famous Captain Singleton.*

Despite all this frenetic scribbling, Defoe thought there was still life in – and money to be made out of – Crusoe. His hero was now too old to embark on yet more 'strange, surprising adventures'. But like Robert Knox writing his autobiographical memoir in his rented rooms, Crusoe could look back on his 'Life of Wonders in Continued Storms' on his 'Island of Despair', and deliver up to the reader all the wisdom and philosophy that his long ordeal had yielded.

The result was *Serious Reflections during the Life and Surprising Adventures of Robinson Crusoe* published, once again, by William Taylor at the Ship and Black Swan in Paternoster Row, on 6 August 1720. Soon after it appeared, the book which Defoe hoped would be a triumphant culmination of his Crusoe trilogy, sank almost without trace. Only one impression of *Serious Reflections* was printed and, according to Taylor's sales catalogue, it did not sell out.[45] The book disappeared from view, except for a few fragmentary passages that were appended to several nineteenth-century editions of the first two Crusoe books. Even William Lee, Defoe's most admiring nineteenth-century biographer, conceded that 'of the myriads of those who have read *Robinson Crusoe*, very few are aware of the existence of his *Serious Reflections*'.[46] When it was finally resurrected in a meticulous new edition in 2008, its editor had to concede that the book is usually considered 'a sequel to a sequel . . . an anticlimactic final instalment'.[47]

The *Serious Reflections During the Life of Robinson Crusoe* is, in fact, probably the least read book ever written by a major British author. It begins promisingly with a spirited riposte to Charles Gildon's parody. Defoe makes the most of Gildon's insinuation that *Robinson Crusoe* is merely a veiled biography of its author and claims that 'there is a Man alive, and well known too, the Actions of whose Life are the just Subject of these Volumes'. The 'Story', he claims, 'though Allegorical is also Historical; . . . it is a beautiful Representation of a Life of unexampled Misfortunes and of a Variety not to be met with in the World.'[48] These words would inspire generations of biographers to interpret the 'allegory' of Crusoe's adventures as Defoe's veiled autobiography — with interesting and inventive, but in the end unverifiable, results.

But after this preface, Defoe subjects the reader to seven moralising essays on Solitude, Honesty, Immorality, Religion, Providence, Paganism and spirits and ghosts in the supernatural or 'Angelick World'. Few if any of the 'reflections' in these long-winded essays have anything to do with Crusoe's experiences in the first two volumes. Sometimes, in fact, as in the essay on Solitude, Defoe seems to contradict the lessons so hard won by young Crusoe. Solitude, Defoe tells us in the *Serious Reflections*, is pernicious and 'inconsistent with a Christian Life', thus completely ignoring the vital role that isolation and loneliness have on Crusoe's psychological and spiritual transformation on his desert island.

Despite its title claiming that the *Serious Reflections* were made 'during' Crusoe's adventures, this book is actually a jumble of afterthoughts hastily cobbled together. *Serious Reflections* shows Defoe at his most tiresome and tedious, recycling earlier work, cutting and pasting and paraphrasing, padding, sermonising, riding all manner of hobby horses. This book also brings to mind old Robert Knox in his rooms in St Peter le Poer, scribbling his memoir, endlessly rehearsing his past, writing and editing, remembering and repeating himself. There is a feeling in both Defoe's final instalment of *Robinson Crusoe* and Knox's *Memoir* of a need to keep the past alive, and to fathom its meaning, or in Defoe's case, to wring it of its last drop of profit. But, ironically, the more Defoe and Knox discourse on and explain their 'strange surprising adventures', the more their early lives seem to recede and disintegrate. Defoe and Knox are like dogs worrying old bones, the meat and flavour of which are long gone.

In his final will, signed 4 April 1720, Knox bequeathed his 'Booke of Ceylon wth [sic] Maniscripts [sic] of my owne Life' to his grand-nephew Knox Ward with instructions to publish them after his death. Knox was ill and failing when he made out this will and he died just over two months later on 19 June 1720. Both *Robinson Crusoe* and the *Farther Adventures of Robinson Crusoe* had been published the previous year, but Defoe's final Crusoe work, *Serious Reflections*, didn't come out until August 1720, after Knox's death.

Did Knox read *Robinson Crusoe* and his *Farther Adventures* when they were published in 1719? He never mentioned either book or any other of Defoe's works – or Defoe himself – in his letters or autobiography. The only books Knox refers to are the Bible, which he read and reread daily, and his favourite devotional works, especially Bishop Bayly's *Practice of Piety*. If Knox heard about *Robinson Crusoe* – a very real possibility because he read the newspapers in which it was advertised – he would surely have obtained a copy – readily available 'at most booksellers' – and read it. But we simply don't know if he got wind of the book and discovered that his own 'life of wonders in continued storms' – or something uncannily close to it – had already been salvaged, resurrected and published by Defoe.

How and when did Knox's story – as he told it – begin all those years before? In 1659, to be precise – the same year that Defoe says Crusoe, too, was cast away.

CHAPTER THREE

'Captivated'

South India and Ceylon, 1659–64

Captivate. †1. a. *trans.* To make captive, take prisoner, capture. *Obs.* or *arch.* †b. To capture, secure, hold captive (animals and things). *Obs.* †2. *fig.* To make or hold captive, put or keep in subjection, subjugate (the mind, mental attributes, etc.) Const. *to.Obs.* exc. as passing into 3. 3. *esp.* 'To overpower with excellence' (J.): to enthrall with charm or attractiveness; to enslave, fascinate, enamour, enchant, charm.

Oxford English Dictionary

19 November 1659. They were anchored at Masulipatam, on the east coast of India, loading goods for their return to England, when the storm rolled out of the sky and hit them in the inky darkness of night. First a howling frenzy of wind and then cutting sheets of rain lashed the ships and boats in the harbour. Some were torn from their anchors and swept out to sea. Others were flung onshore and dashed to pieces on the rocks. On land, roofs and tiles were swept away, chimneys and houses collapsed. Further inland, fields were flooded, crops destroyed, cattle and men drowned.[1]

The *Anne*, a 230-tonne East Indiaman under the command of Captain Robert Knox, was fortunate only to lose its mainmast, which the Captain, at the height of the storm, shouting above the uproar of wind and thunder, ordered cut down to save the ship. The *Anne* survived but it was badly battered and damaged. And without its mainmast there was no hope of it being seaworthy enough to make the long voyage home.

A messenger was dispatched with news of their plight to the nearest East India Company settlement, Fort St George at Madras, further south on the Coromandel Coast. Thomas Chambers, the company agent at Fort St George, sent orders to Captain Knox to sail to Porto Novo, some thirty miles south of Pondicherry. Knox's instructions were to take on bales of cotton cloth at Porto Novo and then sail to Kottiyar Bay in Ceylon. South India lacked suitable trees to make a new mainmast and other repairs, but Kottiyar, 'a very commodious Bay' on the eastern side of Ceylon, was heavily forested with good timber. It was also one of the few places on the coast of Ceylon that wasn't at that time occupied by the rival Dutch East India Company.[2] The *Anne* could trade the Porto Novo cloth at Kottiyar, build a new mainmast and make other necessary repairs to the ship and then proceed on her journey home.

With great care, the disabled and leaking *Anne* made her way to Porto Novo and then to Kottiyar. They had been too close to destruction for the Captain to risk further hazards. He had much at stake in this voyage for he had traded profitably on his own account as well as the Honourable Company's.* Like many East Indiamen captains, Knox hoped to be rich enough to retire after three or four successful voyages to the Indies. It was a risky game these captains played. The odds of ruin – of being taken by pirates or an enemy ship, or of death from disease or shipwreck – were always high. But if an East India Company captain had luck as well as intelligence, imagination and fortitude, he could make a fortune in a matter of years and see the wonders of the seas and distant lands besides.

This was Captain Knox's second voyage in command of the *Anne*. He was also one of the ship's owners, so he stood to gain both as Captain and investor. If he returned safely, and made perhaps just one more voyage to the Indies, he could retire in ease and plenty to his home in Wimbledon, joining the growing ranks of prosperous company nabobs in London. He could also bequeath his share in, and the command of, the *Anne* to his eldest son, Robert.

Like young Robinson Crusoe, Robert Knox's 'inclination' had been 'strongly bent for the seas' from the time he was a boy. But Captain Knox, like Crusoe's father, opposed his son's ambition. Instead of going to sea, Captain Knox wanted Robert to become a London merchant, dealing in the new consumer goods – spices, cottons, silk

---

* East India Company captains were allowed to buy goods and trade them 'on their own account' in the course of their voyages. This enabled captains to make a good deal of money and increase their income far beyond their company salaries.

and tea — brought back to England by the East India Company's ships. Knox Senior had explained all this one day back in London to several fellow sea captains who had called on him at home. As his son later related, the visitors asked the boy whether he wanted to go into trade, and young Robert had answered 'to go to Sea was my whole desire, at which they turned to my father saying . . . when you have done goeing to sea [the *Anne*] will be a good . . . plentifull estate to your Sonn, & it is pitty to crosse his good inclination since commonly younge men doe best in that Calling they have most mind to be in'.[3] This was sound advice and, unlike Crusoe's father, Captain Knox relented.

And so it was that young Robert Knox, aged just fourteen, sailed on the first voyage of the *Anne* to the Indies in 1655, returning 'full laden to London' in 1657. It was while they were away on this long first voyage that, back in London, Knox's mother died and was buried in Wimbledon Church — a loss that he and his father only learned of when they returned the following year. When the *Anne* set sail from the Downs on her second voyage to the Indies on 21 January 1658,[4] young Robert Knox was again on board. This was the voyage that after more than a year of trading 'from Port to Port' in Persia, India and Sumatra, brought the *Anne* to the storm-tossed Indian harbour at Masulipatan in November 1659. It was 'the fatall voiage', as Knox later put it, 'in which I lost my father & my selfe, & the prime of my time for businesse and preferment for 23 years'.[5]

The *Anne* arrived safely at Kottiyar Bay in early February 1660, and anchored on the south-eastern edge of the vast, deep-water harbour of Trincomalee.[6] Initially, the crew who ventured onshore were wary of the local inhabitants, most of them Tamil villagers and farmers though there were also a few Arab and South Indian Muslim traders. But the native Tamil Governor welcomed them and the people supplied them with the best 'provisions and Refreshings as those parts afforded': cows, buffaloes, deer, hogs, antelopes, fowl and all sorts of fruit. Furthermore, the men on the *Anne* had the experience of the first mate John Burford to reassure them. Twelve years earlier, in 1648, Burford's ship had stayed 'many days' at Kottiyar and members of his ship's crew had travelled more than thirty miles inland, without interference.

For the next two months the *Anne*'s boats ferried seamen and carpenters with their tools to the shore where they felled trees, sawed planks and repaired damaged parts from the ship.[7] The seamen came and went 'at their pleasure without any Molestation' from the Tamil inhabitants. In fact, they were 'very kindly entertained' by them. According to young Knox, the Englishmen paid for their food and goods, though later Thomas Chambers, the Fort St George agent, would claim 'the Country people' at Kottiyar 'would receive nothing . . . pressing one gift upon another on' the ship's company as a 'meere baite and delusion to Entrapp Capt Knox and his men'.[8]

In time, however, news of the *Anne*'s presence at Kottiyar reached the King of Kandy in the interior of the island. For years, his kingdom had been steadily eroded by the incursions of first the Portuguese and then the Dutch. Now he feared yet another foreign threat had arrived on the island. The King dispatched a Dissava[9] or general with a small army to the coast to enquire what these new 'outlandish' people in Kottiyar Bay wanted. A messenger was sent by the Dissava out to the *Anne* anchored in the harbour requesting the Captain to come ashore to receive a letter from the King. Captain Knox 'saluted this message' with the firing of the *Anne*'s twenty guns – both a fitting acknowledgement and a show of might. But Knox himself did not – as bidden – go ashore to collect the King's letter. Instead, on the morning of 4 April, he sent his nineteen-year-old son Robert along with the ship's merchant or supercargo,* John Loveland, in a boat to the shore to confer with the Dissava and take receipt of the King's letter.

The Dissava and his guard were camped at a village called Kiliveddi, some twelve miles inland from Kottiyar, and it was to this place that the messenger led young Knox and Loveland on a red dirt track that wound through thick groves of trees and green paddy fields. They passed farmers in white loincloths carrying huge bales of grain on their heads, carts pulled by humpback bullocks and settlements of small, low, thatched huts with women pounding rice in ebony mortars outside and naked children playing amid goats, chickens and pigs.

---

* A supercargo represented the ship's owners on a merchant ship. He looked after the cargo on the ship, and conducted all trade transactions at the ports visited.

At Kiliveddi the Dissava received them cordially, but Robert and John Loveland began to have misgivings. We don't know what language they used to communicate. Before the Dutch occupation of Ceylon, the island had been held by the Portuguese, and the Dissava, like the King, spoke that language. Knox, many years later, communicated with the Dutch authorities in Portuguese, and even at this early date, when he had made two voyages to the Indies and come into contact with Portuguese seamen, he may have been capable of a rudimentary exchange of information in the language. However he communicated with the Dissava, there was considerable confusion and this contributed to his and Loveland's apprehensions.[10] What was immediately apparent, though, was that the Dissava's soldiers had muskets. The Dissava himself was also well armed with a long sword, carved and inlaid with silver, a knife and halberd.

Adding to their doubts, the promised letter from the King of Kandy was not forthcoming. The Dissava now said that it could only be delivered to Captain Knox in person. Robert and Loveland explained that the Captain could not travel the long distance to Kiliveddi from his ship, but that if the Dissava would himself go to the harbour at Kottiyar, the Captain would come onshore to receive the King's letter. The Dissava pretended to agree to this plan, but pointing out that the sun was now low in the sky, he said that it was too late for them to travel back to the sea that day. He assured young Knox and Loveland that they would sleep comfortably in the house where he and his soldiers were lodged at Kiliveddi. The next morning, he promised, they would all set off for Kottiyar together.

In the meantime, the Dissava announced that he was that night going to send ahead presents to the Captain, and he offered to include with them a message if Robert wished to write to his father. Neither Knox nor the Dissava had paper, but Knox tore a leaf out of his 'Table Book' – a pocket notebook – and wrote a letter of warning to his father to be wary of the Dissava's intentions. It would be many years before Robert Knox would use pen or paper again.

The Dissava's gifts of cattle and fruit were duly delivered to Kottiyar for Captain Knox, but the warning message from his son was not. This had merely been a ploy on the Dissava's part to allay Robert and Loveland's anxieties. Instead, the Dissava sent his own message with the gifts, asking the Captain to meet them several miles upriver.

On the morning of 10 April, Captain Knox, still 'mistrusting nothing', was rowed ashore in the ship's boat by six oarsmen and a cox. They anticipated a peaceful parley so came unarmed. The barge went two miles upriver as directed. Here Captain Knox and his men got out and sat under a huge tamarind tree, to await the promised arrival of the Dissava with young Knox and Loveland.[11]

Suddenly, as if out of nowhere, the Dissava's soldiers surrounded the Captain and his men. In his son's words, 'he was seized on and seven men with him, yet without any violence or plundering'. The soldiers then brought the Captain and his party up to another town where young Knox and Loveland had been taken, 'carrying the Captain in a Hammock upon their shoulders'.[12]

The following day, the *Anne*'s longboat came ashore with a gang of men to cut wood to make the ship's new mainmast. They had no inkling – and apparently no fears – of what had befallen the Captain and his party, and so were taken by surprise when they too were seized by the Dissava's soldiers. But unlike the Captain, the gang of seamen put up resistance and were used 'with more violence' and bound with ropes. Then they were marched to the town where the Knoxes and John Loveland were held.

Captain Knox now, at last, saw that they had walked into a trap. The Dissava and his soldiers had cleverly lured eighteen of his crew inland and taken two of the ship's boats. When the Dissava then requested that the *Anne* itself be brought upriver, the Captain realised they wanted to seize his ship and all its cargo as well. To buy time, he sent two messengers to the ship. When the men failed to return, the Captain told the Dissava that the crew left on board would never obey his command as long as he, their commander, was detained onshore.

At this juncture, the Dissava suggested that the Captain's son – who would be obeyed as his father's proxy – be sent to the *Anne* to deliver the order. The Captain agreed to this plan, but in his son's words he 'intended to make another use of this Message'. Captain Knox in fact instructed Robert to tell the first mate John Burford to take charge of the ship and to be on guard because the Captain and his party on land now feared they were at 'the beginning of a sad

Captivity'. If they were not released within twenty days, the Captain directed that the ship should depart without them.[13]

Before dispatching his son with this message, Captain Knox made him swear that he would come back and not abandon him in this foreign land. Robinson Crusoe's father forbade his son from going to sea, but Crusoe disobeyed him and ran away. Unlike Crusoe, the younger Knox did as his father commanded. He 'solemnly vowed', according to his 'Duty to be [an] Obedient Son', to return even if this meant the loss of his own liberty. He went out to the ship, delivered the Captain's secret message to the men, and then immediately returned to his father and the others onshore.

For several more weeks a stalemate prevailed. The King's promised letter failed to arrive; the Captain's ship remained at anchor out in the harbour. The Captain and his men onshore were 'entertained as formerly with the best Diet and Accommodation of the Countrey'. The Dissava continued to 'pretend' that he was merely awaiting the King's order to release them. But as the days passed, their hope ebbed away. The ship would have to depart before the monsoon rains. In early May, when the stipulated twenty days of waiting had passed, the *Anne* set sail, as the Captain had ordered, leaving those held onshore to 'their sad captivity'.

Even after the *Anne* departed, the captives did not give up all hope of escape. On the river near the town where they were held, there was an Arab trading boat with some forty men onboard. Captain Knox secretly bargained with its commander to buy their boat and arms 'and so make our escape'. But this plan was thwarted when the Dissava and his soldiers – perhaps suspecting their plot – suddenly moved them to another town.

It was some comfort that in their new quarters 'the entertainment proved as good as formerly . . . [and] to mitigate our misery . . . the People were courteous to us and seemed to pity us'.[14] In fact, as Knox later reflected, it was hard to say who were the real captives – or 'slaves' as he put it – the hostages from the *Anne* or the 'Country people . . . who by labour and pinching thire owne wives and children['s] bellies ware forced to feede us with the best they had'. The hostages themselves only had 'to eate and not run away'.[15]

Grateful as they were for this hospitality, the remaining band of sixteen men from the *Anne* now had to face the fact that they were prisoners. Until this moment, their thoughts had strained to the future, to departure; they had lived in anticipation: waiting to sail once more, to return to their native country. Now they had to acknowledge that they were, as Knox put it, 'captivated'. The original sense of the word 'captivate' was still current in 1660: 'to capture, secure, hold captive, to put or keep in subjection'. They were trapped in the present moment, fixed in a particular geographical and physical space. Although they had been on the island of Ceylon nearly two months, as if for the first time and with new eyes, they now looked upon this strange, alien world where they were stranded.

For the first time, too, it seems, they searched for an explanation for their detention. Why had the King had them seized? Only with hindsight did it occur to them that they had been guilty of 'Neglect . . . in not sending a Letter and Present to the King' of Kandy, 'who looking upon himself as a great Monarch, as he is indeed, requires to be treated with suitable State'.[6] They knew, of course, about the earlier incursions of the Portuguese and the Dutch. But only now, when it was too late to allay the King's apprehensions, did they see that their arrival must have appeared to the King like the vanguard of yet another invasion by Outlandish People.

In Defoe's novel, Robinson Crusoe is washed up on an uninhabited desert island and his lonely ordeal there is the major event of the book and the source, too, of the potent Crusoe desert island myth. But in an earlier episode Crusoe is captured by Barbary pirates and carried off to Morocco where he is kept as a prisoner and slave for two years until he escapes with the 'black boy' Xury. The raids of the Barbary pirates – both at sea and on coastal towns in Cornwall and Devon – were well known and feared by Britons. As many as 20,000 British captives were taken to North Africa in the seventeenth and eighteenth centuries. 'Barbary appalled,' as Linda Colley says, 'because its corsairs converted the sea from an emblem of commerce, freedom and power . . . into a source of menace and potential slavery.'[7]

But it is not Crusoe's early Barbary captivity – which closely resembles Knox's on Ceylon – that provides the main action of Defoe's *Robinson Crusoe*, but rather his long sojourn on the desert island. If Defoe had made Crusoe's imprisonment in Morocco the central plot or if he had populated the island in the mouth of

Orinoco where Crusoe is shipwrecked, he would have had to describe the peoples and cultures of these places. Defoe himself most likely never travelled beyond Great Britain or confronted a people more alien than the Peakrills in the 'howling wilderness' of the Derbyshire Peak or kilt-wearing Highlanders in Scotland. He plundered books of maritime voyages, but he gleaned from them little other than geographical facts. In Defoe's mind's eye, remote places and islands, if they were populated at all, were inhabited by savages that had to be conquered, civilised, colonised – or killed. This is how Crusoe deals with the groups of cannibals who turn up on his island. Until the cannibals arrive, his island is virgin territory – a kind of *tabula rasa* upon which Crusoe can project his own, quintessentially British civilisation.

Captain Knox and his men knew, of course, that Ceylon was inhabited, but like most servants of the East India Company, they merely passed through the exotic places they traded with. They didn't engage with the people who lived there. The East Indies were a vast treasure trove of spices, silks, cottons and tea: a storehouse to be plundered. In the eyes of sailors on company ships, the generally dark, undifferentiated mass of humanity that lived in these regions – the 'natives' – were merely part of the landscape. Often, it's true, they proved a hindrance or obstacle. To Europeans, their language, customs and beliefs seemed alien, primitive, even barbaric. They had to be dealt with in various ways: appeased, cajoled, cheated, dispossessed or conquered. Very rarely, if ever, was there any need to engage with or understand them.

Now Captain Knox, his son and the other men from the *Anne* would have to acknowledge, and then in some measure adjust to, this strange land where they were 'captivated'. Hostages pass through predictable stages. Initially, there is a 'fight or flight' reaction: in Captain Knox's case, the attempt to flee in the Arab boat. When fight or flight is impossible, a reason for detainment is sought with the underlying hope that the damage of this explanation might be undone. They now concluded that Captain Knox should have sent a message and gift to the King of Kandy when they had first arrived at Kottiyar. But it was too late to remedy this omission.

It is only after these first two stages, and after they have abandoned hope of an early escape or rescue, that hostages begin fully to comprehend their situation. Denial and panic then subside. Disorientation and bafflement give way to observation and the decoding of meanings.'[18] But this happens only gradually, by increments. Young Robert Knox – in all the years that lay ahead – continued to dream of escape, but at the same time, he had to come to terms with the island and its peoples, to *make* a life for himself there, to belong to some extent and in some way in this new world.

This process of comprehension and assimilation began with their march into the Kandyan kingdom at the heart of the island. The King sent a message for all the captives to be 'carried into the mountains'. With their soldier guard, they entered 'the great Woods' of the interior. To their surprise, the route was not as forbidding as they feared: the trails were narrow – they had to walk in single file – but well cleared and 'the way was plain and easy', at times, even, like walking through an 'Arbour'. The soldiers served as bearers and guides as well as guards: they carried the Englishmen's few possessions for them – such things as blankets, cutlery and clothes. Knox describes how 'as they brought us up they were very tender of us, as not to tyre us . . . bidding us go no faster than we [could]'.

At first it seemed as if they had wandered into some primordial world or gone back to the beginning of time. The woods were a labyrinth through which they threaded their way on carefully hewn, narrow paths. Gradually they ascended higher, but for days the terrain was so unvarying they wondered if they were really making any progress at all. The same birds seemed to cry above them, the same owls hooted at night; they heard the same rustle of small creatures in the undergrowth. There were no human inhabitants and every night they made camp 'on the Ground, with [only the] Boughs of Trees over our heads'.

They stopped for 'victuals twice a Day' – and ate as much as they could of rice, salt fish and dried meat. Sometimes there was even better fare when the soldiers shot a deer or antelope and found honey in the trees, which they shared liberally with the captives. Nor did they suffer from thirst, 'there being Rivers and Puddles full of [fresh] Water' the whole way. This forest was a prison to them, but it was also a place of beauty and plenty.

After ten days or so, they emerged from the thick woods and entered inhabited territory. At nightfall they halted at towns or villages full of coconut trees, 'amounge which but not under (for feare of the nuts falling)' stood thatched houses where they slept. Rice fields – 'some as large as a mile' – encircled these settlements, 'very pleasant to view'. The villagers gave them 'victuals ready dressed after their fashion' – boiled rice with meat and herb sauces and 'all kinds of ripe Fruit which [they] . . . fed heartily upon'. This hospitality continued to be 'at the Charge of the country'. They were not expected to pay.

But they soon realised that their mere presence was a kind of reciprocation. Every place they stopped, they created a sensation – like a travelling circus. When they ate the villagers would gather round to gape and wonder at the outlandish men 'sitting on mats upon the Ground', feeding themselves 'with Spoons', which they had brought with their other possessions from the *Anne*.* The Sinhalese had never seen spoons or this curious way of eating, nor had they seen the Englishmen's mode of drinking by putting a pot to their lips, rather than pouring water in a long stream into their mouths from a vessel held at arm's length above, so that their lips did not touch it. 'Thus,' Knox says, 'at every Town where we came, they used both young and old in great Companies [come to] stare upon us.'[19]

Such wonderment was mutual. The men from the *Anne* were surprised in turn by the way their hosts washed the Englishmen's hands for them before and after they ate. This, Knox says, 'we took as a token of theire servitude and respect'. Several even joked that 'they never were so much Gentlemen in their lives'. It was only much later that they could correctly interpret what this seeming courtesy meant. The villagers would not allow the Englishmen to wash their own hands because they didn't want the foreigners to handle their water pots. The Britishers were 'beef eaters' and if they touched the pots they would defile them. It was 'not respect but disdaine', as Knox later put it, that made them wait on their guests.[20] In these early days they misconstrued much of what they saw and were often baffled by what went on around them.

* Cutlery for personal use – especially knives and spoons – were standard items in a seaman's kit.

Eventually they reached the county of Hotcourlay, to the north-west of Kandy. Here an order was waiting from the King that the Englishmen should be separated and distributed to various towns in the province. This dispersal of the captives was to spread the burden of feeding them among the people and also to prevent them from plotting together to escape. Captain Knox, his son, John Loveland and John Gregory were moved together to a place closer to Kandy because, they assumed, they were to be summoned to court and an audience with the King. For two months here they 'were well entertained [and] . . . had no cause to complain'. But their fate remained uncertain, nor did they know what had become of their shipmates who had been dispatched to other places. They were closely guarded, especially at night: two or three villagers always slept in the house they shared. Soon the captives grew accustomed to their guards' nightly routines. Instead of sleeping soundly through the night, the Sinhalese would wake every few hours and sit up and smoke tobacco, chew betel nut, talk and sometimes sing, then grow quiet and drop off to sleep again.

More time passed and still there was no summons from the King. Then an 'order came from the great men in Court' to break up their small group and send them to separate towns. Though they were sad to lose the company of Loveland and Gregory, Captain Knox and his son Robert were greatly relieved to learn that they wouldn't be parted from each other. They were sent together to a 'pleasing and commodious' place called Bonder Coos-wat [Koswatta] – some thirty miles north of Kandy. Their 'black boy' from Porto Novo, who was their interpreter as well as servant, went with them.

From the day he first left the *Anne* at Ceylon, the younger Robert Knox kept careful track of the passing days and months. Thus he was able to say with precision that he and his father arrived at Bonder Coos-wat on 16 September 1660. He continued to keep a scrupulous record of dates for all the coming years, just as Crusoe does on his island. Most captives, like the Knoxes and Crusoe, have no notion of how long their detention will last – or even if it will end at all. With the future so uncertain, you might expect that time would lose significance. With no end in sight, what was the point of keeping track of the date?

Nevertheless, Crusoe notches up his days, weeks, months and

years on the island on a wooden post. When he finally escapes after twenty-eight years, he finds, however, that he 'has somehow lost track of several days. Knox didn't have or make any tangible record of time passing. He had no writing implements and he moved about so he couldn't keep track of time on a particular post or tree. Instead, he kept a running diary in his head and committed to memory the date of every significant event. Knox's Ceylon book and his autobiography, in fact, are riddled with dates, and indeed his autobiography ends with a stark list of key events and when they occurred. Keeping careful track of time gave Knox – even in his captivity – the illusion of having some sort of control. It also kept hope alive. If he took note of, and remembered, what befell him, it made him believe that some day his captivity would end. He already imagined himself at some future date, somewhere else, looking back on these events and describing them one by one in sequence, as they happened over the course of time.

When Knox and his father arrived at Bonder Coos-wat in mid-September 1660, four months had passed since they were taken captive: months of uncertainty and rootlessness. Now, they were made to understand, they had arrived at the place where they would live. They were no longer on the move. They would need to settle and to make some sort of life for themselves here.

Bonder Coos-wat was a poor rural hamlet, surrounded by rice fields and woods. The villagers were under strict orders from the King to supply the Knoxes with their best accommodation and food, so they gave the white men their choice of any house in the village. 'The Countrey being hot and their Houses dark and dirty,' Knox says, 'my Father chose an open house, having only a Roof but no Walls. Wherein they placed a Cot or Bedstead . . . with a mat upon it for him, which in their Account is an extraordinary Lodging.' Captain Knox had brought his pillow and quilt from the *Anne*. His son had also brought a pillow and the villagers gave him a mat to spread on the ground to sleep on. They were fed, as before, liberally and 'without money' – that is they paid nothing for their food and lodging. They could eat as much as they wanted of 'as good as their Countrey yielded: to wit, a Pot of good Rice, and three Dishes of such things as with them is accounted good

Cheer: ... Flesh, Fish or Eggs ... Herbs, pumkins [sic] or such like'.²¹

No work or service was required of them: they were guests as well as captives. The only demand made of them was that they make no attempt to escape. In the heat of the day, Knox and his father stayed in their shaded, open-walled house, dozing and talking. But in 'the cool of Evening' they walked out into the surrounding green rice fields 'for a refreshing'. Among their few possessions they had brought two books: Bishop Bayly's *Practice of Piety* and Richard Rogers's *Practice of Christianity*, both pocket-sized devotional works which had long been staples of pious households back in England. Knox and his father read aloud from these comforting volumes as they walked under the trees. The wisdom and solace of Bishop Bayly's and Reverend Rogers's words touched them deeply in this wild place, and buoyed their belief that, despite their captivity, they had not been forsaken. They now felt in their hearts what Rogers said in *The Practice of Christianity* – that 'God is most sweet, when the world is most bitter'.

And so they might have settled to a new kind of contentment – much as Crusoe does for many years on his desert island, until he encounters a lone footprint on the shore. In Bonder Coos-wat, the Knoxes were grateful they were still together; they reassured themselves of God's mercy, they keenly felt the blessings as well as the sorrows of their captivity. But misfortune overwhelmed them just as it does in Defoe's novel. Crusoe becomes a victim of a terrible tropical fever, and so, too, did the Knoxes. In the summer of 1660 – with the beginning of the heavy rains – a virulent wave of 'Agues and Feavours' devastated Bonder Coos-wat and the surrounding countryside Even the villagers, who were habituated to tropical maladies of all sorts, were decimated by this new sickness which was probably a cholera epidemic. Many people died and those who survived were too ill to look after the outlandish men quartered on them. This meant that the Knoxes often went hungry, 'there being none well enough to boil or bring Victuals unto us'.

Soon the Knoxes themselves were stricken with endemic, virulent malaria. Their symptoms were appalling and utterly debilitating: high fever and sweating followed by acute chills, severe headaches, aching muscles, bones and joints. When their fever was at its height they became delirious and semi-conscious. They had hideous night-mares and woke up in a cold sweat, shaking. Generally they were too weak to eat even when food was brought to them by a rare healthy villager. And if they forced nourishment down, they soon brought it back up. Malnourishment further weakened them, and both quickly lost weight. Captain Knox became especially feeble and frail.

This illness was another kind of captivity – a captivity within a captivity. It confined them to their house because they were too ill to walk out in the evenings. They were also too weak and disori-entated to talk or read: locked up and silenced by their sweating, aching, emaciated bodies.

Acute bouts of fever were followed by two or three days of lassi-tude when they became aware again of each other and their surroundings. But the attacks of 'ague' soon recurred. Captain Knox, who was in his fifty-fifth year, was less able to withstand them than his nineteen-year-old son. Not only was the older man gravely ill physically, he also fell into an acute mental depression. For his son, in fact, 'the sight of my Father's misery was far more grievous unto me than ... my own, that I must be a Spectator of his Affliction, and not any ways able to help him'. To the older man, in turn, the presence of his son was a constant reproach that 'augmented' his grief and misery as he lamented the promise he had exacted of Robert not to abandon him.

Captain Knox's fever began to abate somewhat after several months, but his depression grew even worse. His 'deep grief daily more and more increased upon him'. The Captain now realised that he was dying, and the thought of leaving 'his bones in the Eastern parts of the World', of never seeing his two children back in England and his native country again, 'did even break his heart'.

The older man stopped eating and then refused to leave his bed. For three months never did he 'rise up out of bed, but when the course of Nature required it, always groaning and sighing in a most piteous manner'. For nine days he would consume nothing other than cold water. Young Robert's fever still recurred every three days, but he tended his father as best he could, although, he says, it did 'almost break my heart'.

Another month passed and a change came over his father. He was no better physically but the anguish and despair that gripped him subsided. The 8th of February 1661 was young Robert's twentieth birthday. By this time his father was skeletal: 'he was consumed to an Anatomy having nothing left but Skin to cover his Bones'. But his mind was unclouded. In the evening he called his son to come to his bedside because he wanted to speak to him.

He said that 'he sensibly felt his life departing from him, and was assured that this Night God would deliver him out of this Captivity, and that he never thought in all his Life-time that Death could be so easie and welcome to any Man, as God had made it to him, and the joyes he now felt in himself he wanted utterance to express to me'. He told his son that 'these were the last words that ever he would speak to me, and bid me well regard and be sure to remember them, and tell them to my Brother and Sister, if it pleased God, as he hoped it would, to bring us together in England . . . He charged me to serve God, and next, he bad me have a care of my Brother and Sister. And . . . he gave me a special charge to beware of strong Drink, and lewd Company which . . . would change me into another man, so that I should not be my self. It deeply grieved him, he said, to see me in Captivity in the prime of my years, and so much more because I had chosen rather to suffer Captivity with him than to disobey his Command . . . but [he] bad me not [to] repent of obeying the command of my Father; seeing for this very thing, he said, God would bless me . . . and God Almighty would deliver me.'

Captain Knox also confided that it was 'a great comfort to him to have his own Son sit by him at his Death-bed, and by his hands to be buried, whereas otherwise he could expect no other but to be eaten by Dogs or wild beasts'. He then told him how and where he wished to be buried, to wrap his corpse in a mat, since there was no winding sheet, and to cover his head and face with his shirt. After saying all this, at about nine in the evening, he 'ceased speaking, and fell into a Slumber'. His son sat up through the dark night with his father and was with him when he finally breathed his last shortly before dawn on 9 February 1661.[22]

When morning broke, Robert wrapped his father's slight body up in his mat, and made him 'ready for the Grave'. He felt very 'sick and weak', and had only the black boy to assist him, so he sent the

boy to ask 'the People of the Town for help to carry my Father to
the Grave', because, as Knox explains, 'I could not understand their
Language.'

To Knox's grief and anger, the villagers would do no more than
send a 'great rope' which they used to tie cattle to enable Knox to
drag his father's body into the woods for burial. 'This Insolency of
the Heathen,' Knox says, 'grieved me much.' There was no way that
Knox could understand that the villagers were barred from partic-
ipating in the burial of a 'beefe-eater'.[23] In some ways the Sinhalese
seemed to venerate white men, but in their eyes an Englishman was
also an 'untouchable', of the very lowest, 'scavenger' caste. Such
people were simply dumped into graves dug in the jungle. It was
only much later that Knox learned that 'persons of inferior Quality'
– lower-caste as well as 'outlandish' people – were 'interred in . . .
the woods, there being no set places for Burial, carried thither by
two or three of their Friends and Buried without any more ado'.[24]

Thus was Captain Knox laid to rest in the early evening of 9
February, the same day he died, for it was essential in this climate
to bury him without delay. Knox and the black boy managed to
carry the body to the corner of the rice field near the woods and
river where he and his father had walked in the cool of evening
and read aloud to each other. Here Knox dug the grave, he says,
'with my own hands', having no shovel or other implements,
though a legend today persists – and perhaps is true – that he dug
his father's grave with a tin plate that he had brought with him
from the ship. It was impossible for Knox to erect any sort of stone
or memorial to his father, but he never – in all the years to come
– forgot the precise spot in the corner of the rice field where his
father was buried. He returned to this place whenever he could, and
before he finally escaped from the island many years later, he made
a last pilgrimage to his father's unmarked grave at Bonder Coos-
wat.*

After his father's death, Knox was left 'Desolate, Sick and in

---

* The location of Captain Knox's grave – and the fact that he was buried by his son
– are well known to the people who live there today. Several colonial servants in the
early twentieth century searched out and marked various locales in Ceylon with memorial stones to the Knoxes, but this is one of the few places associated with them that
has no marker.

Captivity' with only 'the black Boy and my Ague to bear me Company'.* For many months, he remained gravely ill with attacks of fever. In his worst moments, when he was too weak to rise from his bed or even 'hold up my head', he 'prayed . . . God would take my life, for it was a burthen to me'. [25]

It is small wonder that he longed for death. He was utterly alone except for the black boy; he had no news of his fellow captives and no prospect of seeing them. Instead of inheriting his father's estate and the command of the *Anne*, all that was left to him was his father's 'Gold Ring, a pagoda,† and some two or three Dollars and a few cloths [clothes]'.[26] The news of Captain Knox's death meanwhile had reached the King's court and two messengers were sent to Bonder Coos-wat to make enquiries. They questioned Knox 'how and in what manner' his father had died, and what he had left. Knox was 'scared not a little' – his 'want being so great' – that they would take away his gold ring, pagoda, dollars and clothes – his only possessions and tokens of remembrance of his father. But the King's messengers 'had no such order nor intent'. They had come in fact 'to renew the former order unto the People of that Town, that they should be kind to me and give me good Victuals, lest I might dye also as my Father had done'. The upshot of their visit was that Knox was given even 'better entertainment than formerly'.[27]

Gradually, as the months passed, his fever subsided, and 'so by degrees . . . wore away'. He went out with the black boy into the

* Despite the devotion of his 'black Boy' – whom he does not name – Knox never considered him a companion. The loyal, resourceful 'black Boy' was another feature that Defoe borrowed from Knox's book, but not for the character of Friday. Before Crusoe is shipwrecked on his desert island, he is taken captive by Barbary pirates and carried to Morocco where he is held captive for two years. There Crusoe, like Knox, acquires a faithful 'black Boy' servant named Xury who goes fishing with him and in time helps him escape from the Moors. It is the 'boy' Xury, rather than his 'Man Friday', who was inspired by Knox's servant. Despite Xury's loyalty and help, Crusoe sells him to the Portuguese captain who picks them up at sea. Knox never betrayed his 'black Boy'. In 1664 he released him to 'seek his fortune'. In the course of Knox's final escape, he encountered the boy again – now a grown man with a family. Knox hired him to guide him to the Dutch settlement at Arippu, but as things turned out, Knox made it to safety without the help of his faithful 'black Boy'.

† This is probably the same gold ring that Knox wears on the last finger of his right hand in the 1708 portrait. A pagoda was a gold coin used in India and Ceylon; its value fluctuated between seven and ten shillings.

woods where there were rivers and streams 'to catch small fish'. One day when they were out fishing, an old man passed by and seeing Knox, asked the boy if Knox could 'read in a Book'. The boy said that he could and the old man explained that he had a book that he had acquired when the Portuguese lost Colombo to the Dutch. He wanted to know if Knox would be interested in buying it from him.

Knox, of course, assumed that the book would be written in Portuguese and so of little use to him since he could not read the language even though he could now speak a few words. But he sent the boy to the old man's house to look at the book anyway. Soon the boy came running back waving the book excitedly in the air and calling out to Knox, 'It is a Bible.' Upon which, Knox says, 'I flung down my Angle [fishing rod] and went to meet him.' The boy had been a servant to an English family in Porto Novo and recognised the familiar volume. Knox could scarcely believe the evidence of his eyes: it was indeed a small octavo English Bible from 'the Reigne of King James the first with no Common prayer or apocryphya'.

With shaking hands, he opened the Bible at random. The first place his 'eye pitched on was a passage in the Book of Acts where the Jailor asked . . . Paul, *What must I do to be saved? And he answered saying, Believe in the Lord Jesus Christ, and thou shalt be saved and thine house.*'[28] When Defoe pilfered this scene in *Robinson Crusoe*, he changed the place the Bible falls open to, but the message is the same. Crusoe too has been suffering from a severe fever and when he searches for some tobacco to use as medicine, he comes upon 'a Cure for both Soul and Body'. In his seamen's chest he finds not just the tobacco but a Bible which heretofore he had had 'no Leisure or . . . inclination to Look into'. When Crusoe opens it, the first words that his eyes see are from Psalm 50: 'Call on me in the Day of Trouble, and I will deliver [thee], and thou shalt glorify me.'

Knox came from an Anglican family. Defoe was a Dissenter. Knox remained an Anglican all his life, but he had the Dissenter's cast of mind which set greater store by direct, personal communion with God – in prayer and Bible reading – than through the mediation of priests and sacraments. Because his father was so often at sea, Knox had been raised and educated principally by his mother – 'a woman of extraordinary Piety; God was always in her thoughts, as appeared by her . . . Godly exhortations to us her Children to teach us the Knowledge of God, & to love, feare, and serve him'. In addition to morning and evening family prayers, as a boy Knox read daily from the Bible aloud to his mother and sister as they sat sewing. When he and his father were 'captivated', they had gained great comfort from the passages of Scripture quoted in their devotional books, *The Practice of Piety* and *The Practice of Christianity*.

Now the whole Bible was within his reach. and Knox didn't know 'which Passion was greater, the joy . . . that I had got sight of a Bible, or the fear that I had not enough [money] to buy it'. Knox would, in fact, have surrendered all his worldly goods – even his father's gold ring – in order to buy the Bible from the old man. But the clever black boy persuaded him to conceal his 'passionate desire' for it, to in fact 'seem to slight' the book, as if it were of little value to him. The old man of course didn't know any better and had no use for it himself and so he felt he had done well when he handed over the Bible to Knox in exchange for a knitted cap the boy had made.

This 'miraculous' appearance of the Bible 'in my own Native Language, and . . . in such a remote part of the World, where [God's] Name was not . . . known and where any English Man was never known to have been' was for Knox like a rope thrown to a drowning man.[29] He took it for a sign or portent. Since his father's death, he had been overwhelmed with despair and hopelessness. Now he felt that Divine Providence had intervened and rescued him by sending the Bible to him in this godforsaken place. He now had in his possession the one book which embodied the world he had left behind. He clung fast to it for all the years he was on the Island and long after.

For months after his father died, Knox had no news of the other men from the *Anne*. Then one day, in the summer of 1662, John Gregory suddenly turned up in Bonder Coos-wat and he brought tidings of the other captives.

At first, Knox and Gregory scarcely recognised each other with their long hair, matted beards, and shabby clothes. The Sinhalese had supplied the captives with food but nothing else and their English clothing had been reduced to rags. They had long since dispensed with their coats and doublets; their loose seamen's breeches were worn thin and full of holes as were their linen shirts. They had also given up wearing stockings and shoes, and after months of walking barefoot, their feet were leathery and calloused. Gregory told Knox that the other captives now lived like natives and 'changed their habit from breeches to clouts [sarongs] like the Chingulays [Sinhalese]'. Held individually in different villages and towns, they had become so despondent in their isolation that eventually they were allowed to visit each other, but they were carefully watched for fear they would try to run away to Colombo.

Gregory also told Knox that he and the other captives had begun to bargain with their captors to gain some ready money with which to buy clothing and other necessaries. Instead of taking their 'victuals brought to them ready dressed', or cooked, they now asked for raw provisions and 'so to pinch somewhat out of their bellies, to save to buy Cloths for their Backs'. Thus they were given two measures of rice a day each, but they only ate one, using the remaining measure to barter for clothes and other essentials. In time they also devised another means of raising income by knitting caps which were popular among the Sinhalese. The thread to knit the caps cost about three pence, but they could sell caps for nine pence, thus making a tidy profit.

By this time Knox had begun to communicate in 'the Language of the Countrey . . . whereby I was inabled [sic] better to speak my mind'. After Gregory left to return to his own village, Knox asked the people of Bonder Coos-wat if he, too, could receive his 'victuals' raw as the other captives did. At first they refused, arguing that his case was different: as the late Captain's son, he had a higher status than the other captives. They said they couldn't allow him to debase himself by preparing his own food. The King might send for him suddenly and promote him to a 'place of honour'. It was for Knox's own 'credit and repute' that his food be brought to him already cooked and prepared. But Knox was insistent and he pointed out, too, that his black boy could prepare his food. After much discussion, they finally agreed to Knox's demand, and he was given two measures of uncooked rice a day for himself and one for the black boy. They were also supplied with fresh coconuts, pumpkin, herbs, limes, pepper and salt, and 'sometimes Hens, Eggs or Flesh'.

The one-room house he had shared with his father was too small both to cook his food and to sleep, so Knox set about building a larger dwelling for himself in a garden of coconut trees. His neighbours not only consented to this plan, they also helped him build it: a small, low thatched cottage, 'built with sticks and daubed with clay'. When it was finished, and the villagers had gone back to their own houses, Knox and the boy coated the outside walls with lime 'according', Knox says, 'to my own countrey [English] fashion'. But in this they had, unbeknown to them, committed 'a Capital Offence: for none may white their Houses with Lime, that being peculiar to Royal Houses and Temples'. Knox, however, incurred no penalty: 'being a Stranger, nothing was made of it, because I did it in ignorance'.[30]

After he was settled in his new house, Knox, like Crusoe, began to keep livestock – hogs, hens and goats. He also cultivated a vegetable and herb garden. From the abundant coconut trees that surrounded his house he extracted oil with which to cook his food and fuel his lamps. The black boy taught him how to knit caps at which he quickly became adept.

'In this manner,' he says, 'we lived, seeing but very little sign that we might build upon, to look for Liberty.' But he hadn't given up hope of escape and of fulfilling his promises to his dying father. Knox had settled in Bonder Coos-wat for the duration because he 'feared to run . . . [away until] I was acquainted with the Countrey'. This, he knew, would take time, planning and patience.[31]

Then suddenly, in 1664, the prospect of release seemed tantalisingly close. In early December, Knox and the other captives were summoned to the town of Nilambe, where the King kept his court, some thirteen miles south-east of Kandy.[32] The King had received a letter from Edward Winter, the new East India Company Governor at Fort St George in India, requesting the release of the English captives. In addition, there was a Dutch envoy at the King's court, one Hendrick Draeck, and he and his superiors in Colombo were mediating with the King on behalf of the captives.[33] Knox says that Winter's letter 'much pleased' the King, who summoned all the English captives to Nilambe, where, they were told, they would soon be allowed to go free.

It is unclear what the King's real intentions were regarding the captives. He suspected – correctly – that the British not only wanted their people released, they also sought to establish a trading factory in Ceylon. The King may have hoped to play the British off against the Dutch, and he might have been willing to release the captives as part of the bargain.

In Nilambe, the captives joined not only their fellows from the *Anne* but also a group of thirteen other English detainees. These were survivors from the East India Company ship the *Persia Merchant* which had foundered in the Maldive Islands in August 1658. After the wreck, fifty men crowded into the ship's two boats and sailed for Ceylon, arriving in mid-September. Thirteen of these came ashore at Kalpitiya on the west coast. Here they were taken captive and marched to Kandy. (The remaining *Persia Merchant* survivors – who didn't come ashore – sailed on to Colombo and then to Madras.) In his book, Knox devotes a whole chapter to the *Persia Merchant* men, their characters and fates, but when he first encountered them in December 1664, he merely learned who they were and that they had been held even longer than he and the men from the *Anne*.

The captives who now gathered at Nilambe – twenty-nine men in all, sixteen from the *Anne* and thirteen from the *Persia Merchant* – were called to the royal court and told by the King's nobles 'that it was his Majesties Pleasure to grant unto us our Liberty and to send us home to our Countrey, and that we should not any more look upon our selves as Prisoners or detained men'. The nobles also told them that they could leave either with the Dutch envoy or in a boat Edward Winter was sending for them.

But at the same time as he held out the prospect of liberty, the King tried to entice some of them to stay on the island by promising them 'very great rewards, as Towns, Monies, Slaves and places of Honour'. The captives all refused these baits, whereupon the court insisted upon interviewing each man separately. They wanted to know their trades and ranks and duties on their ships. The King was in particular need, it seems, of handicraftsmen and trumpeters. But still his nobles failed to tempt any of the British captives – of whatever rank or occupation – to stay. They all preferred to return to their hazardous life as seamen. By this unanimous refusal, as Knox later realised, 'we purchased the Kings Displeasure'.[34]

They were still waiting to be released when a blazing comet appeared
in the sky on the night of 21 December 1664. 'Just at that Instant,
[when] the star was right over our heads,' Knox says a Rebellion against
the King, Raja Sinha, broke out in Nilambe and Kandy, and indeed
throughout his kingdom. A large band of rebels, led by a man named
Ambanvela Rala, marched into Nilambe in the dead of night and
stormed the King's palace. The captives were caught up in the cross-
fire of the ensuing 'Broils and Combustions.' 35

Raja Sinha, King of Kandy

The King managed to escape from his chamber and flee through
a secret tunnel into the thick forest with a charging elephant in the
van to trample down the dense undergrowth. He took refuge in
the mountains at a place called Diyatilaka. The rebels meanwhile
attempted to recruit the English captives to their cause, by giving
them money and clothes and pointing out their shared hardships
under the King. This put the captives in a difficult and dangerous
position, for they had no idea which side – the King or the rebels
– would prevail. They told the rebels they wanted to remain neutral,

'but they would not permitt it. Thus Death,' Knox says, 'stood before us on boath sides.'

They were saved by an unexpected event. The rebels assumed that the King's nineteen-year-old son would gladly take the place of his father on the throne. But this plan was stymied when the Prince secretly fled from Kandy with his aunt, the King's sister, to join Raja Sinha in the mountains. The rebels were now thrown into disarray. Riots and looting engulfed the kingdom. Some erstwhile rebels now declared themselves to be on the King's side. Others remained stalwart revolutionaries. The result was chaos and mayhem. As Knox put it, 'the people were now all up in arms one against another, killing whom they pleas'd'. The hostages were still caught in the middle, but they perhaps were the safest people in the kingdom since they were aligned neither with the King nor the rebels.

After the Prince's flight, the rebellion crumbled in a matter of days. All the ringleaders were hunted down and killed. Ambanvela Rala was also caught, but the King was too astute to make a martyr out of him. Instead, he sent him in chains to the Dutch authorities in Colombo where he assumed the rebel leader would be executed. In the event the Dutch spared Ambanvela who became one of their most valuable advisors on the Kandyan kingdom.

By the end of December 1664, the 'Tumults' of the rebellion had been 'appeased . . . the Rebellion vanished, and the King was in his Throne again', though he ruled now from the security of his impregnable mountain citadel at Diyatilaka. In the meantime, many of the English captives were in desperate straits and reduced to begging for their food. In their great need, they decided to appeal to the King and they got an old Portuguese-speaking Catholic priest[36] in Kandy to write a letter for them.

As for the East India Company coming to their aid, Knox gives the impression in his book that he and the other captives felt they had been abandoned by their employers. He even accuses the company of meanness when he complains that 'noe other means (to save Charges I beleeve) than letters' were used to gain their release.[37]

Time stands still for a captive – at least it does in the world he has left behind. When Knox sailed from England in January 1658 Oliver Cromwell was Lord Protector. He and the other captives had no way of knowing that Cromwell's rotting head now topped a twenty-foot pole on the roof of Westminster Hall. Nor did they have any inkling that the restored King, Charles II, himself had called for 'speedie care to be taken that the [Ceylon captives] . . . bee freed from their bondage'.[38]

Unbeknown to Knox and the others, the East India Company had, in fact, the previous year mounted a rescue attempt that was thwarted by the Dutch. A December 1664 letter from company officials in Madras to the directors in London, describes a 'frustrated expedition to Kottiyar' to release 'our captivated friends'. This letter also includes a substantial 'bill of costs' for the 'losse & Damage by sending a Vessel from Fort St George to Zeilon' which was intercepted by the Dutch before it arrived at Kottiyar. The amount lost on this abortive rescue attempt was substantial – £168.19 – covering such things as the cost of the boat, cables, ropes, lascars' wages and the expense of a Persian horse bought as a present for the King.[39] (The precious horse, the letter writer adds, 'remayning soe long aboard yt . . . hath been diseased & is now dead'.)

Both the Dutch and the King of Kandy suspected – correctly – that the British were not only interested in the return of their captives. Even more, the East India Company sought to establish a trading factory of its own at Kottiyar, and to thwart this, the Dutch captured the ship sent to rescue the captives. This desire of the company for a foothold in Ceylon was, in fact, the main obstacle to their release. Knox and the other captives were pawns caught in the middle of the power struggle between the Dutch and their own English East India Company, both of which coveted the island's cinnamon and other lucrative resources.

Eventually, the King from his mountain citadel sent down a response to the captives' appeal for help. His answer, to their dismay, was not to resume negotiations for their release, but instead 'to quarter us in the Countrey againe'. Knox and his fellow Englishmen were now, however, to be sent to new towns and villages rather than back to the places where they'd been held before the rebellion. It was small comfort that in their new towns they were to be supplied once again with food and accommodation by the local people who had, Knox says, 'as strict a charge . . . given for our good entertainment as before'.[40]

The awful, overwhelming reality they now had to face was that they were still captivated.

CHAPTER FOUR

Shipwrecked by Land

London, 1692–97

> Shipwreck'd often, tho' more by Land than by Sea ... 'tis as
> reasonable to represent one kind of imprisonment by another,
> as it is to represent any Thing that really exists, by that which
> exists not.
>
> *Serious Reflections during the Life and Surprising*
> *Adventures of Robinson Crusoe*

You don't have to go to sea to be shipwrecked. You can court catastrophe and come to grief on dry land, as Daniel Defoe did, not once
or twice, but repeatedly in his adult life.

As a boy, he didn't dream of sailing the oceans. Defoe's father, a
prosperous tallow chandler named James Foe, was a Dissenter who
wanted his only son to become a Presbyterian clergyman. In 1674,
he sent fourteen-year-old Daniel Foe – as he was then – to be educated
at a well-regarded Dissenting Academy run by the Reverend Charles
Morton in Newington Green.* Here young Daniel met, among other
boys, Timothy Cruso who did indeed go on to become a Presbyterian
minister of the congregation at Crutched Friars.[1] Defoe spent five
years at Morton's Academy – the full course for students training
for the clergy – but he was somehow diverted from a religious
vocation – or as he later put it, 'it was my disaster first to be set
apart for, and then to be set apart from, the honour of that sacred
employ'.[2]

Defoe chose Mammon over God, or, rather, he probably thought

---

* Defoe didn't change his name from Foe to De Foe (with a space between De and
Foe) until the mid-1890s, but for the sake of clarity and consistency, I use 'Defoe'
during his early as well as later years.

that he could serve both. Around 1682, at the age of twenty-two, he went into trade, the same occupation that Captain Knox had hoped his son would follow. Initially Defoe set up as a wholesale hosiery merchant and went into partnership with two brothers, James and Samuel Stancliffe. Stocking production was a thriving industry in the 1680s. Hose were an indispensable consumer item, worn by rich and poor alike. Labourers wanted thick socks to keep their feet warm and dry in their shoes. Middling folk sought good-quality stockings and fashionable people wanted the latest colours, style and designs.

Defoe was later sneered at for being a 'hosier', but he was never a humble shopkeeper, sitting behind a counter, selling to the public. He started out as a middleman wholesaler of hosiery, but he soon expanded his business interests to general haberdashery and then to importing and exporting a variety of goods including tobacco, timber, wine, spirits, snuff and cloth.

His rising fortunes were helped along by his choice of a wife. Defoe would in time warn against early marriages for aspiring tradesmen, but he himself married young. On New Year's Day 1684, when he was just twenty-three, he wed Mary Tuffley, the daughter of a prosperous cooper, who brought with her to the marriage a large dowry of £3,700. Perhaps it was a love match; certainly Mary Defoe – who bore her husband eight children, six of whom survived – was long-suffering and loyal in the years to come. Defoe always referred to his wife with gratitude and respect, describing her on one occasion as his 'faithfull steward' and on another as 'a Vertuous and Excellent Mother'.[3] But it was trade, as he himself later admitted, that 'was the whore I doated on'. Whatever his union with Mary Tuffley was based on, one thing is certain: the marriage settlement helped fund the business that Defoe now set up in Freeman's Yard, near Cornhill and the Royal Exchange – the mercantile heart of London.

In 1685, Defoe took part in the Duke of Monmouth's abortive rebellion against James II. Four of his former classmates at Morton's Academy were captured, tried and executed after this debacle. But in the aftermath of the decisive Battle of Sedgemoor on 6 July 1685, while the defeated rebels were being hunted down, tried and sentenced to death by the notorious 'hanging judge', George Jeffreys,

Defoe evaded arrest and escaped back to London and his business premises at Freeman's Yard.[4]

His commercial activities now became increasingly varied and complex and, by the end of the 1680s, Defoe had his mercantile fingers in a number of pies. He was a wholesaler of various goods, the owner or part-owner of several ships, and a dabbler in marine insurance. He exported and imported goods to and from Portugal, Spain, Holland and the Americas. Because of these overseas ventures, many of Defoe's biographers have assumed that he travelled abroad in his early years as a merchant. In his writing in later years, Defoe himself mentioned visiting various foreign cities and distant ports during his early career as a trader. But there is no solid evidence, other than Defoe's often unreliable word, that he ever travelled to Europe or any other foreign land.[5]

In his very last, uncompleted work, Defoe insists, in fact, upon the superiority of what we now call 'virtual' over 'real' travel. For him this meant travel through reading books about places rather than going to the trouble and expense of travelling to them. Instead of taking a 'grand tour of Italy and France', he recommends making 'a tour of the world in books'. 'Travel by land with the historian,' says Defoe, 'by sea with the navigators.' 'Go round the globe with Dampier and Rogers and know a thousand times more' from reading their books than any number of 'illiterate sailors' ever do.[6]

In this rare respect Defoe took his own advice and roamed the world in books: he was an inveterate reader of sea voyages: not merely William Dampier and Woodes Rogers, but Hakluyt's *Navigations*, Purchas's *Pilgrimages*, Exquemelin's *Bucaniers of America*, John Ogilby's *Africa*, Henry Pitman's *Adventures* and Robert Knox's *Historical Relation of Ceylon*, among many others.[7]

What we know for certain about Defoe's early trading years is that by the beginning of the 1690s he had got in way over his head. Years later, in *The Complete English Tradesman*, he warned against many of the errors he himself committed at this time: overtrading, giving and taking too much credit and practising various common or 'customary Frauds of trade'. Defoe overextended himself, borrowed from Peter to pay Paul and to finance yet more ventures that he hoped would recoup his losses. Soon he was mired in debt. Suppliers, creditors, erstwhile business partners, friends and even family members began to lodge suits in the Court of Chancery against 'Daniel Foe, Merchant'. [8]

In July 1688, Defoe owed Joseph Braban, a King's Lynn merchant, £396 7s for goods that Defoe had sold for him on commission. Braban filed a suit against Defoe for this amount, and Defoe in turn filed a counter-suit against Braban. This ploy of filing counter-suits soon became a frequent recourse, not because Defoe believed himself to be in the right, but because counter-suits delayed judgement while he scrambled about for more funds.

In August 1688, Defoe sold a three-quarters share in a ship, the *Desire of London*, to a mariner named Robert Harrison for £260. Defoe himself kept the remaining one quarter. In 1689, after war had broken out between England and France, the *Desire of London*, with Harrison on board, was captured by a French man-of-war. Harrison paid his full portion of the loss, but Defoe owed £62 for his quarter share. Poor Harrison died in prison in France, but his widow and her new husband pursued Defoe for compensation in the courts. In the suit that was later filed on Harrison's behalf, witnesses testified that the ship was 'weak and leaky' and 'not worth more than £150'. Not only did Defoe not pay his share of the loss of the ship, he had sold it to Harrison for £100 more than it was worth.[9]

Defoe was also sued by another mariner named Humphrey Ayles of Redriffe, the master and part-owner of the *Batchelor of London* which had carried goods for Defoe to Boston, New York and Maryland. Because of various delays and demurrage charges, Ayles claimed Defoe owed him £424. Like the Harrison case, there is no indication in the Chancery records of how or whether this suit was resolved.[10]

Successive financial setbacks did not curb Defoe's spending and investing. If anything, they spurred him to take ever greater risks which he hoped would salvage his affairs. His debts continued to mount at an alarming rate. In 1691, he owed £400 to one Peter Maresco, £200 to John Ghiselyn and £300 to Robert Stamper. With these funds Defoe leased sixty acres of marshland in Tilbury, Essex, where he later set up a brick and pantile factory. When Defoe failed to repay Maresco, Ghiselyn and Stamper they obtained subpoenas for him to appear in court.[11] But Defoe failed to appear. This case, in fact, dragged on in the courts for the next seven years.

In 1692, Thomas Nisbett, a merchant in York, brought an action against Defoe in the Chancery to recover £100 owed to him on a bill of exchange belonging to a man named John Hoyle of the Middle Temple. Nisbett maintained in his suit that after Hoyle's death 'one Daniell ffoe of London Hosier' had paid Hoyle's servant, William Marsh, £60 to obtain the bill fraudulently. Then, to cover his tracks, Defoe endorsed the bill over to a London goldsmith named Thomas Williams. The court ruled for Nisbett and Defoe was ordered to pay back the £100, plus £5 13s 4d costs and £48 10s damages.[12]

Years later, Defoe himself poignantly admitted that most of his financial disasters were of his own making when he described the 'Infinite Mazes' of the sinking tradesman: 'what Turnings and Windings in Trade, to support his Dying Credit; what Buying of one, to raise Money to Pay another; what Discounting of Bills, Pledgings and Pawnings; what Selling to Loss for present Supply; What Strange and Unaccountable Methods to buoy up sinking Credit'.[13]

In his desperate situation, Defoe sought desperate remedies. His head, like Robinson Crusoe's, 'began to be full of Projects and Undertakings beyond my Reach; such as are indeed often the Ruine of the best Heads in Business'.[14] In 1692, he branched out from trading in solid consumer merchandise such as hosiery, tobacco, cloth and wine, and embarked on two high-risk schemes: a civet cat business in Newington Green and a diving bell expedition off Cornwall.

On 21 April 1692, 'Daniell ffoe of London Merchant' contracted to buy from John Barksdale 'seventy Civett Catts' for 'eight hundred fifty and two pounds or thereabouts'.[15] This huge sum included a purchase price of £12 per civet and rental of the Newington Green house where the cats were kept. What were civet cats doing in Newington Green? Their native habitat is Africa and the East Indies. More akin to a mongoose than a domestic cat, civets have a pointed snout and masked face like a badger or weasel. According to Court of Chancery legal documents concerning Defoe's civet cat venture, the Newington Green house had been 'fitted and made convenient and proper . . . for the keeping' of the cats, including 'several Coopes with Troughs and Cisterns to feed them in and stoves for keeping of fires in the severall roomes for the preservaon [sic] of the said Catts'.[16]

The £852 price for the civet cat farm probably also covered wages for the servants who stoked the fires, fed the cats and collected the greasy musk that the cats, crammed inside their wooden cages, secreted from their anal glands into pouches under their tails. In the wild, civets excrete musk to mark their territories. In the seventeenth and eighteenth centuries this musk – or 'civet' as the substance as well as the cat was called – was used in the manufacture of perfume, an increasingly popular luxury item. It was also considered, by some, to be a medical panacea which cured 'diseases of the head and brain . . . fits and vapours . . . bad hearing, barrenness and depression of spirits'.[17] Civet musk sold for at least £2 per ounce, so Defoe expected to make a large profit selling it to perfume manufacturers and apothecaries.

Characteristically, he didn't have sufficient funds to purchase the cats outright from John Barksdale. To initiate the transaction, he borrowed £400 from his business partner Samuel Stancliffe, to whom he already owed £1,100. But Defoe then gave Barksdale only £200 as a down payment for the cats. He promised, however, to pay another £300 within a month and the remainder within six months. Several months passed and Stancliffe – who was himself being pursued by creditors – pressed Defoe to pay off at least some of the £1,500 he owed him. But he was able 'to get none of it', due to the 'troubles that daily came upon the said Foe by reason of certain debts he had contracted and then owed to severall others'. Defoe meanwhile was still operating the civet cat business in Newington Green despite the fact that he made no further payments to Barksdale.

Finally Stancliffe – despairing of ever getting back his money – decided to take legal action. He obtained a writ of seizure for Defoe's goods and chattels, and in mid-October 1692, agents from the Sheriff's office took possession of the Newington Green civet cats. After an inventory and appraisal were made, the whole concern was offered up at public sale for the price of £439 7s – little more than half what Defoe had originally contracted to pay.

When Defoe got wind of the seizure and public auction of the civets, he turned to his widowed, solvent mother-in-law, Joan Tuffley, for aid and persuaded her to buy the cats for the asking price of £439 7s. Mrs Tuffley made the purchase on 17 October and sent in a team of servants 'to feed and looke after the said Catts and goods'. Over the next four months she spent an additional £150 'for meate and other things necessary for keeping and preserving the said Catts alive and for servants wages'.

And so things went on until March 1693 when one day the servants of Sir Thomas Estcourt turned up at Newington to evict Mrs Tuffley's people and take possession of the civet cats in Estcourt's name. Estcourt was 'a reputable and wealthy merchant', who had loaned a great deal of money to John Barksdale. When Defoe failed to pay the remainder of the amount he owed Barksdale for the civet farm, Barksdale deeded the cats and Newington Green house – which he still owned since Defoe had never paid the balance – over to Estcourt.

The baffled and dispossessed Mrs Tuffley now went to the Court of Chancery and charged 'manifest fraud' against Barksdale, Estcourt and her own son-in-law, Daniel Foe. Barksdale and Estcourt both duly made depositions in court, but not Defoe.

Nine days after Mrs Tuffley's suit was filed, a subpoena was issued for Daniel Foe, but there is no testimony in the Chancery records from 'Daniel Foe Merchant'. The man at the centre of this intricate web of debt and deception is the only one without a voice. Defoe was again lying low in the hope the storm would pass.

Even before the civet cat debacle had played itself out, Defoe was deeply involved in another high-risk venture. He invested in a newfangled diving bell. There is a certain irony in the appeal for Defoe of this particular 'project' – as such new inventions were called then. Here was a man who metaphorically speaking spent most of his life struggling to keep his head above water. But one of his greatest speculative follies was to invest in an 'engine' designed to enable men to breathe in a container submerged several fathoms beneath the sea.

Why would anyone want to be lowered in such a contraption to the ocean's depths in the first place? Lost treasure of course. In 1687, William Phipps, later a colonial governor of Massachusetts, salvaged the treasure of a Spanish ship which had sunk in the Caribbean. The Phipps expedition recovered more than £250,000 of gold and silver. Phipps's own share totalled £11,000 and he was knighted by James II on 28 June 1687.[18] Defoe later conceded that the Phipps venture was a wild gamble: 'twas a mere Project, a Lottery of a Hundred thousand to One odds; a hazard, which if it had failed, everyone wou'd have been asham'd to have own'd themselves concern'd in it. A Voyage that woul'd have been as much ridiculed as Don Quixote's Adventure upon the Windmill: Bless us! that Folks should go Three thousand Miles to Angle in the open sea for [gold and silver coins] . . . but he had Success and who reflects upon the [folly of the] project?"[9] Phipps' gamble triumphed against its 'hundred thousand to one odds' and made him a very rich man.

Francis Bacon had described a diving bell as early as 1620 in his philosophical work *Novum Organum*, and indeed the history of these submergible machines in which men were lowered beneath the sea went all the way back to Aristotle and Alexander the Great. In 1690, three years after Phipps's salvage of the Spanish treasure, Edmond Halley designed a new, improved diving bell built of wood in the form of a truncated cone, open at the lower, larger end and closed at the top, with a glass viewing window through which the person inside the bell could look out. Halley's diving bell was weighted with lead and had a cock to let out the used air in the cone which was replenished with fresh air contained in two barrels, also weighted with lead that went down with the bell and were attached to it by leather hoses. Air supply was alternated between the two barrels which were refilled on the surface, and raised and lowered from their boats by tackles. Halley explained the workings of his new diving bell in his essay 'The Art of Living Under Water', and reported that he and four other divers had remained submerged in the bell for an hour and a half at a depth of nine or ten fathoms.[20]

A 'diving engine' was precisely the kind of project or invention that would appeal to Defoe. It was ingenious and offered the prospect of making a quick fortune. Luck, rather than hard work, would bring instant wealth. The wrecks of Spanish galleons and other ships littered the ocean's floors just waiting to be plundered. Defoe was the sort of man who in a later age would have invested in a metal detector to comb the landscape for buried treasure. Thus when Defoe heard in 1692 that a Cornish inventor named Joseph Williams had been granted a patent for a new diving bell, he rushed to buy ten shares from Williams for £200. He also persuaded Williams to appoint him secretary and treasurer of Williams's newly formed diving bell company.

Their quarry was a Genoese wreck off Lizard Point in Cornwall which had sunk in 1667 laden with silver coins. A Spanish ship had also been lost at nearby Poleopor Cove with £100,000 worth of silver ingots. But the Williams diving bell scheme foundered before it ever got under way because funds for the projected Lizard Point expedition went missing. Joseph Williams brought a suit in Chancery against Defoe, charging that the secretary and treasurer of his company had appropriated money and notes that were 'for the use of the said Company and not . . . any other use or purpose whatsoever'. When Defoe was asked to return the notes and bills, Williams testified that he first 'pretended they were at his house in the Countrey and therefore could not deliver them up'. Williams then accused Defoe of having 'by Contrivance and designe' made the money 'payable to himselfe', whereupon Defoe changed tack and 'pretended that the notes were given' to him 'on his own account, and that he never promised to hand them back'.[21] The London goldsmith Thomas Williams, who had cashed bills for Defoe in the Nisbett case, also changed the Williams bills for Defoe. Joseph Williams, in fact, sued both Defoe and Thomas Williams in his Chancery case.

Defoe was subpoenaed by the court to account for his actions, but he again failed to appear or make a statement. Defoe was probably referring to this diving bell fiasco when he later wrote: 'I could give a very diverting history of a patent-monger whose cully was nobody but myself, but I refer it to another occasion.'[22] The occasion never arose and Defoe never told his 'diverting history'. But it was almost certainly Joseph Williams, not Defoe, who was duped.

More than ten years later, Defoe belatedly made a general confession of the sort of reprehensible financial practices he was guilty of in his civet cat and diving bell ventures when he wrote: 'I freely rank my self with those, that are ready to own, that they have in the Extremities and Embarrassments in Trade done those things, which their own Principles Condemn'd, which they are not Asham'd to Blush for, with their utmost Diligence.'[23]

In October 1692 Defoe went bankrupt. He owed a total of £17,000 – a staggering amount for his day – to 140 creditors, and was in danger of being arrested and jailed for debt.[24] As crisis loomed, he may have fled to the Mint — the seedy district in Southwark where Henry VIII established a mint in 1543. This building was demolished during the reign of Henry's daughter, Mary I, but up to the early eighteenth century, the area remained a sanctuary for debtors because of its legal status as a 'liberty' outside City jurisdiction. This meant that criminals, fugitives and debtors could not be apprehended and prosecuted if they sought refuge there. Defoe was certainly well acquainted with the filthy, crowded, crime-ridden streets of the Mint which he later described in *Moll Flanders*.

But if he did flee to the Mint or Whitefriars (another debtors' sanctuary), he didn't remain hidden for long.[25] On 29 October 1692 Daniel Foe, Merchant of Freeman's Yard Cornhill, was sentenced to Fleet Prison. The jail records state that he was:

> committed to the prison of the Fleet . . . by John Powell, knight, one of the Justices of the Bench . . . in discharge of the recognizances . . . of Walter Ridley of Cheapside, London, haberdasher, and Cornelius Lovett of Shadwell in the County of Middlesex, Distiller, at the suit of John Selby and £100 upon contract.
>
> And also in discharge of their recognizances, that is, of Jerome Whitchcote of Love Lane, London, merchant, and Nicholas Barrett of Whitechapel in the County of Middlesex, Sailmaker, at the suit of Edward Lambert for £60 upon pledge.[26]

Defoe was transferred to the King's Bench prison in Southwark on the same day he was committed to the Fleet, but he was sent again to the Fleet on 4 November 1692, this time:

> in discharge of recognizances . . . of Walter Ridley, Charles Noakes of Lothbury, London, gentleman at the suit of Thomas Martin for £200 debt. And also in discharge of recognizances at the suit of Henry Fairfax, Esquire. Attached in a plea of debt.[27]

Fleet debtors' prison

More creditors' recognizances followed in the months to come. It wasn't Defoe's exotic ventures — his civet cat and diving bell projects — that finally caught up with him, though they contributed. It was ordinary unpaid traders and merchants — including a haberdasher, distiller and sailmaker — who had run him to ground.

The Fleet was said by a contemporary to be 'the best Prison of any in the City, for good Rooms and other Conveniencies'.[28] But good rooms and conveniences came at a high price because prisoners had to pay for everything in the Fleet, including food and lodging, having keys turned and their irons taken off. The richest man in the prison was the warden but all the jail officers exacted exorbitant fees from the three hundred or so inmates. Most of these, like Defoe, were bankrupts and debtors. The more affluent among them had decided that peaceful incarceration was preferable to being harassed by creditors, and they rented comfortable quarters in the district surrounding the Fleet known as the Rules. Here they lived, often with their families and servants, comfortably and contentedly, safe from those they owed money to on the outside. Prisoners who couldn't afford accommodation in the Rules paid for spacious rooms on the 'Master's Side' of the jail where there was also a coffee and tap room. Debtors who swore they were worth no more than £5 were consigned to wards, but they were allowed the benefit of the begging grate – a grille built into the Farringdon Street prison wall – where they could take turns begging of passers-by. The worst-off group in the Fleet were the completely insolvent debtors who, lacking funds to purchase the freedom of the Rules or comfortable quarters in the jail, were weighed down with chains and fetters in the squalid, dank, prison cellar.

Defoe had some illustrious predecessors at the Fleet, including John Donne who was imprisoned for marrying his wife without the consent of her father, a fact immortalised in his famous line 'John Donne, Anne Donne, Un-Done'. The dramatist William Wycherley was jailed for debt in the Fleet just a few years before Defoe, and wrote a poem there entitled 'In Praise of Prison', in which he claimed that prison was a 'welcome reprieve from marriage'.[29]

A well-known publisher named Moses Pitt was already locked up in the Fleet when Defoe was committed in October 1692, and Defoe may have met Pitt either here or at the King's Bench Prison, where Pitt and Defoe (for the second time) were soon transferred. Pitt was first imprisoned in 1691, and while still incarcerated, he wrote a passionate pamphlet, the *Cry of the Oppressed*, about the appalling prison conditions, in which he described how he had to pay the keeper £2 4s 6d to secure lodgings on the 'gentleman's side' and an additional 8s every week for his room. When he ran out of money after sixteen months, Pitt was sent to the dungeon where he slept on the floor with twenty-seven men 'so lowsie that as they either walked or sat down, you might have pick'd lice off . . . their . . . garments'.[30]

The King's Bench Prison in Southwark was just as 'thronged with Debtors' as the Fleet and run in the same exploitative way. Geffray Mynshul, the son of a Cheshire gentleman and a student at Gray's Inn, was imprisoned here for debt some years before Defoe and vividly described his experience in his *Essayes and Characters of a Prison and Prisoners*. Mynshul claimed that 'every dram of content' in the King's Bench cost 'a pound of silver'. A prisoner even had to pay sixpence for 'an earthen pisse-pot'. Fees were exacted by all the prison staff, including 'cut throat the Steward' and 'Mistress Mutton Chops', the cook, both 'merciless bloodhounds', who drink 'the blood of thy purse', and also the keeper whose 'eyes shoots at two whites, thy person and thy purse, one to guard thee, the other to feed him'.[31]

The King's Bench, Mynshul maintained, had 'more diseases ... than the pest-house at plague-time, and it stinkes more than the Lord Mayor's doggehouse ... A Jailor is as cruell to his prisoners as a dogge-killer ... to a diseased curre ... they are like Bawdes and Beadles, that live upon the sins of the people.' The prison, in fact, is a 'grave to bury men alive, and a place wherein a man for halfe a yeares experience may learne more law, than hee can at Westminster for an hundred pound and ... a young man more villainy if he be apt ... than he can learn at twenty dicing houses, bowling allies, brothell-houses or ordinaries, and an old man more policies than if he had been pupil to Machieavel'.[32]

But what is most arresting about Mynshul's account of the King's Bench Prison is that he repeatedly describes it in terms of storm, shipwreck and desolate captivity on a desert island.

My travels hither to this infernall Iland [King's Bench Prison] hath been but a short Voyage and my abode here as yet but few months, but it seemes longer to mee than an East-Indian voyage, and I am sure farre more dangerous: for if from the Indies of sixty men twenty come home safe it is well; but in this, if eighty of an hundred be not cast over board it is a wonder ... Being once arrived, no starre of comfort here can be seene to sayle by, no haven of happiness neare, no anchor of hope to cast out, top-sayle, sprit-sayle, mizen, maine, sheate, bollings and drablers are all torn by the windes, and the barke itself so weather-beaten, that there is few can come neare to touch the Cape of Bon Esperanza [Cape of Good Hope].[33]

A prisoner, Mynshul insists again and again in his pamphlet, is like the survivor of a shipwreck and his enduring lament is 'What misery can bee greater than to see shore and yet be cast away?'[34]

Defoe may have read Mynshul's *Essayes and Characters of a Prison and Prisoners.* Even if he hadn't, in jail he learned at first hand the catastrophe of being 'shipwreck'd by land'. *Robinson Crusoe* clearly had its autobiographical genesis in Defoe's bankruptcies and incarceration in the Fleet and King's Bench Prisons.[35] Throughout his adult life, the threat of financial ruin 'tossed' and 'overwhelmed' Defoe in 'tempestuous seas'. Years later, he wrote a popular two-volume work *The Complete English Tradesman*, great chunks of which were devoted to the 'worst disgrace' and 'many mortifications' of bankruptcy. In the preface, Defoe said his purpose was to instruct others how 'to avoid all those rocks which . . . tradesmen so frequently suffer shipwrack upon'.[36] Defoe might seem like the last person qualified to write a book on how to be a 'complete' or successful tradesman, but his failure, he argued, actually made him a particularly reliable and expert authority on the subject: 'An old sailor that has split upon a sunk rock, and has lost his ship, is not the worst man to make a pilot of for that coast; on the contrary, he is in particular able to guide those that come after him to shun the dangers of that unhappy place.'[37]

Defoe, however, was a bankrupt rather than an insolvent debtor like Pitt and Mynshul, and though his debts were much greater, being a bankrupt was to his advantage. The distinction is often overlooked, but Mynshul and other debtors resented it heartily. In his *Essays*, Mynshul writes, 'In prisons gentelmen [insolvent debtors] and bursten cittizens [bankrupt traders] meet . . . but the newes of both are not alike, for the gentlman shall be sure to heare of nothing but wracks [wrecks], but the politique cheating bankrupt heares still that his ship comes home with rich lading, this is his safest landing place.'[38]

Mynshul protests here against the inequity of the seventeenth-century bankruptcy laws under which traders, but not 'gentlemen' (non-traders), could bargain for release from prison by reaching 'a composition' with their creditors.[39] This usually involved declaring and surrendering their assets and paying an agreed percentage of their debt to the creditors whereupon the trader would be 'discharged' and free to resume trading again. Insolvent debtors, in contrast, had no bargaining power; they were locked up indefinitely, with no means of earning money and paying off their debts. Many languished in prison for years, or until the ends of their lives. Just as Crusoe feared he would die on his island, and Robert Knox that he would never escape from Ceylon.

In 1693 Defoe was released from prison when he reached some sort of composition or agreement with his creditors, probably paying them fifteen or twenty shillings to the pound.[40] Some years later he claimed to have 'reduc'd his Debts from £17000 to under £5000', and said this was 'evident proof of his honesty', though we have only his own word for this.[41] But however much Defoe repaid, four of his creditors refused to sign the composition. This meant that even after he was free, he was not fully discharged. He remained vulnerable if one or more of these four wanted to pursue him. For the time being, though, Defoe was at large again.

When Defoe emerged from the King's Bench Prison he couldn't resume the existence he'd left behind when he went bankrupt. His business premises at Freeman's Yard, Cornhill, had been closed down. The 1694 Cornhill 'Estreats into the Exchequer' recorded: 'Dan: ffoe Hozier freemans yard gone 19s'.[42]

Defoe's wife, Mary, and their children had moved in with her mother, Joan Tuffley, in Kingsland, a village not far from Newington Green. It is unlikely that Mrs Tuffley, still smarting over the civet cat fiasco, welcomed her newly released son-in-law into her home as well. He may have rented lodgings in the city and made visits to his family in Kingsland. Whatever his specific arrangements, his old life was over.

Defoe later said a tradesman viewed bankruptcy as other men do 'the grave, with a chilness [sic] in the blood and tremor in the spirits. Breaking is the death of a tradesman; he is mortally stabb'd, or, as we may say, shot thro' the head in his trading capacity; his shop is shut up, as it is when a man is buried; his credit, the life and blood of his trade, is stagnated; and his attendance, which was the pulse of his business, is stopt and beats no more; in a word, his fame, and even name as to trade, is buried.'[43]

'Daniel Foe Merchant' of Freeman's Yard was no more. Defoe,

however, did not give up all his business ventures. It was at this time, in fact, that he set up his brick and pantile factory on the marshland that he had leased in Tilbury in Essex.[44] Defoe's livelihood and name both changed at this crucial juncture, as he went about reinventing himself as a man of business, a 'projector' and, most importantly, a writer. For it was now that Defoe embarked on his first book, *An Essay Upon Projects.*

The 1690s were, in Defoe's own phrase, 'a Projecting Age' – a time of experimentation, innovation and all manner of new schemes and inventions. The Royal Society, established in 1660, was flourishing. Newton, Boyle, Hooke and Halley were all active. Applied science, commerce and trade were expanding. As Defoe himself put it, 'new contrivances, new inventions, new trades, stocks, projects' were in the air.

Defoe's involvement with Joseph Williams's diving bell had brought him into contact with two prominent 'projectors' of the day: Thomas Neale and Dalby Thomas, both of whom were, like Defoe, diving bell enthusiasts. In 1693, Neale, who was King William's Groom Porter, launched the first lottery in England. Defoe later denounced lotteries as fraudulent, but if he held this view in 1693, it didn't prevent him from accepting a timely offer of employment from Neale. When advertisements appeared for Neale's lotteries in handbills and the *Post-Boy*, 'Mr D De Foe' was listed as one of the 'Manager trustees' for the lottery.[45]

Defoe's association with Dalby Thomas proved even more lucrative. Thomas was named commissioner of the newly imposed glass duty* in 1695 and he in turn appointed Defoe accountant of the glass tax with an annual salary of £100 (later it rose to £150) and two clerks to work under him. Treasury records indicate, in fact, that 'Daniel de Foe, Accomptant' was the highest paid person in the glass duty office.[46] He held this post with its generous salary until the glass duty was abolished in 1699.

Defoe began to use the new name De Foe – rather than Foe – in this post-bankruptcy period, in connection with his association with Neale and Thomas. 'Daniel De foe' wasn't a disguise or alias of the sort that he would later assume when he travelled incognito as a

---

* This was a tax on bottles, dishes and other glassware, not on windows.

government agent or rented lodgings when hiding from creditors or political enemies. The change of name — from Foe to De Foe* — though slight, was deliberate and significant. It indicated that his life had entered a new phase. Foe, of course, had unfortunate connotations for a man who had gone bankrupt and indeed still had outstanding debts and creditors. Defoe sought to nullify these connotations and the humiliation of bankruptcy by adding the prefix De which gave an air of gentility to his name. He was, after all, now operating on the fringes of a world of men of stature and power such as Neale and Dalby Thomas.[47]

When Defoe took up his pen after his release from the King's Bench Prison, he remained a trader at heart, but he switched commodities: he was now dealing in words rather than hosiery, wine, timber and snuff. He was still, however, on the make. In the coming years he produced an endless stream of books, pamphlets, poems and journalism. All these involved 'the production of saleable commodities'.[48] Defoe wrote for money; he sold his words by the page to a series of booksellers and printers operating in and around Paternoster Row, St Paul's Churchyard and Cheapside. It wasn't so much a matter of 'how can you make catastrophe into art' as how can you make experience pay?[49] 'Necessity', as Defoe says in the very first sentence of *An Essay Upon Projects*, must be 'the Mother of Invention'. Defoe mined his catastrophes and turned them to profit.

An Essay Upon Projects was a startling debut, born out of the ashes of his early business failure. In it he provided not merely a searching analysis of bankruptcy, but, even more ambitiously, what amounted to a blueprint for a new and better social order. Before *An Essay Upon Projects*, Defoe had published very little. Only two earlier works can be attributed to him with certainty. The first appeared in 1688: a short pamphlet entitled *A Letter to a Dissenter from his Friend at the Hague* in which Defoe argued that Dissenters should not be taken in by James II's proposed repeal of the Test Act of 1673 which discriminated against Catholics and Dissenters. James's real aim, Defoe said, wasn't to

---

* Always with a space between the first and second syllables until after Defoe's death when they were joined into one word.

aid persecuted Dissenters, but to give his fellow Catholics places 'of Honour, Profit and Trust in the Nation'. Defoe's second published work, another pamphlet, *A New Discovery of an Old Intreague*, published around 1691, was a verse satire against the Jacobites. After this there is a lull of six years, until 1697 when *An Essay Upon Projects* was published by Thomas Cockerill 'at the Three Legs in the Poultrey', a printer located a short distance east of St Paul's.

According to Defoe's own account, he had begun writing the book five years earlier – at the time of his bankruptcy and imprisonment. In the course of these five years, several of his original schemes were proposed by others. Two of them – the Bank of England founded in 1694 and the registration of seamen – were actually implemented before he published his *Essay*. But Defoe insists he came up with all his ideas independently and did not borrow from others: 'I do not write this to Magnify my own Invention, but to acquit myself from Grafting on other People's Thoughts.'[50] *An Essay Upon Projects* was, as Defoe claims, an original and ingenious work of projection and he dedicated it to one of his new benefactors, the glass commissioner and keen projector Dalby Thomas.

Defoe begins by drawing a distinction between 'meer' and 'honest' projectors. He denounces the 'frauds and tricks' of bogus projectors and charlatans whom he later compared to pickpockets, 'birds of prey' and incendiaries.[51] He even refers obliquely to his own civet cat and diving bell misadventures when he says 'there is a kind of honesty a man owes to himself and to his family, that prohibits throwing away his estate in impracticable, improbable adventures'.[52] Whether fraudulent or simply 'impracticable and improbable', such ventures had brought projection into disrepute in the eyes of men like Jonathan Swift who later lampooned the contemporary projecting craze in *Gulliver's Travels*. In his first book, Defoe set out to rehabilitate the reputation of projection and demonstrate how genuine projects could cure ills, create new institutions, and transform lives and society.

An Essay Upon Projects outlines a number of specific plans that will bring about Defoe's brave new world: a national banking system, schemes for repairing and maintaining the nation's highways, friendly societies to which people would contribute in order to help each other 'in case any disaster or distress fall upon them', a 'fool's home' for the mentally handicapped, the registration of seamen, the establishment of various academies, including a military academy, a college for women and a national academy to purify and preserve the English language.

A Pensions Office would 'prevent the general misery and poverty of mankind'. All labouring people under the age of fifty would pay a sixpence subscription and one shilling per quarter which would provide a fund for the aged, maintain widows of drowned seamen and – significantly – the wives and children of bankrupt tradesmen. Assurance societies would rescue people who suffered calamities such as fire, accidents and injuries. Defoe's dream, in fact, was that 'all mankind, be they never so mean, so poor, so unable, shall gain for himself, a just claim to a comfortable subsistence'. The end result would be to 'banish beggary and poverty out of the kingdom'.

In *An Essay Upon Projects*, Defoe didn't merely identify social ills, he prescribed – often in great detail – exactly how they should be remedied. What distinguishes a projector from a social critic or satirist is his ability – or at least readiness – to propose solutions. A projector is always a supremely practical man. In Defoe's case, he undoubtedly got more satisfaction from his own ingenious plans and schemes than he did from dissecting the social evils that made them necessary. Defoe was a fixer and a problem solver – in theory at least and in his writing.

He proposes, for example, that the national network of roads and highways that he envisions should be built by prisoners under a system whereby 'Corporal Punishments, as of Whippings, Stocks, Pillories, Houses of Correction etc might be easily transmitted to a certain Number of Days Works on the High-Ways'.[53] Defoe then goes on to specify the exact dimensions of his various proposed roads:

From London every way 10 Miles the High Post-Road to be Built full 40 Foot in Breadth, and 4 Foot High, the Ditches 8 Foot Broad, and 6 Foot Deep, and from thence onward 30 Foot, and so in Proportion.

Cross Roads to be 20 Foot Broad, and Ditches proportion'd; no Lanes and Passes less than 9 Foot without Ditches.

The Middle of the High Causeways to be Pav'd with Stone, Chalk, or Gravel, and kept always Two Foot Higher than the sides, that the Water might have a free course into the Ditches, and Persons kept in constant Employ to fill up the Holes, let out Water, Open Dreins, and the like.'

And who, we might wonder, is going to be 'constantly employed' filling up holes in the roads, letting out water and opening drains? More prisoners, including 'such Malefactors, as might on those services be exempt'd from the Gallows'. Instead of sending men to their deaths, give them gainful employment maintaining the roads.[54]

Defoe carefully costs his road system, provides tables of mileage for various sections of it, calls for signposts at every junction, and the erection of cottages at a space of every two miles to serve as sentry posts 'for the safety of the Traveller'. These cottages, he stipulates, should be inhabited gratis by 'Poor Inhabitants', thus giving them housing in return for their provision of shelter to travellers. Defoe was particularly fond of this 'double purpose' or 'killing two birds with one stone' kind of modus operandi. Convicts working on the roads would maintain the highways *and* clear the jails. Sentry cottages would afford aid to travellers *and* accommodation for the indigent.

Other projects often had a distinctive logic to their solutions: a 'Fool-House' or asylum for those with learning disabilities should be funded by 'a Tax upon Learning, to be paid by the Authors of Books'. Defoe includes a helpful table or schedule of the amount of tax to be levied on various categories of book, according to their size: folios would be taxed at £5 each, quartos at 40s, 'octavos of 10 sheets and upward' at 20s, and 'every stitched pamphlet' at 2s.[55] The more ambitious and successful a book, the higher the tax its author would pay. The Fool-House constructed from the funds thus raised would accommodate a hundred inmates to be cared for by the following staff employed at appropriate annual salaries:

A Steward	£30 per annum
A Purveyor	£20
A Cook	£20
A Butler	£20
Six women to assist and clean £4 each	£24
Six nurses . . . £3 each	£18
A Chaplain	£20

Defoe is scrupulously thorough in the design of his projects. No detail is too small for his notice. He lays down the curricula in his various proposed academies. He calculates the per capita charge for diet and clothing of each inmate in his benevolent institutions. He costs everything; makes calculations on subscriptions and interest accrued.

Many of Defoe's proposals were intended to benefit those, like 'fools' or widows, who experienced hardship and want through no fault of their own: people who were in some way vulnerable, disadvantaged or unfortunate, including the poor, the ill and the aged. But Defoe's projecting benevolence also extended to those who participated in − or were even the architects of − their own ruin: bankrupts. Much later, in his novel *Roxana*, he seemed to explain the autobiographical origin for writing his section on bankruptcy reform in *An Essay Upon Projects*: 'when a poor Debtor, having lain long in the Compter, or Ludgate, or the King's Bench, for Debt, afterwards get out, rises again in the World, and grows rich; such an one is a certain Benefactor to the Prisoners there, and perhaps to every Prison he passes by, as long as he lives; for he remembers the dark Days of his own Sorrow'.[56]

Defoe's section 'Of Bankrupts', in *An Essay Upon Projects*, is one of the longest and most heartfelt in the book and this was by no means his last word on bankruptcy: it was a topic that he remained obsessed with in much of his later writing. But he never really modified the essential views he set out in his first book where he condemns the 'barbarity . . . malice and revenge' of creditors who consign debtors to jail and make them 'uncapable of any thing but starving'. Some debtors, he laments, are even driven to suicide. Bankrupt merchants, on the other hand, flee to 'those Nurseries of Rogues, the Mint and Friars', where they mix with a 'Black Crew' of men who only harden and lead them into yet more misfortune.

Instead of flight, Defoe proposes that bankrupts do what he did in order to gain his release from prison: 'offer [creditors] what you can propose in the Pound . . . which if they take, you are a Freeman'. But if the creditors refuse and 'proceed to a Statute', the bankrupt must not take this rejection lying down but instead 'oppose Force with Force, for the Laws of Nature tell you, you must not starve'.[57] This last advice is understandably vague, but it would seem to condone whatever behaviour is necessary to regain liberty. After all, when he wrote this, Defoe had not been fully discharged by his creditors and was still under a cloud himself. He had resorted to dubious stratagems before he was imprisoned and now he seemed to countenance similar action as a last resort in the face of tyrannical creditors.

What was needed, according to Defoe, was a system under which bankrupts and creditors could negotiate in a manner that was fair and just to both parties. Of course Defoe had just the system required up his sleeve: 'A Court of Enquiries' which he goes on to describe and explain at length. This special Bankruptcy Court will receive petitions from bankrupts (Defoe helpfully includes a sample petition for them to use as a model), hear evidence from those involved in the case, arbitrate and hand down binding decisions with justice and equity to all. No detail of this Court of Enquiry is too small to escape Defoe's notice. He stipulates the number and rank of its members: a president, secretary, treasurer, judge, two lawyers '(Barristers at least) out of the Inns of Court' and 'Fifty two citizens out of every Ward two; of which number to be Twelve Merchants'.[58] He specifies that the Court of Enquiries office be located in the Guildhall, 'where Clerks should be always attending', and that the court should meet daily from 'Three to Six a Clock in the Afternoon'.

The court procedure would be as follows. The bankrupt would present his petition, after which the court would send officers to the petitioner's premises to take possession of his house and goods and make an inventory. The bankrupt would have fourteen days to draw up his books and accounts which he was then required to submit to the court. 'After this Account [is] given in, the Commissioners shall have Power to examine upon Oath all his Servants or any other Persons.' Finally 'Upon a fair and just surrender of all his Estate and Effects, bona fide', the commissioners would return 5 per cent of all the estate surrendered – 'in Money . . . or Goods as [the bankrupt] shall chuse' – 'together with a full and free Discharge from all his Creditors. The Remainder of the Estate' would then be 'fairly and equally divided among the Creditors'.[59]

Defoe's discussion of bankruptcy was remarkably foresighted and enlightened and it looked ahead to later legislation, including the parliamentary bill of 1705 which provoked him to write yet more on the subject. Bankruptcy lies at the heart of *An Essay Upon Projects*, and gives energy and life to the book. If a man could survive bankruptcy under the system Defoe presents, he could survive any 'shipwreck' by land or sea. It was all a matter of ingenuity, care and perseverance.

Defoe clearly enjoyed concocting his Bankruptcy Court and other schemes to save the world. He was what would later be called a futurologist, of a distinctly upbeat sort. Instead of predicting doom and gloom, he maps out a new and better world and explains in great detail how to bring it about. *An Essay Upon Projects* was a clarion call for social revolution on a grand scale.

Too grand as it turned out. Despite its far-sighted designs and ingenuity, the book failed to make an impact when it was published in January 1697. Its publisher Thomas Cockerill specialised in theological and educational works and he probably thought *An Essay Upon Projects* an appropriate addition to his list. But when it didn't sell, he let it slip into obscurity. This first 1697 edition was the only one to appear in Defoe's lifetime.

Perhaps he was too visionary in his thinking even for a 'Projecting Age'. Certainly the ordinary reader would have soon grown weary of all the minutiae of Defoe's elaborate plans, programmes and schemes. *An Essay Upon Projects* was not just a mission statement; it was also a collection of technical instruction manuals. Tables, lists, numerical sums and Latin legal phrases littered the text and obscured Defoe's far-reaching vision of a better society.

But this attention to detail – the exact dimensions of things, the statistics, the catalogues and specifications – was a crucial characteristic of Defoe's first novel, *Robinson Crusoe*, twenty-two years

later. Even this early, in *An Essay Upon Projects*, he had an uncanny
gift for making the mundane facts of life speak volumes.[60] It is,
paradoxically, the mundane facts in *Robinson Crusoe* that make the
book so memorable. Those who haven't read it recently seldom recall
Crusoe's early ordeal as a slave in North Africa, success as a Brazilian
planter, his long moralising reflections on the island, or his journey
through the Alps with Friday at the end of the book when he is on
his way back to England. Instead, what sticks in your mind, long
after you have closed the book, are a collection of vivid concrete
images and sensory perceptions: the 'two shoes that were not fellows'
of lost crew members that wash up onshore after the shipwreck; the
protracted process Crusoe contrives to fire pots and bake bread;
the gleaming eyes of the old goat he encounters in a cave; the
abandoned, land-bound boat it took Crusoe months to build but
which he failed to consider how to bring to the shore; the shrill
voice of Poll the parrot breaking the island silence, calling 'Poor
Robin Cruso, Poor Robin Cruso'; the single footprint in the sand
that fills Crusoe with terror. These vivid, emblematic scenes and
moments capture Crusoe's loneliness, fear and yearning, as well as
his ingenuity, cunning and will to survive.

In *An Essay Upon Projects* Defoe made two great discoveries. The
first was that the purpose of writing was quite simply to *use* adversity rather than succumb to it. The second was that the most effec-
tive way of doing this was with a wealth of facts: the steady, careful
accumulation and specification of detail.

Why doesn't Crusoe just lie down in the sand and give up? Well,
there is God of course and Crusoe's 'miraculous' discovery of a Bible
in his sea chest when he is ill and searching for tobacco with which
to dose himself. God and Providence loom large in Defoe's moralising passages in the book. These pious ruminations are sincere,
but for most readers they are not the key to Crusoe's survival. What
really rescues Crusoe from despair is the way he imposes himself
and the world he came from upon the uninhabited wilderness of
the island. Despite the catastrophe of his shipwreck, Crusoe remains
the same, just as Defoe did despite the trauma and humiliation of going bankrupt in 1692. *An Essay Upon Projects* was not a
commercial success, but writing it, Defoe demonstrated for the first
time in print what was to become the dominant obsession of much

of his later work: the only sure way of conquering the harsh blows
life dealt out was to make use of them. When shipwrecked by land,
take up a pen rather than an oar or a sail. Make experience into a
saleable commodity. If life fails you, rewrite it.

Two hundred years after *An Essay Upon Projects* first appeared,
the Victorian critic Leslie Stephen summed up the Crusoe survival
formula when he wrote:

> Robinson Crusoe is Defoe and more than Defoe, for he is the typical
> Englishman of his time. He is broad-shouldered, beef-eating John
> Bull, who has been shouldering his way through the world ever
> since. Drop him in a desert island, and he is just as sturdy and self-
> composed as if he were in Cheapside. Instead of shrieking or writing
> poetry, becoming a wild hunter or a religious hermit, he calmly sets
> about building a home and making pottery and laying out a farm.
> He does not accommodate himself to his surroundings; they have
> got to accommodate themselves to him. He meets a savage and at
> once annexes him . . . Cannibals come to make a meal out of him,
> and he calmly stamps them out with the means provided by civil-
> isation. Long years of solitude produce no sort of effect upon him
> morally or mentally. He comes home as he went out, a solid keen
> tradesman, having somehow or other, plenty of money in his pockets,
> and ready to undertake similar risks in the hope of making a little
> more. He has taken his own atmosphere with him to the remotest
> quarters.[61]

Stephen overstates the case and is even unfair here; Crusoe is by
no means 'sturdy and self-composed' and calm all the time. But
it's true that Crusoe 'does not accommodate himself to his
surroundings; they have got to accommodate themselves to him'.
Crusoe's essential being doesn't alter. Despite being cast away on
a desert island, he undergoes no sea change. It is the island itself
that must change, as Crusoe slowly but relentlessly recreates his
home civilisation.

After he went bankrupt and was imprisoned in the Fleet and
King's Bench prisons, Defoe altered his profession, circumstances
and name. But the fixed, unchanging constant in his character and
personality remained: he always turned – or tried to turn – adversity

into gain. Fate, fortune, his own bad judgement or rash behaviour
– whatever these brought down upon him – Defoe searched for and
generally found in and wrested some sort of advantage out of them.
By hook or by crook, he exploited misfortune for benefit. He was,
like Crusoe, a survivor.[62]

CHAPTER FIVE

'Having But Little and Wanting Lesse'

Ceylon, 1665–79

After the failed rebellion in December 1664, when the English captives were dispersed again throughout the King's realm, Robert Knox was sent to a place called Handapondown to the west of Kandy. Arriving here in early 1665, he found that it was 'much nearer to the Sea' than Bonder Coos-wat, where he had lived with his father, and this consoled him somewhat despite his continued detention because, as he says, 'it gave me some . . . hopes, that in time I might make an escape'.

But for the present, to avoid suspicion, he went to work, 'to Build me another House upon the Bank of a River'.[1] Friendly neighbours helped Knox construct his house which he then fortified like Crusoe does his island home, digging a deep ditch around it and planting a tall, thick hedge beyond this moat. Crusoe feared attack from savage animals or peoples. Nothing threatened Knox in Handapondown, but he still protected his house in this way. He was literally digging in.

For furniture he made simple benches out of bundles of sticks tied together with creepers, rather than labouring for days, like Crusoe does, to make a table and chair. He created doors out of coconut leaves woven into large mats which he then hung at the front and back entrances of his house. Wooden boards, Knox explained, were scarce in Ceylon, not for want of timber but because there were no saws with which to cut them. Only rich men went to the trouble and expense of obtaining planks by having whole trees felled with axes. Each tree then yielded just two planks which were generally used as large wooden doors in 'great mens houses'. In *Robinson Crusoe*, Defoe's hero resorts to the same laborious method of making boards, but when Knox first built his house at Handapondown he says planks were 'to[o] much worke for me'.[2]

He found that local ways were almost always best. Unlike Crusoe, he didn't go to the trouble of making pottery. For plates he used large green plantain leaves. He slept, as his neighbours did, on a mat on the ground, with a stone for a pillow. In this manner, he says, he slept 'many years on the hard ground with onely a matt under me, as well as ever I have done eather before or since my Captivity in sheets one [on] a feather bed'.[3]

By the King's command, his neighbours supplied Knox with food, but he had released his black boy 'to seek his Fortune' before coming to Handapondown, so now he prepared and cooked his own meals: rice and corn and what Knox calls 'Carrees' or curries – the Portuguese word for a stew made of jackfruit, pumpkin, coconut or other vegetables. He also ate an abundance of fruit, which grew everywhere: plantain, bananas, oranges, lemons, mangoes, pineapples, watermelon, pomegranates and grapes and sugar cane. Fresh water to drink was plentiful. Coarse brown sugar was made from the sap of the jaggery palm or kittul tree which also yielded a sweet toddy that could be fermented into arrack or 'racke' as Knox called it.

Knox also adopted the local habit of chewing areca nuts wrapped in betel leaf which he refers to simply as 'betel'. This was actually a preparation of sliced areca nut wrapped up with lime in the leaf of the betel vine. Sometimes cardamom and tobacco were also included. The resulting bundle or wad was then put in the mouth and chewed or sucked. Betel was considered a medical panacea and taken as a painkiller, laxative, aphrodisiac, remedy for bad breath, cure for indigestion, arthritis and worms. But it was also mildly addictive and most commonly used not as a medicine but a stimulant.

According to Knox, betel varied in the effects it produced. If it was eaten when the areca nut was still green and not fully ripe, it made 'people drunk and giddy-headed and give them stools [diarrhoea]'. More commonly, betel gave you a lift, banished sleepiness and fatigue and assuaged hunger. Habitual use stained a regular user's teeth red or sometimes black, and discoloured teeth in turn were considered attractive in Ceylon where betel was consumed by young and old, men and women, alike.[4] When Knox finally left Ceylon years later and was deprived of betel, he suffered withdrawal symptoms, and he always resumed chewing it whenever it was available to him.

By the time Knox arrived in Handapondown, he had been 'captivated' for five years and his English clothes were in rags. The only thing that was still intact was his tricorne hat. But even this was scarcely recognisable because he had unpinned the wide brim so that it could lie flat and shield his face from the sun. Knox describes how he had to improvise 'to cover my Carkas' when his clothing became threadbare and worn. He tore the flaps or tails off his cotton shirts and made breeches out of them 'which did very well for a while', and after these wore out, he cut off the large sleeves of his shirts and found that he could make 'one scant pare of briches' out of them, which, 'with the body of the shirt without sleeves made me a whole suite'. 'In this habbitt,' he says, 'without stockings or shooes I walked up and downe.'

But after a time, even these makeshift garments fell apart. By now his hair reached down to his waist and his beard was a span long, so he began to go naked from the waist up, his back covered by his long hair and his chest with his beard. Then, when his shirt-flap and shirt-sleeve breeches completely wore out, he got 'a Cloute [sarong or long loincloth] & wore the countrey habbett [native dress]'. He also used his 'cloute' as a coverlet to keep him warm when he slept on his mat at night. He soon realised that this new native attire was 'more Convenient heere'. Shoes as well as shirts and breeches were superfluous: 'instead of difficulty I found a great Conveniency to be bare foot'. His feet grew tough and calloused and needed no protection.

Clothes may not make the man, as the saying goes, but they certainly reveal him. It is interesting to contrast Knox's simple clothes with Crusoe's elaborate approximations of English dress. Crusoe describes his apparel in great detail:

> I had a great high shapeless Cap, made of Goat's Skin, with a Flap hanging down behind as well to keep the Sun from me, as to shoot the Rain off from running into my Neck . . . I had a short Jacket of Goat-skin, the Skirts coming down to about the middle of my Thigh; and a Pair of open-knee'd Breeches of the same, the Breeches were made of the skin of an old He-goat, whose Hair hung down such a Length on either Side, that like Pantaloons it reach'd to the middle of my Legs; Stockings and Shoes I had none, but had made me a Pair of

some-things ... like Buskins [half-boots reaching to calf or knee] to slap over my Legs, and lace on either Side like Spatter-dashes [gaiters] but of a most barbarous Shape, as indeed were all the rest of my Cloaths. I had on a broad Belt of Goat's-Skin dry'd, which I drew together with two Thongs of the same, instead of Buckles, and in a kind of Frog on either Side of this. Instead of a Sword and a Dagger, hung a little Saw and a Hatchet, one on one Side, one on the other. I had another Belt ... which hung over my Shoulder; and at the End of it, under my left Arm, hung two Pouches, both made of Goat's-Skin too; in one of which hung my Powder, in the other my Shot. At my Back I carry'd my Basket, on my shoulder my Gun, and over my Head a great clumsy ugly Goat-Skin Umbrella ... As for my Face, the Colour of it was really not so Moletta-like [mulatto] as one might expect from a Man ... living within nineteen Degrees of the Equinox [changed to '9 or 10' degrees in the 4th edition]. My Beard I had once suffer'd to grow till it was about a Quarter of a Yard long; but as I had both Scissars and Razors suffi-cient, I had cut it pretty short, except what grew on my upper Lip, which I had trimm'd into a large Pair of Mahometan Whiskers, such as I had seen worn by some Turks, who I saw at Sallee.[5]

Talipot leaf

Despite the hot climate on his island, Crusoe is fully clothed, including breeches, jacket, gaiters and footgear. He also trims his beard and presumably cut his hair. He is fully armed and carries an umbrella. His skin remains untanned despite daily exposure to the equatorial sun.

Instead of Crusoe's crudely constructed approximation of an English umbrella, Knox adopted the standard Sinhalese equivalent – a large, sturdy talipot leaf that kept off both rain and sun and could serve as a tent when he travelled from home. His silver pocket watch had long since stopped, and he now reckoned time as his neighbours did, by a plant called the 'four o'clock flower'.[6] This was a deep purple or white blossomed flower that opened every day at four o'clock in the afternoon and remained open 'until the morning, when it closeth up it self till four a clock again'. These flowers grew wild in the woods, but people transplanted them to their gardens 'to serve them instead of a Clock'. They were completely reliable because they bloomed even when clouds obscured the sun.[7]

Thus by stages Knox sloughed off his English dress and habits. With his deeply tanned skin, betel-stained teeth and 'naturall dresse', he could scarcely be distinguished from the Sinhalese he lived among. And in spite of what he calls his 'poore & meane . . . food, raiment & lodging', he was 'in good health & strength & I think better than [if he had had] sumptuous Appareil: Voluptuous faire; & delicate and soft lodging'.[8] He 'followed' his 'business in Knitting' caps, keeping livestock and going about the countryside selling his caps. It wasn't long before he felt 'very well contented in this Condition'.[9]

On his deathbed, Captain Knox had warned his son to 'beware of strong Drink, and lewd Company which . . . would change me into another man, so that I should not be my self'. Knox, now twenty-five, had changed profoundly since he arrived in Ceylon five years earlier, but it was not drink or 'lewd company' – the native arrack and liaisons or marriage with Sinhalese women – that wrought this change. It was the island itself and the experience of being 'captivated' there that transformed him into 'another man'.

His life now mirrored that of his neighbours. He ate local food, wore native dress, rose early to work in his garden and retired when the sun set in the evening. During the night he woke every couple of hours, as was the Sinhalese habit, to smoke tobacco and chew betel nut, and lie awake, listening to the murmured conversations and singing from his neighbours' houses. Then when he got drowsy, he lay down and drifted off to sleep again.

Knox later described this kind of life with sympathy and approval. Nature, he said, has 'stored this Island' so plentifully with crops and animal life that the people 'neither need nor have many manuall operations, except tooles to till the ground, to sow Cotten for Clothing, and for rice; for they reach not at more than food and raiment and drinke the water of the brookes. Thuse with these naturall helpes they live with little labour, having less riches and Care than we in England, but are healthfull, Cherfull and Carelesse [without cares] and so live with theire wives and Children tell [till] worne out with old age. Thus they eate to live (not for wantonnesse) and live to eate ... theire Chiefe divertion is to sett and talke with theire friends and neighbours. This kind of life have I had many years experience of, haveing but little and wanting lesse – I meane such things as are absolutely nessary for mans subsistance – and so could very well have Contained my self to have Continued, had not thoughts of slavery so perced my heart that I accounted it better to dye in the attempt to attain liberty than to live with want thare of."[10]

Why did 'thoughts of slavery' pierce his heart? Knox describes himself as free and contented, not enslaved. He didn't have to labour for his food, he was kindly treated, he was healthy and had everything he needed. Many of his fellow captives settled into this simple lotus-eating kind of existence without regrets. It was not thoughts of slavery, as Knox claimed, which prevented him from sinking into this world, but 'duty' and 'home' and the vows he had made to his father to return to England and care for his brother and sister and tell them of their father's fate.

Thus however much he assimilated and accommodated himself to island life, Knox remained ambivalent. Outwardly he 'went native', but not in his heart. Unlike many of his countrymen, he was unable or unwilling to live just in the present moment on the island. This meant that he was torn between the world he had come from and the one where he was cast away. And it never seems to have occurred to him, now or in the years to come, that the land of his birth would have changed beyond recognition during his absence; that his friends would have ceased to think of him; that his siblings would have accepted and adjusted to life without their father and brother. Knox, in other words, didn't lose faith in the stability of his English home and his place in it, and this is why he couldn't let go of his determination somehow to escape from Ceylon.

It was this overriding desire – and faith – that he must one day return to his 'native countrey' that lay behind Knox's unwillingness to marry when his Handapondown neighbours urged him to take a Sinhalese wife. The Sinhalese were baffled by his refusal, arguing that a wife would 'be an ease and help' to him. 'It was not convenient,' they said, 'for a young man ... to live so solitarily alone,' and they pointed out that marriages in Ceylon were easily dissolved so that any union Knox entered into need not be binding. If, at some future date, Knox preferred another woman, or if the King allowed him to return to England, Knox could 'discharge' his wife, take another one, or go away 'without any offence'.[11]

Knox pretended to listen to this kindly meant advice so that his neighbours wouldn't 'suspect ... I had any thoughts of [running away to] mine own Countrey'. But he put them off by saying 'that as yet I was not sufficiently stocked [did not have sufficient wealth], and also, That I would look for one that I could love'. In his heart, however, as Knox says, 'I never purposed any such matter; but on the contrary, did heartily abhor all thoughts tending that way'.[12]

Knox's reasons for 'abhorring' the idea of marrying a Sinhalese woman were complicated. He had strong religious scruples against marrying a non-Christian, though he didn't condemn his fellow Englishmen for taking Sinhalese wives, which most of them did. In fact, he defends them in much the same terms as Crusoe defends his island's colonists' marriages to native women in the *Farther Adventures of Robinson Crusoe*. Knox says that the '[un]lawfulness of matching Heathens and Idolaters' with Christians and the absence of 'Christian priests to join them', might seem an insuperable obstacle to such unions, but 'these cases we solved for our own advantage after this manner, That we were but Flesh and Blood, and that it is said, It is better to Marry than to burn, and that as far as we could see, we were cut off from all Marriages any where else, even for our Life time, and therefore we must marry with these [Sinhalese women] or none at all'. There was even biblical authority to support such marriages: 'there are examples in the Old Testament upon Record, that they took Wives of the Daughters of the Lands where they dwelt'.[13]

Despite his bachelor state, Knox learned a great deal about the sexual mores on the island. When he came to write about the people of Ceylon in his book, he described their intimate lives in detail, including such matters as adultery, sodomy, incest, contraception, abortion, pregnancy and childbirth. He was no prude and the world he paints is very different from the asexual one Crusoe inhabits on his island.[14] How did Knox come by his knowledge of sexual activity in Ceylon? Perhaps at second hand, from his fellow captives who married there. But it is also possible that he himself had personal experience of intimate life on the island.

The years of Knox's captivity were in his own words 'the prime' of his life, the period when, in the normal course of things, he would have established himself, courted, married and raised a family. He could have had all these in Ceylon, but his secret determination to return home made him shun them. This meant that despite his fellow captives and friendly neighbours, Knox remained in some ways as lonely and solitary as Crusoe was on his island.

Two years after Knox first settled at Handapondown, the Dutch established a garrison nearby at Arandara. Only a ridge of mountains separated this new fort from Knox. He was confident the Dutch would help him if he could manage to escape to their outpost. But the only route to it was a narrow path through dense forest. All the trails in the King's realm had manned watch posts at regular intervals. Every traveller had to halt at these and present for inspection an official permit or authorisation for his journey. In addition, everyone had to carry the seventeenth-century equivalent of a photo ID – a passport made out of a clay tablet with a seal or device impressed on it. These seals varied according to the bearer's profession: a soldier's passport showed the image of a man with a pike on his shoulder; a labourer's had a man with two bags hanging on the opposite ends of a pole carried on his shoulders. A 'white man', according to Knox, carried a passport with 'the print of a Man with a Sword by his side, and a Hat on his head'.[15]

If Knox had tried to flee to the Dutch without a permit or

passport, he would have been stopped at the thorn gate of the first watch post and apprehended by the King's sentries. Furthermore, the King foresaw that the English captives might attempt to escape to Arandara, and so he ordered Knox and three other captives who lived in the vicinity to move to a place called Laggendenny which was much further away from the new Dutch fort. This order came without warning, so Knox was forced to leave Handapondown without delay with just the clothes on his back. He set off, under guard, with the three Englishmen who lived nearby – John Loveland, Thomas Kirby and William Day. 'And thus,' as he says, 'I was carried out of this Countrey as poor as I came into it, leaving all the fruits of my Labour and Industry,' including outstanding debts owed to him, 'behind me.'[16]

Laggendenny was a small, isolated settlement of just five houses perched high up on a mountain. The captives' hearts sank as soon as they set eyes upon it: it looked to them 'one of the most dismal places' in the land. The King banished malefactors and others whom 'he was minded suddenly to cut off' to Laggendenny – a fact that depressed them even more as they assumed they were now considered 'malefactors' too. But their 'trouble and dejection' over their exile 'lasted but a day'. For soon the King sent a messenger up to the 'sad and dismal mountain' to inform the native inhabitants that 'they should not think that we were malefactors, that is, such as who having incurred the King's displeasure were sent to be kept Prisoners there, but men whom his Majesty did highly esteem, and meant to promote to great Honour in his Service, and that they should respect us as such and entertain us accordingly'.[17] Thus the captives' status as people of importance was established. But in the three years they lived there, Knox says that the natives grew 'weary of us, who were but troublesome Guests to them', because they had to be fed and 'would not permit or suffer' the natives 'to domineer over us'.[18]

In Laggendenny, Knox shared a house with his 'dear friend and fellow Prisoner' John Loveland. William Day and Thomas Kirby had by this time 'despaired of their Liberty and . . . taken Wives or Bedfellows' with whom they lived.'[19] The captives' food was brought to them by the villagers. Altogether, it was a dull life; they had, as Knox says, 'little to do, only to dress, and eat and sit down to knit'.[20]

Few visitors ever toiled up the mountain to the settlement and they had only infrequent news from below of their fellow captives.

Even today Laggendenny is a remote, inaccessible place, and no one at all lives there now. The winding narrow road up the mountain is potholed and bumpy, with very few vehicles on it. Occasionally a farmer on foot comes round a bend with a bundle of corn or rice on top of his head. If you stop to ask him where Robert Knox's house was, he points further up the mountain. And sure enough, at the summit, where the road forks before it begins its steep descent, a solitary engraved stone monument – erected by a British colonial servant in 1908 – marks the spot where Knox and Loveland had their house.[21] An endless vista of mountains falls away from Laggendenny, range after range of jagged peaks separated by precipitous gulfs and canyons. Winds buffet the mountain top and beat down the tall grass. It is easy to grasp why Knox felt utterly cut off and forgotten up there.

Despite their isolation at Laggendenny, in 1669 Knox and Loveland learned that a captive named William Vassall had secretly received letters and funds from the Dutch authorities in Colombo and the East India Company agent in Madras, which Vassall had not shared with the other English prisoners.[22] Vassall knew that sending and receiving letters was strictly forbidden by the King, and fearing that someone would report him, Vassall himself told the King about these letters and 'pretended excuses and reasons to clear himself'. This stratagem had the desired effect: 'The King . . . seemed not to be displeased in the least, but bid him read them. Which [Vassall] did in the English language, as they were writ; and the King sat very attentive as if he had understood every word.'[23] The King, however, didn't know English, so he comprehended nothing. But Vassall succeeded in cleverly ingratiating himself.

When Knox and Loveland found out about Vassall's treachery, they wrote a letter of their own to the Dutch authorities and the East India Company agent in Madras. This, in fact, was the first of four letters they wrote on ola leaves – the widely used papyrus of Ceylon made out of dried strips of the talipot or palm fan, which had been used for writing since ancient times.[24] Because sending or receiving letters was strictly forbidden – it was considered a serious crime that could carry a death sentence – their letter had to be smuggled out.*

Knox and Loveland's first letter was dated August 1669 and it opens with their grievance against Vassall.

In the year 1664 we received a packet . . . which is all that we have received, although Mr Vassall has received some, but concealed the fact from us, and money also which we have not once received, though our necessity is so great. Our company is all still in life and health. Only Arther [sic] Emery, the Captain [Knox], and Jan [sic] Gregory are dead. At present there are 23 persons still alive who would be glad to regain their liberty. As for news, we dare not write any, fearing that our note may be intercepted or captured on the road, and we refer you to the bearer Perga, who can inform you of all that has passed better than we can write. As he has hazarded his life in carrying this, we beg you to reward him liberally. The Dutch are not unmindful of our being looked after in case your Honor can by any means send some assistance, as the bearer can direct you, to us poor afflicted captives who will not cease to pray for your Honor's long health and prosperity, remaining your Honor's servants

John Loveland

Robert Knox

The direction on the reverse side of the ola leaf was 'Into whatever good Christian hands this note shall come, we pray, for God's sake, to aid in forwarding it'.[25]

Perga, the messenger who carried the letter, made it safely to Colombo where he delivered it to the Dutch Governor, Ryklof van Goens. Van Goens then duly forwarded it, along with a sympathetic, explanatory letter of his own to the East India Company agent in Madras. The Dutch rewarded Perga and gave him fifty pagodas to take back to Knox and Loveland, along with as many clothes as he could carry.[26] In their next letter, dated 23 January 1670, Knox and Loveland revealed that Perga failed to return. Either he was a 'rogue' – as Knox and Loveland were quick to assume – and ran off with

---

* All the captives' letters from Ceylon remained a secret, in fact, for over two hundred years until they were discovered in the East India Company and Dutch colonial archives in the 1890s.

the money and clothes himself, or he was apprehended by the King's guard. Whatever the case, in their second letter, Knox and Loveland complain again of William Vassall's refusal to share news or funds that he received: 'what Mr Vassall hath received we know not . . . whatsoever comes unto him . . . be it monies or letters he keepes from us soe his poore distressed brethren may perish for him'.[27] When Vassall was confronted with his perfidy, however, he flatly denied it. It is unclear just how Knox knew of Vassall's duplicity. Vassall was the only captive who didn't adopt Sinhalese dress. He was known to the Sinhalese as 'the English factor' — a reference to his former position as merchant or supercargo on the *Persia Merchant* as well as to his clothing. He could only have maintained his European dress if he had the wealth to have new garments made — possibly with the money sent by the Dutch which he failed to distribute among all the captives — but it's unlikely that Vassall's clothes alone revealed that he had received funds from the Dutch.

Knox's second letter is signed not only by himself and John Loveland, but also by two other captives from the *Anne*, John Merginson and Thomas March. After protesting against Vassall, they describe their 'hellish condition . . . very poore . . . and miserable', and entreat the authorities to send any future letters for them to Knox or Loveland or to the 'Pilato Engres' — the English pilot, Merginson — or the 'Condestable Engres' — the English gunner, Thomas March. As instructed, the Dutch sent their next letter to Knox and Loveland, along with ten pagodas, but this letter also went astray as Knox reports in his third letter of July 1670. This time Vassall wasn't to blame, but the messenger, who 'not knowing any [of] us', apparently gave the letter and money to another captive who simply pocketed both instead of directing the messenger to Knox and Loveland in Laggendenny.

Finally, at the end of July 1670, in their fourth letter, Knox and Loveland reported that they had received a letter from the Dutch Governor dated 22 May 1670 and enclosed with it a ten-page letter from the new Madras East India Company agent, George Foxcroft. In their reply, Knox and Loveland once again warned against sending any communication through William Vassall 'for if it comes to his hands the rest of the distressed English shall not be the better for it'. And they reiterate their sorry plight: 'our condition is lamentable and very poore like our brothers the Dutch prisoners [of the King] who drinck of the same cupp of want as we do'.[28]

In their letters to the Dutch and the East India company, Knox and Loveland express the hope that they will one day escape, but unlike William Vassall, they do not suggest ransom payments or gifts that the Company might send to the King in order to redeem them. This was because they knew that if any British ambassadors or envoys bearing payments or gifts ventured to Kandy, they would themselves be taken captive by the King. As the company agent in Madras wrote to the East India Directors in London, 'none . . . dare adventure to go with any letter or other thing to ye King of yt [that] Iland [sic], for . . . he suffers never any to returne yt [that] come to him'.[29]

Thus their situation seemed, for the time being at least, hopeless. They remained stranded on their mountain at Laggendenny. But the King's palace at Nelemby was just several miles away, so Knox periodically went to the court in the hope of obtaining a licence to be 'removed' from Laggendenny and 'placed anywhere else'. Though he used his 'utmost skill' to get a permit to visit his old home in Handapondown to recover some of his debts from the people there, Knox was repeatedly denied permission to travel.

Undeterred, he devised a clever plan for going back. He hired a Sinhalese man to go with him so that he would be able to pass through the sentry watch posts. Knox explains that 'altho I was the Master and he the Man, yet when we came into the Watches, he [pretended to be] the Keeper and I the Prisoner'. And so they went together to Handapondown 'into my old Quarters, by pretending that this man was sent down from the Magistrate to see that my Debts and Demands might be duly paid and discharged'.[30] Their ruse was a great success and when Knox and his 'Master' arrived at Handapondown, he was able to collect at least some of the money still owed to him there.

Even more importantly, though, Knox learned in Handapondown that a piece of land was up for sale at a place called Eladetta. The only people who were allowed to own land in the Kandyan kingdom were Buddhist priests, and this particular land had belonged to one such priest who had recently died and left it to his nephew. The nephew in turn now wished to sell it. Knox, in his own words, had been 'some seven or eight years in this Land, and by this time came to know pretty well the Customs and Constitutions of the Nation', but he still went to the Governor of the district in which the land was situated to enquire whether he might 'lawfully' buy it. The Governor, learning that the land had belonged to a priest, 'approved' its sale and even 'encouraged' Knox to purchase it.* And so, Knox says, he bought the land at Eladetta for 'five and twenty Larees, that is Five Dollars, a great sum of Money in the account of the country'. A title deed to the land was written 'upon a leaf' according to the local custom, which was 'witnessed by seven or eight Men of the best quality of the Town', and Knox 'took possession of the Land', which lay ten miles to the south of Kandy, and five miles north of a town called Gampola.[31]

As soon as he had purchased the land, Knox set about building a new house on it with the help of three English captives who lived nearby – Roger Gould, Ralph Knight and Stephen Rutland. From the beginning Knox planned to share his house with these friends. They were not part-owners but by their labour they had purchased their right to live there as long as they wished, provided they did not marry. 'We were all single men,' Knox explains, 'and we agreed very well together.' In order to preserve this harmony Knox says that 'with a joynt consent it was concluded amongst us, That only single Men and Batchellors should dwell there'. They decided, in fact, 'to make such a Covenant to exclude women from coming in among us, to prevent all strife and dissention [sic], and to make all possible Provision for the keeping up of love and quietness among ourselves'.

It would be easy to read all sorts of things into this all-male set-up. But what is most clear is that he was attempting to establish not merely an ideal, conflict-free sort of community but also that he envisioned it as a quasi-permanent one. He was settling in for the duration, literally putting down roots with every seed and tree that he planted in his garden. He assumed now that he would still be there when these flowered and bore fruit.

---

* This would seem to defy the law that only Buddhist priests could own land. Knox's status as a foreigner was probably the reason the Governor granted him permission to buy the land.

Before they had finished building the house, Knox left the other three men still working on it while he returned to Laggendenny to wait for a 'fit season' to move permanently to what he called 'my Estate at Elledat'. The King's order which had banished Knox to the mountain had not been lifted. But Knox had discovered that the King's commands 'wear away by time, and the neglect of them comes at last to be unregarded'. In early 1670, even though Knox wasn't certain that it would be safe to leave Laggendenny, he and John Loveland were 'resolved to put it to hazard', and they came down from the mountain – Knox to his new house at Eladetta and John Loveland to settle at the nearby town of Gampola.

Eladetta, as Knox put it, 'liked me wondrous well'. His land was beautifully situated in the midst of rice paddies and cornfields and intensely green rolling hills. He now extended his homestead: besides the two rooms that he, Gould, Knight and Rutland slept and ate in, they built another house four yards away which they walled only halfway up leaving the upper part 'open for light & air'. Then they made shutters of talipot leaves for these 'windows' so that they could be opened and shut 'like shop windows'. This second house or hall was called a 'mandua' and they used it to receive visitors and entertain guests. In the years to come, when the English captives became free to travel in the King's realm, Knox invited them and their families to Eladetta for the 'festivals' of Christmas and Easter. The men would then sleep in the mandua with Knox and his house-mates, while their wives and children lodged in the main two-room house. Describing these celebrations Knox says, 'I feasted them for 2 or 3 days . . . with goates, hogs, & hens, & the reason I invited theire wives was to dresse the victualls . . . we had every meale Rost, boyled & baked; the latter I did in an earthen pan, made for my purpose, with the fire one the top & bottome, & flower I made myself beaten in a Mortar, which made a very good pie, & we sett the oven or pan in the Middle [of us] & so eate.'[32] Defoe borrowed Knox's baking method wholesale for Crusoe's bread-making in *Robinson Crusoe*.

Knox's Eladetta residence was the last and most elaborate that he built in Ceylon, and he went to considerable pains constructing and furnishing it. The house itself was 'built . . . with better stufes . . . wood & bigger than either of my former houses'. And for the first time he strove to create an English sort of home for himself. He had proper doors built out of wood 'planke[s] with Staples & padlocks to hange thare on'.[33] He even had a bedstead – 'a frame cased with Canes . . . with . . . 4 legs, large and stronge' – though he did without bed curtains and used his mat as a mattress. Instead of the rock he had used up to now for a cushion, he devised a pillow out of 'a sort of wild cotton . . . almost equall to feathers'. He also brought out a small quilt that he had taken from the *Anne* which he now re-covered with coarse native cloth and used as his bedcover. His household goods included earthen and brass pots, basins to eat rice out of, two stools and 'a small table (which latter the Chengulayes [Sinhalese] never use) . . . iron tools, 2 or 3 spare clouts [loincloths or sarongs]'. Altogether his comfortable home and its furnishings greatly pleased him and he felt that he 'had as good lodging as any Gentleman in the Country'.[34]

Eladetta remains a fertile, lush landscape today, little changed, except for the modern bungalow inhabited by a retired police sergeant and his family where Knox's house once stood. This place is not easy to find, but if you stop anyone walking along the road they can give you directions to Robert Knox's house, as if he were living there still. As in Laggendenny, there is another memorial stone to Knox's residence – also 'erected 1908' – at the end of the police sergeant's drive. The sergeant – who is old now and blind – is himself an authority on Knox's life. His son-in-law will take you down the path through the forest to the threshing ground where labourers bring huge stalks of rice to be threshed mechanically rather than by the elephants and cattle that trod the rice in Knox's day. The spring where Knox bathed and washed his clothes is nearby.

For a time after he settled at Eladetta Knox continued to receive his allowance of food from the people of Laggendenny, but at last they told him in 'plain Terms' that 'they could give it to' him no more, and that he 'was better able to live without it than they to give it to me'. They were aware that Knox was prospering in his new quarters and was capable of maintaining himself. Not only did he continue to knit caps and trade cotton thread, he also 'set up in a new Trade' – lending corn to his neighbours at a rate of 50 per cent per annum. This indeed he found a 'most profitable way of Living'. He converted all his stock into 'corn or rice in the Husk' which he then lent out to his neighbours. Then, when their harvests were ready, they had to pay back to Knox 'the same quantity I lent them, and half as much more'. This obviously was a lucrative 'trade', but it also required vigilance. Knox had to keep a close eye on his customers' fields and as soon as their crops were ripe make his 'claim in due time otherwise other Creditors coming . . . will seize all'. 'By this means,' Knox confesses, 'I was put to a great deal of trouble, and was forced to watch early and late to get my Debts and many times miss . . . them after all my Pains.'[35]

By now the people of Laggendenny had stopped sending food to Knox and the other Englishmen, arguing that since they had left the mountain of their own free will, their Laggendenny hosts were not 'bound to carry our Provisions about the Country after us'. Knox decided to take his case to the judge, or adigar, at the King's court, little expecting that this would lead to a 'great danger, out of which I had much ado to escape'. What happened was this. The adigar heard Knox's application for his food allowance and rather than renew the order for the Laggendenny people to supply it, he told Knox that he could henceforth receive his monthly allowance of provisions from the King's court. This meant that Knox had to go to court regularly to collect his food. These visits 'brought him to the notice of . . . the Great men', who were impressed by Knox and decided that he could 'be of use and service' to the King. But this prospect of being given 'Honourable employment' by the King horrified Knox, because he knew that if he joined the court, it would make it even more difficult for him to escape.

Several English captives had already been recruited into the King's service and for a time they prospered. One of these, a man named Richard Varnham, was given command of 970 soldiers, ruled over several towns, and was presented with a silver sword and halberd. Two other captives, Hugh Smart and Henry Man, were personal attendants to the King whose 'clothes and linen-wear [were] under their supervision and custody'. They also slept at the King's feet during the night. But both Smart and Man came to grief in the end. After secretly communicating with the Dutch ambassador at Kandy, Hugh Smart was banished into the mountains. Henry Man was promoted Chief over all the King's servants, but one day he accidentally broke one of the King's china dishes. He knew that this was a grave offence so he ran to a nearby Buddhist temple for sanctuary. The King sent a reassuring message 'not to be afraid for so small a matter as a Dish' and told him to return to his place at the palace. But as soon as Man emerged from the temple he was seized by the King's soldiers and bound so tightly that his arms swelled up and 'the Ropes cut throw [sic] the Flesh into the Bones'. For months Man was kept in chains and when he was finally released, though he was restored to his former position, he had lost the use of both arms.

An even worse fate awaited him. A Portuguese man who lived some distance from Kandy was sent for by the King who wanted him to enter his service – a prospect, Knox says, that he 'had no stomach at all' for and 'was greatly afraid of'. The Portuguese fellow wrote to Henry Man and asked him to use his influence with the King, but before Man could take any action, someone else at court reported this correspondence and suspected intrigue to the King. The King's reaction was swift and merciless: he ordered that all three men be executed: the Portuguese writer, Henry Man who received his letter, and the person who informed on them. They were condemned to a particularly gruesome form of execution: trampling to death – or 'torn in pieces' in Knox's account – by the King's elephants.[36]

Richard Varnham, Hugh Smart and Henry Man had nothing to qualify them for high positions at the King's court. Varnham indeed, Knox tells us, was 'given to drunkenness' and wasted all his income on women and alcohol. But all three men were, in Knox's phrase, 'very propper Comly persons', and it was their attractiveness that 'prevailed with the King'. The King clearly singled out for royal service those captives who were particularly handsome. This criterion of physical beauty also determined his choice of young male Sinhalese attendants. Knox doesn't say why the King was eager to recruit him into his European retinue, which included not only the three English captives but also the Dutch ambassador Hendrick Draeck who had first arrived at the King's court in 1664 to plead the cause of the captives and was never allowed to leave. Presumably all of them were handsome men. Poor Draeck died while still in detention in Kandy in 1670.

It was, then, almost certainly Knox's own 'comly person' that brought him to the notice of the King. When he became aware of the King's intentions, Knox realised he was in real danger, and 'fearing I should suddainly be brought in to the King, which thing I most of all feared, and least desired, and hoping that out of sight might prove out of mind, I resolved to forsake the Court and never more to ask for Tickets [for food] especially seeing God had dealt so bountifully with me as to give me ability to live well enough without them'. And thus, as Knox explains, 'I was driven to forego my [food] Allowance'.[37] This meant that he now had to earn his own way and buy his provisions which he did by continuing his trade in knitted caps, lending corn, and also 'Pedling and Trading in the Country.'[38]

In September 1670, when Knox was well established at Eladetta, he received a letter from John Loveland who lived just five miles away at Gampola. Loveland wrote to say that he had fallen 'sickely, & had mind to come to' stay with Knox at Eladetta. He had only a 'blacke Boy' servant to help him at Gampola, and feeling melancholy as well as ill, he wished for 'English company'. Knox, of course, 'will-ingly assented' to Loveland joining their household, 'knowing we could bee more helpfull & Comfortable'.

Soon after he arrived at Knox's house, Loveland's condition deter-iorated: 'his disease increased to runing paine from one part of his Boddy to another exceeding violent'. He was seized with agonising fits that 'made him roare out', with only short pauses of peace. The heartbreaking task of nursing his 'dear friend' now fell to Knox. Loveland didn't fade away quietly as Knox's father had nine years earlier. For days he was racked by paroxysms of pain which rendered him speechless, though 'he was in his perfect sences'. In the brief intervals between fits he 'prayed to God either to ease him or remoove him hence by death'.

When it became clear that he was dying, Loveland told Knox that he wished his few possessions to be divided equally among the English captives they lived with – Stephen Rutland, Ralph Knight and Roger Gould – because all three were poor men. He asked that his clothes be given to his black servant boy 'who had served him well'. The only thing that he bequeathed to Knox was his silver pipe to remember him by. This might seem a meagre legacy, but Loveland made it 'not for want of Love' of Knox, 'but to releeve the Needy' Gould, Rutland and Knight. His pipe was of less value but it was his only personal possession. It would also survive the ravages of time and Loveland knew Knox would use it often and remember his lost friend.

When Loveland's last 'very violent' fit came upon him, Knox 'tooke him up in my armes & his head lay on my left sholder'. Loveland said no more, but for some hours he muttered 'grones & earnest prayers'. He finally died in Knox's arms early in the morning on 22 October 1670. Knox was now, if possible, even more heart-broken than when his father died. As he said, 'In all my life I never had such an intire [sic] intimate friend as he [John Loveland]; I may compare us like Jonathan & David.'

Knox's only consolation was that he was not left entirely alone after Loveland's death, as he had been when his father died. Knox, Rutland, Gould and Knight buried their friend that same evening 'as Decently as our Circumstances would permit just behind my house'. No stone marks the spot where John Loveland lies. We only know the circumstances of his death and his final resting place because years later Knox described it in his manuscript autobiography. His reason for recording his friend's death, Knox says, is that 'some of Mr Loveland's Relations have wished to heare more of him'.[39]

Loveland's illness was not contagious and after his death, Knox himself remained in good health though much depressed in spirits by the loss of his friend. Knox indeed was seldom ill during all the years of his captivity in Ceylon, a fact which he ascribed to his healthy diet and physical exercise – farming his land and walking long distances in the course of his trading. He doesn't mention any more attacks of 'ague' or malaria after the bad bout he had at the time of his father's death. But he does mention another sort of 'severe Feavor' that people got during times of drought when streams of fresh water dried up and they were forced to drink from ponds of thick, muddy rainwater. Such fevers could swiftly prove fatal.

Knox soon discovered, however, that there was 'an Antidote and Counter-Poyson' for this terrible affliction – a 'dry leaf beaten . . . to a Powder' and mixed with jaggery. The Portuguese called it 'Banga' and the Sinhalese 'Consa'. This miracle cure was actually the plant called hemp which we now know as cannabis. Hemp had been used widely in India and Ceylon for centuries.[40] But Knox's glowing and detailed description of it is one of the first to appear in English. Whenever he feared he had drunk contaminated water and might come down with fever, Knox ate cannabis 'Morning and Evening upon an empty stomach'. According to him, it quickly banished the fever, though it had other effects as well: 'It intoxicates the Brain, and makes one giddy . . . deprives a man of memory [so] that in disscourse he cannot remember what hee hath sayed . . . It procures a great appetite.' Despite these side effects, Knox considered cannabis 'very holsome . . . [it] is good for those that are posesed with griefe or trouble in the mind'. It was, he says, 'much used by the moores [Muslims] all over India and is in most parts Generally Called . . . Gange'.[41]

Although Knox mentions the intoxicating effects of cannabis, he gives the impression that it was consumed by the Sinhalese principally as a medicine. Another Englishman, Thomas Bowrey, who travelled in India and Ceylon during the same period, also described 'Bhang', as he called it. But Bowrey thought that people used cannabis to 'besott themselves'. And because it had, according to Bowrey, a 'more pleasant Operation' than arrack and other spirits, it was 'more addictinge . . . and sold at fives times the price'.[42] Bowrey, however, merely visited India and Ceylon – he didn't live there as Knox did – and he may have misinterpreted cannabis use. Knox, at any rate, viewed cannabis as a medicine. And the only people who, Knox says, 'besotted' themselves in Ceylon were some of his fellow English captives who drank large quantities of arrack.

In 1672, two years after John Loveland died, Knox's 'family [at Eladetta] was reduced to two', when Roger Gould and Ralph Knight 'seeing but little hopes of Liberty, thought it too hard a task . . . to lead a single life' and married. In accordance with Knox's bachelors-only 'Covenant', Gould and Knight moved out to live with their wives. This meant that all the work of the household now fell to Knox and Stephen Rutland 'whose inclination and resolution', Knox tells us, 'was as stedfast as mine against marriage'. They began to breed goats, as Crusoe does, and also to keep hens and hogs. They fetched their own firewood and water, beat their rice out of the husk, tended their cooking fire, prepared their meals and washed their own pots and pans. Knox also became 'very expert' at the 'great arte' of washing stones from the rice which, he explains, 'generally our rice is full of, which doth very much anoy the teeth unlesse clean washed out'. [43]

Knox and Rutland thus lived together as a couple in Eladetta, but Knox says little about Rutland himself or his feelings for his house-mate. They plotted how they might escape together and they trusted each other, but they don't seem to have been close friends the way Knox and Loveland had been. Besides the two of them, the only other inhabitant of the Eladetta household for the next three years was their tame red monkey which Knox taught to bring a firebrand to light their pipes when Knox said to him in Sinhalese: *'Ghindera penula genning'* — 'a firebrand bring'.[44]

But something else happened in 1672. At about the same time that Gould and Knight left to marry, Knox himself may have become a father. In his published book, *An Historical Relation of Ceylon*, he records that in January 1676, he 'adopted' a child who he says was 'one of my poor Countrey-men's Children'. There is informa-tion in Knox's manuscript autobiography, however, that suggests that this child, a little girl named Lucea, may in fact have been his own daughter.

Knox tells us that she was three when she came to live with him in January 1676. If Knox *was* Lucea's father he would have known and remembered the precise date of her birth. At the very end of his manuscript autobiography he records 'Certaine Passages I would Keepe in Memory'. This takes the form of a list of all the signifi-cant dates that occurred during his captivity and what happened on each of them. But three dates are merely written down with no indication of what transpired on them or why they were important to him.

The first date Knox recorded is 4 April 1660, next to which he wrote: 'I came on Shore at Cuttiar on Zelone when & whare I was Detained Captive.' Then he notes 10 April, the day his father came on shore, followed by 11 April, when the men from the longboat were detained. After this there is a gap until 9 February 1661, the day his father died. The next date is 16 September 1664, when Knox says he 'received letters from England'.[45] Then there is another gap of six years until John Loveland's death on 22 October 1670. This is followed by 22 September 1679, the day Knox 'sett out from my house in order to make escape', after which he records his precise movements over the next four months until he finally sailed for England.

Knox also lists the following three dates with no explanation of what happened on them: 'October the 2th Anno 1672; Janua the 26th Anno 1676; May the 13th Anno 1679.'[46]

Knox wrote down his list of dates sometime between 1709 and 1720 – long after they occurred. Those with brief explanations make perfect sense as milestones in his life in Ceylon. But what of these three dates recorded at the end? What happened on them, why did he want to remember them, and why did he not write down why he wanted to 'Keepe [them] in Memory'? At some point in the last decade of his life – when he was upwards of seventy – Knox in his lodgings in St Peter le Poer wound up his autobiography with these mystery dates. The only other thing he wrote at the end of his auto-biography was that he had found 'by the Church booke in Nacton . . . in Suffolk' that his grandfather was born there in 1581 and that his father was 'borne there also & Baptised the 15th March 1606'. This information is followed by just four words in his hand – 'By Mee Robt Knox'. Knox thus formally signs his long account of his life.

Why did he fail to write down what happened on 2 October 1672, 26 January 1676 and 13 May 1679? These were secret dates that he wished to put on record, but not to explain. The only events that seem to fit these dates are ones connected to Lucea. We know that when she came to live with him she was three, which is how old she would have been in January 1676 if she was born on 2 October 1672. Three, of course, is the age at which she would have been weaned. Knox finally escaped from Ceylon in 1679, and 13 May 1679 could have been the last time he saw Lucea, though he did not actually embark on his escape until September. Several months before he set off, he must have arranged for Lucea to be adopted by one of his countrymen and taken her to settle in with her new family.

In his unpublished autobiography, Knox also copies out a letter he wrote to the English captives many years after his escape, in

December 1698, when he – by this time the captain of his own East India Company ship – was in Cochin in south India. After giving the captives news of their families in England, Knox tells them:

> I find a man in his Native Country [England] amounge his Relations is not free from trouble, many of which I was free from whilst on Zelone [Ceylon], in so much that I still Continew a single man. I have heere with sent my picture [small portrait or miniature of himself] to the Girll I brought up, Lucea, and you know I loved the Child and have no cause to hate her.[47]

Ostensibly Knox is here consoling his friends for their continued captivity by saying that life back in England is difficult and lonely. But there seems to be more going on in this letter. The three central points that leap out over the gulf of centuries are that Knox is announcing that he has not married, that he is sending his picture to Lucea – who he names for the first time here – and that Knox 'loved the Child' and has 'no cause to hate her'. The only thing that could have diminished Lucea's place in his heart is if he had had more children when he returned to England, especially a son or sons. In this letter Knox is explicitly communicating the fact that he has not married or had children since he returned to his 'native country'. His real 'family' – his daughter Lucea – was left behind in Ceylon.

Another clue that suggests that Knox may be Lucea's father is the fact that, before he left Ceylon, Knox made a will and went to the trouble of having it authorised by a judge or adigar and witnessed by several of the other English captives. In this will Knox stipulated that in the event of his death or his departure from Ceylon, Lucea should inherit his land and house at Eladetta and all his possessions. In his manuscript autobiography he reports that he later learned that Lucea did indeed receive this handsome inheritance. This news was brought to him by several captives who escaped some years after Knox and made it back to England.

In his published book Knox says that he adopted Lucea when he 'began to consider how helpless I should be', if he failed to escape and instead 'grew old and feeble' in Ceylon. Who would care for

him in his decrepitude when he was no longer able to look after
and provide for himself? He describes how 'I entred [sic] upon a
Consultation with myself for the providing against this [old age]'.
One way was to take a wife, but this, he says, 'I was resolved never
to do'. Next he 'began to enquire for some poor body to live with
me, to dress my Victuals for me', and do other chores – someone
who could then care for him in his old age. But he could find no
one who suited him. It was, he says, only after he had ruled out
these first two options – marrying and finding a servant – that he
decided 'to take one of my poor Countrey-mens Children, whom I
might bring up to learn my own Language and Religion. And this
might be not only a Charity to the Child, but a kindness to my self
also afterwards.' According to Knox, several of the English captives
with families were 'glad to be eased' of one of their children and
so he says he chose one 'by whose aptness, ingenuity and company
I was much delighted at present, so afterwards I hoped to be served'.[48]

This was Knox's official version of how and why Lucea came into
his life in January 1676. But certain things don't ring entirely true.
Or at least leave unanswered questions. A three-year-old child – even
in rural Ceylon where children grow up quickly – is still a very
young one to take on and she would certainly need a great deal of
care. If Knox wanted a child to help him why didn't he 'adopt' one
that was older – seven or eight perhaps – who could assist him right
away and not have to be tended to herself? When Lucea came to
live with him, she did in fact take up much of Knox's time and
attention, not that he in any way begrudged her this. He taught her
English and 'haveing no primer I made letters on a tallapot [sic]
leafe' and taught her how to read and write. Soon 'she could read
any plaine Chapter in my bible'.[49] Crusoe of course also teaches his
man Friday English. But Lucea was not Knox's Friday. When she
came into his life in 1676, she created more – not less – work in the
household. Knox at this time, in fact, also hired 'an old man to dress
my victuals [cook]' and do other chores, including no doubt looking
after Lucea when Knox was away from home.

An alternative account of Lucea's parentage and birth would go
something like this: In early 1672 Knox had some sort of liaison
with a Sinhalese woman, and their child, Lucea, was born on 2
October of that year. He couldn't 'adopt' her of course until she was

weaned. But when she was weaned – in January 1676 – Lucea came to live with him. If all this did in fact happen, who was Lucea's mother? Knox never mentions any individual Sinhalese women. If he had a relationship with one, there is simply no way of knowing her identity or anything about her. But it is interesting that Knox does say in his book that pregnant women in Ceylon never have the cravings for certain foods that Englishwomen commonly have. He also describes the 'exquisite' methods used by the Sinhalese for contraception and their customs at childbirth. Such information may well have come from his own experience.

The identity of Lucea's mother – or her father – cannot be conclusively resolved. And perhaps her biological parentage isn't really the important issue. The crucial thing to grasp about Lucea's entry into Knox's life in 1676 is that in his heart she *was* his daughter. And she remained his only child long, long after he escaped from Ceylon. Nineteen years after he had last seen her, he sent her a picture of himself and reasserted that he 'loved her well'. If the three unexplained dates at the end of Knox's autobiography mark Lucea's birth, her coming to Knox's home and the last time he saw her, they make a moving conclusion to his autobiography. A little girl, who came to live with him when she was only three and whom he left behind when she was just six, continued to haunt Knox for the rest of his life.

In 1676, then, Knox was faced with two possible futures. Either he would grow old in Ceylon and live out his days there with Lucea, or he would escape and return to England. He never says which fate he wished for most. And in his own mind, what he desired was less important than what he had promised his father. It was his duty to do his dying father's bidding and make every possible effort to return to his native country.

By this time Knox and Stephen Rutland had 'brought our House and Ground to such a perfection that few Noble mens Seats in the Land did excell us'.[50] Their Eladetta neighbours often observed to Knox that they were sure 'I lived better thare [in Ceylon] than I ever did in my owne country, which I would owne to be true that they should have the lesse suspition [sic] that I intended to runaway'. Thus Knox and Rutland 'did Plot and Consult . . . between our selves with all imaginable Privacy and . . . laboured by all means to hide our designs'.[51]

They worked on their escape plans by gradually extending their peddling trips further and further until they could be absent from Eladetta for a whole month without arousing suspicion. They travelled throughout the King's realm and 'speaking well the Language and going with our Commodities from place to place', they literally learned the lie of the land by talking to the local peoples in the various areas where they traded. From them they learned the best routes, which areas were least populated and 'where and how the Watches' were situated. They pretended that they were gathering all this information to learn what goods were most in demand in each region and Knox says, 'None doubted but we had made these inquiries for the sake of our Trade . . . Neither was there [the] least suspistion of us for these . . . questions: all supposing I would never run away and leave such an estate as . . . I had.'[52]

'By diligent inquiry', Knox and Rutland learned 'that the easiest and most probable way to make an escape was by travailing [travelling] to the Northward [of Kandy], that part of the Land being least inhabited'. So they obtained the trade goods that were most 'vendible in those parts, as Tobacco, Pepper, Garlick, Combs, all sorts of Iron Ware etc and being laden with these things we two set forth, bending our course towards the Northern Parts of the Island'. Their ultimate goal was to make it to a Dutch settlement at Mannar on the north-west coast.

In the late 1670s they made, according to Knox, 'eight or ten' trading trips to the north and in the course of one of these they reached the edge of the King's dominions some miles from Anuradhapura. But here they encountered a severe drought and since there were no springs, they ran out of water. They drank dirty pond water instead – so thick and muddy 'that the very filth would hang in our Beards when we drank'. And this contaminated water in turn gave them 'fevers' and agues that prevented them from going any further. They had to call a halt where they fell ill, and 'both lay Sick together', unable even to help each other.[53] They dosed themselves with cannabis, and when they had finally recovered enough to walk again, they were so weakened they had to retreat back to Eladetta.

On another trial run north, Knox and Rutland encountered the 'black boy' Tamil servant Knox had brought to Ceylon on the *Anne* from south India and then released to pursue his own fortune after the 1664 failed rebellion. By now this Tamil boy had grown up, married and had children. He seemed as glad to see Knox as Knox was to find him, and he explained that he had now lived in this northern region for many years. Knox could see the man was poor and scarcely able to maintain his family, and he asked him if he would be willing to guide Knox and Rutland to the Dutch settlement at Mannar. Knox promised a good reward and his Tamil friend was 'very joyful and promised to undertake' this job. But he said that as it was then harvest time and many people were out in the fields and on the roads, it was not safe to pursue their escape plan now. He suggested instead that they meet again at the same place in two months' time.

Two months later Knox and Rutland kept their rendezvous with their Tamil guide, but on the eve of their flight, Knox was taken by a 'grievous pain in the hollow of my right side [so that] for five days together I was not able to stir from the fire side'. This was Knox's first attack of 'the stone', or 'the graviell' as he called it. Bladder stones plagued Knox for the rest of his life, but this ill-timed attack in Ceylon was his first. Samuel Pepys and Daniel Defoe, among other contemporaries, also suffered from 'the stone'. Pepys had his stone surgically removed in 1658 – a risky operation without anaesthetic – and he survived both the operation itself and its aftermath when a patient could easily be carried off by infection. Defoe suffered from 'the stone' for years before he submitted to surgery in 1725 when he was in his mid-sixties. Knox, as far as we know, never had surgery. This first attack in Ceylon was acute but after five days of 'warming' his 'grievous pain' and 'fomenting and chafing it', he says he got 'a little ease'.[54] By then, though, it was too late and he was too weak to continue further north.

Knox and Rutland made several more escape attempts, one in company with their fellow captive Ralph Knight, but because Knight was married they did not 'acquaint him of our design', intending not to tell him 'till the Business [final escape] was just ready to be put in action'. But when they reached the spot where they had arranged to meet their Tamil guide he was not there. They waited for a time, then gave up and retreated again to Eladetta where they delivered Knight 'to his wife, but never told him anything of our intended design, fearing lest, if he knew it, he might acquaint her with it'.[55]

By this time Knox had settled Lucea with her new family. He and Rutland continued to bide their time. A serious drought thwarted another escape attempt. They tried, without luck, to communicate with their Tamil guide but he seems to have completely disappeared, for Knox never mentions him again.

Having decided to 'persist in our . . . Northern Discovery', Knox and Rutland finally felt the time was ripe to set off once again without a guide. As Knox explains, 'having often gone this Way to seek for Liberty . . . we again set forth to try what Success God Almighty would now give us, in the Year MDCLXXIX [1679], on the Two and twentieth of September, furnished with such Arms as we could well carry with safety and secrecy . . . [and] several sorts of Ware to sell as formerly.' They had waited until the full moon so 'that we might have a light . . . to see the better to run away by'.[56] Knox left his old manservant to look after his house and goats, as he had done before, just as if he were embarking on another trading expedition and would soon return. And so, on the morning of 22 September 1679, Knox, now thirty-eight years old, along with Stephen Rutland, left Eladetta for the last time.

CHAPTER SIX

Escape

Ceylon and Java, 1679–80

They left Eladetta by the most arduous route – a crooked, winding trail through 'great woods' and up a hill called Bocawl (Bokawala) which Knox says was so high and steep that 'very few people goeth that way'. Because the track was rarely used, there were no watch posts or thorn gates. Their plan was to follow such overgrown, lonely trails the whole way north to the coast. What they lost in speed and ease of travel, they gained in security. Escape from Ceylon could be achieved only by calculation, cunning, patience and stamina. They had been held captive for nineteen years and had learned not to be in a hurry.

After descending from Bocawl, they came to Bonder Coos-wat – the town where Knox had lived with his father and where his father had died. Eighteen years had passed since he had dug his grave. For what he knew was the last time, Knox wanted to see the place in the corner of the rice field near the stream. He thought that when he left Ceylon, no one would visit this green spot or remember that it was a burial place.* Knox had promised his father that he would return to England, yet the heavy cost of keeping this promise was to feel he was leaving his father behind on the island.

There was no time to linger at Captain Knox's grave. They had to press on towards Anuradhapura which marked the boundary of the King of Kandy's territory. In all their escape trial runs, they had got no 'nearer than twelve or fourteen miles' of Anuradhapura

* Knox, however, was mistaken. The people who live in Koswatta have remembered where Captain Knox is buried, and will still take anyone who asks to the place where his son dug his grave more than three hundred years ago.

for fear of the watch posts. Leaving Bonder Coos-wat, they entered an uninhabited 'wilderness . . . full of Elephants, Tigres [sic] and Bears'. They emerged at a town called Colliwilla (Kaluvila) which was surrounded by impenetrable forest. Here they knew they would be stopped and questioned not just by inhabitants, but also by the Governor, a prospect that filled them with trepidation. But they had no option but to 'go boldly and resolutely' to the Governor's house, and 'not to seem daunted in the least . . . but to shew such a behaviour, as if we had authority to travail [travel] where we would'.¹

Thus with their packs of trade goods on their backs, they entered Colliwilla, and laid out their knitted caps and other wares for sale. A crowd gathered to see the 'outlandish' visitors, and when they asked the whereabouts of the Governor's house, several men led Knox and Rutland there. Here the 'Great Man himself' received them in his mandua, or reception hall. Knox presented the Governor with some knives with carved handles and a red Tunis cap they had brought specially as gifts, along with a parcel of tobacco and betel. They told the Governor that they had come to buy dried flesh – the 'chief commodity' of this region – to sell back in Eladetta whence, they claimed, they would return as soon as they had purchased enough dried meat. But this was a ruse. Knox and Rutland knew it was the middle of the dry season, when it was difficult to catch deer, so dried meat was scarce. They were really buying time in order to explore possible routes to lead them further north. The Governor, however, took Knox at his word and 'suspected us not'. They were eager to get to Anuradhapura, but they didn't want to appear 'too hasty, lest it might occasion suspition'. So they stayed at Colliwilla for three days knitting caps and going to nearby towns to enquire if there was any dried meat for sale.

The night before they had secretly decided to depart, the Governor, 'being disposed to be merry', held an entertainment with dancers and magicians and they stayed up most of the night watching the performers. The next morning Knox and Rutland packed up a portion of their cotton yarn, cloth and other goods into a bundle which they left with the Governor 'as a pledge for [our] returne'. They also presented him with four or five charges of gunpowder, 'intreating him rather than we should be disappointed of Flesh' when they came back, to use this gunpowder to shoot them some deer. In the meantime, they said they would 'make a step to' Anuradhapura to see if there was any dried meat to be had there. Reassured by all the goods they were leaving behind and thus confident they would return, the Governor 'like a good natured man bid us heartily farewel'.[2]

The way from Colliwilla to Anuradhapura was uncertain but they 'durst not ask [for directions] lest it might breed suspition'. They tramped on through a 'desolate Wood', and luck was with them, for they came out 'directly at the Place'. Anuradhapura was the site of the ruins of the ancient capital of Ceylon. Knox describes it as 'a vast great Plain', in the middle of which stood a large tank or pond that had been dug to water the fields. The plain was surrounded by the woods with small towns in clearings 'on every side'.

The people who lived here were Tamils, or 'Malabars' as Knox calls them, and when they saw Knox and Rutland emerge from the forest, they were 'amazed . . . because White men never' had come as far as Anuradhapura. Knox and Rutland pretended not to notice their astonishment and set up shop under a tree and 'proclaimed our Wares'. But no one could understand Sinhalese so they and the gaping townspeople spoke to no purpose until a man came along who did know Sinhalese and could serve as an interpreter. He asked the Englishmen where they had come from. When they said they came from Kandy, no one believed them. Everyone assumed that they had really come from the Dutch fort at Mannar.

Word of their arrival spread quickly and soon the Governor of Anuradhapura himself appeared with whom they conversed through their interpreter. Like the townspeople, the Governor suspected Knox and Rutland had come from the Dutch rather than from Kandy as they claimed. He proceeded to interrogate them, demanding what news they had of the Kandyan court, who were the regional governors in the Kingdom, what had been the fate of certain noblemen who had provoked the King, and other queries meant to expose the strangers. But to all these questions they were able to give 'satisfactory answers'. They also told the Governor that they had been given leave to travel so far from Kandy by the King himself, who, they said, allowed them to 'Trade in all his dominions'. Despite his initial distrust, the Governor was convinced by Knox and Rutland's explanations and gave them permission to stop in the town and trade.

They stayed in Anuradhapura three days, during which Stephen Rutland traded their goods while Knox 'went abroad' pretending to seek dried meat, though he was really trying to ascertain the route further north and find out where the watches were located. He also wanted to get all the provisions they needed for their final flight to the Dutch – rice, meat, a pot to boil rice in and deer-skin with which they could make themselves shoes. Knox purchased all these 'necessaries', and it was also his 'good hap' that the dried flesh he was pretending to seek was nowhere to be found.

In the course of his wandering round Anuradhapura, Knox worked out that the coast was a two- or three-day journey via the main or 'great road' north. But this road had manned watches on it, and Knox wasn't able to get close enough to investigate the terrain to see if they would be able to circumvent the watch posts. In the end, he decided it wouldn't be safe to take the 'great road'. They then considered going through the woods, but it was the dry season and they feared they would be unable to find drinking water. Finally, after long consultation and deliberation, they decided to backtrack some distance to a place near Colliwilla where they had seen a river. Their plan was to follow this river, the Malwatu Oya, all the way down to the sea.

They left Anuradhapura on Sunday 12 October 1679 at the time of the full moon They had carefully planned for this final stage of their escape and had 'furnished [themselves] with all things needful': 'Ten days Provision, Rice, Flesh, Pepper, Salt, a Bason [sic] to boil our Victuals in, two Calabasses [calabashes] to fetch Water, two great Tallipats [talipot leaves] for tents . . . to sleep under if it should rain, Jaggery and sweet-meats . . . Tobacco . . . and Betel, Tinder-boxes and deerskin to make us Shooes to prevent any Thorns running into our feet as we travelled . . . for our greatest Trust under God was to our feet [to carry them to freedom].'³ Like Robinson Crusoe and Friday, they also armed themselves with small axes and knives.

They detoured round Colliwilla and arrived at the river at four in the afternoon, taking care not 'to tread on the Sand or Soft Ground, lest our footsteps should be seen'. And where they couldn't avoid leaving prints, they walked backwards, 'so that by the print of our feet, it seemed as if we had gone the contrary way'. In another sandy place they trod on both sides of the river, backwards and forwards, so that it looked as if many men had walked on both riverbanks.[4] Defoe may have got his idea for the lone footprint on the shore that terrifies Crusoe from Knox's account. Crusoe's peace of mind on his island is destroyed when he comes across this stark, solitary footprint – a kind of inversion of Knox's account of his and Rutland's multiple footprints going in all directions.

They felt exposed on the riverbank, so as soon as they could find a path, they went into the forest again. Here in the undergrowth they abandoned their remaining trade goods, keeping only those things they needed for themselves. Their wares, as Knox says, had merely been 'a pretence', but now that they had embarked on the final stage of their escape, they 'ware past all pretence'. Then they had a supper of 'Portuguese Sweet-meats', and waited for the moon to rise. When it appeared in the sky, they 'commended' themselves 'into the hands of the Almighty ... took up our Provisions upon our shoulders, and set forward, and travelled some three or four hours'.[5]

But they had to call a halt when they came upon an elephant which they tried unsuccessfully to scare away. There was nothing for them to do but kindle a fire to keep the elephant at bay and to sit down, smoking their pipes as they waited for morning. The next day they continued northward through the woods alongside the river. The country seemed completely uninhabited until suddenly, after several twists and turns of the river, the trees opened up on 'a Parcel of Towns' called Tissa Wewa and they could hear the sounds of people all about them. Thus as Knox says, 'while we were avoiding Men and Towns, we ran into the midst of them'.[6]

They were now trapped. With 'the noise of People on every side ... it was not safe ... to stir backwards or forwards for fear of running among People', but it was just as 'unsafe to stand still where we were, lest some body might spy us'.[7] They desperately looked around for some place to hide and finally spied a tree, the base of which was so huge that they hoped it might be hollow. And sure enough, when they inspected it, the tree 'was like a tub'. It was actually a tree stump – only three feet or so high – but both Knox and Rutland managed to crawl into it 'and made a shift to sit there for several hours, tho very uneasily, and all in mud and wet'.[8] Defoe may have recalled this episode in his 1722 novel *Colonel Jack* when the eponymous hero hides a cache of stolen money in a hollow tree.

When night fell, Knox and Rutland crept out of the tree stump. They could hear elephants roaring close by and then men's voices shouting some way off. They decided to erect their talipot-leaf tents because the elephants would prevent anyone coming nearer, and if they kept a fire burning, the elephants would also stay away. By the time Knox and Rutland had set up camp they were famished, so they boiled rice and roasted meat and then slept in shifts: one man keeping watch and the fire burning while the other slept. Throughout the night they could hear the stamping and roaring of the elephants and the 'hollowing' of the men who, high in the trees in their 'elephant huts', kept watch over their cornfields. At daybreak, Knox and Rutland arose, packed up their few things and retreated again into the forest.

They didn't feel entirely safe, however, even in the woods, for they feared that here they might encounter some of the aboriginal people of the island – the Veddahs, whom Knox refers to as 'wild men' in his book. The Veddahs, the earliest inhabitants of Ceylon, were forest-dwelling hunter-gatherers. As Knox explains, they lived in crude shelters made from the boughs of trees. Veddahs didn't farm. They subsisted on the plants and fruits they scavenged and the deer they killed with their bows and arrows. In his manuscript revisions to his book, Knox made sketches of the Veddahs' distinctly shaped arrows, and his published book had a detailed illustration of 'A Vadda or Wild Man'. Knox had seen several Veddahs, when they brought presents to the King at Kandy, so he knew what they looked like, how they dressed in a short loincloth, and the small axe, bow and arrows they always carried.

As Knox and Rutland made their way through the woods, they saw a number of abandoned Veddah huts around which were scattered cattle bones and fruit stones from the food the Veddahs had eaten. One afternoon, when they had sat down on a rock by the river to smoke their pipes, they suddenly glimpsed further downstream several Veddah women who had come to the river to bathe. Fearing that the women might see them, Knox and Rutland fled in the opposite direction.[9]

In the forest, they encountered bears, deer, wild hogs and buffaloes, but to their relief they met with no more elephants. In the evenings they pitched their talipot-leaf tents and made a great fire both before and behind them to scare off wild beasts. For the next four days they trekked further north. At first they stuck to the forest, but when the woods became 'full of Thorns and shrubby Bushes with clifts and broken Land', they had to leave it and walk in the river.

By the evening of their fifth day, they calculated that they had probably crossed the boundary of the King's realm and entered the Malabars' [Tamils'] country. The following morning, Friday 17 October, they came upon signs of settled territory: footprints along the riverside, cattle with bells about their necks, and corn plots in the forest clearings. But they didn't feel safe because they knew that although the Tamil Prince paid tribute to the Dutch, he also feared the King of Kandy and sometimes returned runaways to him. Thus, as Knox explains, 'great was our terror . . . lest meeting with People we might be discovered'. Yet they had no alternative but to follow the course of the river wherever it led because the 'woods [now] were so bad, that we could not possibly Travel in them for Thorns: and to travel by Night was impossible, it being a dark Moon, and the River a[t] Nights so full of Elephants and other Wild Beasts coming to drink'.[10]

And so they carried on until about 'three of the Clock' that afternoon when they came upon two naked holy men sitting under a tree, boiling rice over a fire. These two ascetics were as amazed and startled to see Knox and Rutland as the Englishmen were to encounter them. But Knox quickly realised that the naked men were itinerant mendicants who would do them no harm. So instead of running away, he and Rutland stopped and greeted them in Sinhalese. But the Tamil-speaking holy men didn't understand them, so Knox and Rutland then attempted to communicate by gesturing with their hands. To explain the great distance they had travelled, they turned and exposed their 'bloody backs' which had been cut up by briars and branches in the woods. At the sight of their wounds, the holy men 'seemed to commiserate', beckoned them forward and offered them rice and herbs to eat. Knox in turn gave them tobacco and made signs to ask if they could guide them to the Dutch fort. But the holy men were reluctant and only one of them could be prevailed upon to take them four or five miles, in return for which Knox gave him a red Tunis cap, a knife and five shillings – all the money he had left.

That night, after the holy man left them, Knox and Rutland camped on the riverbank. They set off the next morning as soon as it was light, trekking down the middle of the riverbed which at this point had completely dried up. The 'sand was . . . loose, and . . . very tedious to go upon', but they had to stay in the riverbed because the banks were 'all overgrown with Bushes'. After several hours, they came upon a man who was not in the least startled to see them, a sure sign that they had entered 'the Hollanders jurisdiction', since this man seemed 'used to see White-men'. They greeted him in Sinhalese and enquired 'to whom he belonged', to which the man responded, again in Sinhalese, 'to the Dutch'. He told them 'all [this] Country was Under [Dutch] . . . Command', and that the Dutch fort at Arrepa [Arippu] was just six miles further on. This information, as Knox says, 'did . . . rejoyce us'. At last they felt they 'were out of all danger'.[11] They explained to the man that they had escaped from Kandy after 'many years captivity'. But despite their entreaties, they could not persuade him to guide them to the Dutch settlement. Instead, he took them to a path which he said would lead them there.

Knox and Rutland followed this route, but came to no towns. There were 'so many cross paths' that they couldn't tell 'which way to go', and they got hopelessly lost. Finally they came upon some Tamils who understood Portuguese and Knox told them he and Rutland were Hollanders and asked for guidance to the Dutch fort. In exchange for a knife one of the men took them to the next town, and 'from thence', as Knox says, 'they sent a Man with us to the next [town] and so we were passed from Town to Town until we arrived at the Fort called Arrepa: it being about four of the clock on Saturday afternoon October the eighteenth MDCLXXIX [1679]'.

Thus, at last, Knox and Rutland were delivered 'from such a long Captivity, of nineteen years, and six months, and odd days, being taken Prisoner when I was nineteen years old and continued . . . among the Heathen till I attained to Eight and Thirty'.[12] In his later revisions to his book, Knox was even more precise in his calculations: 'I was prisoner one [sic] Ceilon [sic] nineteene years six months and fourteene days, which is fower [sic] months and seventeene dayes longer than I had lived in the world before I was taken prisoner thare.'[13]

Defoe is similarly exact in *Robinson Crusoe*. When Crusoe is finally rescued, he records: 'thus I left the Island, the Nineteenth of December . . . in the year 1686, after I had been upon it eight and twenty Years, two Months and 19 Days . . . I arriv'd in England, the Eleventh of June in the Year 1687, having been thirty and five Years absent.' Crusoe was twenty-seven when he was shipwrecked on his island in 1659. Thus when he finally escapes, he, like Knox, has spent more than half his life in captivity.

The Dutch settlement at Arippu was an outpost of a larger fortification to the north at Mannar. Pearls were one of the Dutch East India Company's most lucrative trade goods in Ceylon and there was an abundance of them in the sea at both Arippu and Mannar which the Dutch hired local Tamils to dive for.* When Knox and Rutland arrived at the gates of the small Arippu fort, the handful of Dutch there were amazed. No one in living memory had ever escaped from Kandy. Knox and Rutland were warmly received and 'entertained . . . very kindly that Night'. The next morning a corporal escorted them the sixteen miles further north to the fort at Mannar.

Mannar is a small island that pokes out like a finger from the north-west coast of Ceylon towards India. Today it is connected by a bridge to the mainland with the town of Mannar at its eastern end. It is now a derelict region, ravaged by the Sri Lankan civil war, with no trace of its colonial past, but in Knox's day, Mannar had an imposing garrison originally built by the Portuguese, which the Dutch had taken over, strengthened and enlarged. When Knox and Rutland arrived, the Dutch Commander was away, so they were received by 'the Captain of the Castle', who immediately invited them to dine with him in his 'fair and sumptuous House'. It all seemed new and strange to the two escaped captives who 'had dwelt so long in straw cottages . . . and [were] used to sit on the Ground and eat our Meat on [plantain] leaves'. Now they were ushered into a formal dining room with 'Chairs and eat [ate] out of China Dishes

* Mannar is said to have inspired George Bizet's opera *The Pearl Fishers*, the only opera set in Ceylon.

at a Table where were great Varieties [of food]'. After they had eaten, the Captain conversed with them in Portuguese, asking them many questions about Kandy and the Dutch captives remaining in the King's custody. Then he gave them money and urged them to go out into the town and 'drink and be merry'. The Dutch in Ceylon, as Knox and Rutland soon discovered, were great drinkers – so much so that there was a Sinhalese saying that 'Wine [arrack] is as natural to White Men as Milk to Children'.[14]

At the castle courtyard, Knox and Rutland asked the guard whether there were any Englishmen among them, and to their delight, a Scotsman named Andrew Brown and an Irishman named Francis Hodges were summoned. These two invited Knox and Rutland to stay with them in their lodgings where they entertained their unexpected guests with copious amounts of arrack and tobacco. The news of Knox and Rutland's escape quickly spread throughout the town and, as Knox describes, 'the people came flocking to see us, a strange and wonderful sight!' Many came not only to gawk at their long beards and hair and scanty loincloths, but also to enquire about 'their [own] Husbands, Sons, and Relations' who had long been held prisoner in Kandy.

For as Knox explains in a later chapter in his book, there were even more Dutch captives detained in Kandy than there were English. Over the years the Dutch had sent a number of ambassadors to the King, all of whom he detained. Knox describes the fates of five of these poor envoys in some detail, and he calculated that there were probably 'about Fifty or Sixty' more Dutchmen still living in the Kandyan Kingdom – 'some whereof are Ambassadors, some Prisoners of War, some Runaways and Malefactors that have escaped the [Dutch] hand of Justice'.[15]

For the next ten days in Mannar Knox and Rutland were 'gallantly entertained both with Victuals and Lodging'.[16] But now, when they had finally made it to safety, Rutland 'fell very Sick' with fever and Knox thought he 'should have lost him'. Rutland was still very ill when the Commander returned to Mannar from Jaffna further north. The Commander planned to go to Colombo the very next day and he invited Knox and Rutland to sail with him, saying that from Colombo they would be able to embark on their long journey home to England. Though Rutland remained unwell, on the morning of

29 October he and Knox went on board with the Dutch Commander. It was the first time they had set foot off the island in more than nineteen years. When they boarded the ship, they expected to 'be Sea-sick, being now as Fresh men, having so long disused the sea'. But it proved otherwise, and on the voyage south they 'were not in the least stirred'.[17] Indeed, they thrived in the sea air, and at last truly believed themselves free men.

They sailed into Colombo on the evening of 2 November 1679 and anchored in the harbour. Knox and Rutland, who was still ill, spent one last night on the ship and the next morning went ashore by boat, going straight to the guardpost where, Knox says, 'all the Soldiers came staring upon us, wondring to see White-men in Chingulay [Sinhalese] Habit'. As he had done in Arippu and Mannar, Knox communicated with the Dutch in Portuguese, and the first thing he asked was if there were any Englishmen at the fort. He was told there were several in the city but none at the fort. At this point a Dutch trumpeter, who had served on English ships and spoke English, greeted them and invited them to his lodgings where he gave up his own bed to the ailing Rutland.

The Dutch had captured the Portuguese fort at Colombo in 1656 after a seven-month siege and made it their East India Company headquarters in Ceylon. The area where their garrison stood is still called the Fort, bounded by the sea on the west and north. But there are few traces now of the Dutch castle, its nine bastions connected by ramparts, the residences of the Governor, the Commander and all the employees – or 'servants' as they were called – of the company.[18] The entire Dutch community lived within the garrison from the Governor at the top down to foremen, storekeepers, the apothecary and the keeper of the prisons.[19] There was a hospital, stable, coach house, book bindery, a Dutch school and everything else needed to sustain the fort and its inhabitants.

From this stronghold, the Dutch East India Company ran their lucrative trade in cinnamon, pearls and other goods with smaller outposts dotted around the island. Colombo was the hub of this commercial enterprise, and the man in charge of it when Knox arrived there in November 1679 was Governor Ryklof van Goens Jr, the son of the famous Ryklof van Goens who had driven the Portuguese out of Ceylon in 1658 and gone on to become its first

Dutch Governor. It was van Goens Sr who had attempted without success to negotiate the release of the English and Dutch captives in 1664. In 1675, he handed over the governorship of Ceylon to his son in order to take the higher appointment of Governor General at Batavia, the Dutch East India Company headquarters in Java.

As soon as he learned of their arrival, Governor van Goens summoned Knox and Rutland to his palatial residence where he received them in 'a large and stately Room, paved with black and white stones'.[20] He gave them a warm welcome and assured them that both he himself and his father had done all in their power to free the English captives, 'having endeavoured as much for us as for his own People'. Knox and Rutland 'thanked him heartily, telling him We knew it to be true'.[21]

But this exchange was merely the polite preamble to what soon turned into a much more thorough interrogation than the one Knox had undergone at Mannar. The Dutch authorities were keen to welcome and play host to Knox because they assumed that he could give them much detailed information about 'the Affairs of the [Kandyan] King and Countrey'. The impeccably uniformed Governor invited the bedraggled captives to sit on elegant upholstered chairs at a vast oval table. Refreshments were served. The heavy air was stirred and cooled by the motion of the punkah wallahs working their huge fans in the corners of the 'Stately Room'.

The Governor and Knox conversed in Portuguese, and this question-and-answer session went on for hours. Van Goens' aim was to wring the maximum amount of useful intelligence out of his informants. Knox's objective was to obtain from the Dutch as much aid as he could for his and Rutland's speedy and safe return to England. He answered all the Governor's questions honestly, but he also responded with great care and diplomacy. As far as possible, he told the Governor what he knew the Governor wanted to hear.

Thus when van Goens asked 'how the hearts of the People [of Kandy] stood affected', Knox replied, 'Much against their King. He being so Cruel.' And when van Goens asked Knox 'What I thought would become of that Land after this King's Decease? I told . . . [him that the King] having no Issue, it might fall into their [Dutch] hands.' (Knox at this time still believed that the King's son was dead.) When Knox couldn't give answers that he knew would gratify the Dutch, he pleaded ignorance. When the Governor asked why the King had resisted all Dutch overtures of peace, Knox responded, 'I was not one of his [the King's] Council, and knew not his meaning.' When asked about the King's appearance and habits and the men in his court, Knox told the Governor that he 'had never had a near sight of him', and that he 'was too small [insignificant] to have any Friendship or Intimacy or hold Discourse' with members of the court. When van Goens pressed Knox further and asked who specifically were the King's main advisors, Knox insisted that he 'was a Stranger at Court, and how could I know that?' Van Goens then pressed Knox to hazard an opinion on the royal advisors, to which Knox astutely replied that he thought the King 'was so great that there is none great enough to give him counsel'.[22]

The Governor also wanted to know the fates of certain Dutch renegades who had fled into the kingdom, and Knox again told the Governor what he would want to hear. The King, Knox said, looks upon 'the Dutch Runnawayes . . . as Rogues'. Knox gave van Goens much precise, valuable information concerning not merely the Dutch captives, but also the remaining English, French and Portuguese prisoners, where they lived, the trails and paths through the jungle, the locations of the watch posts, and the best escape route out of the kingdom. And despite his confessed ignorance of the King and his court, Knox spoke at length about the King's tyranny and cruelty, including his various methods of executing his enemies.

This long interview finally drew to a close when the Governor asked Knox 'what was [his] intent and desire' to do now. To which Knox immediately replied: 'To have Passage to our own Nation [England] at Fort S[t] George [Madras],' the nearest East India Company settlement in India from which Knox and Rutland could readily find a company ship to take them to England. But van Goens explained that he planned to sail to Batavia soon, where his father was Governor General, and it was his 'desire that' Knox and Rutland 'go with him to Batavia, where the General, his Father would be very glad to see us'. The prospect of sailing thousands of miles out of their way to Java must have dismayed Knox, but as he says in his book, it was 'not in our power to deny' van Goens' wish. He and Rutland were in the hands of the Dutch now and although sailing east to Batavia would delay their return to England by months, Knox felt they had no choice but to do the Governor's bidding.

After they agreed to go to Batavia, van Goens sent for a Dutch captain in the fort and ordered him to take Knox and Rutland 'to his House, and there well to entertain us and also to send for a Tailor to make us Cloth [clothes]'. Knox at this point tried one last time to plead for their going to Madras, telling the Governor that 'his Kindness . . . was more than we could have desired; it would be a sufficient favour now to supply us with a little Money upon a Bill to be paid at Fort S[t] George' where they could easily get clothes. To which van Goens answered, 'That he would not deny me any Sum I should demand, and Cloth [clothe] us upon his own account besides.' Knox thus had no choice but to 'humbly thank' van Goens and acquiesce to his plan to take them to Batavia.

He and Rutland went home with the Captain where they 'were nobly entertained'. The next day all the English in Colombo came to visit and invited them out 'to walk and see the City' where, as Knox describes, 'We being barefoot and in the Chingulay Habit, with great long beards, the People much wondred at us.' In even greater numbers than at Mannar, everyone 'came flocking to see who and what we were, so that we had a great Train of People about us as we walked in the Streets'.[23]

As promised, the Governor sent Knox and Rutland money and a tailor who took their measurements and went away to make them clothes. When Rutland's malarial fever returned, the 'chief Chirurgeon' at the Dutch fort visited daily and dosed him with 'such Potions of Physick that . . . he soon recovered'. By this time the tailor returned with their new European clothes and also shoes. But to their dismay, Knox and Rutland found their new clothes and shoes 'very troublesome & uneasy like as a Coller to a dog, or a yoke to a hog', and so they alternated their European and their Sinhalese dress, going 'some dayes . . . with shooes [and trousers, doublets and shirts and some days] without' until they could wear their new garments without discomfort. From this experience, Knox later reflected that God intended man to go 'in a naturall dress' or naked, like 'the rest of his Creatures', and that it is 'fashion' rather than 'health of body that puts people to the troublesome way of apparelling & dressing theire Carkasses, for I was never better in health & ease of body than when I went ... bare foot, with a Clout wrapt aboute my body'. [24]

They spent three weeks in Colombo and during this time Knox wrote a letter to his 'fellow Prisoners' left behind in Kandy in which he described in great detail the escape route that he and Rutland had taken 'so that they might plainly understand [it]' and he 'advised them, when God permitted, to steer the same course'. Knox handed over this letter to the Governor who promised to see that it was conveyed to the English captives. According to Knox, the Governor also had the letter translated into Dutch for the benefit of the Dutch captives in Kandy.

The Governor then asked Knox to write out in English all the information that he had given during his interview with him. A transcript of Knox's testimony in Portuguese had already been made, but van Goens also wanted a signed statement from Knox himself. This, however, as Knox says, 'I was unwilling to do.' He doesn't explain his refusal and it must have been an awkward moment when he declined the Governor's request. But Knox knew that he had not been completely candid with van Goens. He was also reluctant to sign his name to a document that might later be altered or doctored.

The night before they were to sail to Batavia, the Governor invited Knox and Rutland to a farewell feast with great 'Varieties of Food, Wine, and sweet Meats and Musick'. The following morning after a ceremonial firing of guns, they boarded the *Nieuw Middelburg*, an 800-tonne Dutch East India Company ship anchored in Colombo harbour. Knox and Rutland were given choice accommodation in a cabin near the Governor's with a soldier standing sentinel at their door.

They sailed for Batavia on 24 November 1679. For the next fifty-two days the winds carried them further and further East in the opposite direction from England. It was a smooth, uneventful voyage during which Knox and Rutland dined at the Governor's own table where they had 'ten or twelve Dishes of Meat' at every meal 'with a variety of Wine'.

Without calling at any ports en route to Java, they reached Batavia at midday on 15 January 1680. When Knox and Rutland first came ashore with Ryklof van Goens Jr they might well have wondered if they had somehow been magically transported to Europe after all. Batavia* was the Dutch East India Company's headquarters in the Indies, from which it ruled all its factories and possessions from Arabia to Japan. The Dutch settlement was protected by a huge castle built of coral slabs with four bastions and surrounded by strong fortifications. But within its impregnable walls, Batavia looked like a Dutch city with its tall, thin brick houses and tiled roofs, its market-place, exchange, infirmary, orphan asylum and churches. The streets were lined with trees and there were even canals as in Amsterdam. Despite the intense heat and humidity, the European population of Batavia – soldiers, merchants, clerks and artisans – all dressed in the same heavy woollen clothes and wooden shoes they wore at home. The rainforest outside the city encroached on this transplanted European outpost, but never breached its ramparts. Tigers, monkeys and rhinoceroses roamed outside in the jungle. But for those who dwelt within, they could have been living on another planet. Most of the Europeans in Batavia never saw anything of what lay beyond its walls.

One thing, however, couldn't be barred from Batavia: diseases, including all manner of tropical fevers and illnesses, ran rampant through the city. It was, in fact, one of the deadliest places in the world. The rule of life for the Dutch here was *carpe diem*: they drank and smoked to excess and took local women as mistresses and wives.

After their long, uneventful voyage, Knox now descended into the maelstrom of Dutch Batavia. This was not civilisation as he remembered it. But he and Rutland were received with great hospitality: 'as we came to greater [more important] Men so we found greater Kindness: for the General of Batavia's Reception of us, and favours to us exceeded (if possible) those of the Governor [of Ceylon] his Son'. When they were ushered into Governor Ryklof van Goens Sr's presence, he took Knox 'by the hand and bad us heartily welcome, thanking God . . . that had appeared so miraculously in our deliverance'. Van Goens also insisted that he himself 'had omitted no means for our Redemption and that if it had layd in his Power, we should long before have had our Liberty'. Knox of course took these protestations with grace and 'humbly thanked his Excellency, and

---

* Batavia today is Jakarta, the capital of Indonesia.

said That I knew it to be true . . . our obligations being ever to thank and pray for him'.[25]

After this warm reception, the Governor ordered his own personal tailor to measure Knox and Rutland 'and furnish us with two Sutes of Apparel. He gave us also Moneys for Tobacco and Betal [nut], and to spend in the City', and arranged for them to stay at the house of the Captain of the castle. In the days that followed the Governor often invited Knox 'to his own Table, at which sat . . . himself and his Lady; who was all bespangled with Diamonds and Pearls. Sometimes his Sons and Daughters-in-Law were also present . . . The Trumpet sounding all the while' they ate their lavish, multi-course meals.

Knox and Rutland had by this time become habituated to their new European clothing and now, at last, they decided to 'cut off our Beards which we had brought with us out of our Captivity; for until then we cut them not.' In Batavia, with their escape from Ceylon sealed and 'God having rolled away the reproach of Cande [Kandy] from us', they shaved and also cut their long hair, thus removing the last vestige of their Sinhalese camouflage. The only outward manifestation that remained of their long sojourn on Ceylon was their sun-darkened, weathered skin. In every other respect, they had been transformed into proper European gentlemen.

After welcoming, clothing and entertaining Knox, Governor van Goens got down to questioning him closely about Kandyan affairs and his long detention in the King's realm. They conversed in Portuguese, as Knox and van Goens Jr had in Colombo, but two secretaries were also present in Batavia who wrote down in Dutch everything that Knox said. Knox patiently rehearsed the same answers that he had given in Colombo, taking care not to diverge in even the slightest detail from his original account. The Dutch transcript of the statement ran to a number of pages and Governor van Goens asked Knox to put 'his hand to the same'. But Knox refused, just as he had refused to sign anything in Colombo, using the excuse that 'I understood not the Dutch language'. Governor van Goens then 'persuaded' Knox to sign a separate sheet of paper or 'certificate' testifying that what he 'had informed them of was true'. Reluctantly, Knox complied and signed this document.

The Governor then attempted to persuade Knox and Rutland to

return to England via Holland 'that I might better satisfie their Company [there] . . . concerning the Affairs of Ceilon, which they would be very glad to know'. The Governor's youngest son was due to sail for Holland soon, and Knox and Rutland were offered free passage and 'entertainment at his Son's own Table' on the ship. The prospect of yet another Dutch interrogation in Amsterdam and further delay to their return to England dismayed Knox. It seemed now that he had not only to escape from Ceylon and the Sinhalese but from his nominal saviours, the Dutch, as well. Luckily he was able to decline the Governor's offer when two British merchants from nearby Bantam turned up in Batavia at about this time and invited Knox and Rutland to return with them to the English factory there.

Bantam was the headquarters of the English East India Company in the Indies, the twin port to the larger settlement that the Dutch held at Batavia. Strategically placed, Bantam was a crossroads and depot for trade with the Spice Islands further east. But it had little other than its location in its favour. Bantam's climate was even deadlier than Batavia's. 'Here the sick died and the healthy sickened.'[26] The coastline was a morass of mudflats and marshes that were breeding grounds for swarms of mosquitoes. Four months out of twelve Bantam was scorched by terrific heat, and during the remaining eight months, it was drenched in rains. Nearly everyone who passed through Bantam got malaria and often dysentery as well. Waves of typhoid and cholera regularly decimated the settlement. In addition to tropical diseases, there was a constant danger of fires, whipped up by the dry winds or set by hostile Javanese arsonists.

When Knox and Rutland arrived at Bantam in early 1680 the factory consisted of a compound with a timber warehouse and adjoining living quarters surrounded by a high palisade of stakes. It was a much smaller, drearier and unhealthier place than Batavia. But Knox and Rutland were grateful to be taken to Bantam by the English merchants because the company agent there insisted that 'since God had brought us to our own Nation' at Bantam, they must sail back to England on the company ship *Caesar*, a 530-tonne East Indiaman then lying in Bantam harbour and 'bound for England, the land of our Nativity, and our long wished for Port'.[27]

Knox says very little of his brief stay in Bantam, though the authorities there must have questioned him closely not only about his long captivity in Kandy, but also about what he had observed of the activities of the Dutch in both Colombo and Batavia.[28] But once he had finally reached British-held territory, Knox wastes few words on the remaining stages of his escape from Ceylon. Instead, he simply concludes his dramatic account by saying that he and Rutland sailed from Bantam on the *Caesar* and 'by the Providence of God . . . arrived safe [in England] in the Month of September [1680]'.[29]

The voyage home took about seven months. The only thing Knox says about it is that during his passage he wrote his 'Booke' – *An Historical Relation of the Island of Ceylon*. For the first – and last – time in all his travels at sea, Knox was simply a passenger with no responsibilities on board. There was no reason for him to keep a log of the ship's course, to record the weather, or their stops to take on cargo at India and fresh supplies at St Helena.

Knox could have used these seven months to question the Captain and officers about the world he was returning to – an England that had been utterly transformed since he last saw it in 1658. As he sailed east, he must have learned of the major events that had occurred in the past twenty-two years. Oliver Cromwell was dead, Charles II had returned from his European exile in 1660 and still reigned. During the Great Plague of 1665, 100,000 people had died in London alone. Knox had no idea if his brother and sister were among those who perished. He also learned of the Great Fire of 1666, but he couldn't have begun to grasp the extent to which the medieval London of his boyhood with its tall timbered houses, narrow congested streets and old-fashioned churches had disappeared. Nor was there any way of imagining the new modern city that had risen – and was still rising – in its place.

For the most part, though, Knox's hours and days on his long voyage home were not spent looking ahead to the world that awaited him in his 'native country', but were devoted instead to gazing back at the one he had left behind in Ceylon. In good weather and bad, on deck and in his cabin, in the morning soon after rising, during the long afternoons and at night by candlelight in his cabin, he painstakingly resurrected in his mind's eye and then recorded on page after page of paper the world he had spent so many years endeavouring to escape.

Why did Knox remain absorbed, even haunted, by his past? His own explanation is that 'In my passage to England from Bantam . . . I wrote this Book, 3 reasons Induced mee so to do: first to record Gods great mercies in so plentifully sustaining me in the land of myne enimies . . . after a Detainement of 19 yeares 6 months & 14 dayes [when] . . . [God's] providence so disposed of & directed me to escape thence . . . & conducted me safe whome to my Native Country . . . Secondly, that after my death if I died by the way [en route back to England] my Relations might know what became of my Father . . . Thirdly to exercise my hand to wright for in all the time of my Captivity I had neither pen Inke nor paper & now as a man new borne I came into the world, so made it part of my busi-nesse to learne to write.' When he had fulfilled these three reasons for writing his account, Knox claimed he 'intended it [to go] noe further'.[30]

All that Knox says regarding his motives is undoubtedly true: he believed he had escaped from Ceylon through the mercy and providence of God; he wished to leave an accurate record of what had befallen his father and himself in Ceylon, and he wanted to practise writing again after a long period of abstinence. (Strictly speaking, though, he had sometimes written things down in Ceylon on ola leaves – letters to the East India Company and Dutch authorities and also letters to fellow captives in other places on the island; he had also taught Lucea the alphabet and how to write. But this threefold rationale for writing a manuscript of several hundred pages is incomplete and inadequate. Furthermore, if these three reasons had been Knox's only motivation, he would have had no cause to retain the manuscript, much less show it to others and then publish it after he had safely arrived back in England.

No matter how much he questioned the crew and officers and how much they told him, Knox could not know what awaited him in his 'native country'. For him, the only real, palpable world was Ceylon. On the *Caesar* he was suspended between the known past and an unknowable future, between an archaic England that no longer existed and a new modern country that he had no means of envisioning. His way of riding out all the uncertainty bearing down on him, of fortifying himself to face whatever fate awaited him in England, was to write down, describe, explain and relive his long years of captivity on Ceylon. He had no way of knowing now that he was also embarking on what would become – in all the coming years – his life's work.

CHAPTER SEVEN

Another Escape

London, 1703–4

At midday on Thursday 29 July 1703, a short, slight man – it was difficult to tell his age, but he was no longer young – stood on a wooden platform before the Royal Exchange in Cornhill, the financial centre of London. For the past two days there had been 'violent showers' in London, and Daniel Defoe – in a tight spot again – was standing in the pouring rain. With his wet, wigless head and dripping, shabby clothes, he looked anything but a man of letters.

Defoe's posture on the platform was strangely contorted and he was also immobile. He couldn't move because his neck and wrists were gripped in a cross-shaped wooden frame. From a distance the wooden structure might have been mistaken for a gallows. At closer range, Defoe appeared to be crucified. His arms were invisible behind the horizontal strut of the frame, but they had clearly been pulled out at right angles to his body. His hands poked through two holes on either side of his head. The writing on the piece of paper above his head made it clear that, unlike others who suffered this punishment, he was not a sodomite, fraudster or felon. The legend simply identified him as the author of *The Shortest Way with Dissenters.*

Daniel Defoe was standing in the pillory – a dangerous, shameful place to be. Men had died in the pillory. More often, they were wounded or maimed by stones and bricks, smeared with rotten eggs, slaughterhouse refuse, dead cats, mud and excrement hurled by spectators. Their mental pain was as intense as their physical suffering. Many people, including Defoe himself, considered the pillory 'a fate worse than death' because it brought the extinction of a man's reputation, dignity and honour. The infamous Titus Oates – the man who invented the Popish Plot hoax – had stood in the pillory on the very same spot twenty-five years before. And some thirty years before Oates, the Puritan zealot William Prynne had stood there with his ears 'cropt' and cheek branded into the bargain.

Defoe in the pillory

In 1703, Defoe had to suffer the ignominy of the pillory not once, but three times. On 29, 30 and 31 July, between the hours of eleven in the morning and two in the afternoon, he stood in the pillory in three of the most public places in London: before the Royal Exchange in Cornhill; in Cheapside, the busiest market street in the city; and finally, on the third day, in Fleet Street, in front of Temple Bar, the ornate gate at the western edge of the walled City of London.

Imagine him on that first day, before the Royal Exchange, which he used to frequent as a city merchant. Businessmen and traders making their way home for a noon dinner pause to wonder who the poor wretch in the pillory is. A contemporary woodcut of Defoe in the pillory shows a grotesque head with goggle eyes, long beaked nose and lank hair

framed by dangling hands on either side. Above the head is the unnecessary description 'A Deformed head in the Pillory'.

Alexander Pope vividly if inaccurately captured the scene some
years later in *The Dunciad*: 'Earless on High, Stood Unabash'd Defoe'.
Unlike William Prynne, however, Defoe's ears were still intact.
The practice of mutilating men in the pillory had ceased by the
eighteenth century.

Another of Defoe's contemporaries memorialised him in the
pillory as a popular hero: 'The shouting crowds their advocate
proclaim / And varnish over infamy with fame.[1]

More than 150 years later, the Victorian artist Eyre Crowe will
reproduce this triumphant view in his painting of Defoe in the
pillory.[2] In Crowe's idealised version, instead of the typical rabble
that congregates for pillory and execution events, the crowd is full
of clean, well-dressed, wholesome-looking folk. Even more importantly, instead of hurling stones and filth at Defoe, they are cheering
him. Men drink his health and women hold up offerings of flowers
as if to a temple idol. Soldiers with rifles and swords try in vain to
drive back this enthusiastic crowd. Up on the platform, Defoe gazes
down on the scene with a look of patient resignation and benign
satisfaction. No one could look less like the 'Seditious man . . . of a
disordered mind . . . a person of bad name, reputation and
Conversation' described in his Old Bailey indictment.[3]

There is another gratifying sight for Defoe beyond the edges of
Crowe's painting. In the midst of the crowd, street hawkers are doing
a brisk trade selling two of his most recent works: a new edition of
The Shortest Way with Dissenters, and a spirited defence of himself
written in Newgate Prison especially for this occasion: *A Hymn to
the Pillory*.

The Shortest Way with Dissenters, published in early December
1702, is a scathing satire on High Church partisans and Tories who
promoted the government's persecution of Nonconformists or
Dissenters — those who 'dissented' from the strict Anglican creed and
worshipped at their own Presbyterian, Congregational or Quaker
'conventicles' or meeting houses. When Queen Anne ascended the
throne upon the death of William III in 1702, Dissenters once again
came under fire. The new Queen was a zealous Anglican and hostile
to Nonconformists. She and her Tory ministers wanted to curb the

toleration that had marked William's reign, and in particular, they sought to abolish the practice of 'Occasional Conformity' – which made it possible for Dissenters to hold government positions as long as they took Anglican Communion and subscribed to Church of England doctrine once a year. By resorting to this practice of 'Occasional Conformity', prominent Dissenters such as the Presbyterian Lord Mayors of London, Sir Humphrey Edwin and Sir Thomas Abney, were able to receive preferment and hold office.

In November 1702, a bill prohibiting occasional conformity was passed in the House of Commons, and in December it came up for debate in the House of Lords. Defoe decided to seize the moment and publish a broadside not only against the Tory and High Church party but also against what he felt was the religious hypocrisy of Dissenters who practised 'Occasional Conformity' to advance themselves – something that Defoe in an earlier pamphlet had scathingly described as 'a new sort of Religion that looks two ways at once'.[4] Defoe should have known better than to stick his neck out and dabble in controversy over the occasional conformity bill. Just five months earlier, in May 1702, he had been in legal trouble and arraigned before Justice John Blencoe – some of Defoe's creditors from a decade earlier had resurfaced and were pursuing him again.[5]

Despite this recent skirmish with the law, in early December 1702 Defoe published his twenty-nine-page pamphlet *The Shortest Way with Dissenters*, which landed him in the pillory because it preposterously called for the wholesale 'Destruction' of the 'viprous Brood' of Dissenters. Nonconformists, its anonymous author asserts, are the 'true Enemies' of the Established Church and must be 'rooted out from the Face of this Land for ever'. If recalcitrant Dissenters refused to see the error and sinfulness of their ways, they must be banished, hanged, destroyed or sent to the devil.

Defoe published his scathingly ironic *Shortest Way with Dissenters* a good twenty years before Swift's 'modest proposal' that Irish babies be eaten as a 'cheap, easy and effectual' way of dealing with the poor. Whatever his other virtues as a writer, Defoe was seldom guilty of subtlety. In spite of the crudeness of his far-fetched polemic, some took this diatribe for what it purports to be – the work of a half-crazed High Church fanatic. Some Tories and High Church Anglicans even praised *The Shortest Way*. Then, when they belatedly realised it was 'a satyr', they pronounced it a 'criminal document, a Seditious, pernicious and Diabolical Libel', that sought 'to make and Cause discord between the Queen and her ... subjects'. It was, in short, a gross insult to both monarch and Parliament.[6]

The pamphlet was published anonymously, but Defoe's authorship was soon revealed. On 30 December 1702, John Tutchin in his newspaper the *Observator* named Defoe as the author of *The Shortest Way*. Tutchin was himself a Dissenter – his father and grandfather had both been Nonconformist ministers and Tutchin had participated, along with Defoe, in the Duke of Monmouth's rebellion in 1685.[7] But despite being natural allies, Defoe and Tutchin had fallen out after Defoe published his hugely popular poem *The True-Born Englishman* in 1701. This verse satire was actually a spirited riposte to Tutchin's own xenophobic, anti-Williamite poem *The Foreigners* published in 1700.

Defoe and Tutchin were inhabitants of the seedy world of eighteenth-century journalism known as Grub Street which took its name from the geographical location where many of the hacks lived – the region of Grub Street, just outside the City walls, close to Moorfields and Bedlam.[8] Defoe was literally born into this world, a stone's throw from Grub Street on Fore Street in the parish of St Giles' Cripplegate. A thick fog of print warfare hung over Grub Street, a domain, as Samuel Johnson would later put it, 'much inhabited by writers of small histories, dictionaries and temporary poems'.

Tutchin's *Foreigners* was one such mediocre, 'temporary' poem. Like Defoe, Tutchin paid for his folly when he published it. His attack on the government of William III and the King's Dutch favourites led to Tutchin's arrest for libel, but he managed to avoid prosecution and imprisonment because he had used 'covert' (or fictional) names. Today Tutchin and his poem are remembered only because they incited Defoe to write his answering verse lampoon *The True-Born Englishman*.[9]

In late December 1702, three weeks after *The Shortest Way with Dissenters* was published, Tutchin seized the opportunity to get back at Defoe. In the *Observator*, he announced that 'the plot' or 'pretty sham' of the *Shortest Way* was the work of none other than Daniel Defoe.[10]

On 3 January 1703, four days after Tutchin's outing, a warrant was issued for Defoe's arrest by Daniel Finch, Earl of Nottingham, a Secretary of State in the Queen's government. Queen Anne herself had found Defoe's hoax offensive and reprehensible and she took a personal interest in seeing that that whoever perpetrated it was punished. She and her ministers believed Defoe was in the pay of Whig conspirators – followers of the late William III – who sought to undermine the Queen's new regime.

On 11 January, the official government newspaper, the *London Gazette*, published a detailed notice offering a reward of £50 'for whoever shall discover . . . Daniel de Foe alias de Fooe' who was charged with 'writing a Scandalous and Seditious Pamphlet entituled [sic], The Shortest Way with the Dissenters'. A helpful description of the accused was included: 'He is a middle Siz'd, Spare man, about 40 years of age, of a brown Complexion, and dark brown coloured Hair, but wears a Wig; a hooked nose, a sharp Chin, grey Eyes and a large mould [mole] near his Mouth, was born in London, and for many years a Hose Factor in Freeman's-yard, in Cornhill, and now is Owner of the Brick and Pantile Works, near Tilbury-Fort in Essex.'[11]

Defoe's house was raided and his papers seized. But Defoe was nowhere to be found. As soon as Tutchin exposed him, he went into hiding. And despite the £50 bounty on his head (five times the reward for turning in an army deserter and more than twice what the notorious thief and escape artist Jack Sheppard would later fetch), Defoe continued to elude capture.

Defoe had escaped, but a known Whig agitator and an associate of Defoe named Edward Bellamy was taken into custody. Under interrogation, Bellamy admitted that he had carried Defoe's manuscript of *The Shortest Way* to a printer named George Croome. On 14 January, Croome's house and shop were searched, and Croome was arrested to give evidence against 'Daniel Deufoe [sic] [for] publishing a Scandalous Booke'. Croome was released the next day after paying £80 bail and agreeing to testify against Defoe in court.[12]

But first Defoe had to be apprehended. After Croome's arrest and release, the trail went cold. At the end of February, Defoe was still on the run. Since the author couldn't be found, revenge was taken on his work. On 25 February, the House of Commons charged that *The Shortest Way with Dissenters* was 'full of false and scandalous Reflections upon this Parliament', and that it 'promoted sedition'.

Defoe's pamphlet was ordered to be burned by the common hangman in New Palace Yard, Westminster.

For several months Defoe remained in hiding and saw little or nothing of his pregnant wife and six children, though Mary Defoe bravely (but vainly) attempted to intercede with the Earl of Nottingham on her husband's behalf. Meanwhile, Defoe's prosperous brick and tile factory in Tilbury failed in his absence. His family was forced to take refuge with Mary's mother in Kingsland, a few miles north of the City, just as they had done in 1692 when Defoe went bankrupt.[13]

Defoe continued to evade arrest by moving from one cheap lodging house to another. He ventured out only at night and even then in disguise. Though he refused to turn himself in, Defoe wrote to the Earl of Nottingham pleading for clemency. He explained that the 'Oneley Reasons' for his 'Withdrawing My Self' were a 'Body Unfitt to bear the hardships of a Prison ... a Mind Impatient of Confinement ... and the Cries of a Numerous Ruin'd Family'. 'Prisons, Pillorys and Such like,' Defoe wrote with anguish, 'are Worse to me Than Death.'[14]

He attempted to negotiate his way out of punishment by bargaining. In his grovelling letter to Nottingham, Defoe offered 'to Surrender my Self as a Voluntier at the head of her [Majesty's] Armyes [sic] in the Netherlands', or 'even Raise her ... a Troop of horse, at my Own Charges and at the head of Them Ile Serve her as Long as I Live'. 'He vowed to serve the Queen in whatever way she desired: 'with my hand, my Pen or my head'.[15]

This is the very first of 250 surviving letters written by Defoe – a letter written in hiding, in desperation and terror. Few things frightened or daunted Defoe in his life, but he would rather have perished than endure confinement, prison and the pillory.

Defoe also wrote pleading letters to influential men such as William Paterson (one of the founders of the Bank of England) and the Quaker William Penn, whom he thought might intercede with the authorities on his behalf. He confessed to Paterson that the 'Jayls, Pillorys and Such like' with which he had been threatened have 'Convinc't me, I want Passive Courage, and I shall Never for the Future Think My Self Injur'd if I am Call'd a Coward'.[16]

The earliest personal words we have from Defoe's pen, written in his own voice and signed with his own name, are ones of fear, claustrophobia and self-confessed cowardice.

In May 1703, still undercover, Defoe went to stay with a friend named Nathaniel Sammen, a French Huguenot weaver who lived in Spitalfields. But someone who had read the *London Gazette* notice for Defoe recognised him when he took refuge there. On 21 May, two government 'messengers' arrived on Sammen's doorstep, entered and captured Defoe. He was arrested and sent to Newgate Gaol under close guard. (The informer, 'who did not care to appear himself', later collected his £50 reward.)

Defoe was interrogated for two days by the Earl of Nottingham who demanded that Defoe reveal the identity of his co-conspirators. It is unclear whether Defoe alone was responsible for *The Shortest Way*. He always claimed to Nottingham and others that he acted on his own, or as he put it later in a letter to William Penn, he had 'No Person to discover ... no Accomplices, No Sett of Men (as my Lord [Nottingham] call'd Them) with whom I used to Concert Matters'.[17] Nottingham reluctantly ordered Defoe's release from Newgate on 5 June, but the bail he set was exorbitant – £1,500 – and he probably hoped Defoe would be unable to pay it. Defoe, however, somehow raised £500, and the remainder was paid by contributions from one Joseph Whitaker, 'a broker', Thomas Powell, 'Gentleman', a baker named Nicholas Morris, and Defoe's long-suffering brother-in-law Robert Davis, a shipwright who had come to Defoe's rescue in the past and would continue to do so in the future.[18] Defoe's release on bail, however, was only a temporary reprieve. As Nottingham sternly warned him, in a month's time, he would have to appear in court again for his trial.

In his previous run-ins with the law, at the time of his bankruptcy in 1692, Defoe ignored court summonses and laid low. In 1703, however, he obeyed Nottingham and appeared for his trial 'for sedition and libel' on 5 July at the Justice Hall, or Criminal Court, at the Old Bailey. The courthouse, just west of St Paul's Cathedral, was a 'fair and stately building', according to John Strype, located on Newgate Street next to the prison. Trials at this time were held on the ground floor of the Old Bailey in a three-walled courtroom supported by Doric columns. The fourth side of the chamber was open to the elements. The rationale for this exposed architecture was to provide plenty of fresh air which, it was hoped, would thwart the spread of 'gaol fever' or typhus that prisoners often brought with them to the proceedings. The accused stood in the dock directly across from the judges' bench. Jurors sat along the sides of the courtroom and spectators crowded into the yard. There was always a large audience for Old Bailey trials.[19]

When Defoe took up his position in the dock on the morning of 5 July, he was dismayed to see that the judges' bench was packed with men he had ridiculed and insulted in print: judges, justices and London aldermen such as Sir Simon Harcourt, Sir Salathiel Lovell and Sir Robert Jeffreys. Defoe had mocked and accused all of them of vices and misdemeanours in earlier works (now largely forgotten) such as *The Pacificator* and *Reformation of Manners*. Defoe and his legal counsel William Colepepper, however, had been led to believe that Defoe would be treated leniently if he pleaded guilty and confessed to the charge of 'seditious libel'. So, as he later confided to William Penn, 'upon promises of being us'd Tenderly . . . [I] agreed to give the Court no Trouble but to plead Guilty to the Indictment, Even to all the Adverbs, the Seditiously's [sic], the Malitiously's [sic] and a Long Rapsody of the Lawyers et Ceteras'.[20] But Defoe's antagonists had lured him into a trap. After pleading guilty, he was sentenced on 7 July by the eighty-four-year-old Justice Lovell, a twisted, sadistic man, who had sentenced the pirate William Kidd just two years earlier and lived on to sentence a man to death ten years later when Lovell was still meting out justice at the age of ninety-four.[21]

Lovell's sentence on Defoe was harsh even by his own and the day's standards. Defoe was fined two hundred marks* (about £133), confined again for an indefinite period in Newgate Prison, and ordered 'to be of good behaviour for the space of seven years', which meant that Defoe was not to publish anything controversial. In effect, this was a gagging order. But worst of all, Defoe was sentenced to stand in the pillory in three of the most densely populated, conspicuous places in London. As one of Defoe's biographers put it, this ferocious sentence 'was meant not to punish but to destroy'.[22]

This severe verdict and sentence were meant to frighten Defoe into naming his putative accomplices. During the days following his

---

* A mark was not a coin but an amount of money, equal to 13s 4d.

show trial, he languished in Newgate where his persecutors hoped that being locked up with murderers and felons would make him change his mind and name names. On 12 July, Defoe was called again to testify before the Privy Council. But he still insisted that he had no co-conspirators and 'no Person to Discover'.

William Penn's son visited Defoe in prison and attempted to negotiate on his behalf. To no avail. After this visit Defoe wrote again to Penn, who had himself been an inmate at Newgate (and other gaols) but was now in favour at court. According to Nottingham, William Penn Sr reported that 'de Foe was ready to make [an] oath . . . of all that he knew, & to give an Account of all his Accomplices . . . provided . . . he may bee excused from the punishment of the pillory'.[23] But Defoe had either misled Penn or Penn had misinterpreted his letter. Defoe never divulged the names of any accomplices.

Defoe's terror of the pillory was perfectly rational. To be exposed in the pillory was considered 'a public means of degradation . . . a greater penalty than imprisonment or large fines. Pilloried men [also] lost their right to vote and to serve on juries.'[24] They were, in short, the lowest of the low. As Adam Smith later observed, the pillory was considered a worse fate than the gallows: 'A brave man is not rendered contemptible by being brought to the scaffold; he is by being set in the pillory. His behaviour in the one situation may gain him universal esteem and admiration. No behaviour in the other can render him agreeable.'[25] The pillory could also prove as lethal as the scaffold. Pilloried men had died from injuries they'd received when drunken, hostile spectators hurled bricks and stones and other missiles at them.

After William Penn's intercession, Defoe's case was deferred until 21 July when he was conveyed from Newgate to Windsor where not only the Earl of Nottingham but Queen Anne herself heard his testimony. She was not impressed. Indeed, the Queen judged that Defoe's protestations that he alone was guilty of writing the *Shortest Way* 'amounts to nothing', and that his vows in future always to 'deserve her Majesty's favour' meant just as little'.[26] Defoe was taken back to Newgate.

Despite incurring Her Majesty's displeasure, on 23 July at Newgate, Nottingham interviewed Defoe yet again, giving him one last chance to divulge his 'intentions and collaborators'. But Defoe stood his ground. No doubt he had always told the truth when he said he acted independently and he was too honest a man to implicate anyone else now. The result of this impasse, as Nottingham wrote to the Sheriff of London on 27 July, was that 'Her Majesty does not think fitt to delay any longer the execution of the Sentence upon Mr Fooe'.[27]

Back in his Newgate cell on the night of 27 July Defoe considered his options. Anyone else in his position would have concluded that he had none or that he had just two equally bad ones: submitting to the degrading, public humiliation of standing in the pillory or taking his life to avoid it. Defoe, however, did not abandon hope, collapse into despair or consider suicide. Though his plight seemed irredeemable, he decided to use this latest calamity – in a life riddled with misfortunes – to his own advantage.

Defoe's appearance in the pillory would be a public spectacle. He decided to turn infamy into martyrdom with yet more words: by writing A *Hymn to the Pillory*, a Pindaric ode of more than 450 lines that bristles with moral indignation and intellectual integrity. It was also, of course, an act of immediate defiance of his court order to be of 'good behaviour' and desist from engaging in controversy for seven years. Despite his ignoble predicament, in *A Hymn to the Pillory* Defoe celebrates the unassailability of spiritual liberty and truth. The poem was the weapon with which Defoe battled and defeated his persecutors and transformed what should have been the darkest experience of his life into a personal triumph.

A Hymn to the Pillory opens with Defoe addressing the pillory directly, with the defiant boast that 'Men that are men, in thee can feel no Pain' because the pillory 'never frights the Wise or Well-fix'd Mind'.

> Thou art no shame to Truth and Honesty,
> Nor is the Character of such defac'd by thee . . .
> And he who for no Crime shall on thy Brows appear,
> Bears less Reproach than they who placed him there.

With consummate nerve and wit, Defoe turns the tables on 'the scandalous Magistrates' who condemned him. They are the real villains while Defoe is the hero of the drama. The pillory is transformed from a site of ignominy into a pulpit and a law court, and

the martyred author – Defoe – preaches, judges and passes sentence
on his enemies – and triumphs.

> Tell them he stands Exalted there,
> For Speaking what we wou'd not hear;
> And yet he might ha' been secure
> Had he said less, or wou'd he ha' said more
> Tell them that this is his Reward
> And worse is yet for him prepar'd
> Because his . . . Vertue was so nice
> As not to sell his Friends . . .
> And thus he's an Example made
> To make Men of their Honesty afraid . . .
> Tell 'em the M[en] that plac'd him here,
> Are Sc[ande]ls to the Times

The poem is a dazzling performance. Small wonder that in several
contemporary reports of the scene, as well as in Eyre Crowe's painting,
the crowd huzzahed Defoe's defiance and pelted the smiling hero in
the pillory with flowers.

You have to admire the legerdemain of Defoe's feat in writing
his *Hymn to the Pillory* which was distributed, along with a new
edition of *The Shortest Way with Dissenters*, to the crowd while he
stood, pinioned and helpless, before them. Defoe not only proclaimed
himself moral and principled, he also revealed how clever and ingenious he was. This was the man – Daniel Foe – who had been bank-
rupted ten years earlier, only to reinvent himself as Daniel Defoe
and go on to be a government servant, a projector and an author.
Now up in the pillory in 1703, Defoe once again transmuted adversity into victory. He was no mean scribbler or hack, but an author
who rewrote experience as it happened and convinced those looking
on that his version was the truth. Not only that. Defoe's version
remains the truth today, long after he himself has ceased to be and
the issues he championed have been forgotten.

In December 1702, Defoe had dashed off an obscure religious
pamphlet one winter's afternoon that no one today would remember
if he hadn't been sent to the pillory for it. It is unlikely that the
crowds who cheered Defoe on three consecutive days in July 1703

at the Royal Exchange, Cheapside and Temple Bar were Nonconformists or even that many of them bothered about religion at all. They were, for the most part, a typical London street crowd: a heterogeneous assortment of merchants and tradesmen, gentlemen on their way to coffee houses, common folk going about their business, servants on errands, and also the pickpockets, idlers, drunks and beggars who always gathered to gawk and heckle men (and sometimes women) exposed in the pillory. But the throng that stopped to see Defoe found another spectacle entirely: a beaming defiant hero, wreathed in flowers. This unruly mob wasn't jeering and shouting obscenities or hurling stones and bricks. They cheered their new hero pinioned up on the wooden platform because he refused to be a victim.

The moral of *A Hymn to the Pillory* — and indeed of the pillory episode in Defoe's life — was that the Ingenious inherit the Earth. Survivors are those who create in the face of all the dark forces that seek to destroy them — those who, like Defoe, are resourceful, determined and patient. They ride out the roughest storms. They make it to land and, once there, they patiently and creatively make a paradise out of desolate exile, a kingdom out of their captivity. [28]

Newgate prison

In August 1703, however, Defoe had more storms ahead to weather, the first of which he endured in Newgate where he was confined for the next three and a half months. Newgate was the most notorious of all London's gaols, and over the centuries a long line of famous, notorious and obscure individuals were incarcerated within its walls — traitors, heretics, burglars, murderers, Protestant martyrs, legendary criminals and highwaymen, as well as countless ordinary malefactors, felons, prostitutes, thieves, pickpockets, perjurers and debtors. A prison had stood on Newgate Street since the twelfth century. The Newgate Gaol that housed Defoe was its third incarnation, having been completely rebuilt after the Great Fire of 1666 destroyed its predecessor. This third Newgate was five storeys high and designed with 'great magnificence' at a cost of £10,000. The Main Gate was decorated with elaborate Tuscan pilasters, battlements and life-size statues representing Peace, Security, Plenty, Mercy, Truth and Liberty. No exterior could have been so misleading. Outwardly Newgate cruelly mocked what transpired inside. Or as one poor inmate put it, 'the sumptuousness of the outside but aggravates the misery of the wretches within'.[29]

Just below the entrance gate there was a dungeon known as Limbo or the Hole with an open sewer running through it. This is where both new arrivals and the condemned were held. There were no individual cells in the prison — just large areas or quarters. Inmates were confined by manacles, shackles and irons on their ankles, legs, necks or arms, and these irons in turn were attached to rings and staples in the stone walls or floor. Irons varied in both their weight and size. Prisoners were required to pay 'easement' fees to the keeper to get their fetters removed or, if they could not afford this, exchanged for lighter ones.

The place was horribly overcrowded. Newgate was designed to hold 150 prisoners but there were usually 250 or more crammed inside, and many brought their families into prison with them. Men and women were kept in separate accommodation, though in 1700, just three years before Defoe entered Newgate, a keeper named William Robinson was charging male prisoners sixpence for admission to the women's quarters.[30] There were also animals wandering about — dogs, cats, pigs, pigeons and poultry, not to mention vermin like rats and bats. The stench was such that neighbouring shops closed in warm weather and no doctor would visit to tend the ill. Disease was rampant. Gaol fever carried off far more prisoners than the gallows.

Like the Fleet and King's Bench prisons where Defoe had served time when he went bankrupt, accommodation in Newgate varied according to a prisoner's means. Wealthier miscreants paid 22s 6d a week to stay in the relatively comfortable 'Masters' Side', though such luxury as it offered was expensive: an additional charge of 3s 6d a week for beds and a daily charge of 1s 6d for visitors. Extra fees or 'garnish' were required for coal and candles.[31] Far less fortunate were the impoverished inmates who lived on the 'Commons' Side' of Newgate, where there were no beds, no windows, no light or ventilation and the food was a thin soup made of bread and water. Rats, cockroaches and lice added to the misery of the prisoners. One survivor of this squalor named Batty Langley later wrote of the Commons Side 'such wickedness abounds therein that the Place seems to have the aspect of Hell itself . . . the Augean Stable could bear no comparison to it'.[32]

It is in the Commons Side of Newgate that the heroine of Defoe's novel *Moll Flanders* (published in 1722) is born when her mother 'pleads her belly'. (The execution of a pregnant woman was delayed until her child was born, or sometimes, as is the case with Moll's mother, her sentence was commuted to transportation to the colonies.) Many years later, when Moll is locked up in the Commons Side after she steals two pieces of silk brocade, she vividly describes Newgate's 'hellish Noise, the Roaring, Swearing and Clamour, the Stench and Nastiness . . . joyn'd together to make the place seem an Emblem of Hell itself and a kind of Entrance to it'.[33] Moll finds her fellow inmates 'odious . . . Company . . . [and] harden'd Wretches', and she herself is soon brutalised by her surroundings and the 'crew of Hell-Hounds' she lives among. She is reduced to a 'meer Newgate-Bird', overcome with 'a strange Lethargy of Soul . . . so thro [thorough] a Degeneracy . . . possess'd me'.[34]

While in Newgate Defoe closely observed the horrendous conditions on both the Masters and the Commons Sides and became acquainted with a number of their inmates, but he himself was confined in the very best and most expensive accommodation that Newgate had to offer – the Press Yard. This was actually part of the keeper's residence. Its name derived from the fact that it was here that the gruesome torture of *peine forte et dure* had in the past been carried out on those felons who refused to enter pleas. All guilty felons had to forfeit their property to the Crown, thereby leaving their families destitute. The only way to avoid this was to refuse to enter a plea at their trial. But the consequence of this intransigence was that these felons were taken to the Press Yard where they were made to lie almost naked on the stone floor. A heavy board was placed on top of them and loaded with iron or metal weights. More weights were added each day and the prisoner was given only a minimum of water and bread. This torture continued until he either entered a plea or died. If he capitulated and made a plea his family was disinherited and he died a quick death on the gallows at Tyburn. If he was 'pressed' to death in Newgate, his end was protracted and agonising but his family was saved from destitution. By Defoe's day, this torture had ceased and the Press Yard had been converted into the most luxurious and expensive quarters in the prison with glazed windows, beds, quilts and other amenities.[35]

The price of admission to stay in the Press Yard was high. Indeed, it was more expensive to live in the Press Yard of Newgate than it was to rent a fashionable London town house or stay in the best inn in the city. Presumably the same friends who had stood Defoe's bail now came forward to pay for his keep. There was an entrance fee of twenty guineas and a weekly charge of 11s. Cleaners cost another 1s a week. The wealthier inmates of the Press Yard brought their servants, cooks and families with them and lived in some style. The anonymous author of *A History of the Press Yard* – who described himself as a writer or, in his own phrase, one of the 'Brethren of the Quill' – made the place sound almost like a gentlemen's club. His fellow prisoners included former army officers, wealthy merchants, a mathematician and a classical scholar. They passed the time amiably together, smoking, playing skittles and drinking. Defoe wasn't a 'clubbable' sort of fellow, and may have felt a bit out of his element in the Press Yard. Certainly he wasn't complacent and he remained alert and receptive to any means of getting out of Newgate.

Despite his comfortable quarters, at midnight on the nights before executions, Defoe, like the other inmates of Newgate, was awakened by the tolling of the great bell at St Sepulchre's Church which stood opposite the gaol. This melancholy death knell went on for hours and along with it a chorus of 'dismal groaning and crying' rose up from the condemned hole, where those who were to be hanged the next day were spending their last night on earth.

Defoe was a religious man, so this mournful tolling of the Death Bell – and the cries and groans of the condemned – would have haunted him. But despite his piety, he didn't attend the Sabbath services held in the prison chapel. These, in any case, were noisy, chaotic affairs. Complaints have survived of prisoners eating and drinking at the Communion table and urinating in the corner of the chapel.[36] On the Sundays before a scheduled execution, a coffin was carried into the chapel and placed directly in front of the condemned pew. Then a sermon was preached exhorting those who were soon to die to repent. These pre-execution, condemned services were open to the public who were charged an admittance fee that fluctuated according to the notoriety of the condemned and the number of eager spectators. One turnkey was reported to have collected £20 in ticket fees on a single Sunday.[37]

Defoe of course was a Dissenter, a Presbyterian, and the religious observances at Newgate were strictly Anglican ones. Newgate in fact had its own chaplain, or 'Ordinary' as these chaplains were called, who was appointed by the Bishop of London and received a salary of £35 a year, together with a house on Newgate Street. The Ordinary preached at the daily and Sunday services, visited and counselled prisoners, and accompanied them to the scaffold at Tyburn. He also wrote a lurid account of each condemned criminal's career, confession and repentance which included a hair-raising description of the deceased's last moments at the gallows, closing with the statement 'the Cart drew away, and he [or she] was turn'd off'. These accounts were then rushed into print as broadsides, chapbooks or pamphlets the morning after an execution, and sold in the streets and at book-sellers for between 2d and 6d.[38] Some 2,500 of these criminal biographies were published over the years under the general title *The Ordinary of Newgate's Account of the Behaviour, Confession and Dying Words of the Condemned Criminals Executed at Tyburn.*

In 1703, when Defoe entered Newgate, the prison chaplain was a French Huguenot named Paul Lorrain, an educated man who had previously been employed by Samuel Pepys as a secretary, translator and copyist. When Pepys reached his declining years, Lorrain had to find a new job so he took holy orders in the Anglican Church. Pepys furthered Lorrain's career by praising his 'sobriety, diligence and integrity'. When he was appointed Ordinary of Newgate in November 1700, Lorrain welcomed his 'new and important work . . . for the good of those wretched souls that shall come under my care'.

But it wasn't only the wretched prisoners in Newgate who bene-fited when Lorrain was made chaplain. Lorrain discovered that crime could pay: he profited hugely by publishing and selling his *Ordinary's Accounts* which were said to earn him up to £200 a year. Defoe didn't attend Lorrain's religious services or turn to him for spiritual comfort or advice in Newgate, but he read his *Accounts* and learned their impor-tant lesson – you could make a killing out of crime if you wrote it up and packaged it with both salacious detail and moral homily.[39]

Lorrain also made money from the various advertisements listed at the end of his *Accounts*. He charged substantial sums of those who placed these notices, including quack doctors, apothecaries and booksellers. One of these notices earned him the lasting enmity of Defoe when it was published in the *Ordinary's Account of John Peter Dromett*, a Frenchman who was convicted of murdering his wife and was executed on 21 July 1703. This advertisement was for a 'nearly published' book entitled *The Shortest Way with Whores and Rogues for a new Project of Reformation containing the Shortest Way with the Atheists, Murderers, Thieves, Whore-masters, Strumpets, Sodomites, Drunkards* – the title goes on to include scolds, usurers, cowards, Sabbath-breakers, cuckolds and many more and finally ends with 'The whole dedicated to Mr Daniel de Foe, Author of the Shortest Way with the Dissenters'. *The Shortest Way with Whores and Rogues* etc – a parody of several of Defoe's recent titles – was the work of a hack and bookseller named John Dunton who, like John Tutchin, had a score to settle with Defoe.[40]

Defoe soon took revenge against Lorrain for advertising Dunton's scurrilous book. While still in Newgate, Defoe published his satiric poem *A Hymn to the Funeral Sermon* in which he accused Lorrain of taking bribes from condemned prisoners in return for writing flattering accounts of them.

... Pulpit praises may be had
According as the Man of God is paid ...
He can the Stains of Humane [human] Vice explode,
And from a cart exalt them [the condemned] to a Cloud; ...
... if you'll be Sainted, I dare say for't
L——n [Lorrain] will do it; if you'll pay for it

Nearly twenty years later, when he was writing *Moll Flanders*, Defoe still harboured a grudge against Paul Lorrain. When Moll is incarcerated in Newgate the Ordinary visits her. He tells her God will never forgive her until she makes 'a full Discovery' of her 'Crime as he call'd it (tho' he knew not what I was in for)'. But after 'preaching Confession and Repentance' to her in the morning, Moll finds the chaplain 'drunk with Brandy and Spirits by Noon ... so ... that I began to Nauseate the Man' and she tells him 'to trouble me no more'.[41] Later, Moll receives genuine consolation from a Dissenting Minister who visits her in Newgate and tells her that the prison Ordinary's 'business ... [was] to extort Confessions from Prisoners for [his own] Private Ends'.[42] It is also this Dissenting man of God who saves Moll's life, first by getting Moll a reprieve and then by arranging for her death sentence to be converted into a transportation order to the colonies.[43]

Defoe's months in Newgate brought him into close contact with the criminal underworld, and for the rest of his life he was obsessed with the minds, behaviour and experiences of those who ran foul of the law. Moll Flanders is often said to be modelled on the notorious seventeenth-century lawbreaker Mary Frith, aka Moll Cutpurse. But Defoe didn't have to go back to old broadsides and ballads about Mary Frith for copy. While in Newgate Defoe encountered many women on the Commons Side who, according to their trial records, had been born into humble and deprived circumstances, 'kept bad company', been drawn into 'lewd and wicked ways', taken up the 'Practice of Stealing and Whoring, two things that generally go together', 'been burnt in the Cheek several times for diverse Robberies', and finally ended up on the scaffold.[44]

We can read in the Proceedings of the Old Bailey and the *Ordinary's Accounts* about young women such as Ann Holland (her surname may have inspired Moll's) who was indicted for stealing a trunk that contained 'a pair of Flaxen Sheets value 12s'. This was Ann Holland's second offence and she got off lightly with being branded. She may even have repented and reformed because she doesn't appear again in the court records. Less fortunate and more common were the fates of Elizabeth Tetherington and Jane Bowman – both condemned for felony and executed at Tyburn on 21 October 1703. Elizabeth Witherley, Mary Bunch and Elizabeth Stanton were found guilty of housebreaking, whoring and thievery. They were all hanged. As was Mary Raby for stealing a tippet worth five shillings.

Defoe is believed by some to be the author of biographies of two of the most famous Newgate criminals, Jack Sheppard and Jonathan Wild, both of whom met their ends at Tyburn – Sheppard in 1724 and Wild the following year. Numerous lives of both men were rushed into print after they were executed, but there is no solid evidence that Defoe wrote any of them.[45] What is certain is that he used what he learned in Newgate not only in *Moll Flanders*, but also for creating criminal heroes and underworlds in his novels *Colonel Jack* and *Captain Singleton*. But these books lay twenty years or more in the future and had nothing to do with Defoe's release from Newgate in early November 1703, just three and a half months after he was sentenced to remain in prison for an 'indefinite' period.

How did he make this audacious escape? It was Defoe's pen that got him out of trouble as well as into it in 1703. The man who rescued him, Robert Harley, Speaker of the House of Commons, was a member of the same government that sent Defoe to prison, and it was Defoe's writing that brought him to Harley's notice. The two men had already briefly encountered each other in 1701 when Defoe wrote a document called 'Legion's Memorial' that stated various grievances of the 'People of England', and made demands on their behalf. These included a vigorous resistance to the growing power of France and the release of all persons who had called for such resistance, especially the Kentish Petitioners, a group of men from that county who had peaceably petitioned the Commons and been arrested and jailed for their efforts. On 14 May 1701, Defoe, accompanied by a guard of sixteen 'gentlemen of quality', delivered his 'Legion's Memorial' to the Speaker of the Commons, Robert Harley. As a result, the Kentish Petitioners were released from gaol and feted at a 'lavish dinner in Mercers' Hall' where their champion, Defoe, 'sat next to the guests of honour'. According to one journalist present, you 'might have read the downfall of parliaments in . . . [Defoe's] very countenance'.[46] Overnight, Defoe had become both the Peoples' spokesman and their hero.

Harley was too clever and cunning to hold a grudge against Defoe for this political victory. Instead, he made a mental note to himself that Defoe might prove useful if he could be recruited to write *for* rather than *against* the government. This impression was further enhanced by the controversy surrounding Defoe's *Shortest Way with Dissenters* and *Hymn to the Pillory* when they were published in 1702 and 1703. Defoe may have been aware of Harley's interest in him because, while still in hiding in April 1703, he wrote to his friend William Paterson, who had connections with Harley. Defoe told Paterson that he'd been made 'Desperate by This Disaster' following the publication of the *Shortest Way*, and he asked his friend to 'make my Acknowledgements to a Certain Gentleman [Harley] who I allwayes Honour For his Character Among Wise Men, More Than the Greatness of his share in the Royall Favour'. Defoe pressed Paterson to plead his case with Harley: 'in your Conversation with the Gentleman [Harley] . . . Venture in My Name in the Humblest Terms to Ask his Pardon'.[47]

Paterson did not send Defoe's letter to Harley until 28 May, four days after Defoe was arrested. Harley then bided his time. Defoe was now just where Harley wanted him – cornered and trapped in prison. He knew that the longer he left Defoe to languish in Newgate, the more eager – or desperate – he would be to grab any hand that was extended to help him.

In August, Harley wrote of him to his Tory ally Lord Godolphin: 'I believe his circumstances are very difficult at present . . . Her majesty's bounty to him would, I believe, be seasonable and quicken his diligence to serve her.'[48] Godolphin responded, 'If you have any means of sounding him, I wish you would try it.' Harley reported back that Defoe's morale was very low and that there was some sort of 'private attempt' afoot (presumably by Defoe's friends) to raise two hundred marks to pay his fine. Harley then proposed the solution to the 'Defoe problem' that he had had in mind all along.

[He] is a very capable man, and if his fine be satisfied without any further knowledge but that he alone be acquainted that it is the queen's bounty to him, and grace, he may do service [to the government], and this may engage him better than other rewards and keep him more in the power of an obligation.[49]

Harley knew that not only was Defoe's 'morale' poor, his brick and tile business in Tilbury had failed since his arrest and imprisonment, and his pregnant wife and children — camped out with Mary Defoe's family in Kingsland — were in dire need of assistance. On 26 September, Godolphin wrote to Harley: 'What you propose about Defoe may be done when you will and how you will.'[50]

Twelve years later, in his autobiographical *An Appeal to Honour and Justice*, Defoe gave a rather florid account of this crucial episode when Harley intervened in his life.

While I lay friendless and distress'd in the Prison of Newgate, my Family ruin'd, and myself, without Hope of Deliverance, a Message was brought me from a Person of Honour [Harley] . . . the Message was by Word of Mouth: *Pray ask that Gentleman* [Defoe] *what I can do for him?* . . . this Noble Person made it his Business to have my Case represented to her Majesty and Methods taken for my Deliverance . . . I soon felt the Effects of her Royal Goodness and Compassion . . . her Majesty was pleased particularly to enquire into my Circumstances and Family, and by my Lord Treasurer Godolphin to send a considerable Supply to my Wife and Family, and to send . . . Money to pay my Fine, and the Expenses of my Discharge . . . Here is the Foundation on which I built my first Sense of Duty to Her Majesty's Person and the indelible Bond of Gratitude to my First Benefactor [Harley].[51]

By 9 November, Defoe was a free man and he wrote fulsomely to his saviour, Harley: 'I can Not but Profess my Self a Debtor wholly to your Self . . . And . . . as I have Rec'd Such an Obligation as few Ever Receiv'd, I [desire to] Make Some Such Sort of Return as No Man Ever Made.' Defoe pledged that he was 'Ready to Dedicate my Life and all Possible Powers to The Intrest [sic] of So Generous and

So Bountifull Benefactors' [the Queen, the government and, above all, Harley himself].⁵²

Thus Robert Harley won over Daniel Defoe, the one-time thorn in the government's side, and brought him in from the cold. Some of Defoe's enemies would later brand him a mercenary. But he wasn't merely a hired pen, nor did he sell his soul to the Devil when he 'dedicated' himself to Harley's service. He admired Harley and there is no doubt that his lifelong gratitude and loyalty to his 'benefactor' was genuine and profound.

As for Harley, we have no way of knowing his personal feelings for Defoe – if he had any. But it is clear that Harley had two purposes in mind for him. He wanted to use him in intelligence work, as an undercover government agent, but even more importantly, he wanted him to become the government's unofficial apologist, propagandist and polemicist. Defoe was soon to become Harley's eyes and ears on the ground in England and his 'man in Scotland'. Even more importantly, in February 1704, Defoe began to publish the pro-government news-sheet the *Review*, an influential periodical which he produced single-handedly for the next nine years. He had become what we would today call a spin doctor for the same government that had been issuing warrants for and hunting him down a few months earlier.

A key element of Harley's strategy with Defoe was to dispense his largesse irregularly and tight-fistedly. He refused to give him a sinecure or indeed any real financial security. Instead, he kept him at a distance and sporadically forwarded just enough funds to keep him from complete destitution. Over the coming months and years Defoe begged his benefactor for a fixed appointment, some sort of salaried post, or a 'private allowance'. To no avail. Harley ignored his importunate letters, refused to settle a regular stipend on him, and sent money to him at unpredictable intervals. Defoe was never sure whether financial relief would arrive in time to save what he described to Harley as his 'Large and Promiseing family ... Seven Beautiful and hopefull Children' and their 'Vertuous and Excellent Mother'. As for himself, Defoe confessed to Harley at one point that he was 'Sure the Gulph is too Large for me to get ashore again'. The 'black Case', he said, was that 'Not less Than a Thousand pounds will Entirely Free me', though he added 'Tis True ... £500 or 6 ... will Open the Door to Liberty'.[53]

In November 1703, however, when he was released from prison, Defoe was full of hope. He had yet to learn the vague, erratic terms of Harley's patronage. His 200-mark fine was paid and he was free. Defoe was as buoyant and optimistic as ever.

Then, just two weeks after he walked out of Newgate, Defoe was hit by yet another storm – this time a real one.

There had been 'terrible Weather' – rain and violent gusts of wind – in southern England for months. When Defoe stood in the pillory on the last three days of July, it was in the pouring rain. At the beginning of November, the rain and high winds got worse and they kept up all month. On the afternoon of Wednesday 24 November, Defoe was in Kingsland, at the home of his mother-in-law Joan Tuffley, where his 'large and promising family' was staying. That evening, when he was out walking in the neighbourhood, the strong winds turned into a gale that ripped tiles from roofs and hurled them through the air, shattering windows in their way. Defoe himself 'narrowly escap'd ... Mischief' when a large section of a house that he was walking past collapsed almost on top of him. The winds blew with 'unusual Violence' all that night and the next day. On Friday 26 November, it 'continued to blow exceeding hard'. At about ten that night, when Defoe checked his barometer, he found the mercury sunk lower than he'd ever seen it before, and he thought at first that his children must have been tampering with it.[54]

Despite the shrieking winds outside, the Defoes, like most other Londoners, went to bed as usual on the night of 26 November. But at one or two the next morning they were jolted awake when 'the Fury of the Tempest Encreased to Such a Degree' that most people 'expected the Fall of their Houses'. The Tuffley home in Kingsland was 'a well-built brick House', but even so, when 'a stack of chimneys' fell in upon the house next door, Defoe was certain theirs too would come 'down upon their Heads'. He ran to the door 'to attempt an Escape' only to see that the danger outside was even greater than that indoors. Wind-borne tiles, pieces of timber, iron and sheets of lead were flying about in the dark, wet night. These missiles, torn from damaged and demolished buildings, were carried great distances by the gale. Viewing the devastation outside, Defoe realised that it was better for his family 'to surrender to ... Almighty Providence and expect their Graves in the Ruins of the House ... than to meet most certain Destruction in the open Garden' and streets.[55]

There was no question of going back to bed or sleep now. 'From two of the Clock the Storm continued and encreased till Five in the Morning; and from Five to half an Hour after Six it blew with the greatest Violence: the Fury of it was ... exceeding great for that particular Hour and a half.' Finally, 'at Eight a Clock' in the morning, the wind began to subside and gradually 'it ceased so much that our fears were also abated and People began to peep out of Doors'. Venturing out to inspect 'the Havock the Storm had made', Defoe could scarce believe his eyes: 'the Streets [were] covered with Tyle-sherds, and Heaps of Rubbish, from the Tops of the Houses'. Windows were broken, shutters ripped off; chimneys had toppled over or caved in on houses. The 'Distraction and Fury of the Night' was mirrored in 'the Faces of the People'. And it soon became clear that some poor souls lay dead and buried in the bricks and rubble of their homes – in their own beds, in cellars, in shattered doorways through which they had tried to flee.

Stunned as he was by this general devastation, when Defoe emerged from his mother-in-law's house the next morning, one of the first things that must have occurred to him was that if he hadn't lost his prosperous tile and brick factory in Tilbury while he was in Newgate, the storm would have made him a very rich man. On the morning of 27 November, the streets 'lay . . . covered with Tiles and Slates . . . Houses were so universally stript'. Roofs and tiles indeed were the largest casualties of the storm, and slates and tiles the commodity most in demand for repair work in the coming weeks and months. Demand far exceeded supply, resulting, as Defoe tells us, in 'the sudden Rise of the Price of Tiles . . . from 12s per Thousand to £6 for plain Tiles and from 50s per Thousand for Pantiles, to £10'.[56]

Undaunted by his ill luck in losing his tile factory just as he could have made a fortune, when Defoe grasped the full enormity of the storm of 1703, he decided to make money out of it another way. He later claimed of the storm that 'No pen can describe it, no Tongue can express it, no Thought conceive it'.[57] But this impossible task of capturing the storm in words was exactly what Defoe now set out to do. He realised that he had lived through and witnessed an unprecedented historical event – one that should be recorded not just for a contemporary audience but also for posterity. Hence the opening lines of the book he now embarked on, *The Storm*: 'Preaching of Sermons is Speaking to a few of Mankind: Printing of Books is Talking to the whole World . . . a Book Printed is a Record . . . [It] conveys its Contents for Ages to come, to the Eternity of mortal Time, when the Author is forgotten in his Grave.'[58]

Defoe had in mind an entirely new sort of book: a meticulous, documented historical account of an unparalleled catastrophe. He would record the terrible events of 26–27 November which occurred not just in London, but in all the regions hit by the storm, including the devastation to shipping and loss of life at sea. To this end, in early December – less than a week after the storm – Defoe put the following appeal for information in the *London Gazette* and *Daily Courant*.

To preserve the Remembrance of the late dreadful Tempest, an exact and faithful Collection is preparing of the most remarkable Disasters which happened on that Occasion, with the Places where, and Persons concern'd, whether at Sea or on Shore. For the perfecting so good a Work, tis humbly recommended by the Author to all Gentlemen of the Clergy, or others, who have made any Observations of this Calamity, that they would transmit as distinct an Account as possible . . . to the Undertakers, directed to John Nutt near Stationer's hall, London. All Gentlemen . . . are desired to write no Particulars but what they are well satisfied to be true, and to set their Names to the Observations they send, which . . . shall be faithfully recorded, and the Favour publickly acknowledged.[59]

While waiting for responses to his advertisement, Defoe embarked on fieldwork of his own. The day after the storm he went to inspect the scene at the Thames and counted seven hundred ships between Shadwell and Limehouse in 'a posture not to be imagined'. The high winds of the storm had torn ships and boats from their moorings and driven them in upon each other 'in heaps . . . the number of

Masts, Boltsprits and Yards split and broke, the Staving Heads and Sterns ... the tearing and destruction of Rigging ... is not to be reckoned'. The Thames ferrymen he met told Defoe they had lost five hundred wherries, 'most ... dasht to pieces'. Three hundred ships' boats were sunk, along with sixty barges.[60] Defoe was amazed, however, to see that London Bridge had survived the storm with little damage. This was all the more surprising because there were houses and buildings perched on top of the bridge, and these, as Defoe observed, stood 'high and are not sheltered, as [the houses] ... are in the Streets'. Defoe's theory for the 'remarkable preservation' of the bridge and its houses was that the arches that supported it allowed the winds to pass through below it, thus 'diverting the Force of the Storm'.[61]

Defoe roamed all over London, surveying the damage, counting collapsed buildings, toppled chimneys and steeples. Many 'Houses', he says, 'looked like Skeletons, and an universal Air of Horror seem'd to sit on the countenances of the People; all Business seem'd to be laid aside for the Time', as everyone was busy trying to repair their 'Habitations'. Fortunately the foul weather had ceased. After the storm it was 'fair and temperate' for nearly a month, which gave the homeless the opportunity to seek new shelter and those whose houses were damaged time to fortify them with deal boards, old tiles, tarred pieces of sailcloth and canvas. Defoe also inspected the city's major churches and buildings. The lead roofs of Westminster Abbey, St Andrew's Holborn, Christ Church Hospital and 'abundance of other Places' he found had all been 'roll'd up like a Roll of Parchment'.[62]

What of those who had perished in the storm? Defoe studied the weekly Bills of Mortality to find out the toll the storm had taken in human life. Here he read how a distiller in Duke Street was killed when his house collapsed; his wife survived but was taken out 'very much bruised'. A Mr Dyer in Fetter Lane paused to strike a light before he fled from his tottering house, only to have 'a Stack of Chimneys' fall upon and kill him before he made it out. Mr Simpson, a scrivener in Threadneedle Street, was 'unconcern'd at the Danger' of the storm and 'could not be prevailed with to rise' when his family woke him up. His wife and children escaped but Mr Simpson – 'too fatally sleepy' – was 'kill'd in his bed', when the house chimneys fell through the roof on top of him.[63]

In early December, Defoe went down to Kent to view the damage the storm had wrought in the countryside. He was staggered by the 'Multitude of Trees blown down' and began to count them, stopping only when he got weary at 17,000. He calculated that some four hundred windmills had been destroyed – they'd either blown down or gone up in flames when the friction of their whirling blades caught fire. Hundreds of cattle and 1,500 sheep had drowned. Sea salt was carried as far as twenty-five miles inland, coating the grass so that the cows couldn't eat it. In every direction, houses, barns and outbuildings were blown down.

By the time Defoe returned to London, letters about the storm written in response to his advertisement had begun to pile up at his printer and bookseller, John Nutt, near Stationers' Hall. Hundreds of people sent in detailed descriptions of what they had endured, witnessed or had reliable reports of. Much of Defoe's book in fact consists of lengthy excerpts from this correspondence. Many of his informants were clergymen, but Defoe also included a number of letters from ordinary folk in their own words, with the result that the account of the storm we get in his book is one of the earliest examples of 'You Are There' journalism – reportage directly from the scene, as related by eyewitnesses. The story is told from different geographical locations – London, the provinces and out at sea – and also from different points of view.

One Mr J. Bagshot in Oxford wrote to Defoe of Bishop Kidder and his wife who were both killed when a chimney collapsed in the Bishop's palace at Wells and fell through the roof into their bedchamber. The seventy-year-old Bishop apparently 'perceiv'd the fall before it came, and accordingly jump't out of Bed, and made towards the Door, where he was found with his Brains dash'd out; his Lady perceiving [her husband's death] wrapt all the Bed-cloaths about her and . . . smother'd in her Bed'. Mr Bagshot closes his letter with the assertion 'This account is Authentick'.[64]

Even greater dramas were suffered out at sea. Fourteen miles south of Plymouth, Eddystone Lighthouse, which its designer Henry Winstanley had boasted was indestructible, was relentlessly battered by the storm. Winstanley just happened to make a visit to the 120-foot lighthouse tower on 26 November. The next morning there was no sign of lighthouse or men. At some point during that fateful night, the tower, Winstanley and five other men were all swept into the sea.

An even worse drama was played out in the Downs, a four-mile-wide channel between the notorious Goodwin Sands and Deal off the Kent coast. Defoe received a long letter recounting the general calamity there when scores of ships were driven on to and then broken up on the Sands. An 'abundance of poor Wretches' from these ships hung on to pieces of masts and rigging and then swam to where they could stand up on the Sands when the tide went out. Here they gesticulated and made signals for help. They could be clearly seen with 'the assistance of glasses [spyglasses]' by those on land, and several boats full of men were then launched from the shore for the Sands. But these boats came 'in quest of Booty, and in search of Plunder, and to carry off what they could get . . . no Body concern'd themselves for the Lives of [the] . . . miserable Creatures' stuck on the sands who would be drowned when the tide went in again.

Then a hero arrived on the shore, one 'Mr Thomas Powell of Deal, a Slop-Seller by trade'.* Powell recruited volunteers from the crowd of men onshore, offering 'out of his own Pocket 5 s per head for all the Men whose Lives they could save'. They rescued 'above 200 Men' in the night and when they were safe on land Powell 'furnish'd them with Meat, Drink and Lodging . . . at his own Charge'.[65] Despite Powell's heroism, many more seamen perished that night in the Downs and on Goodwin Sands.

There was, indeed, no way of calculating overall how many lives were swallowed up by the sea. The Royal Navy lost fifteen warships and 1,500 seamen, but it was impossible to estimate how many ships and men were lost in the merchant service. On land the storm proved less fatal. Defoe recorded that the death toll in London was 123. The total number of lives lost − both on land and at sea − was somewhere between 8,000 and 15,000. As the storm swept across the south of England, it toppled 2,000 chimneys and 800 houses and rolled up or blew away the lead sheeting on a hundred churches. Queen Anne herself had to take shelter in the cellar of St James Palace.[66]

*   *   *

* A slop dealer was a tradesman who sold ready-to-wear clothing for seamen.

Defoe was not the only person to write on the great storm. Many who lived through the dreadful night of 26–27 November recorded their experience of its fury. Among these was Lady Rachel Russell who wrote to a friend that 'Hampshire is all desolation . . . many killed in the country as well as town. Lady Penelope Nicholas killed in her bed in her country house, and he [presumably Lord Nicholas] in the same bed saved; a piece of timber falling between his legs.' The courtier, diarist and gardening enthusiast, John Evelyn, then in his eighty-fourth year, witnessed the storm at his estate in Wotton, Surrey. Evelyn, who was a founder member of the Royal Society and the author of a work entitled *Sylva or A Discourse on Forest Trees*, lamented the destruction of 2,000 oak trees at Wotton which he described on the morning of 27 November as lying 'like whole regiments fallen in battle by the sword of the conqueror . . . crushing all that grew beneath them'. His losses, he said, were 'tragical, not to be paralleled', and after enumerating the devastation in great detail he claimed, 'I am not able to describe it; but submit to . . . Almighty God.'[67]

Samuel Pepys – the other great diarist of the age – died five months before the storm, though Pepys had ceased to keep a regular diary many years earlier. Robert Hooke, another founder member of the Royal Society, was an assiduous student of the weather – to the point of obsession. But like Pepys, he had the bad luck to miss the storm – which he undoubtedly would have relished – because he had died on 3 March 1703.

Hooke's close friend Robert Knox, however, was still alive and at home with his landlords, the Bartlett family, in St Peter le Poer in London. In his seafaring days Knox had survived many tempests and, like Hooke, he was something of a storm connoisseur. On 27 November, on the other side of London from Daniel Defoe, Knox sat in his rented rooms and wrote down the following account of the storm:

Att aboute one this morning began a very violent Storme of wind aboute WSW & SW. It so frighted many people that they durst not lay in theire beds but came downe & many Chumnies ware blown downe which by the fall Broake through the roofes & killed some people; it blew the tiles of[f] from many houses which after they

Covered with Boards & nere 20 saile of the Queenes Ships were lost,
4 on the Goodwin Sands besides many Marchant Ships & thousands
of men.[68]

Defoe wasn't privy to Lady Russell's, John Evelyn's or Robert
Knox's descriptions of the storm, but in his mother-in-law's house
in Kingsland he carefully read through all the piles of letters –
many of them eyewitness reports – that had been sent to him after
he'd advertised for information. Defoe also read and later incorpo-
rated extracts from several learned articles in the *Transactions of
the Royal Society*. As he amassed this huge body of information,
he became convinced of the unprecedented nature and historical
importance of the storm. He correctly asserted that 'the Damage
done by this Tempest far exceeded the Fire of London' of 1666.[69]

But what caused it and what did it signify? In addition to *The
Storm*, published in July 1704, Defoe wrote two other related works:
a pamphlet, *The Layman's Sermon Upon the Storm*, and a long
poem, *An Essay on the Late Storm*. In both of these he explicitly
stated his belief that the storm, like the great fire, was an act of
God, inflicted on mankind as punishment for their sins. Few, if
any, of his countrymen would have disagreed with him. The Queen
herself declared that 19 January 1704 be a day of fasting and
repentance for the sins of the nation that had provoked the great
storm.

But which sins – and whose – were the sins that had incurred
such divine wrath? In *The Layman's Sermon*, Defoe lamented how
different factions – Jacobites, Whigs, Occasional Conformists and so
forth – judged the meaning of the tempest each 'according to their
own Fancy'. He himself, however, believed that it was sent by God
to reprimand the entire nation for its 'feuds and Storms of parties'.
He called, instead, for moderation: 'Peace, Love, Charity and General
Union.'[70] This argument was recycled in *An Essay on the Late Storm*
in which Defoe asserted in bold capitals that the message of the
storm was to 'REFORM' and 'REPENT'. Even more importantly,
though, Defoe explains what a boon the storm has been to him
personally because it liberated him from his sentence of 'good behaviour' – the seven-year ban on his writing.

Rise Satyr from thy sleep of legal Death
And reassume Satyrick Breath;
What tho' to Seven Years sleep though art confin'd
Thou well may'st wake with such a Wind.[71]

The Layman's Sermon and *An Essay on the Late Storm* were not
really about the storm of 1703 itself but rather about what it meant
– or what Defoe and his contemporaries thought it meant. Defoe
wrote three works in all on the storm in order to get the most out
of it. He used the pamphlet and poem to vent his moral and satiric
interpretations of the event with the result that his book, published
nine months after the storm in July 1704, was for the most part free
of pious reflections and tedious moralising.

Title page of the first edition of The Storm

Instead, *The Storm* was something entirely new and arresting: an
eyewitness catastrophe book, perhaps the first example of a true-life,
'reality' blockbuster. There was something for almost every reader:
suspense, catastrophe, horror, tragedy, heroism, villainy, martyrdom

and plunder. The immediacy of the book gave it an almost voyeuristic feel. The reader could experience – and thrill to – the storm without risk or danger. The result was a compulsive page-turner.

As for the significance of the storm for Defoe himself, it gave him both the central drama and metaphor for his best writing. *The Storm* looks straight ahead – over a gulf of sixteen years – to *Robinson Crusoe*. It unlocked for Defoe the secret of survival: turn adversity to advantage, seize profit from the teeth of calamity. Exploit catastrophe and make it pay.

The storm of 1703 brought Defoe back to life. He made the most of it. In all his years to come he remained obsessed with storms – and catastrophe – and surviving them. He knew that both real and metaphorical tempests were inevitable in human life, and although nearly all his fictional heroes and heroines are alive and well (albeit old) at the end of their stories, Defoe knew that he would perish in the end, as we all do. Ultimately, the only way to survive is in the written word. As Defoe says in the opening pages of *The Storm*: 'Printing of Books is Talking to the whole World . . . a Book Printed is a Record . . . [it] conveys its Contents for Ages to come, to the Eternity of mortal Time, when the Author is forgotten in his Grave.'[72] *Ars longa, vita brevis* – art is long, life is short.

Or as H. F., the narrator of Defoe's other great documentary work, *A Journal of the Plague Year*, writes in his closing 'coarse but sincere Stanza':

> A dreadful Plague in London was,
> In the Year [16] Sixty Five,
> Which swept an Hundred Thousand Souls
> Away; yet I alive![73]

CHAPTER EIGHT

Stranger, Author, Captain

London, 1680–81

Robert Knox arrived back in his 'native country' on 6 September 1680, twenty-two years after he had left it as a boy of eighteen. Now a man of nearly forty, he was middle-aged by the standards of his day. The *Caesar* docked at the small port of Erith in Kent, on the south bank of the Thames and several miles downriver from London. Here, the heavier cargo would be unloaded before the ship went on to the Customs House and Billingsgate Dock in the city. But Knox was eager to be in London, and the only thing that prevented him from setting off immediately was that he was penniless. The boatswain, however, kindly loaned him five shillings to make his way to the city.

Then, just as Knox was getting ready to disembark, a 'drugster' named Mr Short came on board the *Caesar*. Drugsters – pedlars of popular remedies – were always eager to learn of new medicines and nostrums from returning seamen and travellers, so they were often among the first to board newly arrived ships. When Short caught sight of Knox with his 'old fashion[ed] beard' and 'long whiskers', he asked the Captain who this strange figure was,* and was amazed to learn that it was none other than Captain Robert Knox's long-lost son, home at last from Ceylon. Short happened to be acquainted with Knox's family, and he welcomed him heartily, explaining that he 'knew my Brother & that my Sister was Married to a second husband [after being widowed] & had severall Children'. Short also told Knox

---

* Knox cut off his beard in Batavia, but on his long voyage to England he let it grow and trimmed it into the style current in the 1650s when he had sailed to the Indies. The fashion in the 1680s was to be clean-shaven.

where his sister and her family lived in London and gave him directions to find the house. This chance encounter seemed to Knox an amazing 'providence', for he himself had no idea whether his brother and sister were still alive 'nor Whare to Inquire after them'.[1]

By the time Knox was able to leave the *Caesar* it was dark and too late to go on to London, so he and Stephen Rutland lodged that night at an alehouse in Erith. Early the next morning, they hired a boat to take them to London. As they approached it by river, the city that emerged bore little resemblance to the medieval town Knox had last seen when he sailed on the *Anne* in 1658. London in 1680 was well on its way to becoming the 'monster city' Defoe later described in his *Tour through the Whole Island of Great Britain*. The boat carrying Knox and Rutland had to make its way through a 'forest of masts' on the Thames: the river itself was 'almost hidden by merchant vessels from every country'.[2] London had become, in the words of a contemporary, 'the epitome of England, the Seat of British Empire . . . the greatest Emporium . . . of Trade in the whole world.'[3]

When Knox and Rutland disembarked, the grim underside of this 'great Emporium' assaulted their senses. Over the past twenty years migrants from all over England had swollen the city's population from 200,000 to nearly 500,000. The resulting overcrowding and congestion produced a hellish atmosphere, 'a region of dirt, stink and noise'. Knox made his way through 'a Babel of . . . serpentine Streets, close, dismal . . . Lanes, stinking allies, dark, gloomy Courts and suffocating Yards'. Rich and poor, high and low were all thrown together: 'Here lives a Personage of High Distinction; next Door, a Butcher with his stinking Shambles.'[4]

The main thoroughfares were clogged with people, carts, 'sedan chairs', horses, beggars, hawkers, pedlars and pickpockets. The din of human voices, animal, cart and wagon noises was deafening. Mouldering heaps of rubbish and horse droppings lay everywhere. Even the air was noxious. The city's coal- and wood-burning furnaces, kilns, ovens and forges produced beer, bread, soap, glass, lime, dyes, pottery, ironwork and other desirable consumer goods. But all this combustion turned the air into what John Evelyn described as 'an impure and thick mist', a stinking, choking atmosphere. One French visitor wrote that 'this smoke forms a cloud which envelops London like a mantle . . . which suffers the sun to break out only now and then'. Another visitor found himself 'writing by the light of a candle at half-past ten [in] the morning'. The polluted air left a sooty, greasy layer of grime on people, houses, shops, taverns, horses and animals, so that 'everything in the streets seemed dark even to blackness'.[5]

To add to his confusion and disorientation, Knox encountered a multitude of unfamiliar streets and buildings. Much of the London of his childhood had been destroyed in the Great Fire of 1666. In its place, a new modern city was still in the process of being constructed; Christopher Wren's vast, new St Paul's Cathedral would not be completed until 1710. Knox's return was supposed to be a homecoming, but he felt, he says, like Moses in the Old Testament, a 'stranger in a strange land'. Some of the old streets and lanes and a few of the landmarks he remembered survived, but they all appeared diminished in size, as places do when you have last seen them as a child and then return as an adult. By these, however, he managed to navigate.

In his autobiography, Knox describes how 'without inquiry, by my memory', he found the new Royal Exchange on Cornhill though its 'magnificence . . . appeared to me very strange'. This new Royal Exchange was much grander and larger than the one he remembered.[6] Everything, indeed, looked 'outlandish' or foreign to Knox.

In Threadneedle Street, he stopped a passer-by who pointed the way to the house of his sister's husband, Mr Lascelles. When he knocked on the door, Knox found only an apprentice at home who told him that the family was at their country house, but he expected them to return later that day. Without identifying himself, Knox then asked the apprentice if he knew Mrs Lascelles' maiden name and the boy immediately said, 'Yes, it was Knox.' Then, as Knox turned to go, the apprentice begged leave to ask him if he was Mrs Lascelles' brother. He explained that he had heard 'his mistresse had a Brother longe Absent in the East-indies, & my Speech was so like to hers'. Knox of course was both astounded and heartened by this unexpected recognition. He then asked the boy where his brother James Knox lived. When the apprentice told him that James lodged close by, near St Mary Aldermary Churchyard on Bow Lane, Knox decided to seek him out and then return to the Lascelles'.[7]

James Knox, a limner* and artist, was probably at his easel or drawing board when he heard the knock on his door. When he opened it, he had no idea who the strange man before him was. His caller, however, knew immediately that this was his younger brother. Now thirty-two, James Knox had changed beyond recognition since Robert last saw him, but one thing immediately betrayed his identity. One Christmas Eve thirty years earlier, nine-year-old Robert Knox had come upon a gun that a servant had carelessly left leaning against a wall. Knox took it up and began playing with it, aiming at some nearby pigeons as if to shoot them. Just then the maid came to fetch the two-year-old James who was watching his older brother, and when the maid gathered the child into her arms, the heavy gun Robert was holding slipped, struck his brother's head and discharged all its shot, some of which hit James directly in his left eye. A surgeon was summoned who saved the child's life, but not his eye.

It was only 'by the unhappie marke I had given in his eye', that Knox says he recognised James. He decided, however, not to reveal himself immediately. Instead, he said that he had come from Ceylon where he'd known both his brother and father. As soon as James began to respond to this news – first with amazement and then joy – Knox could no longer keep up his pretence. He began to weep as he spoke and then 'fell on my Brothers necke & kissed him, blessing God that had brought me to see my Brother, my owne Mothers Sonn againe'.[8] The brothers embraced over and over, weeping with joy. Finally, when they had composed themselves, they decided to go together to their sister's home on Threadneedle Street.

Here they found that Abigail Lascelles had returned with her son John. The apprentice had already told her that her brother had come back from Ceylon and that his 'speech was so like hers'. But now that Knox was standing before her, instead of displaying the least hint of pleasure, Mrs Lascelles insisted that she didn't recognise him. Nor could Knox see any likeness in this impassive, middle-

---

* In the seventeenth century, a 'limner' was a painter of miniatures. 'Limning' was the skill of 'painting in little'. The term was later replaced with miniature, from *minium*, Latin for red lead or vermilion, the pigment used to decorate the first letters of illuminated manuscripts.

aged matron to the sister he remembered. Perhaps Abigail Lascelles was wary because she suspected he was an impostor. If he was, on the other hand, truly her brother, she had reasons for not being pleased that he had returned, as it were, from the dead. Whatever the case, she demanded proof of Knox's identity, and asked if he had a 'pockehole [pockmark]' on his left temple. Knox pulled his hair back from his forehead so that his sister could examine him, exposing a small indented scar above the corner of his eye. The eventuality that Abigail had probably ceased to think or worry about had now come to pass. This stranger was indeed her brother, Robert Knox.

It was clearly his sister who Knox had in mind when, some years later, in a letter to his cousin John Strype, he described the 'cold reception' he received from his family and how they had 'started from' him when he returned from Ceylon.[9] At the time, however, Abigail must have recovered herself quickly and at least partially concealed her dismay. Soon her husband, Edward Lascelles, arrived home and warmly welcomed his brother-in-law to his home. Lascelles also insisted that Knox must live with them in Threadneedle Street.

Captain Knox had made his son promise to return to England in order to take care of his brother and sister and tell them what had become of their father. But as Knox put it in his autobiography, 'when I came home to my Native Country ... I was Destitute of mony & friends ... how could I performe this Charge of my dying father, when they [Abigail and James] boath ware in a fitter Capassity to take care of mee who had nothing to helpe my selfe'.[10]

Captain Knox had also told his son that he had 'settled his Estate by Letters which he sent from Cotier [Trincomalee]'.[11] But these letters had never arrived and Knox now learned in addition that his father had not made a will before leaving England. In 1662, Abigail Knox (as she still was then) began to petition the East India Company for the money owed to her father. To no avail. When news of Captain Knox's death finally reached London in 1664, she took out letters of administration on his estate, but the company directors still refused to release funds because, they claimed, Robert Knox Jr was his father's rightful heir as the eldest of his three children and he was still alive in Ceylon. Abigail, however, did not give up harassing the company, and finally, in March 1667, they 'ordered a warrant to be made out

to Abigail Knox Administratrix to Captaine Robert Knoxe deceased'
for £180 11s 1d.[12]

Knox now learned that this 'patrimony', as he calls it, had been
divided equally between his brother and sister. Abigail's husband
Edward Lascelles was a prosperous grocer and merchant, who was
eager not only to provide a roof over Knox's head but also to pay
him the share due to him out of Abigail's inheritance. But James
Knox was a struggling, jobbing illustrator without the means to give
anything to his brother.

When Robinson Crusoe finally returns home from his long island
exile, he, too, finds that his patrimony has been divided among his
relatives and that his family – after the passage of so many years –
is now nearly 'extinct'. But Defoe's hero doesn't suffer the disorientation and estrangement Knox felt when he returned. Crusoe finds
that his Brazilian plantation has prospered, that he himself is now
a wealthy man, and without much ado, he replaces his 'extinct'
family with a wife and children of his own with whom he settles
for some years until his wife conveniently dies, thus releasing Crusoe
'to be on the Wing again'.

Things did not go so easily and smoothly for Knox. His brother-
in-law provided him with lodging and some ready cash, but Knox's
share of his sister's inheritance wouldn't last long. He now turned
to the East India Company, not only for compensation for his twenty
years of captivity on Ceylon but also for future employment. Without
wasting any time, the day after he arrived back in London, Knox
and Stephen Rutland, accompanied by Edward Lascelles, went to
the company's headquarters in London.

East India Company House on Leadenhall Street was one of the
few buildings in the city to escape the Great Fire of 1666. Knox
recognised it as soon as it came into view: a half-timbered Elizabethan
mansion with an imposing front decorated with a fleet of company
ships, topped by a wooden statue of a sailor standing between two
carved dolphins.[13] No company records survive of this first visit Knox
made to East India House on 8 September 1680. But a week later,
on 15 September, a Company clerk recorded in the official court
book that 'Mr Rob Knox & Mr Steven Rutland who were prisoners
on ye Island of Zeilon & lately escaped thence, coming into Court,
were directed to attend the Comtees for Shipping to communicate

what they had observed of affairs in those parts'.[14] No mention is made of payment to or future employment for Knox. The company's first concern was to collect information from him.

Knox duly appeared before the company committee and was interrogated much as he had been in Colombo and Batavia by the Dutch and by the English in Bantam. It was during this lengthy interview that Knox told the company directors that on his voyage home, he had 'been diligent in writing papers' about his long sojourn in Ceylon. These, the directors immediately realised, must contain valuable information and they told Knox that they 'desired a sight of what I had wrote'. Knox duly delivered to them the thick stack of manuscript pages that he had produced on the *Caesar*. Sir Josiah Child, one of the most prosperous and influential members of the committee, was especially intrigued by Knox's manuscript and took it back to his country estate at Wanstead Abbey in Epping Forest to study carefully.

Knox, meanwhile, discreetly indicated to the company directors that he was in financial difficulties. He may not have anticipated a hero's welcome home by the company, but he did expect compensation for his long years of detention. On 5 October 1680, the following entry was made in the Company Court Book records: 'It is ordered that the sum of 20lb be paid unto Robert Knox & 10lb to Stephen Rutland (who lately made their escape from Zeilon) for their relief.'[15]

Knox's own account of this transaction in his autobiography was written in 1696, when he was still in the company's employ.

> At my first appearing before them [the company committee], they all bid me welcome to England, & told me they would not detaine me with discours of inquiries to keepe me from my Relations, but defered that to hereafter, & the next time I appeared before them they ordered twenty pounds to be paid to me & ten pounds to Stephen Rutland which we received accordingly; but Sir Jeremy Sambrooke [one of the company directors] called me a little to one side & put two Guineas into my hand, who then I knew not, but afterward I went to his owne house to thanke him againe for that Great faviour.[16]

Only Knox's closing description of Sir Jeremy Sambrooke's generosity hints at his real feelings. As he later confided to his cousin John

Strype, Knox was shocked and angered by his paltry remuneration. Legally, however, the East India Company did not owe Knox or Rutland a penny because they had been captured before completing their voyage. According to the Conditions of Service, which applied to every man who sailed on an East India Company ship, if the men were wrecked or captured 'before the [ship] . . . arrives at her port . . . neither the master nor the mariners are intituled to any wages'.[17]

Why, then, had the company paid Abigail Knox her late father's £180 in 1667? Most likely because Captain Knox had been a part-owner of the *Anne*, and despite the fact that he was taken captive and died in Ceylon, Captain Knox's crew, following his orders, sailed on from the island to their next port in south India where the ship's cargo was unloaded and traded or sold. (The only cargo that had been unloaded in Ceylon, and thus lost, was the Porto Novo Indian cloth which was of negligible value). Despite the loss of the sixteen men taken captive in Ceylon, the *Anne* and her cargo survived. The Captain's heirs back in London were thus entitled to their father's share of the ship and its cargo.

The company handed over all that was due to Abigail Knox in 1667, as Captain Knox's executor, without reserving any portion for Robert Knox Jr should he ever escape from Ceylon. When he did finally return, Knox bitterly resented the miserable 'reward' of £20 the company gave to him. It was an insult he nursed for the rest of his life, though he concealed his anger in the autumn of 1680 for the simple reason that he needed employment. He evidently lost no time in applying for this because the next company Court Book entry for 22 October records that 'Robert Knox who was many years a Captive on ye Island of Zeilon is entertained as a 4th Mate on board ye *new London* . . . bound for Bantam'.[18]

Knox, however, did not take up this post. He had made only two voyages, some twenty years earlier, so the rank of fourth mate was probably suitable, even taking into account the fact that he was the son of a captain. But Knox aspired to higher things. He asked John Strype, who knew Sir Josiah Child – the powerful company director who would soon become its Governor – to go with him to visit Child and 'intreat his favour & offer my service'.[19]

Josiah Child had originally made his fortune as a brewer and victualler to East India Company and Royal Navy ships. He invested in company stock in the early 1670s, and by the end of the decade he owned shares worth £23,000. As the principal shareholder, Child dominated and shaped company policy, which included flagrant bribery of Members of Parliament. His despotic rule at East India House made him many enemies, but there was no one strong enough to challenge his supremacy. In 1673, he bought Wanstead Abbey for £11,500. Three years later, he purchased a baronetcy for £1,095. By this time Child was worth something like £200,000 and he lived in a grand style. John Evelyn described how he improved his estate at Wanstead Abbey at 'prodigious cost in planting walnut-trees about his seate, and making fish-ponds, many miles in circuit'.[20]

It was to this opulent manor that Robert Knox and John Strype came to seek Child's favour. Child received them cordially and reassured Knox that he had no cause to worry: 'he would provide to imploy me'. Child, however, hoped to persuade Knox to become the company agent at their East Indies factory in Bantam. He tried to entice Knox by saying that Bantam would give him an 'easier life & more profett' than a life at sea.[21] But the truth, as Knox well knew, was that Bantam had a deadly climate, with tropical diseases of every sort, and also a hostile population of natives just outside its fortress walls.

Knox politely declined Child's offer, explaining that he had a different future in mind and was already diligently preparing for it. Soon after he arrived in London in September 1680, Knox had turned for help to one of his father's old friends, Captain John Brookehaven, who, 'taking pity' on Knox's 'forlorn Condition', arranged for him to study navigation with the mathematician John Colson. Soon after he began these studies, Knox left the Lascelles home where he had been living and took lodgings at Mr Colson's house.[22] Thus when Knox visited Child at Wanstead he parried the offer of the Bantam post by explaining that he was studying with Mr Colson 'to improove myselfe to be fit to serve [the company] at sea'.[23]

Soon after Knox and Strype visited Wanstead Abbey, Child reported back to the company directors his high opinion of Knox's 'Papers' which he said contained 'many new and Strange Stories' about Ceylon. He recommended that they should be published as a book, with sponsorship from the East India Company. Quite apart from the intrinsic merits of Knox's account, which Child fulsomely praised, he was keenly aware that such a book would provide excellent publicity for the company's activities in the East Indies and undoubtedly promote trade.

In his autobiography, Knox claims that Child's proposal to publish the manuscript came as a complete surprise and that he had 'never thought' his 'scribled papers . . . worthy of troubling the world with'.[24] But when Child proposed the idea of publication, Knox offered no resistance, and Child's verdict was soon endorsed by the other company directors. Knox's papers, however, were, in his own words, 'promiscuous and out of forme'. They needed editing and 'several inlargements on such heads as I had but touched briefly'. This meant that at the same time as he was busily studying mathematics and navigation with Colson, Knox was also industriously revising his book for publication with the help of the indispensable John Strype who 'Composed it into heads & Chapters'.[25]

At this juncture, Knox encountered another character who was destined to play a major role in his life: Robert Hooke, Curator of Experiments and Fellow of the Royal Society, Cutler Lecturer on Science and Trade and Professor of Geometry at Gresham College. To look at, Hooke was a strange bird. His contemporary John Aubrey described him as 'crooked, pale faced . . . his head is large, his eye full and popping . . . he has a delicate head of hair'. Hooke's admiring friend and first biographer, Richard Waller, conceded that 'as to his person he was but despicable, being very crooked . . . This made him low of stature, tho' by his Limbs he should have been moderately tall . . . He was . . . pale and lean . . . with a meagre Aspect . . . with a sharp ingenious Look . . . his Mouth meanly wide, and his upper Lip thin; his Chin sharp, and Forehead large . . . He went stooping and very fast.'

Hooke's deformed body, however, housed a keen, enquiring mind.[26] By the time Knox first met him in the autumn of 1680, Hooke had established himself as one of the leading 'natural philosophers' — as scientists were then called — of his day. Although he had been a sickly child growing up on the Isle of Wight, he was a highly intelligent, inventive boy, with a gift for drawing and mechanics. When he entered Christ Church at Oxford, Hooke, still in his teens, became the paid assistant of the wealthy gentleman philosopher Robert

Boyle. It was young Hooke who 'contrived and perfected the air pump' for Boyle with which they performed experiments on vacuums, air pressure and combustion.

At Oxford, Hooke was also drawn into a group of scholars including Boyle, John Wilkins and Christopher Wren who followed the methods and philosophy formulated by Francis Bacon in the 1620s. Bacon argued that the fundamental laws of the universe could be discovered by observing and recording natural phenomena rather than through abstract theorising. The 'Wadham Group' at Oxford (so-called because they met in John Wilkins's rooms at Wadham College) were all committed Baconians who believed that experiment, observation and measurement were the keys that would open up the secrets of the earth and the cosmos.

In this new, exciting world at Oxford, Hooke learned how to use magnets, pendulums, air pumps, telescopes, microscopes and other instruments. At the same time that he was experimenting on the air pump with Boyle, he worked on barometers and microscopes with Christopher Wren and astronomical instruments with Seth Ward, Master of Jesus College and Professor of Astronomy. Hooke attempted to solve the problem of determining longitude by devising a clock that would keep accurate time at sea. He later claimed that he also invented the spring-regulated watch while he was still at Oxford. Encouraged by Wilkins, who had published a book in 1640 on flying to the moon, Hooke drew up plans for various flying machines. He even made 'one contraption of springs and wings which he managed to keep up in the air' for a short space of time.[27]

After the Restoration, the Wadham Group at Oxford migrated to London. On 28 November 1660, twelve of them, including Robert Hooke, met at Gresham College, and after a lecture by Christopher Wren, they voted to found 'a College for the Promoting of Physico-Mathematicall Experimentall Learning'.[28] Two years later, in 1662, the new college received a charter from Charles II and became known as the Royal Society. Their Latin motto '*Nullus in Verba*' – 'Nothing upon another's word' – enshrined the society's empirical, experimental philosophy. Hooke was appointed the society's 'first Curator of Experiments' and his duties included performing three or four experiments before the membership at their weekly meetings held at Gresham College. In addition to the core group of Boyle,

Wren, Hooke and Wilkins, early members of the Royal Society included Samuel Pepys, John Evelyn and Henry Oldenburg. And to attract funding, the society also welcomed wealthy gentlemen and aristocrats who dabbled in science.

When Hooke was appointed the Society's 'Curator of Experiments', he was still employed as Boyle's assistant. After the Great Fire of 1666, he had a third responsibility to squeeze into his hectic life when he was chosen as one of the principal architects and surveyors to rebuild the city. The new modern London that so amazed Knox when he returned in 1680 was in part Hooke's creation. Among his contributions was the new Bethlehem Hospital (known as Bedlam), which he not only designed but supervised the construction of – from the sewers and cellars to the turrets and clock tower, as well as the famous statues of Melancholy and Raving Madness at Bedlam's gates. Hooke also collaborated with Christopher Wren on the tall, imposing Monument to the Fire on Fish Street – a 202-foot pillar of Portland stone topped by a flaming urn of gilt bronze symbolising the fire.[29] But the monument wasn't just a memorial. Within its base, Hooke set up a telescope to view the stars and planets, and the internal staircase enabled him to climb to the summit in order to drop objects of various weight and measure the speed at which they plummeted to the ground.[30]

During the same period that the Royal Society was emerging in the 1660s, another arena for discussion of a less rarefied sort came into being: the coffee house.[31] Seventeenth- and eighteenth-century coffee houses were places where men from all sorts of backgrounds and classes met for fellowship and debate, to read newspapers, conduct business and engage in what we today call 'networking'. Here they could drink a dish of coffee or chocolate, smoke their clay pipes, gossip, read the latest news-sheets and pamphlets, collect their post, meet friends and business associates, and even, in Robert Hooke's case, conduct experiments before a packed audience. (Hooke's lectures at Gresham College were often sparsely attended – sometimes, in fact, no one at all turned up – so he appreciated his attentive coffee-house spectators.)

It was at a coffee house that Robert Hooke and Robert Knox first met.[32] Knox, indeed, might never have encountered Hooke had it not been for this new social phenomenon that had sprung up in London during his years in Ceylon. Hooke was a coffee-house

Defoe in 1706; frontispiece to *Jure Divino*

Eyre Crowe's Victorian engraving of Defoe in the Pillory

Disputed portrait of Robert Hooke

East India Company ships

Knox memorial stone at Lagendenny

Seventeenth-century
coffee house

East India Company House

OLD EAST INDIA HOUSE.

Sir Josiah Child

Robert Harley

Robert Knox in 1695

See Knox'es Aspect here by White designd, (Like those at last by Grace he Freedom Gaind
Peruse his Book, there'll better see his Mind. Pursuing for Spoils they Aegypts Jewels took
Captive, like Jacob's Offspring, long detaind) His Cephein left, yet (changd by) in his Book.
Rich. Stere 1695.

Portrait of Robert Knox in 1709

THE

LIFE

AND

STRANGE SURPRIZING

ADVENTURES

OF

ROBINSON CRUSOE,

Of *YORK,* Mariner:

Who lived Eight and Twenty Years,
all alone in an un-inhabited Island on the
Coast of America, near the Mouth of
the Great River of Oroonoque;

Having been cast on Shore by Shipwreck, wherein all the Men perished but himself.

WITH

An Account how he was at last as strangely deliver'd by PYRATES.

Written by Himself.

LONDON:
Printed for W. Taylor at the *Ship* in *Pater-Noster-
Row.* MDCCXIX.

First edition title page and frontispiece of *Robinson Crusoe*, 1719

St Helena

The 1703 Great Storm

habitué and went to one or more of them daily – most frequently to his two favourites, Jonathan's and Garraway's in Exchange Alley near Cornhill, not far from Gresham College where he lived. Coffee houses extended Hooke's range of contacts and informants beyond scientific circles to a wider world of artisans, craftsmen, instrument and clock makers, and also to merchants and travellers who had been to distant lands and seen strange new sights. Among the men that Hooke befriended at Garraway's Coffee House was James Knox, the limner and engraver, who first appears in Hooke's diary in 1677. Hooke himself was a careful draughtsman who used diagrams and drawings in his lectures and published work. His 1665 book *Micrographia* – which Pepys stayed up until 2 a.m. reading and pronounced 'the most ingenious book' he'd ever read – included, among other things, Hooke's detailed drawings of a flea, a drone fly, a nettle sting and a patch of blue mould as seen through a microscope.[33] James Knox showed Hooke how to draw shells and fossils and gave him technical tips and information such as how to clean pictures with a mixture of water, 'castle sope' and flour.[34]

On the evening of Sunday 12 September 1680 – just four days after Robert Knox arrived at Erith on the *Caesar* – Hooke returned to his rooms in Gresham College and wrote in his diary: 'Perused 1st Journal DH. Haak chesse. Knox his brother escaped out of Ceylon after 22 years detainder. Tisons 2nd account.'[35]

Hooke had learned of Robert Knox's astonishing return from Ceylon during his usual evening coffee-house visit, probably from a mutual friend of Hooke and James Knox. He noted it in his diary entry alongside the other events of his day: reading the first journal published by the Royal Society; dining at home [DH]; playing chess with his friend, the German scholar Theodore Haak; and going through the second draft of the anatomist Edward Tyson's *Anatomy of a Porpess* [*Porpoise*], another friend. With his insatiable thirst for new knowledge, Hooke was eager to question Robert Knox. A meeting was arranged, at Jonathan's or Garraway's, and either at this first encounter or at another soon after, Knox told Hooke that he had written a long, detailed account of Ceylon that included discussion of nearly every aspect of the island – its geography, animal and plant life, agriculture, society, government, laws and religion.

Thus began a friendship and collaboration which became in some

ways the most important relationship in both men's lives. Robert
Knox and Robert Hooke seem, at first glance, an unlikely pair. Hooke
was a seventeenth-century polymath scientist. His voracious curiosity
meant that he always had a number of projects simultaneously on
the go. Among other experiments, he dissected a porpoise one day
at Jonathan's (hence his interest in Tyson's account), and cut open
a dog at Gresham College, keeping it alive by pumping air into its
lungs with bellows. In his attempt to determine the nature of gravity,
Hooke dropped various objects from high buildings, including his
own Monument to the Fire, St Paul's Cathedral and Westminster
Abbey. Using different types of telescopes, he tried to determine the
distance of stars from the earth. In the interests of science, he even
had himself sealed up in a closed chamber. After a quarter of its
air was pumped out (on his instructions), Hooke was gratified when
both his ears began to ache.

Knox, on the other hand, had been thrust into unusual situations
by chance rather than choice. As the son of a sea captain, he also
came from a different social background from Hooke whose father
had been an Anglican curate on the Isle of Wight. Six years younger
than Hooke, Knox was knitting and peddling caps in Ceylon while
Hooke was surveying and rebuilding London, making weekly demon-
strations before the Royal Society and having himself sealed up in
airtight chambers. But dissimilar as their pasts and experiences had
been, when these two men met in the autumn of 1680, they discovered that they had much in common, including a shared curiosity
about virtually everything, acute powers of perception and a passion
for close and detailed observation.

Superficially at least, Hooke and Knox shared a way of life in
that neither ever married. Their temperaments were also similar:
in their later years they became disappointed and embittered, and
felt themselves undervalued by the institutions they had served: in
Knox's case the East India Company and in Hooke's the Royal
Society.[36] There were, however, also significant differences between
the two men. Though both were bachelors, we know from Hooke's
diary that he was not celibate. Knox, for the most part at least,
probably was. Hooke was miserly while Knox was generous: in later
years, Knox paid for the education of various young relatives and
also sponsored promising young men who were no relation but

needed assistance. Knox also came to the rescue of a number of his impoverished elderly cousins, aunts and uncles and helped his land-lady and her family. Hooke was quarrelsome and competitive while Knox, even when provoked and angered, avoided confrontation and argument.

There were certain areas of Hooke's life that Knox probably never knew about, including the suicide of Hooke's brother John in 1678.[37] Knox was aware that Hooke's twenty-year-old niece, Grace Hooke, lived with her uncle at Gresham College, where she occupied her own rooms in one of the turrets. Knox, indeed, probably met Grace because she sometimes acted as her uncle's hostess. But he never would have suspected that Hooke, who was nearly forty years Grace's senior, was having a sexual relationship with his niece – one that began when she was just sixteen and ended only with her death at the age of twenty-six in 1687.[38]

After Josiah Child returned Knox's Ceylon 'papers' to him, Knox showed them to Hooke who wholeheartedly endorsed Child's opinion that they should be published and promoted the idea of publication among the other members of the Royal Society. Hooke not only encouraged Knox to publish, he also offered to work closely with him on the revisions, to write a preface for the book and to negotiate and oversee its publication by Richard Chiswell, printer to the Royal Society.

Knox's original account, written on the *Caesar*, has not survived, but the bulky manuscript of his revised 'second edition' has, complete with Hooke's numerous corrections, additions, queries and explana-tory passages, and we can see from these the sort of contribution Hooke must have made to the first edition. Nothing was too large or too small for Hooke's scrupulous attention. He was an indefatigable editor who worked on the overall structure and organisation as outlined in the detailed Table of Contents that he drew up. But he also laboured on Knox's choice of words, sentence structure and even punctuation. On the pages of the manuscript, Hooke's bold angular handwriting was like the man himself, in contrast to Knox's tentative, spidery, meandering script.

From his first reading of it, Hooke realised that Knox's work was original and quite unlike previous travellers' accounts of distant lands. Knox had not been a mere visitor to Ceylon. He had lived there many years, learned the language and observed the land, peoples and culture at close hand. In addition, Knox's narrative was an unusually impersonal – and for his day, a remarkably unbiased, non-judgemental – one. Instead of focusing on his own experiences – his adventures, trials and feelings – for most of his account, Knox looked steadfastly outward and described in great detail the world where he had been 'captivated'. When it was published, three-quarters of Knox's book was devoted to the island and only the last section covered his own life there. Knox's was one of the most objective as well as exhaustive reports that had ever been made of a distant land, its geography, climate, plant and animal life, its human inhabitants and their culture.

Robert Hooke was not by nature a generous-hearted man and he did not lavish hours on Knox's book out of kindness. He devoted time and energy to it because, from the opening pages of the manuscript, Hooke realised that it was an unprecedented source of new information about a little known part of the world. He also grasped something even more significant about Knox's text: he saw that valuable scientific principles and facts might emerge from it. Like Darwin's Galapagos Islands 150 years later, Knox's Ceylon was a kind of vast laboratory from which important scientific knowledge could be drawn.

According to Hooke's diary, he met Knox and Knox's cousin 'Bunneal' [James Bonnell] on Thursday 6 January 1681 at the Crown Inn, Holborn.[39] Like John Strype, Bonnell was another cousin who became involved in the editing of the book.[40] The following Monday, Knox and Bonnell called on Hooke at his rooms in Gresham College. These meetings were not just to confer over Knox's manuscript. Hooke was going to exhibit one of Knox's more remarkable specimens at the next Royal Society meeting and he needed to ask him various questions beforehand.

The society records describe how at the meeting held on 12 January:

Mr Hooke shewed a piece of a talipat leaf, which one Mr Knox, who had been nineteen years and an half captive in Ceylon, brought with him from thence. It was about seven feet long and nine feet wide at one end, shaped like a woman's fan, closing and opening like that. The whole leaf was said to be a circle of twenty feet diameter.[41]

Nothing like this huge plant had previously been seen in England, and it caused a sensation when Hooke exhibited it to the Royal Society. He also demonstrated its various uses: as an umbrella against rain and sun and as a tent. Talipot leaves, he explained, could also be dried and cut up into smaller pieces which could then be written upon and bound together as books.

Knox had brought back a number of other artefacts from Ceylon which he handed over to Hooke, including his 'habit' (presumably his 'clout' or sarong) and 'utensils'. Hooke was delighted by these specimens and added them to the society's repository — a museum of 'natural rarities' or 'curiosities' that included a stuffed armadillo, a preserved crocodile, 'a giant's thighbone', a stone in the shape of 'the secret parts of a woman', and a 'child [foetus that was said to have] stood 25 years in its mother's body'.[42]

On 13 January, the day after Hooke exhibited Knox's talipot leaf, Hooke dined at home with Christopher Wren. Knox had also been invited, but Hooke notes in his diary that 'Knox came not'. Knox, however, called on Hooke at his rooms in Gresham College on both 21 and 22 January. By now they were working hard on Knox's book. For nineteen years Knox had meticulously studied the interior of Ceylon, and he had included many of his observations and conclusions in his manuscript account. But as they collaborated together, Hooke questioned Knox further about every aspect of his experience. What other sort of flora and fauna were found on the island? What were its climate, rainfall and atmospheric conditions? Who were the inhabitants and what languages did they speak? What did they look like, what sort of clothes did they wear, how were they governed, what God or Gods did they worship? What kind of agriculture did they practise, what trades and crafts and professions did they follow? What were the relations between men and women, adults and children? What was their family and social life like, what arts and entertainments did they enjoy?

Knox and Hooke worked relentlessly on the manuscript, with additional editorial help from John Strype and James Bonnell.[43] They revised and completed the book in just a few months. Hooke's diary records meeting with Knox to make the finishing touches at his rooms at Gresham College on 8 March 1681 and again at Garraway's Coffee House on 13 March. Five days later Knox presented the manuscript to the Governor and committee of the East India Company. In his accompanying letter, he explains that it was his 'Friends and Acquaintances' who had urged him to 'make it . . . Publick'. Knox went on to say that he had organised his account of Ceylon under 'four Heads: The first concerning the Countrey and the Products of it. The second concerning the King and his Government. The third concerning the Inhabitants and their Religion and Customs, and the last concerning our Surprize, Detainment and Escape.' Knox closes his letter by asking for the company's favour and patronage, upon which, he says, all 'his Future Hopes and Expectations' depend.[44]

The finished manuscript of the *Historical Relation* was more akin to a learned history and a scientific treatise than a traveller's tale. Each of the book's four parts was further broken down into chapters. Parts I and II both have seven chapters, Part III has eleven and Part IV has fourteen. Knox's own experience in Ceylon is mainly confined to Part IV, though there are brief personal references in the earlier sections and there is also a good deal of general information about Ceylon in the last section. The major focus of the book, however, is the island itself rather than the captive Robert Knox.

Like Robinson Crusoe, Knox is an autobiographical narrator but, unlike Crusoe, he is a neutral observer and commentator, rather than a hero. His task is to record and analyse with precision a hitherto little known, unexplored world. Knox makes this originality of his work clear in his very first paragraph: 'my design [is] . . . to relate such things onely that are new and unknown unto these European Nations. It is the Inland Countrey [rather than the coasts which the Portuguese, Dutch and English had all visited] therefore I chiefly intend to write of, which is yet an hidden Land even to the Dutch themselves that inhabit . . . the Island.'[45]

The scope of Knox's book is extraordinary, covering as it does geographical, biological, zoological, botanical, anthropological and ethnographic descriptions of Ceylon. He has, however, been accused by some modern readers of incomprehension, inaccuracies, bias and racism. Read with post-colonial eyes, the *Historical Relation* can be interpreted as a record of 'the colonial encounter' and how 'the relations of power [are] embedded in' it. It can even be considered an attempt 'through writing . . . to conquer . . . the Other'.[46] But this is not the book that Knox laboured to produce with the help of Robert Hooke and 'Cosin[s] Strype' and Bonnell in three or four months during the winter of 1680–81. Knox, to be sure, got some things wrong. He was especially blinkered when it came to religion and failed almost entirely to understand Buddhism. He also undoubtedly exaggerated the tyranny and cruelty of the Kandyan King, Raja Sinha.[47] Like every writer, Knox was a product of his own personal circumstances and historical milieu. But what is striking about the *Historical Relation* even today is how much he got right – the depth and extent of his interest, vision and knowledge.

On 23 March, five days after Knox delivered his manuscript to the East India Company, his brother James died suddenly at the age of just thirty-two. According to the parish register of St Mary Aldermary, he was buried three days later.[48] Knox mentions his brother's death only once in his autobiography, and he gives neither the date nor the cause.[49] Hooke's diary has two references to the death but these entries merely concern Hooke's purchase of James Knox's paintings and drawings from Edward Lascelles. This transaction was negotiated when Hooke met Knox and Lascelles at Tooth's Coffee House on 16 May. The next day Hooke delivered the agreed payment of £8 to Lascelles.[50]

His brother's death was not just a personal blow to Knox. James had done many of the illustrations in Knox's book, so when he died new illustrators and sources of illustrations had to be hastily found. When the book was published it contained fifteen copperplate engravings strategically placed throughout the text. These included depictions of a Sinhalese farmer ploughing his land and another threshing rice, a man sheltering himself from the rain with a huge talipot leaf, the Sinhalese 'manner of . . . fishing', a Veddah or 'wild man', a Sinhalese nobleman and gentlewoman, Raja Sinha the King of Kandy, several gruesome scenes of execution and a cremation. A number of these illustrations closely correspond to Knox's descriptions, and he probably contributed additional information as the drawings were being produced. But other illustrations were lifted from earlier sources, including major features of the map of Ceylon taken from the one in Philippus Baldaeus' 1672 work *Description of Malabar and Coromandel and the Great Island of Ceylon*.[51]

After his brother's death, Knox became even closer to Hooke. Hooke, for his part, had much to gain from their friendship. He knew that Knox was studying navigation in order to go to sea again for the East India Company. Even before he met Knox, Hooke and the Royal Society were eager to gain information from travellers and seamen. Hooke himself had produced a document entitled 'Directions for Sea-men bound for farre voyages'. This was a four-page to-do list, which included such items as keeping a diary, recording compass readings, observing tides, describing unusual meteors, and directions on how to sound sea depth without using a line.[52]

Now Hooke had a friend and agent in Knox to follow all these instructions and be his eyes and ears abroad. When Knox set sail again for the Indies, he would be an extension of Hooke's own enquiring mind and serve him in a capacity similar to that of Hooke's long-suffering, faithful research assistant Harry Hunt, who lived with him at Gresham College. Hooke was a difficult, competitive man who quarrelled with other Royal Society Fellows, including Henry Oldenburg, Christian Huygens and, most famously, Isaac Newton. But Hooke trusted and relied on Knox and Harry Hunt – both of whom were devoted to him – because they didn't compete with him and were never a threat. In Hooke's mind, they knew their place and fulfilled their role of collecting data and doing tasks for him.

On 30 March, just a week after James Knox's death, the East India Company 'Court were pleased to entertain Mr Robert Knox to serve them in the East Indies at Sea or on shore, at the salary of £40 per annu [sic] to commence from ye time of his arrival at Bantam'.[53] It seems that the directors still hoped Knox would take a post at their Bantam factory, though this offer was not as specific as the earlier ones and it allowed for the possibility of work 'at sea or on shore'. But Knox was preoccupied with his brother's affairs and he also wanted to remain in England to see his book through to publication and personally present it to the Court of Directors. Thus, despite the generous salary of £40 a year, he declined this rather vague post.

In April 1681, Sir Josiah Child was elected Governor of the East India Company, and the following month he came up with an offer for Knox that was exactly what he hoped for. As Knox relates in his autobiography, 'Sr Josiah Child . . . told me he had this day bought a small ship, building at Blackewell [Blackwall, the company dockyard on the Thames] to put me in Commander & wished me good successe in her, & bid me goe and looke after the finishing & fitting of her.'[54] The company records for 11 May state: 'Mr Robert Knox being presented to be Comandr of the new ship letten to freight . . . for ye Compan[y's] service, on a voiage to the So Seas, the Court approved thereof.'

On 20 May, the court wrote to their agent at Fort St George (Madras) that this new ship was 130 tonnes and would be commanded by Robert Knox. It was scheduled to sail in late August or September from Gravesend, in convoy with five other East Indiamen, for Bantam where it was hoped it would arrive in March 1682.[55]

This new ship was named the *Tonqueen Merchant* because it was destined for Tonqueen [Tonkin] in China. At 130 tonnes, it was a small East India Company ship – with a crew of just twenty-five men. But what mattered to Knox was not its size but the fact that he was to be Captain. It would remain under his command for the next thirteen years, during which he would make four voyages on it to the East Indies. Knox would not only receive a captain's salary, he would also be able to trade on his own account. In the late spring of 1681, he thus had a prosperous future before him, and precisely the sort of life at sea that he had longed for since he was a boy.

On 12 May, the day after the East India Court approved Knox as Captain of the *Tonqueen Merchant*, Knox told Hooke his good news when they met at Garraway's Coffee House.[56] But Knox's appointment also meant that publication of his book had to be expedited. He wanted to see it in print before he sailed. During June and July, Hooke and Knox made the final revisions to the text which was then delivered to the Royal Society printer, Richard Chiswell, whose premises were at the sign of the Rose and Crown in St Paul's Churchyard.

On Monday 25 July, Hooke made a two-word entry in his diary: 'Knoxes praeface', indicating that he had completed his introduction.

This was a glowing endorsement of the book which Hooke recommended as a 'Generous Example' for future sailors to follow when they wrote accounts of their own voyages. Although Knox escaped with almost 'nothing upon his Back or in his Purse', Hooke described how he 'did yet Transport the whole Kingdom of Cande Uda [Kandy] in his Head and by Writing and Publishing this his Knowledge, has freely given it to his Countrey, and to You Reader in particular . . . Read therefore the Book it self and you will find your self taken Captive indeed, but used more kindly by the Author than he himself was by the Natives.' Hooke also praises Knox's objectivity: 'I conceive him to be no ways prejudiced or bypassed by Interest, affection or hatred, fear or hopes, or the vain-glory of telling Strange Things, so as to make him swarve from the truth of Matter of Fact.'[57]

When Hooke's preface was published as part of the preliminary material to the book, Hooke dated it 1 August 1681, the same date that Knox affixed to his 'Epistle Dedicatory'. Chiswell had by now typeset Knox's manuscript. As Knox explains in his dedication to the Governor, Deputy Governor and twenty-four directors (all named in full) of the East India Company, 'What I formerly Presented you in writing, having in the pursuance of your Commands now somewhat dressd [sic] by the help of the Printer and Graver, I a second time humbly tender to you . . . I hope you will not deny it a favourable Acceptance, since 'tis the whole Return I made from the Indies after Twenty years stay there; having brought home nothing else.'[58]

A week later, on 8 August, Robert Hooke met Christopher Wren, the newly elected President of the Royal Society, at Child's Coffee House. After conferring with Hooke, Wren wrote to Richard Chiswell that Knox's book was 'Written with great Truth and Integrity; and the Subject being new, containing an Account of a People and a Countrey little known to us; I conceive it may give great Satisfaction to the Curious, and may be well worth your Publishing'.[59] Hooke visited Chiswell at his shop in St Paul's Churchyard on the same day, and Knox called on Hooke at home that evening.

Two days later, on 10 August, the East India Company officially voted that Knox's book be made 'Publick'.[60] On the same day, company records show that warrants were signed for payment of £260 to the owners of the *Tonqueen Merchant* and £9 15s to its Captain, Robert Knox.[61] Its departure was clearly imminent.

On 16 August, Hooke 'gave Capn Knox querys for ye Indies' – a written list of instructions and directions for him concerning the kind of observations and findings he should record in his journal in the course of his voyage. Two days later, Hooke received an early printed copy of Knox's book from Chiswell.[62]

On the 22nd, the East India Company granted permission to the owners and commander of the *Tonqueen Merchant* to lade '2150 Dollars freight free' on board, and two days later, the court of directors ordered the ship to proceed to the Downs. It was to sail to the East Indies in convoy with five other ships, and on 31 August the company sent further orders that the 'six Ships . . . [should] sail out of the Downs as wind and weather will permit'.[63]

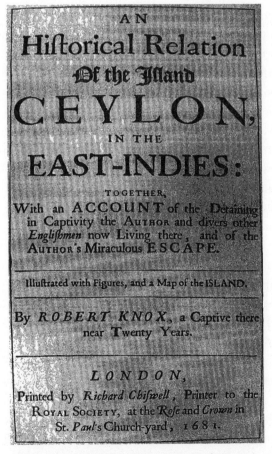

Title page of the first edition of Knox's
An Historical Relation of Ceylon, *1681*

Meanwhile, Knox's *Historical Relation of the Island of Ceylon* was officially published. On Thursday 1 September the *London Gazette* ran an advertisement for:

> An Historical Relation of the Island Ceylon, in the East-Indies: together with an Account of the detaining in Captivity the Author, and divers other Englishmen now living there, and of the Authors Miraculous Escape. Illustrated with fifteen large Figures, and a Map of the Island. By Robert Knox, a Captive there near twenty years. Sold by Richard Chiswell, Printer to the Royal Society, at the Rose and Crown in St Paul's Church yard. (Book priced at 10 shillings in ordinary binding)

Even in 'ordinary', plain, hard covers it was an impressive volume: a large folio of nearly two hundred pages, including the East India Company's and Christopher Wren's imprimaturs, Hooke's six-page preface, a nine-page table of contents, a page of errata and, at the end of the book, a two-page list of other books published by Richard Chiswell. Many of the early volumes had been purchased by subscription and those readers who wanted more elaborate editions than the plain, ten-shilling one, could order vellum or calf binding with gilt lettering and ornate tooling.[64] The impressive, folio-sized copperplate illustrations were placed at appropriate points in the text while the large, fold-out engraved map of Ceylon was inserted at the end.

Thus, in early September 1681, Robert Knox's careers as an author and an East India Company captain were launched simultaneously. On board the *Tonqueen Merchant*, he waited in the Downs for three weeks for the other convoy ships to arrive and then for the weather and wind to allow them to depart. Finally, on 21 September, a bright, sunny day with a good wind, the *Tonqueen Merchant* and the five other ships set sail.

A special copy of Knox's *Historical Relation* sailed with him. As he explained many years later to John Strype, 'the first voiage I went to sea after my booke of Ceylon was printed, Mr Chiswell gave me a booke interleaved with . . . blanke leafe [leaves or folio sheets] & desired me to make additions there on which I did'.[65] Chiswell had promised to publish a new, expanded edition upon Knox's return, and though Knox had no instructions to call at Ceylon on this voyage − nor any intention of doing so – he would have time during his days at sea to go over his book and revise and expand it. He had a great deal more to add that he hadn't included in the first edition because of the pressure he'd been under to complete the book before he departed. No doubt additional material would also come to mind in the weeks and months ahead.

When Knox sailed from the Downs in September 1681, just a little more than a year had passed since his arrival back in England from his 'long and desolate captivity' on Ceylon. Twelve months earlier he had been penniless, homeless and without friends. He had described himself then as 'newborne'. In the year since this strange 'homecoming', Knox had grown up with remarkable speed. He had been transformed from an impoverished former captive into a published author, a man who was praised by the Governor of the East India Company, Sir Josiah Child, and the President of the Royal Society, Christopher Wren. He was now a friend and associate of men of learning such as Robert Hooke, an official authority and collector of data for the Royal Society, and what perhaps mattered most of all to Knox, he was a fully qualified captain in the East India Company.

CHAPTER NINE

Captain Knox Recaptivated

Knox was at sea again. He'd been right to hold out for a captaincy, and wrote to his cousin John Strype, 'I found my reckoning fell as right as any mans in ye ship & ye time I spent at mr Colsons [his navigation teacher in London] was not in vaine.'[1]

In late October, they sighted the Cape Verde Islands – a small archipelago some 375 miles off the coast of West Africa. When the Portuguese discovered them in 1456, the islands were uninhabited, but they soon became an important market for the transatlantic slave trade, and also a Portuguese colony with a large slave population working its plantations. On 28 October 1681, the *Tonqueen Merchant* arrived at the easternmost island, Maio.

In his journal, Knox carefully followed Hooke's instructions on what to observe and record. But his account, though perceptive and detailed, lacks objectivity because he compared everything he saw to Ceylon, usually unfavourably. He was struck by the fact that the difference in longitude between Ceylon and Maio had little effect on climate and vegetation. He saw numerous 'plants growing wild here wch grow in ye same manner upon Zeilon'. But these clearly hadn't been transplanted from South Asia because the inhabitants 'know nothing of [the] use and virtue in them'. Cape Verdeans, in fact, were largely ignorant of the medicinal benefits of plants, though they told Knox about the oil of a seed called endratta, 'wch is excellently good against aches & paines in ye body and limbs . . . annoynted with it'. As for the rest of Maio, Knox says 'I saw nothing else remarkable here' and didn't think it 'worth my time to go up into the Country, it appearing to bee a barren, dry & rocky land'.[2]

From Maio, the *Tonqueen Merchant* sailed to nearby Santiago which gets more rain than Maio and has a greater variety of fruit, including oranges, limes, coconuts, grapes, plantains and water-melons. Knox was so impressed by the watermelons that he took one 'as big as a man's head', slung it up in his cabin with rope, and when he reached Bantam six months later, it was 'as fresh & good, as the day it was gathered'.

They anchored at the south end of Santiago and Knox rode on horseback ten miles through the mountains to the capital Ribeira Grande (now Cidade Velha). On the way he had 'a prospect of . . . Country villages' which he says were 'far inferior to those of Zeilon'. The houses were made of rough stones with roofs of long grass. 'A whole house [was just] big enough for a man to creep into.'

When they reached the capital they found 'some small Fortifications wth Guns & a few curle-pated pockified [curly-haired, pockmarked] soldiers to stand by ym. For ye Pox . . . is the principal disease [here].' Besides the pockmarked soldiers, the rest of the popu-lation consisted of a few Portuguése magistrates and soldiers and a much larger number of black slaves who Knox says 'very much resemble' the people of 'Guinea [West Africa] in complexion, hair & features'.[3]

Altogether Knox was unimpressed: the town he judged 'very mean'. As for the inhabitants, 'I see nothing of ingenuity among the people,' he told Strype, 'unless it be . . . they are very expert in snatching a Coat, or hat or Cap or the like, from any of our men & as nimble to run away with it.'[4] Despite his low opinion of the people, Knox recorded that they spun the cotton grown on the island, extracting the seeds on a flat stone using a 'small round stick' like a rolling pin.

On the way back to the harbour, Knox spotted several plants that grew on Ceylon, including one with broad, heart-shaped leaves called 'allacola'. The Sinhalese boil and eat these leaves, but 'this people', Knox says, 'understand them not'. He also saw another plant common on Ceylon called 'attang-cola': an intoxicant that was used medicinally. Knox had seen the plant in India too where the Portuguese called it dotra and Portuguese women mixed it into their husbands' food 'to lull ym asleep, while they cuckold them'.

After leaving Santiago, the *Tonqueen Merchant* travelled down the west coast of Africa, round the Cape of Good Hope, past Madagascar and on into the Indian Ocean. Ceylon had been the yardstick by which Knox measured the Cape Verde Islands. He reflected now on the ingenuity of the Sinhalese which contrasted so sharply with what he considered the ignorance of the dispirited Cape Verdeans. The Sinhalese were at home on their island and had mined its resources and created a complex culture. The inhabitants of the Cape Verde Islands – Portuguese soldiers, officials, plantation overseers and African slaves – had all been sent there under duress and the landscape remained foreign and alien to them.

As the *Tonqueen Merchant* sailed eastwards in the months that followed, Knox spent whatever time he could spare from his captain's duties working on his book, filling in page after blank page of his interleaved edition of the *Historical Relation* with corrections, revisions and additional material. In his mind's eye, Ceylon travelled with him. It was the other life he lived, that haunted his dreams, that woke him in the night with memories and ideas. He would fumble in the dark for a candle so that he could scribble down things he might otherwise forget in the morning. Even as he slept, the book seemed to carry on in his sleeping mind, just as the ship carried him on through the dark hours and light. This is the double life a writer lives and it would be hard for anyone who leads such a life to say which of their two existences seems the most real, or which is the greater struggle.

In early May 1682, six months after leaving the Cape Verde Islands, the *Tonqueen Merchant* reached Bantam. To their great surprise here they found that the English settlement, where Knox had stayed on his voyage home two years earlier, was now in the hands of the Dutch. Knox wrote to John Strype that the Dutch occupation was 'a great loss to us all as well as ye East India Company; for . . . ye Dutch will not suffer us to bring any goods on shore, neither any to come on board to buy'.[5]

In a cryptic postscript to this letter, squeezed into the left margin of the page, he also told Strype that 'Agent Boyour is mad'. Francis Bowyer had been the company agent at Bantam and his 'madness' had led to the Dutch taking possession of the British settlement. According to company records, Bowyer had to be 'sent home in regard of his . . . distemper'. Nor was this the whole story. Bowyer and another company employee named Cheney had also been guilty of 'frauds . . . committed at Bantam'.[6] It was only now that Knox realised why Josiah Child had tried so hard to persuade him to take the post of company agent at Bantam. News of Bowyer's mental 'distemper' and 'frauds' had obviously reached London by the spring of 1681, and the company directors were eager to have him dismissed and replaced before the Dutch could step in. What better man than industrious, sober, hardy Robert Knox to make the best of this messy situation? While he was still in London, Knox of course had no idea why Child was so keen for him to go to Bantam. When he arrived there and learned of Bowyer's madness and the Dutch intervention, Knox was vastly relieved he had refused, in this instance, to do Child's bidding.

When the *Tonqueen Merchant* was turned away at Bantam, she sailed the next day to nearby Batavia, and after a brief stay there on to Tonkin (today's North Vietnam and southern China) which Knox says they reached safely 'with God's Blessing', though no one on board had ever been there before. At Tonkin, the British agent came out to the ship in a boat with a Chinese pilot who guided them safely over the bar and then twenty miles upriver. Here, Knox says, 'I buried about 8 of my men, most principall officers, as Chiefe mate, Carpenter & Boatswaine'.[7] The loss of eight men – nearly a third of Knox's crew of twenty-five and those not ordinary seamen but officers and skilled craftsmen – was not uncommon on long voyages to the East Indies. But behind Knox's bald statement lies a darker experience of illness – probably malaria and dysentery – as well as anxiety and overwork on the part of the remaining crew.

Tonkin proved a rich market and they stayed there until January 1683, when they sailed back to Batavia, heavily 'laden with very rich goods, as wrought silks & Muske & . . . lackered wares'.[8] At Tonkin Knox had also hired a number of Chinese seamen to help sail the ship. They 'gott safe to Batavia againe' by mid-February. But here the company agent ordered Knox's valuable cargo to be transferred to a larger, better-armed ship, the *Surat Merchant*, which was about to depart for England. At 430 tonnes with thirty guns and a crew of seventy-eight, it was three times the size of the *Tonqueen Merchant* and carried more than three times its number of crew and guns.

Knox was unhappy at having his valuable Tonkin cargo removed, and his displeasure increased when he was told there was no pepper or any other valuable goods at Batavia. The only cargo they could find was 'some few parcell of Cassa lignum' — a tree related to the cinnamon plant with berries that were sometimes used as a coarse and inferior substitute for cinnamon itself when that spice wasn't available.[9] But there was scarcely enough of it to fill a small part of the hold. So the *Tonqueen Merchant*, which had arrived at Batavia heaving with valuable goods, departed for home more than half empty. It was a disappointing and anticlimactic end to what had been up until then a highly successful voyage.

At Batavia Knox also 'gott a recrute of men for those I had buried' in Tonkin. These new crew were English sailors, and they replaced the Chinese sailors brought from Tonkin who now disembarked. On 23 February 1683, the *Tonqueen Merchant* was finally 'dispeeded ... directly home' from Batavia.[10] The long voyage was uneventful and Knox once again devoted his leisure time to the revisions to his Ceylon book. As he records in his autobiography, six months later 'I safely arrived with my small ship to England againe'.

Knox then immediately goes on to tell us the fate of the *Surat Merchant*: 'But note this by-the-by: that the small ship [the *Tonqueen Merchant*] which they [the company] Distrusted to bring theire rich goods home but sent almost empty away ... arrived very safely, without any losse or hazard, & the Great Ship, the Suratt Marchant, which was intrusted with all the rich goods I had brought from Tonqueene, Perished by the way home with all her men, and was never since heard of.'[11]

When Knox returned to England in September 1683, it was to a very different reception from the chilly one he'd had three years earlier when he escaped from Ceylon. Now he discovered that his book, *An Historical Relation of Ceylon*, had continued to sell briskly in his absence and that he himself was a celebrated author. John Locke, among others, had read and admired it. The Royal Society was eager to hear of his new experiences in the East Indies, to read his journals and to see the artefacts that he'd brought back. And Knox's publisher Richard Chiswell was — initially at least — eager to see the new, revised version of his book, and rush it into print.

Fortunately, the artefacts that Knox had collected remained on the *Tonqueen Merchant* when its cargo was transferred to the *Surat Merchant* at Batavia. Soon after he arrived in London, he handed over these specimens to Robert Hooke who immediately set to work examining and cataloguing them. At a packed meeting of the Royal Society held on 21 November, Hooke presented a total of twenty-nine items brought home by Knox from 'Tonquin upon the main of China'. These included a complete Tonquin plough, 'varnished with the true lacker varnish' that was also used for making the 'curious [lacquered] cabinets, screens, [and] boxes' that were so popular in Europe. This Tonquin plough was 'so light and easy to be made and used' that Knox thought 'it might be of very good use here in England. The share is cast of iron very curiously."[12] In order to give some impression of Chinese culture, Knox also brought back 'two Tonquin pictures': the first a group of Mandarins on a barge, the second another group of Mandarins travelling by land with their guard and retinue. Hooke also displayed 'a small pipe [piece] of Tonquin marble' that had been broken off 'from one of the steps of their temples', presumably by Knox himself."[13]

The remaining items were botanical and zoological specimens, including 'a true dolphin's skin'. The dolphin had been caught on the voyage home and then stuffed and preserved on board. This specimen was of particular interest because it varied markedly from the body and skin of porpoises with which dolphins were often confused. Knox's 'true dolphin', in fact, appeared to be an altogether new species.

Knox also brought back a large number of plants and seeds, including the root of the tea tree, 'a stick of wood with which they make their gun-powder in Tonquin', a branch from a bodhi tree (worshipped by the Sinhalese but not by the Chinese), a plant called 'Ki-may' which when 'bruised with salt and applied to the legs . . . alleviates pains [caused by] . . . the strains and weariness . . . [of] walking', and 'a sprig of a shrub called Ki-vong of strange virtue'. When this last plant was submerged in water, something in it attracted crabs, so the Chinese used it to catch crabs by placing it at the mouths of watery holes. Another plant called 'Ki-coy' was used to 'tar' or dye cloth black. And 'the seed[s] of . . . Tonquin oranges' were presented as 'the best in the world'. Knox also brought back lentils of various sorts, watermelon seeds and lychee nuts, or 'plumbs' as Knox calls them – 'the best plumbs of China'. The oil of another seed could be burned as fuel in lamps, mixed with paints and rubbed into painful body joints."[14]

Knox's artefacts were a valuable contribution to the Royal Society's collection, and the day after Hooke presented them, the committee met to vote that 'a present be made from the Society to Mr Knox . . . of about 50 s or £3 value'.[15] A week after Knox's 'curiosities' were shown at the Royal Society meeting, they were delivered to the society repository where they would be permanently housed.[16] In the meantime, the extensive journals in which Knox had recorded his observations during his voyage were circulated among select society members, including the Earl of Clarendon. News of Knox's travels and artefacts had by this time reached the court and in late November he was summoned for an audience with the King himself. In early December 1683, James Bonnell wrote to John Strype that Knox had had 'an hours discourse' with Charles II, 'many flocking about to hear it'.[17]

In the midst of all this acclaim, however, Knox was occupied by two matters of serious concern: his book and his ship. He must have delivered the thick interleaved folio volume of the *Historical Relation* – crammed full with his corrections and new material – to his publisher Richard Chiswell shortly after he got back to London. It was also scrutinised, of course, by Hooke. In his letter to John Strype about Knox's audience with the King, James Bonnell reported that Hooke had persuaded Knox 'to make . . . [more] additions' to his book and said that Hooke would 'furnish . . . head[ings], wch, with a new title page' and an engraved portrait of Knox would complete the work necessary for the second edition. According to Bonnell, Chiswell 'was present' at this discussion between Hooke and Knox, and 'thout [thought] well of it'. Bonnell was writing to Strype to ask him to take down Knox's 'additions' 'in shorthand' as Knox dictated them, which Bonnell assured Strype could be done in one or two evenings at Strype's home. What happened next with the revised manuscript is a mystery. All we know is that the second edition was not published and that the interleaved folio volume sailed with Knox again when he embarked on his next voyage.

In the meantime, Knox became embroiled in a heated dispute that erupted between Sir Josiah Child and the other owners of the *Tonqueen Merchant*. Child, who owned the largest share in the ship, had decided that Knox had acquitted himself so well on his first voyage that he should be entrusted with a larger vessel – or so Knox understood when Child told him that the *Tonqueen Merchant* was to be enlarged. Child asked Knox to procure a builder and contract with him to have the ship cut in two and lengthened by twelve feet.

Child owned 10 per cent of the *Tonqueen Merchant*. The other, smaller shareholders, who collectively held 90 per cent, were unanimously opposed to Child's enlargement plans. Knox followed the instructions of his patron, Child, but the consequence for him was that 'this highly displeased severall of my [other] owners and their anger grew hot against me for following Sir Josiah's orders, without their concurrence'. These enraged shareholders then took legal steps to arrest Knox and halt Child's plans for the ship, but Child posted bail for Knox, so the ship was lengthened after all though only with 'a great deall of trouble and vexation and ill will into the bargain' for Knox. He eventually had to put up bail for himself in the High Admiralty Court and his legal troubles connected with this dispute dragged on for several years. By the beginning of 1684, however, Child had his way: the *Tonqueen Merchant* was lengthened by twelve feet which increased its size from 130 to 160 tonnes. It could now accommodate a crew of thirty-three men and carry up to eighteen guns.[18]

It was only in April 1864, when Knox received the company directors' written instructions for his next voyage, that he fully grasped why Child had decided to make the *Tonqueen Merchant* larger. Robert Knox, the erstwhile captive, was now to be the Captain of a slave ship.*

His orders were to sail to Madagascar, buy slaves there for the East India Company and then transport them back round the Cape

---

* When Robinson Crusoe is shipwrecked on the island, he is sailing to West Africa to buy slaves for his own and his neighbours' Brazilian plantations. Crusoe's and Knox's slave-trading voyages are just one of many clues that suggest Defoe had not only read Knox's published book on Ceylon but also knew the details of his later career after he had escaped.

of Good Hope to the remote South Atlantic island of St Helena, in the middle of the Atlantic. More than a thousand miles off Angola in Africa and 1,800 miles from Brazil in South America, St Helena was already a refuelling station for East India Company ships, especially on their return voyages from the East Indies. Then in 1673 Charles II issued a royal charter for St Helena to be developed as a British colony. Slaves brought from Madagascar would provide the labour force for the island's plantations.

Knox's specific instructions were to purchase '250 Negroes' according to the following specifications: 'We would not have you buy any old Negroes or Children male or Female. Ye males not under 14 years of age, nor Females under twelve years nor any of either sex above 24 years if you can help it.'[19] In addition to the slaves themselves, Knox would have to buy provisions to feed this human cargo during the voyage. He was also instructed to take a number of plants from Madagascar to St Helena for transplantation: ginger, cassava, cinnamon, nutmeg and cloves. All these, as Knox knew, would have to be stored in wire cages to protect them from rats and mice on the ship. When the *Tonqueen Merchant* was thus duly laden with slaves, provisions, seeds and plants, Knox was to proceed to St Helena.

It was only at this point in his long complicated list of instructions that Knox was informed that before he even reached Madagascar, on his outward-bound voyage, he should attempt to land at the remote island of Tristan da Cunha, some 1,500 miles south-west of St Helena. Despite its isolated location, the East India Company thought that Tristan da Cunha, as well as St Helena, might be turned into a profitable colony and Knox was urged 'if you can without . . . loss of much time' to stop at the island, 'take a Survey' of it, see if it had a good natural harbour and fertile soil and what 'Wood, Water, Vegetables or Animals you find there and advise us thereof with your opinion whether it may be advatangeous for ye Compa[ny] hereafter to make any settlement' there.

Knox was also told that if he judged Tristan da Cunha suitable for colonisation, he should leave '2 sowes and 1 bore pig' on the island and also a letter 'enclosed in a Glass bottle fixt upon a Stanchon fastened in ye ground in some conspicuous place one ye East Side of [the] Island'. This document would establish the company's right to the island and inform others who might arrive later of the East India Company's prior claim. And if all this wasn't enough to ask of Knox, it was further suggested that if he *did* find Tristan da Cunha promising, on his homeward journey to England, he should take a number of soldiers, planters and Negroes from St Helena to Tristan to begin colonising the island.[20]

It is clear from Knox's autobiography that he was not keen to make one diversion to Tristan da Cunha, let alone two. Even today, this isolated island without an airport and well off the main shipping routes is very difficult to get to. There is simply no way to visit it 'without . . . loss of much time'. In 1684, very little was known about the place other than the fact that it was first sighted in 1506 by the Portuguese explorer Tristão da Cunha who was prevented from landing by rough seas. He nevertheless named the island after himself and then sailed on to India.

Did Knox actually attempt to make this time-consuming, risky excursion to Tristan? He says he did and there is no reason to doubt him. But he hastily dismisses the episode in his autobiography when he says that he followed the company's instructions and tried to reach Tristan da Cunha on his outward-bound voyage, but was prevented from landing by 'very hard gales of wind, a great Sea and thicke weather'.[21]

On this second voyage Knox was both Captain and supercargo of the *Tonqueen Merchant*. At some stage, too, he had also acquired a share in the ship, probably in the midst of the controversy over enlarging it when one or more of the disputing owners sold their shares. Knox's dual post as Captain and supercargo meant that he was in control of every aspect of the voyage. It was a powerful position to be in, but also one fraught with responsibilities. Knox would make all the important decisions on the ship while at sea and he would determine all commercial transactions on land. He would also decide how long to stay in each port, what price to pay for goods and how much to buy.

As the ship's supercargo he would soon be inspecting, bargaining and paying for the human cargo that he took on board. He would examine all prospective slaves: peering down their throats, flexing their muscles, inspecting their heads for grey hairs (as a check on their age), assessing their strength and agility. It would be Knox too who determined how much to pay (in guns, ammunition, beads or brandy). On this voyage, there is no way he could stay aloof from, or ignorant of, any aspect of the slave trade.

And yet in his letters and autobiography Knox says almost nothing about his experience as a part-owner, captain and super-cargo of a slave ship. This means we have no way of determining how he felt about his involvement and no way of knowing whether he made any connection in his mind between his own years of captivity on Ceylon and the fate of the human beings he bought at Madagascar and then sold at St Helena. Knox was a man of integrity and it's difficult if not impossible to imagine him pursuing a course of action that he believed was morally wrong. Like most of his contemporaries, Knox probably thought that slavery was an economic necessity for an imperial power such as England, and considered his participation in the slave trade unobjectionable. It is worth remembering, too, that organised opposition to the slave trade scarcely existed in seventeenth-century England. It would be another century, in fact, before the abolitionist movement got under way. This doesn't exonerate Knox, but he would have had to be a much more unconventional man than he was to object to an institution that even the Church of England invested in and endorsed.

There is a great irony, however, in the fact that Knox lost his liberty once more when he was engaged in buying a cargo of slaves on Madagascar. Here the new slave trader, Captain Knox, was himself taken captive once again.

Madagascar lies some 250 miles off the south-east coast of Africa. Almost a thousand miles long and 350 miles across at its widest point, it is the fourth largest island in the world, nearly two and a half times the size of Great Britain. It was uninhabited until sometime around AD 500 when the earliest settlers arrived from Indonesia more than 4,000 miles away. The first Europeans to visit the island were the Portuguese in the early 1500s. Slavery was established on the island long before the Portuguese and other Europeans arrived, and the population generally was divided into two classes: one known as 'white' or *fotsy* and the other 'black' or *mainty*, a distinction based on the inhabitants' different skin colour and hair texture.[22] Some slaves were prisoners of war; most, however, had been carried to Madagascar from Africa.

The *Tonqueen Merchant* arrived at St Augustine's Bay in southwest Madagascar in November 1684. The King of the Sakalava Empire, who ruled this part of the island, had been selling slaves to visiting English ships since the 1660s. But when Knox arrived trade was slow and there were few slaves to be had, so in January 1685, the *Tonqueen Merchant* sailed further north along the west coast of the island. They then ran into a storm that rapidly escalated into a hurricane 'so outrageous', according to Knox, that the ship's gunwales were submerged and the men working the pumps on deck had to be secured by ropes to prevent them from being washed overboard. In order to save the ship, Knox ordered the mainmast cut down. It was all uncannily like the terrible storm off southern India in 1659 when his father had to cut down the mainmast of the *Anne* and then sail on to Ceylon to make repairs.

Shorn of its mainmast, the *Tonqueen Merchant* was forced to seek refuge on Madagascar at the latitude of twenty degrees, fifty minutes south. This was a sparsely populated, arid region of sand dunes interspersed with slightly more fertile patches of land, from which vast baobab trees rose up. It was a forbidding landscape which Knox described as 'daingerous by Sea as well as by land, as will appeare by the usage I had from the . . . people'.[23]

After anchoring several miles off the coast, Knox sent a boat onshore with several members of his crew, one of whom spoke a few words of Malagasy. They soon returned with one of the 'Country people' who Knox entertained 'kindly with Brandy & Victuals & adorned . . . very Richly with . . . Beads . . . about his Necke, armes & legs'. This man told Knox that Lahifotsy, the King who had traded with the English in the past and was known to them as King Lightfoot, 'was but lately dead'. King Lightfoot's three younger sons, including Rybassa, the one who ruled this territory, had combined in opposition to their eldest brother with whom they were now at war. As a consequence, King Rybassa was in great need of arms, and Knox's informant encouraged him to bring his guns and ammunition onshore and meet with the King.

Knox, however, was cautious. He didn't rush to meet King Rybassa, who he now learned lived a day's journey from the sea. Knox undoubtedly recalled how twenty-five years earlier the King of Kandy had lured away men from the *Anne* anchored in the harbour at Trincomalee. Knox now decided to send a present of a bottle of brandy to Rybassa along with a message requesting the King to come down to the shore to 'discourse' about trade. The very next day he had a reply from the King who was delighted with the brandy and sent back to Knox a present of six slaves – three men and three women. He also promised to come to meet Knox.

So far so good, and Knox felt encouraged. King Rybassa and his retinue duly turned up a day later in a canoe, followed by a fleet of more canoes full of armed men. As soon as he arrived, the King sent one of his men out to the *Tonqueen Merchant* to ask the Captain and his 'great Dog (wich he had heard I had)' to come and meet him. Early the next morning, Knox and his huge English mastiff went ashore with more presents for the King: 'choice foulling peeces, Gunpowder, bullets, flints, beads of all sorts, & Brasse wire which they use for Braselets . . . and brandy'. He found King Rybassa waiting for him, sitting on a low stool under a tree, flanked by two of his wives and surrounded by about 150 armed men.

Knox's first impression was how arresting the King looked: his hair was elaborately plaited with wires and coloured beads, his arms loaded with silver bracelets and his legs adorned with more beads 'of divers Coullers . . . that made him show very Antickely [colourfully]'. The King's clothes, however, consisted of just a dark, greasy cloth wrapped round his waist, 'for they all grease them-selves boath head & body with beefe fat so thicke that the heat melteth it all about them'. As Knox drew closer to the King, he also saw that he had a loaded 'Brasse Barrell Blunderbusse' on his knees.[24]

The King looked intimidating, but he gave Knox a warm welcome. First he embraced him, and then vigorously rubbed his nose against Knox's, coating his face with beef fat in the process. Knox presented his gifts, spread out the carpet he had brought for himself from the ship, and sat down on it across from the King '& wee began to drinke Brandy which was the Kings Chief delight'.[25]

The King was eager to befriend Knox's dog, no easy task since it was a large, fierce animal held by a strong chain. The sight of the garishly adorned King seemed to agitate the dog, and when Rybassa tried to stroke him, the dog growled and foamed at the mouth. Knox hastily jerked him away and ordered the animal to be taken back to the ship, but it seems the dog's ferocity had made the King 'love him more for his Courage'. He wouldn't allow the dog to be banished and instead wooed him with roasted rib of beef and a calabash full of milk served by the King himself. The dog wolfed down the meat but refused the milk, so the King then brought him a calabash of water and 'held it himselfe while the dog drunke'. 'By this manner of treatment,' according to Knox, 'the dog soone knew his benefactour ... [and] in a few dayes the dog forsooke me & followed the King wheresoever he went & thare [on Madagascar] I left him.'[26]

It was only at this point – after Knox gave the King presents, drank brandy with him and relinquished his dog – that the negotiations to buy slaves got under way. Knox said he needed to purchase slaves and provisions, and he assured the King that he had plenty of arms, gunpowder and brandy to pay for a great number of them. The King said he had many slaves to sell and that he would send for them to come from the surrounding towns and villages. But first he was keen for Knox to bring all of his goods onshore. He ordered his men, in fact, to build a house of sticks and rushes in which Knox's wares could be stored.

Knox, however, was 'mistrustfull of the King lest his want of my Armes ... might be greater than his abillity to buy them', so he was unwilling to bring all his trading goods onshore. Several days passed but the promised slaves failed to arrive. Concealing his anxiety, Knox reassured the King that he would always have enough arms onshore 'to buy all [the] Negrow Slaves he or any other should bring' for sale, but he explained that he couldn't bring 'all [his guns from the ship] at once for fear of Spoyliing with weet [wet or rain] or Sand in the locks'.[27]

Instead of sending for all of his guns, Knox ordered forty to be brought onshore, along with gunpowder, beads and brandy. In the weeks that followed, a trickle of slaves arrived and eventually Knox was able to buy about fifty, but he needed four times this number to fill the ship. More time passed but 'trade came one [on] very slowly' and soon it was clear that what he had feared at the beginning was in fact the case: the King did not have a large supply of slaves to sell.

Meanwhile, King Rybassa's two younger brothers arrived on the scene. Knox had no choice but to entertain them too. He ordered more brandy from the ship. All '3 men ware great drinkers', but to Knox's relief, they didn't insist that he keep them company and drink with them.

King Rybassa and his brothers continued to reassure Knox that consignments of slaves were on the way from the interior: they gave him 'their Royall word that they would fill my Ship with Slaves in ten dayes more'. In the meantime, they pressed Knox to bring more arms onshore. And so the uneasy stalemate dragged on, day after day, under the burning sun. The King continued to demand more guns while Knox despaired of procuring more slaves.

Things came to a crisis suddenly one day when, without any warning, Rybassa's men seized Knox's boat and dragged it up on the beach far above the high-tide mark. Knox and the nine other men from the *Tonqueen Merchant* who were onshore with him were now trapped. There were too few of them to haul the boat back down to the sea. Then, to their dismay, they watched as Rybassa ordered that all of the guns and ammunition in the rush house be removed, leaving only beads, brandy and brass wire behind. Knox and his men were left standing about 'like Sheepe in a little flocke expecting when the Dogs would be sett one to Worrey us; but none medled with us yet but let us turmoile in our own thoughts, which was torment . . . to see ourselves wholy in the hands of such inraged barbarians'.[28]

In this crisis, Knox decided that it was 'best to goe & make my Addresse to the King who was sitting at a distance'. He tried to reassure him and explain that 'if I had not intended the Guns and ammunition for him I would not have brought them hither to his port'. But no sooner had he begun his explanation than Rybassa lunged at Knox, threw him down on the ground, and taking hold of Knox's neckcloth, twisted it about his neck 'as if he intended to Choake mee', which he might well have done, but the neckcloth tore in half. Then the King yanked Knox's hat off his head, flung it down, stamped it flat with his feet and buried it under the sand, after which he began to rifle through Knox's pockets. He pulled out a watch, turned it about in his hand as he examined it and then shoved it back at Knox, saying 'he could not keep it alive'. Finally he grabbed Knox's wrist and twisted his arm violently behind his back, and at the same time, drew out his lance, pointing it at Knox's chest, as if he were about to stab him.

The other men from the *Tonqueen Merchant* meanwhile stood at a distance, gaping helplessly at Knox and the King. It was small consolation for them to be told that King Rybassa only intended to kill Knox and that the rest of them would be made slaves.

For the next half-hour, the King continued to threaten Knox, poking and prodding him with his lance. Then suddenly, with no hint or warning, his mood changed again. He threw down his lance, dug up Knox's hat, pushed out its crown and, shaking off the sand, clapped it back on the captain's head. With a big grin, he embraced Knox and rubbed noses with him again, 'Calling me Brother and shakeing me by the hand'. To Knox 'this seemed . . . a Strange Change and the Stranger because it came so of a sudden & he bid mee not to be angry saying he loved me well'.[29]

After keeping Knox at the end of his spear for half an hour, Rybassa no doubt realised that the threat of violence – even of death – wasn't going to make him bring all the arms onshore. Where brutality hadn't worked perhaps cajoling and protestations of love and friendship would. Knox went along with this because he was playing for time: he called Rybassa 'Brother againe & told him I was not Angry with him, but told him if he ware not angry with mee why did he pull my boate out of the water', whereupon the King immediately ordered the boat brought back down to the sea again, 'but he would not lett my men be in her onely to moore her fast by the Graplins'.[30]

Knox sent for more brandy for the King and 'sat downe to drinke . . . & not as if I did resent any thing ill that [the King] . . . had done, for I thought it my intrest to Conceale both my feare & Anger being yet wholly in his power'. The King was as eager to drink Knox's brandy as before, but he now made Knox drink the first cup of every bottle himself 'for feare of poyson'.[31]

Thus the two men resumed their deadlock: King Rybassa kept asking for more guns from the ship while reassuring Knox that more slaves were on the way, while Knox kept fobbing off the King's requests. Then he thought of a new tactic. He pretended to comply at last with the King's demand and told him he would send all but two of his men back to the ship to request more arms be brought ashore. The King of course readily agreed to this, and Knox's men departed in the boat. But Knox had given them secret orders and also exacted their promise not to leave him stranded on Madagascar and sail away with the others on the ship.

Knox was now in a similar situation to the one his father had been in on Ceylon when he sent his son back on board the *Anne*. Following Knox's secret direction, his men did not come back to the beach with the guns. Instead, after fetching more guns from the ship, they armed their boat and then rowed back only halfway to the shore from where they sent a message to the King that they wouldn't deliver the guns unless Captain Knox was allowed to return to the ship. This was 'not pleasing to the King', who, however, continued to 'fawn' on Knox and rub noses with him.

And so their cat and mouse game continued. The King offered to send his wives out to the ship as a pledge, but Knox knew that 'he valewed not his 2 wives since he had had many more and could have as many as he pleased'.[32] Knox's men – still out in the boat offshore – held out for his return and eventually the King agreed to this, but Knox had to go alone; he wasn't allowed to take his last two men along with him. When Knox got back to his ship, he sent the King a case of brandy and asked for the two men to be released. The King sent a slave, who had recently turned up, instead. In 'this manner', Knox says, 'we treated some dayes. I presenting him with Brandy & he always making returnes to mee in one Slave at a time.'

At this point Knox had almost given up hope of filling his ship with slaves. What he sought now was to get his two remaining men back on board and then escape. The King meanwhile 'was in as great paine fearing lest the Ship should goe away as I was for my Men, so when they [the King's men] came in my boate with the old arguements "noe angry & much love", I ordered my men to lay hold on 2 of the Chiefe of the King's men'. This meant that Knox now had two of the King's men on the *Tonqueen Merchant* (one of whom was a noble who Knox knew Rybassa wouldn't abandon) while the King still had Knox's two men onshore.

The King sent a new message that more slaves had arrived and begged Knox to come ashore. Knox responded that the King should send the slaves to the ship where he would pay for them. 'And thus we continewed treating some dayes.' No slaves, of course, appeared. Finally Knox and Rybassa agreed to negotiate an exchange of prisoners. They swapped the first of their two prisoners without mishap, but then had a protracted discussion of who should release his last remaining prisoner first 'for we ware boathe afraid of a trepan [being tricked]'. After 'a long debate' they decided to bring their prisoners close to each other in canoes 'so they ware each to leap into the Sea and Swime to each others boate'. But which prisoner would jump first? 'At length', Knox agreed 'to let my prisoner leap first', because he was attached to a rope and they could always haul him back if the King's prisoner wasn't allowed to jump into the water. Thus the final two prisoners were exchanged and safely made it to their respective boats.

With all his men now restored to him, eager though he was to leave, Knox didn't depart immediately. He knew it was unlikely that more slaves would arrive, but he stayed on for two more days 'for I was loath to loose my voiage & goe with so few Negrows'. King Rybassa sent messengers to the ship who pleaded with Knox to come ashore. Knox countered, as before, that if there were any more slaves, the King should send them out to the *Tonqueen Merchant*. None was forthcoming. Knox at last decided he had no choice but to leave with the fifty-odd slaves he had, even though this number fell far short of what he had hoped to buy. By this point, he was heartily relieved just to have 'escaped a second Captivity, though short, yet far more dreadful than the first one on Zeilon'.[33]

It had been an incredibly close call. Indeed, for much of his harrowing time on Madagascar, Knox was haunted by the memory of what he and his father and the men on the *Anne* had all undergone twenty-five years earlier. He couldn't believe that God had preserved him for nineteen years on Ceylon only to allow him to perish on this wild, godforsaken island ruled by a grotesque, lying King who drank himself senseless on brandy. Despite the fiasco of his slave-trading venture, then, Knox sailed for St Helena without regret. The mainmast which he ordered cut down in the storm had been replaced by the mizzenmast and thus Knox and his ship 'made the best of my way for St Helena'.

* * *

After Knox's ordeal on Madagascar, the predictable routine of life at sea soothed his shattered nerves, and he resumed work on his book. But he soon had to put it aside. Just as they were rounding the Cape of Good Hope, when they still had about 1,700 more miles to go before reaching St Helena, Knox fell gravely ill with scurvy. This disease had been the seaman's curse – and often cause of death – ever since the advent of long European sea voyages in the fifteenth century. Vasco da Gama lost two-thirds of his crew to scurvy when he sailed to India in 1499. In 1520, Magellan lost more than 80 per cent of his men to it while crossing the Pacific. The English mariner and slave trader John Hawkins dubbed scurvy 'the plague of the Sea, and the Spoyle of Mariners'.

Knox had seen scurvy strike down and kill others, but this was the first time he had succumbed to it. The symptoms were appalling: lethargy and malaise, muscle and joint pains. His body was soon covered in bruises, his gums swelled up and bled, his teeth loosened and then began to fall out. Jaundice turned his skin and the whites of his eyes a sickly yellow. His arms and legs also swelled up and he couldn't urinate. Fever brought sweating, shivering and delirium. His sensory impressions were distorted: sounds became unbearably loud; bad smells turned into loathsome stenches; nausea overwhelmed him in great waves. He could scarcely eat, and when he did force some salt fish or hard biscuit down, he vomited them back up.

Knox lay for days in his dark, airless cabin on his sea bedstead, sweating, shivering, hallucinating. During the brief intervals when his fever subsided and he could think clearly again, he wondered if he would reach St Helena in time to consume the fruit and vegetables that alone could save him – even if he had to be carried on land half dead. He had buried men in the past who had died of scurvy on shipboard and he had also seen diseased men who were barely alive return to full health within days of arriving onshore.

Knox was too ill to leave his bed and go on deck so he didn't see the sheer, barren cliffs of St Helena rise dramatically from the ocean one fine morning. Compared to gigantic Madagascar, St Helena was a mere speck of an island – just forty-seven square miles – buffeted by the trade winds, shrouded in clouds, stranded in the lonely vastness of the South Atlantic.

There is only one harbour at James Bay, on the sheltered, leeward side of the island, and landing at St Helena is a matter of chance even today. A ship has to struggle to anchor in the 'road' off Jamestown. Boatloads of seamen and passengers are tossed wildly in the waves as they make their way towards the small landing beach almost hidden among the rocks at the bottom of the steep, narrow valley that descends from the mountain peaks high above.

Knox was carried into the ship's boat in a hammock and then rowed to shore. Here he was immediately taken into the care of the Governor's household. In a matter of days fresh fruit and other food overcame his worst symptoms. His jaundice and bruises faded, his gums stopped bleeding. Day by day he regained strength. He sold his cargo of fifty-odd slaves, rode out into the island to inspect the embryo plantations with their South Asian crops and instructed the planters. Knox also saw to all the 'troublesome cares . . . to provide & refit [the ship in order to] proceede on my intended voiage for the unknown South parts of India'.[34] These included the crew's labours to replace the makeshift mizzenmast of the *Tonqueen Merchant* with a new mainmast hewn out of one of the tall ebony trees that grew on St Helena.

Days and weeks passed on the cold, windswept island. Waves crashed ceaselessly against the rocks. The air was alive with the cries of gulls and other seabirds.

Finally, at the end of May 1685, Knox had transacted all his business and work on the *Tonqueen Merchant* was completed. On the evening of the 29th, Knox stood on the beach, waiting for the boat to come and carry him out to the anchored ship. He planned to sail the next morning. As he waited, he looked through his perspective glass out to sea.

To his amazement, he saw 'the Men in the Ship cut the Cables & loosed the Sailes & run away with the Ship'. He could scarcely believe his eyes. They had set sail without him!

'So soone as I could get a boate,' Knox says, 'I went and followed her.' As he watched the distance between himself and the *Tonqueen Merchant* grow larger and larger, he shouted at his men to row faster, and still faster.

But the ship receded further into the distance and then disappeared altogether over the edge of the horizon. Knox was forced to return 'on Shore again haveing visibly seen Riches make themselves wings and fly away.'[35] It was only then that the full enormity of what had happened dawned on him. During the days and weeks that he'd been consumed with all his business on St Helena, a mutiny had been hatched and carefully planned out by his crew.

Knox not only lost his ship with all of its cargo. The *Tonqueen Merchant* also sailed off with his book – the thick, interleaved copy of *An Historical Relation of Ceylon*, with all of Knox's handwritten additions and revisions.* He'd sailed from England in 1684 as an East Indiaman captain, a celebrated author and a scientific investigator for the Royal Society. Now he had nothing. He was, in his own words, 'stript . . . [all] at once of all my worldly riches & Injoyments . . . exposed . . . to poverty & Contempt . . . all my Worldly Substance & Worldly Dignities vanished, togeather in a moment & left me with onelly the Cloaths on my backe'.[36]

In this complete and comprehensive dispossession, the worst loss was his book. The story that it told – of another world and people, of suffering, faith, transformation and survival – was more valuable than all his 'Worldly Substance & Dignities'. Knox's book gave his life meaning. It was the only thing he had that was potentially imperishable, that could survive him when he was gone and keep alive his name and existence, and those of his father, John Loveland, the child Lucea and a whole island world, for those who came after him – for us.

---

* This was undoubtedly an inadvertent theft because few, if any, of Knox's crew would have been aware that he was working on an enlarged, revised edition of his book during the voyage.

CHAPTER TEN

St Helena

Stranded on St Helena, Knox had no way of knowing how long this new 'captivation' would last. Most East India Company ships stopped at the island for 'refreshment' on their way home – to take on fresh water, food and other provisions, to offload their cargo of men sick with scurvy, and to pick up any seamen who had been left by other ships and were now restored to health. But it was impossible to calculate when the next company ship would come to Knox's rescue. The vagaries of the winds and the hazards of sea travel made a mockery of the sailing schedules and orders drawn up in East India House back in London. The company spanned the globe, but its far-flung outposts were connected by wooden ships that sailed like toy boats through thousands of miles of ocean.

Years later, when he was writing his autobiography, Knox said that he stayed on St Helena for only a month. But scattered references to him in the company records indicate that he was stuck there for at least three months and possibly longer.[1] His immediate problem was that he had no money or means of support. Knox had sold his Madagascar slaves on St Helena for a good price – £12 to £14 a head, paid in 'pieces of eight',* and calico which he had intended to use to trade for pepper in the East Indies.[2] But the pieces of eight and the bales of calico, like the interleaved copy of his book with his copious manuscript additions and revisions, were on the *Tonqueen Merchant* when his crew ran away with it. On St Helena Knox was left, as he plaintively says, with only the clothes on his back.

---

* The Spanish dollar, also known as 'pieces of eight', was a silver coin minted in Spain. By the seventeenth century it was widely used in Europe, the Americas and the Far East and was considered an international currency.

His plight was recorded in the records of the company council meeting held on 8 June which Knox himself attended.

> Captain Knox presenting a writing subscribed by himselfe setting forth his inauspicious condition, by reason of the falseness & treachery of his officers and merchants running away with his ship the Tonqueen Mercht ... on friday ... the 29th last month carrying away all that he had in ye ship to ye cloths on his back. Also [Knox] owes inhabitants money for provisions. [He has] no money to supply himself on the island ... Therefore [he has been] granted some money from the Company's account ... Knox granted up to one hundred dollars and his ... diet at the Company table.[3]

The Governor of St Helena when Knox was stranded there was Major John Blackmore and every evening he presided over a long dining table at his residence not far from the fort in Jamestown. All the company employees ate at the 'Company table', with the exception of those who had 'an infectious distemper', were drunk or 'not cleanly drest'.[4] But even on St Helena – in the middle of nowhere – rank was strictly observed. Governor Blackmore and his lady and the members of the council sat at the top of the table. Next came the company's 'principal servants and officials', including the chaplain and surgeon, and high-ranking soldiers from the garrison, followed by the 'chief blacksmith and other head artificers' and the sergeant of the guard. The position of the salt cellar* on the dining table marked the

---

* When I checked on this word, I came across the following mini-history of salt containers in the 1911 edition of the *Encyclopaedia Britannica.* 'The word [saltcellar] is a combination of "salt" and "saler", assimilated in the 16th and 17th centuries to "cellar" (Lat. *cellarium*, a storehouse). "Saler" is from the Fr. (mod. *saliere*), Lat. *salarium*, that which belongs to salt, cf. "salary". Salt cellar is, therefore, a tautological expression. There are two types of salts, the large ornamental salt which during the medieval ages and later was one of the most important pieces of household plate, and the smaller "salts", actually used and placed near the plates or trenchers of the guests at table; they were hence styled "trencher salts". The great salts, below which the inferior guests sat, were, in the earliest form which survives, shaped like an hour-glass and have a cover. New College, Oxford, possesses a magnificent specimen, dated 1493. Later salts take a square or cylindrical shape. The Elizabethan salt, kept with the regalia in the Tower of London, has a cover with numerous figures. The London Livery Companies possess many salts of a still later pattern, rather low in height and without a cover. The "trencher salts" are either of triangular or circular shape, some are many-sided. The circular silver salt with legs came into use in the 18th century.'

demarcation line between the higher and lower echelons of diners and this line also determined the amount of punch or wine they were allowed to drink during the meal. According to the company regulations, the salt was strategically placed 'below the Council [members] and the Chaplain'. Those who sat above the salt were entitled to 'drink as [much as] they think proper' or wanted. But those seated below the salt were limited to one bowl of punch (a bowl contained three pints of punch) for two or three persons, two bowls of punch for four or five persons, or three bowls of punch for six or more persons. If wine rather than punch was consumed, one bottle of wine equalled one bowl of punch.[5]

Despite his destitute circumstances, Knox, like every other company ship captain who called at St Helena, became a member of the governing council for the duration of his stay on the island. This meant that he sat at the upper end of the Governor's table, probably next to the Governor himself. He was positioned, then, well above the salt, and free to drink as much punch or wine as he pleased. Given his situation, he might have been forgiven for drowning his sorrows, but Knox was an abstemious man, even in the midst of a crisis, and at St Helena he drank and ate with his habitual moderation.

Knox's asceticism, in fact, was said to have been the main reason for the mutiny of his crew. They had accused him of keeping them on short rations. This came out at an inquiry that was conducted into the causes of the mutiny and flight of the *Tonqueen Merchant*. Knox's men, it was reported, said that he'd been 'brought up in Slavery [on Ceylon and] could live upon turnip tops' and that he expected his crew to survive on the meagrest portions of plain seamen's fare. A man named Matthew Pouncey also testified that he had heard some of Knox's men curse him as a 'Portuguese rogue'.[6] These and other accusations were recorded in the proceedings of the formal inquiry that was held into the mutiny.

But no conclusions were reached nor any action taken because the evidence gathered was deemed 'inconsistent'. Those who would have been judged guilty – the mutineers – were, in any event, long gone. Knox, however, was clearly exonerated because he was generously provided for and made a member of the council. There is no record of where he stayed on St Helena, but it seems likely that he lodged with Governor Blackmore at his residence.

Knox was mortified by the mutiny and loss of the *Tonqueen Merchant*, but to the inhabitants of St Helena and its company council, mutinies and rebellions were common events. The island colony had originally been conceived as a kind of utopia. Captain Thomas Cavendish, who visited it in 1588 on his way home from circumnavigating the world, described St Helena as 'an earthly paradise . . . a marvellous faire and pleasant valley', loaded with 'oranges, lemons, dates, figs, basil, sorrel, partridges, pheasants, hogs and goats'. According to Cavendish, it also provided a 'great store of fresh water' and timber. St Helena was like 'a boye [buoy] in the middle of the seas . . . miraculously placed for the refreshing and service of ships'.[7]

St Helena looked like an idyllic land of plenty, but ever since its establishment as an East India Company colony in 1659, it had been racked by conflicts and unrest. 'A spirit of insubordination' among the inhabitants was 'heightened by their excessive use of intoxicating liquors'. Drunken troublemakers or 'incendiaries' provoked 'violence and riot'.[8] The different groups that made up the island's population – company officials, settlers, planters, soldiers, slaves and a small number of free blacks – were perpetually at odds with each other. In 1672, thirteen years before Knox came to the island, Captain William Bass of the company ship *London* arrived to find that the Governor Richard Keigwin – who was accused of abusing the soldiers 'very much and for no cause' – had been seized, stripped of his arms and imprisoned in a house in the interior of the island. Captain Bass soon restored order, reinstated the Governor and banished his usurper, a Lieutenant Curd.[9]

Twelve years later, in 1684, another rebellion broke out, the after-shocks of which were still reverberating when Knox arrived in St Helena the following spring. The spark which set off the mutiny was a petty dispute between the unpopular Deputy Governor, Captain Robert Holden, 'a man of very evil reputation', and a soldier named Allen Dennison who accused Holden of saying that the primary allegiance of the people of St Helena was to the East India Company rather than the Crown. This pronouncement was viewed as tantamount to sedition. Despite his unpopularity, Holden was exonerated but his accuser, Dennison, was cashiered and locked up in the island prison. On 21 October 1684, a crowd of discontented islanders who backed Dennison stormed the fort at Jamestown. Governor Blackmore ordered them to disband and when they failed to do so, he gave a second order for the guard to open fire on the assembled protesters. Three 'rebels' were killed and fourteen wounded. Many others, however, managed to escape.

Their ringleader, William Bowyer, who is described in the records as 'a malitious, vile person', and several of his confederates were soon tracked down, arrested and jailed. They were tried on 23 and 24 December at a court martial with a military jury consisting of six members of the garrison and six officers from a visiting ship, the *Royal James*, including its Captain, James Marriner. All of the accused were found guilty and William Bowyer was hanged on 31 January 1685.[10] But several others who were also condemned to death managed to have their sentences commuted to transportation to Barbados. A planter's wife, a Mrs Martha Bolton, who had accused the Deputy Governor of being 'a traitorous knave', received twenty-one lashes, was ducked three times in the sea and then jailed.[11]

Given St Helena's tumultuous past, it is perhaps not surprising that Knox's predicament as the victim of a mutiny was viewed sympathetically by the company council. The island, as Knox soon discovered, was still a hotbed of discontent and a remarkably contentious place – the result of a small population, splintered into conflicting groups, confined on an isolated, small area of land. St Helena, in other words, couldn't have differed more from the idyllic desert island that Crusoe remodels and transforms to suit his own needs. The only troublesome people on Crusoe's island are the cannibals who turn up at infrequent intervals and rarely stay long.

In contrast to Crusoe's generally peaceful, uninhabited island, on St Helena Knox pitched up in a social chaos where everyone seemed to be at each other's throats. The Saints – as the island's inhabitants are still called today – were far beyond the range of the company headquarters in London and at times the council members on St Helena were outnumbered or overruled when various groups of islanders – settlers, planters, and even soldiers – formed alliances and revolted against the rule of the company council. This unstable situation was exacerbated by the endemic drunkenness on the island. Planters and soldiers distilled their own arrack, mainly from potatoes, so there was never a shortage of 'intoxicating liquors'.* Drunkenness in turn led to more social problems — blaspheming, gambling and brawling, among others.

The resident chaplain on the island was supposed to impose moral and social order, in addition to providing spiritual guidance, but most of the clergymen sent out to St Helena were themselves given to drunkenness and other vices. Thomas Brooke, an early historian of the island, described the general run of St Helena's clergymen as 'insubordinate, profligate, disrespectful, insolent sots and liars'.¹² The chaplain when Knox was there was one Dr Thomas Sault whose 'fiery orations' had contributed to the rebellion of the previous year. Brooke records that Sault 'scurrilously insulted' the company council, 'condemned their authority, and, by his disrespectful and insolent demeanour . . . fostered a discontent productive of the most serious and alarming mutiny that had hitherto disturbed the settlement'.¹³ By the time Knox arrived in the spring of 1685 Sault was in prison for debt, and no other clergyman had been sent out to tend St Helena's unruly flock.

The feuds and social chaos on St Helena would have been repellent to a man like Robert Knox, and it's unlikely that he ventured far from Jamestown or that he took advantage of his time on the island to tour and inspect its plantations and advise the planters and settlers as he had originally been charged to do. Knox, instead, was too busy vindicating himself in Jamestown, sitting on the company council and scanning the horizon for the next company ship that could rescue him and carry him away from this tiny, volatile outpost of the East India Company in the middle of the South Atlantic.

Soon after you arrive in St Helena you hear about Fernando Lopez. This is still the case today just as it was when Knox was stranded there in 1685. Fernando Lopez — or Fernao Lopez or Lopes, as he is

---

* The number of arrack stills on St Helena became such a nuisance and drunkenness so prevalent that the company eventually sent orders to close down many of the stills and prohibited new ones from being built.

variously called depending on how closely you stick to his original Portuguese name – is one of the few Robinson Crusoe prototypes not mentioned by the indefatigable Defoe scholar, Arthur Wellesley Secord, in his definitive book on the historical and fictional models for Crusoe, *Studies in the Narrative Method of Defoe*, published in 1924. Secord doesn't say why he omits Lopez from his list of candidates for the original Robinson Crusoe (it's unlikely that the ever-vigilant Secord didn't know of Lopez). The story of this first castaway, prisoner and inhabitant of St Helena was recorded by the early Portuguese historian Gaspar Correia and also in the *Chronicles* of the Portuguese naval commander Alfonso de Albuquerque.[14] These admittedly are obscure sources and neither is mentioned in the catalogue of Defoe's library made after his death, but Defoe was always ferreting out information from little known tomes. It is also possible that Defoe found out about Fernando Lopez from Robert Knox, though we have yet to establish a friendship or even an acquaintance between Knox and Defoe.

In 1503, Fernando Lopez, a Portuguese nobleman and soldier, went to Goa on the south-west coast of India, in the service of General Alfonso de Albuquerque. When Alfonso sailed on to Malacca, Lopez was left in charge of the Portuguese fort at Goa. Shortly after Alfonso departed, the fort was attacked by the army of the Muslim Sultan Rasul Khan. In the face of Khan's superior force, Lopez decided to surrender rather than fight. He and his comrades turned renegade and converted to Islam. When Alfonso eventually returned to Goa in 1512 he discovered their perfidy and that the fort was now held by Rasul Khan. Alfonso negotiated the return of Goa to Portuguese power but, as part of the deal, Rasul Khan made him promise to spare the lives of Lopez and the other traitors. Alfonso agreed not to execute them, but he subjected them to three days of brutal torture which included cutting off their right hands and left thumbs, their noses and their ears. Their hair was then shorn off and their beards and eyebrows pulled out, hair by hair. Half of those subjected to this severe punishment died, but Lopez survived and for the next three years, while Alfonso reigned in Goa, Lopez skulked about the city, eking out a subsistence as a beggar.

In 1516, after Alfonso died, Lopez stole on board a ship bound for Lisbon. His original plan seems to have been to return to his wife and children in Portugal, but as the ship approached St Helena, Lopez grew fearful of the reception he might receive from his family, returning home after such a long absence mutilated and in disgrace. He decided instead to seek refuge on St Helena. When they reached the island, Lopez jumped ship and hid himself in the island's forests until the ship sailed away without him. His shipmates, however, had come to pity their mutilated stowaway and when he didn't return to the ship, they left onshore for him a barrel of biscuits, some dried meat, salted fish, clothes and a fire. Until he discovered stones with which he could make fire himself, Lopez zealously tended the one left by his shipmates. With the stump of his right hand and his maimed, four-fingered left hand, he dug out a cave, like Crusoe does, in the soft volcanic rock, which became his home.

For the next ten years, Lopez lived alone on St Helena, hiding whenever a ship visited the island. But the sailors on these ships knew about Lopez and his story, and they always left him supplies, including chickens, seeds, clothes and tools. Like Crusoe, Lopez explored his kingdom; he began to grow his own crops, he domesticated the wild goats and kept chickens. He adopted a cockerel that fell out of one of the ships that called at the island. The cockerel would have drowned if Lopez hadn't rescued it from the sea. According to Correia, it was soon 'on such loving terms with [Lopez] . . . that it followed him wherever he went, and would come at his call, and at night it roosted' with him, perching on his head.'[5] Lopez's cockerel was the original of Robinson Crusoe's parrot Poll.

Like Crusoe, Lopez transformed the island from a prison into a paradise and found peace and happiness there. But when a Javanese slave boy escaped from a ship to live on St Helena, Lopez didn't make him into a manservant like Friday. Instead, he resented this intruder and the slave boy in retaliation revealed Lopez's hiding place to others who came to the island. After this, he was often sighted by those who came to St Helena. He became, in fact, a legendary figure and his fame even reached the King of Portugal who sent him a letter inviting him to return home and promising him safe conduct. When Lopez read the letter he relented and sailed on the next homeward-bound vessel that called at the island.

When he arrived in Lisbon, poor Lopez was stunned by the noise

and crowds and would only venture out at night. He was received
by the King and Queen who offered to set him up in his own
hermitage with a house of friars, but Lopez wanted only to visit
the Pope, confess his sins and make peace with God. With the
Portuguese King's blessing and financial help, he travelled to Rome,
had an audience with the Pope and confessed his 'double crime of
apostasy and the taking up arms for the infidels [Muslims]'. The
Pope gave him absolution and also granted Lopez his sole request:
to return to the island.

Thus Lopez went back to St Helena, but his life there now was
not as solitary as it had been before. He began 'to shew himself and
converse with people . . . [from] the ships which passed by, and all
gave him things to plant and to sow'. Lopez settled down to 'live
happily, tending his orange trees, his pomegranates and his poultry,
or sitting and basking in the sunshine in peaceful solitude, alone
except for the . . . visits of the ships from India, until he died in the
year 1545, after living on St Helena for nearly thirty years'.[16]

Though it has the aura of myth or fable, Correia insisted that
his account of Fernando Lopez's life was the unvarnished truth.
Defoe, however, wanted Crusoe to have things both ways: island
peace and happiness *and* worldly success. Crusoe is spiritually
redeemed on his lonely island but when he escapes and returns
home he is also rewarded with prosperity and good fortune. He
establishes his colony 'kingdom' on the island and then goes back
to England, where thanks to the Brazilian plantation he left behind*
and the trusty, diligent friends who had taken charge of his affairs
in his absence, Crusoe discovers he is a man of considerable wealth.
Like Lopez, in *The Farther Adventures of Robinson Crusoe*, Crusoe
goes back to his island, but he stays just long enough to check on
his colony, and then he sails off blithely to other adventures which
closely resemble Knox's later, post-Ceylon travels.

A very different tale of island exile is embodied in the fate of an
Englishman named John Segar whose story Knox heard – as he did
Lopez's story – when he was stranded on St Helena. Defoe also knew

* When he leaves Brazil, Crusoe goes as a slave trader, like Knox. He sets sail to West
Africa in order to buy slaves for his own and his neighbours' Brazilian plantations,
but a storm drives his ship far off course and he is cast away on an island off the
coast of Venezuela.

about Segar, having read about him in Hakluyt's *Principal Navigations and Voyages.* In 1591 John Segar, a humble tailor from Suffolk, sailed on the *Royal Merchant,* one of three vessels under the command of Sir James Lancaster. This small fleet was making the first trading voyage to India undertaken by English merchants. By the time the trio of ships reached the Cape of Good Hope, on the outward voyage, so many of the crew were ill with scurvy that it was decided that the *Royal Merchant,* under the command of Captain Abraham Kendell, should turn round and carry the invalids back to St Helena where they could recover. Kendall duly sailed to the island and landed fifty men, all of whom rapidly regained their health, with the exception of Segar; so it was decided to leave him on St Helena where he could easily be picked up later. Segar apparently agreed to this plan and before his shipmates departed, they made him two suits of clothing out of goatskins, with the hairy side outwards 'like unto . . . Savages' [clothes]'.[17] Defoe no doubt got his idea for Crusoe's island apparel from Segar's story.

Poor Segar was stuck on St Helena much longer than he expected. In fact, it wasn't until nearly two years later, on 3 April 1593, that Captain Lancaster, on his journey home from India, arrived at the island. But Segar's sojourn on St Helena had not brought him peace and serenity, as it had for Fernando Lopez. One of the men from Lancaster's ship recorded that:

in a house by the chapel, I found an Englishman one John Segar of Bury in Suffolk, who was left there eighteen months before by Abraham Kendall, who left him to refresh him on the island, being otherwise like to have perished on shipboard: and at our coming we found him as fresh in colour and in as good plight of body to our seeming as might be, but crazed in mind and half out of his wits, as afterwards we perceived: for whether he were put in a fright of us, not knowing at first what we were, whether friends or foes, or of sudden joy when he understood we were his old consorts and countrymen, he became idle-headed, and for eight days space neither night nor day took any natural rest, and so at length died for lack of sleep.[18]

Crusoe, like John Segar, is 'crazed in mind and half out of his wits' after his ship is wrecked in a great storm and he alone of all the crew makes it to shore.He compares his 'idle-headed' state to that of a man about to be hanged who is pardoned at the last minute on the scaffold and needs the attentions of a surgeon when he is stunned by the good news of his reprieve: 'For sudden Joys, like Griefs, confound at first' – a line that Defoe lifted from Robert Wild's 1672 poem 'Wild's Humble Thanks for his Majesty's Gracious Declaration for Liberty of Conscience'.[19]

Fernando Lopez and John Segar were both accidental inhabitants of St Helena. By far the most famous detainee on the island was, of course, Napoleon Bonaparte, who was exiled there by the British after his defeat at Waterloo in 1815. If it hadn't been for Napoleon, St Helena would have slept on in undisturbed historical obscurity in the remote South Atlantic. Napoleon could be said, in fact, to have put St Helena on the map. If people today have heard of the island at all, it is probably because they know Napoleon spent his last six years there and that, far from turning into an island hermit like Lopez or going mad like Segar, he transformed the island into a miniature replica of his lost empire.

According to a modern guidebook on St Helena, Napoleon, on arrival, surveyed his 'island prison' with the spyglass he'd used on many battlefields and said, 'It is not an attractive place; I should have done better to remain in Egypt.'[20] He promptly set about seeing that the island outcrop of volcanic rock be made as 'attractive and accommodating' as possible. Unlike Fernando Lopez and John Segar, Napoleon was not stranded alone. He brought his court with him – an entourage of people, including his closest political advisors and personal physician, his staff and their families, two priests, a chef, valet and various servants. The British meanwhile sent nearly 2,000 troops to guard their famous prisoner and built him a lavish residence, Longwood, complete with a billiard room and a huge bathroom with a copper tub panelled in oak in which Napoleon spent long hours bathing, reading, lunching, receiving callers and dictating his memoirs to his secretary. He planned an elaborate garden in the grounds of Longwood. However, the advent of a new British governor, Sir Hudson Lowe, brought humiliating restrictions on Napoleon's movements; a curfew was imposed and his mail censored. But Napoleon was a difficult man to demean, even when he fell ill.

His final illness has given rise to considerable debate. Was Napoleon poisoned by the arsenic used in the coloured wallpaper at Longwood? Did he have hepatitis or cancer? His sickbed was moved to the drawing room so that he could look out at his garden. Here, on 5 May 1821, Napoleon died, surrounded by attendants and members of his entourage. Controversy raged over the cause of his death, but when an autopsy was performed, the official cause was given as stomach cancer and a perforated ulcer. The former Emperor was buried on the island in a peaceful resting place of his own choosing – a simple tomb in a valley beneath two willow trees. A special road was built to reach the grave and it was guarded round the clock. But Napoleon was not left in peace. Nineteen years later, in 1840, at the behest of the French government, his body was disinterred and his remains returned to France.[21]

The fallen Emperor was a Crusoe-like figure on St Helena. Instead of adapting to the island, as Knox had on Ceylon, Napoleon re-established his imperial world of pomp and ceremony, albeit on a reduced scale. His courtiers and servants saw to his every need. Protocol was rigidly followed. Even the English collaborated with Napoleon in his folly by building his magnificent residence and sending out an army to guard him. They may have been his gaolers but they colluded with his fantasy island and bolstered his majestic, VIP status.

Napoleon's exile on St Helena turned out to be its most illustrious period. His fallen greatness gave the island notoriety and gravitas which survive to this day. The major tourist attractions are Napoleonic sites – the Briars (the house where he stayed when he first came to the island), his residence, Longwood, and his empty tomb. Visitors still climb the narrow dirt track to look at the hole in the ground where he was once interred. A haughty tyrant who felt only contempt for his final place of residence has made the island famous.

Napoleon may have put St Helena on the map but both before and after him the island was visited by a number of other famous people. It is quite uncanny, in fact, how many have stopped off there given its remoteness. Nine years before Knox was stranded, Edmund Halley arrived in 1676 and stayed a year, mapping the stars of the southern hemisphere. In 1691, six years after Knox, William Dampier went to St Helena where a number of his crew promptly fell 'Head over Ears in Love with the Santa Hellena Maids'. Dampier describes these ladies as 'well shaped, proper and comely', and several of his men took island women home as wives.[22]

Captain James Cook came to the island in 1771 on the HMS *Endeavour* which also had on board the pioneering botanist Joseph Banks.* Captain William Bligh arrived in 1792, three years after the controversial mutiny on board his ship the *Bounty*. In the early years of the following century the Duke of Wellington and a very young William Thackeray both visited St Helena.[†] Charles Darwin arrived for a six-day visit on 8 July 1836 during which he made a remarkably thorough investigation of the island. He saw many partridges and pheasants but he failed to catch sight of St Helena's indigenous plover, the wirebird.

Darwin didn't confine his observations to the animal and plant life. He also noted that many of the inhabitants were poor and subsisted on a diet of rice and a little salted meat. He was struck too by the number of blacks on St Helena. The island, in fact, had a long-established population of black people, all of them connected with slavery.

The very first blacks to come to St Helena were runaway slaves who escaped from slave ships that stopped at the island on their way to South America or the West Indies. In the 1550s '2 Kaffirs from Mozambique', two women slaves and a Javanese slave escaped from a slave ship and swam ashore and hid themselves in the woods. In the following years their number multiplied and soon there was a

---

* Joseph Banks's heavily annotated copy of Knox's *Historical Relation of Ceylon* is one of the three original 1681 editions held by the British Library. In the Rare Books Reading Room, any British Library reader can order it, as I did, and read Banks's scribbled notes and comments in the margins of the text and on the endpapers of the book.
† Sir Arthur Wellesley, the Duke of Wellington, stopped at St Helena in 1805, on the *Trident* on the way home after his victory at Assaye. In 1816 Thackeray, a child of just five, sailed from Calcutta where his recently deceased father had been in the service of the East India Company. His mother had remarried and her son was being sent back home to school in the custody of a family friend. When the little boy and his Indian servant went ashore at St Helena, he saw Napoleon from afar, and his servant told him that Napoleon ate three sheep a day and all the children he could get his hands on. Thackeray later wrote about this episode in his *Roundabout Papers*.

community of twenty who always hid themselves at the first sight of a ship on the horizon.

In the seventeenth century, however, these escaped slaves were outnumbered by slaves from Madagascar and Africa brought by the East India Company to work on the plantations. In 1659, '10 lusty young black men and women' arrived from the Cape Verde islands and West Africa. Three years later, another '12 lusty young Negroes, the major part women', came, followed by 'two Blacks skilful in planting'. By 1679, there were eighty slaves on the island. In 1685, Knox's cargo of Madagascar slaves increased their population to well over a hundred and the islanders began to fear the possibility of slave rebellions if any more blacks were to arrive. Despite persistent rumours, there was never a real threat of a revolt, though periodically slaves would be rounded up and severely punished or even hanged for allegedly planning an uprising. By 1723, there were 224 slaves on St Helena. Most of these were males who worked on the plantations, though a few were stone layers and cutters, carpenters and workers in the lime kilns. The smaller population of women slaves did dairy work, tended poultry and worked as domestic servants.

Inevitably, this growing slave population produced offspring, which were deemed worthless by the East India Company. There was nothing on St Helena like the communities of slave families later found on plantations in the American South. Instead, in 1699, a policy was introduced on the island to convey 'useless Black children' to Benkulen on Sumatra where no doubt most of them died in the pestilential climate.[23]

The British abolition of the slave trade in 1807 didn't stop the influx of blacks to the island. From 1825, British naval ships hunted down and seized slave ships in the Atlantic, arrested their captains and liberated all the Africans on board. In 1840, a Vice Admiralty Court was established on St Helena to try the Captains of slavers captured off West Africa. Large numbers of these ships were intercepted by the British Naval Patrol and brought to the island where they were sold or broken up. Their human cargo – the slaves on board – were freed, fed, clothed and housed at the Liberated African Depot in Rupert's Valley close to Jamestown. Between 1840 and 1850, 15,000 Africans landed on St Helena.[24] Many of these freed slaves were taken to Sierra Leone where a colony of 'liberated Africans' had been established in 1792. Others were sent to labour as free blacks in British Guiana and the West Indies. But some stayed on St Helena and had children – and their descendants still live on the island today.

Thus, St Helena has played an important role in the history of slavery. The island has provided a hiding place for fugitive slaves, been a prison for imported slave labourers, and finally a depot and safe haven for liberated slaves.

St Helena was and still can be a paradoxical or ambiguous place, not just for blacks, but for all sorts of people: mariners, scientists, missionaries, colonial servants, renegades, the black sheep of families, people seeking their fortunes, tourists, cruise ship passengers and those just passing through. The island's historical significance contrasts sharply with its remote, inaccessible location and small size.* At one time or another it has been a utopian paradise, a sanctuary, a prosperous colony, a naturalists' and scientists' laboratory, and a chance to begin a new life. But it has also been a living hell, a social chaos, a place of exile and imprisonment, and a grave. Defoe never went to St Helena or sent any of his travelling heroes there. Knox was there for just a few months and he spent this short time mentally elsewhere, yearning to escape. But St Helena, despite this, is central to both Defoe and Knox and their books: it is the geographical counterpart of the Crusoe myth.

But we must return to 1685 and Knox stranded in the middle of the South Atlantic. How did he spend his days? Little is known about his time on the island. A formal inquiry was held at which he testified; he attended the monthly council meetings; he dined every evening at the top of the 'Company Table' in the Governor's residence. This is all we can be certain of.

But surely Knox was haunted by his lost book with all his hand-

---

* There is no airport on St Helena and today it remains accessible only by sea. I was able to visit by accepting a short-term job lecturing on a cruise ship that stopped at St Helena on its way to South Africa. Recent plans to build an airport on the island and the first stages of its construction were officially 'paused' in 2009. Then in July 2010 they were apparently revived, but work hasn't recommenced. Today St Helena has fewer links with the outside world than it did two hundred years ago.

written additions and revisions which the mutineers had carried off with them on the *Tonqueen Merchant*. He would have gone over in his mind, again and again, what might have happened to it. After the mutiny, the ship may well have foundered at sea with every-body and everything on board lost. Even if the ship hadn't mis-carried, it was unlikely that Knox's personal effects, including his books and papers, would have survived. Nor did it seem probable that the ship would ever return to England. The mutineers would more likely have turned to piracy and preyed on ships from Madagascar or some other popular pirate base.

Knox, then, must have thought he would never see his book with all the manuscript material again. Indeed, it was all too easy to imagine the possible fate of its folio pages with their margins and blank sheets crammed with his scrawled notes. They could have been torn out and used to kindle fires, as scrap paper to wrap up bits of food or freshly caught fish, or to line the bottom of the chicken coops on board.

To lose a manuscript, for an author, can feel like murder or suicide. It can seem a more grievous and irreplaceable loss than life itself. A writer's immediate impulse would be to make a desperate attempt to revive or resuscitate it — somehow to bring it back to life. Did Knox spend his days and weeks and months on St Helena attempting to remember, conjure up and write down all the words that he'd lost? In his mind's eye, could he literally *see* and *read* his lost manu-script pages? And did he laboriously struggle to decipher and copy them down on blank sheets of paper in his rooms in the Governor's house in Jamestown?*

---

* When I was writing this chapter, I suddenly remembered a book I'd read years ago and scarcely thought about since: Viktor Frankl's *Man's Search for Meaning*. I decided to reread it. Frankl was a Jewish neurologist and psychiatrist who spent three years in Auschwitz, Dachau and other concentration camps during the Second World War. The long first section of his book is an account of his experiences in the Nazi death camps. Frankl describes in harrowing detail how when he first came to Auschwitz he tried to hide and preserve the manuscript of the book he was working on when he was arrested. He explained to one of the old prisoners in the camp: 'this is the manu-script of a scientific book. I know what you will say: that I should be grateful to escape with my life . . . But I cannot help myself. I must keep this manuscript at all costs: it is my life's work. Do you understand?' The old prisoner does understand, but he's

Finally, one fine morning in late August or early September 1685, a ship was sighted far out to sea. As it approached Jamestown's harbour, its East India Company flag could be seen snapping to and fro in the wind. Soon Knox would no longer be marooned.

When the ship anchored in the harbour and its launch came ashore, Knox was amazed to learn that it was none other than the *Caesar*, the very same ship that he had sailed on in 1680 from Java when he'd made his circuitous voyage home from Ceylon via Batavia and Bantam. Not only was it the same ship that had delivered him out of his first and longest captivity, it was also commanded by the same Captain, Jonathan Andrews, who now was almost as surprised to find Knox on St Helena as he had been to come to his rescue four years earlier on Java.[25]

Of course, Captain Andrews was more than happy to carry Knox back to England, and as soon as his ship's 'refreshment' and business were done, Knox boarded the *Caesar* as a passenger of high status who would share the Captain's table at sea. No doubt he also recognised and remembered many of the crew of nearly a hundred men. Indeed, the 530-tonne *Caesar* with its forty guns and three main decks was almost as familiar to him as his own lost *Tonqueen Merchant*. Not only did Captain Andrews entertain Knox at his table, upon seeing that Knox had only 'the Cloath [clothes] on my backe', he gave him 'a suply of Cloaths to Shift me'.[26]

After sailing by way of the West Indies, the *Caesar* eventually reached Plymouth, the first port they called at in England. Shortly after their arrival there, Knox and Captain Andrews were standing on deck, looking 'out into the Sound' when they saw, in Knox's words, 'a Ship comeing in which to my eyes appeared very much

become hardened and bitter. He cruelly jeers back at Frankl, 'Shit!' The manuscript is taken from Frankl when he goes through the disinfection process all the Jews submitted to when they first entered the camps. But eventually, despite the brutal forced labour and starvation diet imposed on him and later when he had typhus and was confined to bed, Frankl mentally reconstructed his manuscript in his head, and whenever he could manage to, he scribbled down what he'd mentally composed on scraps of paper. This, along with the memory of his love for his wife, sustained Frankl and was a key factor in his survival. Knox's situation was very different from Frankl's; he was sustained by his love of God and sense of duty to his father's wishes, but for Knox, too, his book – *An Historical Relation of Ceylon* – with all its revisions and additions, became his 'life's work'.

like my Ship the *Tonqueen* which was carried away from me at St Helena'. Knox, indeed, remarked to Andrews that 'ware it not but that I knew it to be impossible, I should affirme it was my Ship I had lost . . . but it was my misfortune as she was thus coming in to the Sound, [that] a fishing boate came on board [the *Tonqueen Merchant*] to offer theire Service as Pilot, by whome upon inquiry they ware informed that thare was an East India Ship newly arrived which they Concluded came from St Helena . . . & [they] feared lest I should be on board her; whareupon immediately they stood out againe into the Sea . . . & went to the island of white [Wight] to the port of Cowes . . . and all [the men] run away with their plunder leaving the Ship at Anchor with only some boyes in her'.[27]

This was the sort of coincidence that would seem implausible, even impossible, if it appeared in a work of fiction. And yet it really happened. At the very first English port that Knox arrived at after being rescued from St Helena, he saw − although he couldn't at first believe the evidence of his own eyes − his own ship, the *Tonqueen Merchant*, still in the hands of the mutineers, who, fearing Knox was on board the *Caesar*, ran off with his ship for the second time, while Knox helplessly looked on.

Before leaving, Knox sent a letter to the East India Company directors in London, informing them of his return, and some days later, when he arrived at the Downs, he was given a message to go on to Deal where a reply awaited him. This was a letter 'from Sir Josiah Child himselfe wherein he advised' Knox that the ship he had seen at Plymouth *was* indeed the *Tonqueen Merchant*. Child now directed him to go to Cowes on the Isle of Wight and retrieve it and whatever money or goods he found remaining on board. At Deal, too, Knox ran into one of the crew who had sailed off with the mutineers at St Helena, though this man assured him that he had been forced against his will. He told him how the ship had gone to the Cape Verde Islands after sailing away and how the mutineers had divided up the money and goods and then argued with each other over who should be the Captain and where they should go, and finally they 'fell into Confusion' and sailed back to England where they abandoned the ship at Cowes. Knox also learned how the mutineers had attempted to disguise the *Tonqueen Merchant* by breaking off its figurehead, carvings and galleries and renaming it the *Greyhound.*

Knox proceeded to Cowes and there found and took possession of the *Tonqueen Merchant.* The very first thing he did was search for what, if anything, had been left behind by the mutineers. As he expected, the ship had been stripped nearly bare. Indeed, his informant at Deal had already told him how at Santiago, in the Cape Verde Islands, they had disposed of '4 Bales of . . . Callicoes, the Chyrurgery Chest, all sorts of armes & ammunition & all [Knox's] . . . Cloaths, Chest & Bedding'.[28]

The only things Knox recovered at Cowes were 'some of my old cloaths' and – miraculously as it seemed to him – his intact *Historical Relation of Ceylon* with all its extra pages covered with his hand-written additions and revisions. To the mutineers, the book was as worthless and useless as his worn-out shirts and breeches. For Knox, however, it was invaluable – his most precious possession and 'life's work'.

In due course he made his way to London where the first thing he did was to visit Sir Josiah Child at his country seat, Wanstead Abbey. According to Knox, Child 'welcomed me with Expressions of great Kindnesse & Compassion, & bid me Comfort myself saying he would Continew to be my friend & I must now begin againe'. Lady Child 'did also exceedingly Commiserate my Condition & speake Comfort to my very heart'.

However, when Knox met the directors of the East India Company at the Leadenhall Street offices in London he had 'another Kind of reception'. He was castigated and blamed for the mutiny. He was accused of giving his men 'Scant allowance of provisions', and assailed with various 'Contumelious reports that the men had raised on me to Justifie themselves & make theire Barratry [seem] an act of necessity'. It was all a very complicated, nasty business. Another inquiry was held and according to Knox's confusing account, he 'put the Seamens Bonds in suit & arrested severall of their Securities upon Breach of Bonds which stood good in Law against them'. 'By this means,' Knox says, 'I got a little money to Suply my wants,' but he was forced to sell his one-sixteenth share in the ship at a loss. The most important thing, however, was that despite the other directors' objections, Child insisted that Knox retain command of the *Tonqueen Merchant*. In the event, he managed to keep both his ship and his rank of Captain.[29]

Thus in a storm of acrimony and writs, Knox's third voyage was concluded. He had endured and lost much. But by luck and through his own efforts he had retained what he valued most: command of his ship and his book.

Knox would go to sea again, but his life as a captive was over. He was a captive now only in the sense that we are all captives – not on islands, held against our will, but captives of the unavoidable, imprisoning, destructive forces that interrupt every human life: time, ageing, fortune, luck (or lack of it) – the storms and wreckages that threaten, confine and ultimately defeat or drown us all.

CHAPTER ELEVEN

Captain Knox and Captain Singleton

Defoe's novel, *The Life, Adventures and Pyracies of the Famous Captain Singleton*, was published in June 1720, a year after *Robinson Crusoe* and its sequel *The Farther Adventures of Robinson Crusoe*. The book's plot is summarised in its long, cumbersome title: *The Life, Adventures, and Pyracies of the Famous Captain Singleton: Containing an Account of his being set on Shore in the Island of Madagascar: his Settlement there, with a Description of the Place and Inhabitants: of his Passage from thence, in a Paraguay [pirogue] to the Main Land of Africa, with an Account of the Customs and Manners of the People: his Great Deliverances from the Barbarous Natives and Wild Beasts: of his Meeting with an Englishman, a Citizen of London, among the Indians, the Great Riches he Acquired, and his Voyage Home to England: as also Captain Singleton's return to Sea, with an Account of his many Adventures and Pyracies with the Famous Captain Avery and others.*

Like the Crusoe books, *Captain Singleton* purported to be an authentic autobiographical account, so there was no author's name on the title page. But word was soon out that it came from the same pen as the man who wrote *Robinson Crusoe*. Defoe had written it, as usual, at great speed, just before the final book in his Crusoe trilogy, *Serious Reflections during the Life and Surprising Adventures of Robinson Crusoe*, which came out two months after *Singleton* in August 1720. *Captain Singleton*, then, is sandwiched between the second and third instalments of Crusoe's story. Perhaps Defoe was worried that his audience was beginning to tire of Crusoe's exploits, so he introduced a new version of his hero. But Singleton's name is misleading. Far from being singular or unique, he is really a

variant of Defoe's survivor hero – the same old Crusoe under another
name. And just as *Robinson Crusoe* was based on Robert Knox's
long captivity on Ceylon, so too was much of *Captain Singleton*.
Towards the end of the book, Defoe actually introduces Knox into
the story, summarises his years of captivity on Ceylon, and plagiarises a long passage from Knox's *Historical Relation* nearly word
for word.

But *Captain Singleton* was also inspired by Knox's various post-
Ceylon voyages as an East India Company ship's captain. It shows,
in fact, that Defoe was familiar with all the major events Knox
recorded in his unpublished autobiography. Defoe must have known
Knox – or have read the memoir. At the very least he had detailed
second-hand knowledge of Knox and his adventures. The ways in
which Captain Singleton and his travels echo Knox's entire career
– before and after Ceylon – are simply too striking to be coinci-
dental.

In order to trace the parallels between Knox's life and Singleton's,
we need to take up the thread of Knox's story after he recovered
the *Tonqueen Merchant* (with his book and manuscript additions
and revisions) on the Isle of Wight. Singleton is Crusoe under a
different name, but there is one new facet in his life: his later career
as a pirate. Pirate stories were hugely popular in the early eighteenth century, and Defoe was cashing in on the new vogue for these
tales, some of which he himself may have written.[1] Was Knox, of
all people, ever a pirate? Not exactly. But after his return from St
Helena, his next voyage was as a privateer – a form of legalised
piracy whereby the British Crown granted commissions to merchant
ships to attack and capture enemy vessels during times of war. This
was a cheap way of fighting at sea without incurring the expense
of a standing navy. Usually the enemy ships in question were French
or Spanish; Britain was intermittently at war with both powers at
this time. But in the 1680s the East India Company fell out with
the native rulers of India, especially the Great Mogul, and declared
war against them. The company then licensed some of its merchant
ships to, in Knox's words, 'make War against the Grand Mogoll &
his Subjects, & to take all Ships & vessels belonging to them'. In
order to prepare the *Tonqueen Merchant* for its privateering voyage,

in 1686 thirty soldiers were added to the crew so that Knox had sixty-three men in all on board and the arms were increased to twenty-four guns.[2]

As Knox confesses in his autobiography, 'this designe [of sailing as a privateer] pleased me very well being very sutable to my present [straitened] circumstances haveing but little Stocke to trade with & this in all appearances seemed a ready way to raise my decayed fortune'. On privateering voyages, a British ship carried a government commission or licence – a legal document sometimes called 'a letter of marque'. Privateers hunted down and captured the ships of nations with whom Britain was at war. As Knox put it when he received his orders to sail as a privateer, he would now have 'the Kings, as well as the Companies Authority to take booty from the Indians'. Knox also knew that the Great Mogul would not be able to put up much of a fight against the company's superior force. He may have questioned the morality of privateering, but if he had any doubts, he quickly shrugged them off. He says that he 'would not suffer my thoughts to wade far into the Equity & Justness of such Actions since my Commission according to human law would beare me out'.[3] In other words, he wasn't going to refer his actions to any higher law. He would just be following orders.

In addition to its legality, the main difference between privateering and piracy was that a large percentage of the 'booty' taken by privateers from captured ships went to the East India Company and the Crown. The rest of the takings were then shared among the Captain and his crew according to their rank. Pirates, of course, were criminals – they kept everything they took from a captured ship, or 'prize', for themselves. Serving on a privateer wasn't as lucrative as being a pirate could be, but it offered the chance of making far more money than being an ordinary sailor on a merchant or naval vessel. And unlike pirates, privateers seldom ended up on the gallows.

Knox's privateering career was far from successful, however. He summarises it in just a page or two in his autobiography, but East India Company records tell a more complicated story.[4] The *Tonqueen Merchant* pursued several of the Mogul's treasure-laden ships but captured only one and then took it to Persia rather than to Bombay, where Knox's instructions had required him to take prizes. Even more importantly, company records indicate that Knox's crew

embezzled 115 toumans – gold Persian coins worth ten shillings each
– and various goods from the captured ship. In his autobiography
Knox dismisses this episode, complaining that when he returned to
England the company 'made me pay Considerabley for goods said
to be plundered by my men out of her, wharas I think wee deserved
a reward for saveing her when she was on the shore'.[5]

Knox makes no mention at all of another serious episode that
occurred during this privateering voyage. After the *Tonqueen
Merchant* had finally arrived in Bombay, she was supposed to return
to Persia. According to company records, the ship was 'deceived by
ye Currants [currents]' and forced to stop at Sindh* where it
anchored and sent a boat with eight men ashore. Knox waited for
eight days for the men and boat to return, but when they failed to
do so, he set sail without them. As the company records put it, the
directors were 'heartily concerned at ye loss of soe many of our
Countreymen'.[6]

Bad luck continued to dog Knox on this voyage. Stormy weather
forced him to spend the entire winter at Mauritius, during which
time he incurred considerable demurrage charges. Then when he
finally sailed, the ship sprang a leak and he was forced to divert the
voyage to Barbados in order to make repairs. But here in the West
Indies most of his crew were 'pressed' – or forcibly conscripted –
into the navy and transferred to naval ships so that Knox was further
delayed while he recruited new crew members. When he finally
made it back to England he got stuck at Falmouth – incurring yet
more demurrage charges – because Britain was now at war with
France and it was unsafe for him to proceed to London until more
ships arrived at Falmouth with which he could sail home in convoy.
In June 1689, he wrote to his cousin John Strype from Falmouth
that 'I longe to be at whome wch I hope now will not be longe for
I am tired with these kind of East India voiages'.[7]

Knox returned from his privateering voyage in 1689 and during
his brief interval in London he discussed cannabis again with
Robert Hooke, presumably because when Knox was in India on
this latest trip he learned more about the uses (and sampled them

---

* Sindh is the region which today is covered by the Indian state of Hyderabad and
its next-door neighbour Sindh, the south-east province of Pakistan. Its southernmost
border is on the Arabian Sea.

himself) of this 'wonder drug', as he considered it. Not only did
Knox discuss cannabis with Hooke, he also gave him some dried
specimens of the plant which he had brought home with him. It's
likely that he also carried living cannabis plants on board the
Tonqueen Merchant.

Knox of course had already praised cannabis in his *Historical
Relation* as an 'antidote and counter-poison' against typhus and other
diseases. He had also described how the dried cannabis leaves were
beaten into a powder with some sweeteners and then eaten 'morning
and evening on an empty stomach'. On 26 October 1689, Robert
Hooke recorded in his diary how at Jonathan's Coffee House that
evening Knox spoke 'of a strange, intoxicating herb like hemp [that
is] . . . accounted wholesome, though for a time it takes away
memory and understanding'.[8] This was, in Hooke's view, an important scientific discovery and on 18 December 1689 he devoted a
whole Royal Society lecture to the subject of cannabis. He began by
saying that 'the person [Robert Knox] from whom I receiv'd it, hath
made many Trials of it on himself with very good Effect'. According
to Hooke, the leaves and seeds of the cannabis plant should be ground
into a powder and then chewed or swallowed with water. Like Knox,
Hooke noted that cannabis took 'away Memory and Understanding'
and produced a kind of 'Extasie', but 'that which troubled Stomach
or Head . . . is perfectly carried off . . . and he [Knox] assures me
that he hath often taken [it] when he has found himself out of
Order, either by drinking bad water or eating something which have
[sic] not agreed with him'. Thus the generally abstemious Knox, was
a habitual user of cannabis, at least for medicinal purposes.[9]

Knox did not linger in London after returning from his privateering voyage. In early 1690, he embarked on another slave-trading
voyage and went again to Madagascar to purchase slaves which
he was then directed to take to Benkulen in Sumatra. When he
reached Madagascar, Knox encountered the elder brother of his old
captor King Rybassa, one King Tomanuallarebo. Knox dispatched a
messenger to tell the King he had arrived to buy slaves and
Tomanuallarebo sent back a message saying 'his eares had seene me
before when I came to his Brother and he would come downe to see
me with his eyes'. Which in due course he did, and received Knox
warmly; as Knox describes, 'we rubed noses and shaked hands in

testimony of friendship'.[10] Knox spent some three months at Madagascar and bought a hundred slaves. When he departed he prudently took no formal leave of the King, lest he attempt to detain him as his brother, Rybassa, had done. Instead, the *Tonqueen Merchant* slipped away from Madagascar in the middle of the night, and proceeded directly to Sumatra.

They spent four months at Benkulen where they sold the slaves at profit and took on board a cargo of pepper. But Benkulen was, in Knox's words, a 'most sickely Country' and Knox himself, as well as many of his men, came down with fever. In fact, he had to bury a number of his crew in Sumatra. Finally they departed on the long voyage back to England, stopping en route at Bengal in India, St Helena and Barbados in the West Indies. Here Knox received word that his sister had died. It was Abigail Lascelles who had 'started from' her long-lost brother and then checked his pockmark as proof of his identity when he returned from Ceylon. Despite the fact that they clearly weren't close, Knox wrote to John Strype from Barbados that the news of her death had 'greatly greeved mee'.[11]

When Knox finally returned safely to London in late 1693, he was stunned to learn that while he'd been gone the East India Company had changed its regulations and in particular, revoked the privilege or 'freedom' of its captains and officers to trade 'on their own account' on company voyages. Heretofore, captains and officers could buy and carry goods and sell them for a profit along with the company's cargo. A sizeable section of each East India Company ship's hold, in fact, had always been reserved for the cargo of its captain and officers. But with this change of policy Knox's income would be reduced to his captain's salary alone. This was a serious blow because captains and officers often made more by trading on their own account than they did from their company salaries.

This new policy marked the beginning of the end of Knox's long association with the East India Company, as well as the friendship and patronage of Sir Josiah Child. Like many ruptures, it did not happen all at once or without considerable acrimony, but once Knox realised that Child could not waive the ban on captains' private trading, even for his faithful friend and servant, the break with the company became inevitable. Knox indeed relates his grievances against the East India Company and Child in great detail in his autobiography. It is clear that he took the withdrawal of trading on his own account as a personal affront and thought for a time that an exception would be made in his case. But the new regulation was across the board and inviolable. If Knox continued in the company's service, he would not be able to engage in private trade and his salary would be his only remuneration.

After a great deal of thought, he made a momentous decision: he announced that he was going to retire altogether. Not only would he leave the East India Company, which he and his father had served for most of their lives, he would also leave the sea – the only life he had known for the past fourteen years – and settle in London. Knox in 1694, was, after all, a man of fifty-three. Many sea captains retired earlier, especially if they had acquired considerable wealth. And Knox, for all his anger at the company and the revocation of the privilege to engage in private trade, had to concede that he was well off, if not wealthy.

Thus he found lodgings somewhere in London (we don't know precisely where) and settled down. He had decided now to work intensively on the second edition of his *Historical Relation* and he had another project in mind as well. Oliver Cromwell's daughter, Lady Fauconberg,* had some time before suggested to him that he write his autobiography and in it record the story of his life before his fateful voyage to Ceylon in 1659 as well as the events that had occurred after his escape in 1680. He intended to publish the second edition of his book as soon as possible, but he doesn't seem to have envisioned having his autobiography, or 'memoir' as he always called it, published until after his death.

This then was his plan in the winter and spring of 1694 after he had broken with the East India Company and settled in London. For the next two years, Knox worked on his two books, socialised with Robert Hooke and John Strype, attended Royal Society meetings and met other friends from his seafaring days at London coffee

---

* Lady Fauconberg, born Mary Cromwell in 1637, was the third of Cromwell's four daughters. She married Viscount Fauconberg in 1657. The fact that Knox socialised with Viscount and Lady Fauconberg indicates how far he had risen in aristocratic as well as intellectual and scientific circles in London.

houses. It was probably during these years, too, that he first encountered – perhaps at a coffee house one evening – an enterprising
man named Daniel Defoe, who had published little at this time, but
was seemingly on the way up as the accountant of the newly imposed
glass duty and one of the trustees of the state lottery. Defoe was
also in the midst of writing his first important work: *An Essay on
Projects.* He was keenly interested in, among other things, sea voyages,
ships lost at sea with treasure on board and the construction of diving
bells.

Knox completed the first draft of his autobiography on 8 August
1696. He had been back in London for two full years now. He had
also prepared the *Historical Relation* for a second edition and gone
to the trouble and expense of having himself painted and engraved
by the celebrated artist Robert White, presumably so that his image
could serve as the frontispiece. But to Knox's dismay, his publisher
Richard Chiswell and his associates turned down this new version
of the second edition, once again on the grounds that his text was
too long and disjointed. Knox probably put up an argument, but it
was to no avail. The book wasn't going to be reissued despite all his
labours. Knox, for the time being, allowed the second edition to lie
dormant. Meanwhile, he grew tired of what he called his 'idle and
dronish' London life. He decided to return to the sea. But he had
burned his bridges with the East India Company and been dismissed
or had resigned – it isn't certain which. What is clear is that they
refused his tender to take command of a new ship in need of an
experienced captain. The only way Knox could sail again now was
as captain of an independent, non-company ship – or 'interloper' as
they were called.

And this is precisely what he did in 1698 when he took command
of a new ship 'of 500 tuns built by Mr Samuel Shepherd, Designed
for East India as an Interloper or free ship'.[12] His orders were to
depart in early May, and in April Knox made out his will. On 22
April, he wrote to Strype, 'this I pen to you to take my Leave; my
ship *Mary* is now below Gravesend . . . and I shall suddenly repare
onboard . . . The inclosed is a Copie of my Will signed & sealed by
my selfe, which I commit to yor Keeping; the orginall is in ye hands
of Brother Lascelles [Abigail's widower] . . . all sealed up & not to
be opened tell my Death, but on my returne if God permit [it] to

be delivered sealed to me.' There is no record of Knox making out a will before this time. Perhaps he had a presentiment that he would not return; or perhaps now that he was the last survivor of his immediate family, he felt the need to specify which relatives and friends should inherit his wealth. Whatever the case, his seal was not broken and the will remained unread. On the back of the sealed document John Strype wrote, 'Restored this Will to Cap Knox Jan 17 1701."[3] With this last piece of business accomplished, Knox was ready to depart.

As he records in his autobiography, in 'Anno 1698 on the 3 day of May, I set saile out of the Downs on the ship *Mary* bound first for Cadis [Cadiz], thare to take in silver & from thence for Suratt in the East Indies on a private [ie, non-East India Company] account, Alias Interloper'. On this last voyage, Knox stopped briefly at Ceylon on 30 October 1698 – the only time he ever returned to the island – but he was behind schedule and had no time to linger or enquire about his lost friends, still held captive in Kandy.

They remained, however, in the forefront of his thoughts and when he came to Cochin in south west India in December he thought all the more about them when he encountered there one of the former Dutch captives held on Ceylon, a Captain Cornelius Blicklant. They reminisced about their life on the island and Blicklant told Knox what news he had of the remaining captives. He also offered to send a letter to them if Knox wished to write one, through the Dutch authorities on Ceylon. Knox eagerly took up this opportunity and wrote the following letter which he carefully copied out for himself as well and later included in his autobiography.

To all my fellow prisoners and Lo[ving] Countrey-men on Zelone
Mr John Merginson, Mr William Vassall & Mr Tho. March etc
    Lo[ving] Brethren
    I am Sencible you heard of my safe arrival with Stephen Rutland to the Dutch. . . . We had passage in theire ships to Batavia & came in an English Ship from Bantam to London . . . The English Company put me in Command of a small ship of 200 tunes [the *Tonqueen Merchant*] presently & Stephen went with mee the first voiage, but he followed his old Course of Drinking that we parted when [we] came home & since he is dead . . . I was 4 Voiages

Commander to India in the ship Called the Tonqueen & then I left her God haveing blessed me with Successe & being a time of Warr with france for 9 years. 4 years I stayed on shore till the wars was ended & came out Commander of this ship Called the Mary 500 tuns with above 100 men, in May last 1698, bound for Suratt.

Mr Merginson's wife was Married to a Capt of a man of warr but dead before I came to England. Mr Marches wife was long living after my first arrivall but now is dead; his son hath bin Commander of an East India ship of 600 tuns but foundered by leakes coming home, & since he died ... but his sister is yet alive as is Mr Merginsons sister. Mr Vassalls Brother I saw at my first arrivall, but since hee & his father are dead. I know little of the Relations of the rest.

In anno 1692 I saw a letter from Zelone at fort St George mentioning that you are but 11 living. I have often mentioned your Case to the English East India Company but without effectt, therefore I advise you to rely onely upon God who worketh all things after the Councell of his owne will. & Consider the difficulty of aged persons to get a living ... now in England. I doubte not you will take this not well, but I assure you if you ware within my reach you should not have cause to say I have forgott my fellow Captives.

The Circumstances of which Captivity during my time I have published in print ... I find a man in his Native Country amonge his Relations is not free from trouble, many of which I was free from whilst on Zelone, in so much that I still Continew a single man. I ... heere with send my picture [a miniature of the Robert White engraving] to the Girll I brought up, Lucea, and you know I loved the Child & since have no cause to hate her.*

We have had a Strainge Change of governments in England since you left it, as King Charles the 2nd, James the 2nd who is now living in france & flead from his throne & now happie under King William the 3rd, Prince of Orange and at present all Chrisendom is at peace. Capt Blickland ... now heere [at Cochin] hath promised mee to

---

* Knox probably wishes to indicate here that he has had no more children who could have displaced Lucea in his heart.

indeavior to Convey this [letter] to you, which I wish may come to any of your hands, praying God to Comfort & Suport you all, Committ you to his protection & Rest.

    I am & shall be your most
    affectionate & true friend R K

Cochin Rode
one board ship Mary
the 12th Decembr 1698[14]

We have no way of knowing if this heartfelt letter ever reached its intended recipients, and if it did, whether it brought comfort – or more despair – to them with its news of remarried wives and dead loved ones. The world they had left behind in 1659, Knox tells them, has moved on and forgotten them. Home is no longer home and if they returned they would be as strangers in a strange land. This letter was Knox's only recorded attempt to reach out across the years to his fellow captives and the child Lucea – now a grown woman – whom he had 'loved well', and to tell them that life was probably better for them in Ceylon than if they had returned to England as he had.

We know little more of this voyage on the *Mary* because as an interloper its movements and fate weren't recorded in the East India Company records. Knox himself drily dismissed it by saying 'the voiage in the ship Mary to East India, which seemed so much to my satisfaction before I went to Sea, proved otherwise . . . for although by Gods good providence we went well out & Came as well home, yet could not make our first mony we sent out in the ship'. In other words, he invested more in the voyage than he earned back in his private trade and returned home poorer than he was when he departed.

The failure of this last voyage was, he said, solely the fault of the ship's supercargo, a 'great and haughty' man named Thomas Lucas who decided which ports to call at and how long to remain in them. On the *Tonqueen Merchant*, Knox had been both Captain and supercargo, so he had been in complete control of the ship in port as well as at sea. Knox says that Lucas had formerly been a factor for the East India Company but had been sacked 'for some

Action he had Committed'. Lucas proved as disreputable or at least as inefficient as a supercargo and Knox ascribed his own losses on this voyage to Lucas's ineptitude, hostility (Knox accused him of trying to turn his crew against him) and mismanagement. Indeed, Knox felt complete contempt for Lucas who he describes as so uncouth that at table he ate with a horn-handled knife and an iron fork whereas Knox's cutlery was all silver.[15]

When Knox returned from this unprofitable voyage on the *Mary* in 1700, he retired for good. He was now nearly sixty. He was still, as he said, 'well in health' and he had 'wharewith [the wherewithal] to live plentifully without goeing any more to Sea'. Now, he says, that God has blessed him with 'a Competencie & I come to the evening of my age', he intends to settle down '& injoy it in my Native Country of England & thare to end my dayes'.[16] He reflects too on how his life has fallen into twenty-year segments which made it all the more fitting that he retire after twenty years at sea. As he wrote in his autobiography, his childhood and young adulthood – before he was taken captive on Ceylon – lasted twenty years. Then he was confined on the island for nearly twenty years, and after he escaped in 1680, he spent the best part of twenty years as a sea captain. Now it was time to rest, and to reflect.

How, then, did Defoe use all this information from Knox when he came to write *Captain Singleton*? He didn't reproduce Knox's adventures sequentially in the novel. Instead, he appropriated a number of key events, actions and locales and then rearranged and refashioned them into an entirely new narrative which nevertheless was largely derived from episodes in Knox's life.

Bob Singleton, however, comes from a very different background from Knox's: he is a rootless, picaro sort of hero. As a very young boy he is abducted from his real family by a child-snatcher and sold to a beggar woman and then to a gypsy and various other foster-parents until he is taken in hand by a kindly sea captain. After several voyages, this captain dies and Bob ends up with a band of Portuguese seamen who are accused of plotting a mutiny on Madagascar because they'd been kept on 'short rations'. Insufficient food, of course, was said to be the reason why Knox's men mutinied and ran off with his ship at St Helena. After their mutiny fails, Bob and his mates are marooned on the same stretch of Madagascar's west coast where Knox had been held captive by King Rybassa. Singleton and his men are treated kindly and generously by the Madagascar natives, just as Knox and the other captives are well cared for by the Sinhalese on Ceylon.

Next, Singleton and his Portuguese sailors build a boat, pursue other vessels, and after they have captured a sufficiently large one, they sail in it from Madagascar to Africa. Their plan then is to trek across the entire continent from the west to the east coast, ending up at a Dutch or English settlement and then making their way back to England by sea. Before they set off on their African march, they fashion shoes for themselves out of animal skins with the hair turned inwards just as Knox and Rutland had made footgear for themselves before their escape from Kandy.

In his scrupulous study of Defoe's novels, Arthur Wellesley Secord concluded that Defoe didn't base Singleton's trek across Africa on a particular historical or fictional source.[17] But Singleton's journey is remarkably similar to two separate treks in Knox's *Historical Relation*: his account of the captives' initial march into the interior of Ceylon to Kandy after their capture at Trincomolee, and then his escape nineteen years later from Kandy with Stephen Rutland to the Dutch fort of Mannar on the coast of Ceylon, from where Knox and Rutland eventually return to England.

Early on in their march across Africa, Singleton and his men enslave a number of natives to carry their luggage for them, just as Knox's Sinhalese captors carried the luggage of the captured men from the *Anne*. Singleton in particular is well served by a handsome Black Prince who is reminiscent of both Crusoe's Friday and Knox's faithful servant, the 'black Boy', in the *Historical Relation.*

In the middle of their epic march, Singleton and his band come across the arresting sight of a white man who has 'gone native' in the heart of the continent.[18] Like Knox on Ceylon, this man is scarcely recognisable as an Englishman. He is completely naked (Knox wore a loincloth on Ceylon but was otherwise unclothed). Also like Knox, the Englishman's long hair covers his back while his beard covers his chest. His skin is deeply tanned or, as Defoe puts it, 'discoloured'. He speaks the Africans' language and after joining Singleton and his men he serves as their guide and interpreter. He also knows the terrain and geography of the country and in particular where to find gold dust, gold nuggets and ivory. Thus with their new guide, Singleton and the others proceed to enrich themselves as they make their way across Africa.

As they travel, they learn the curious story of this Englishman (who is never named) and it is remarkably similar to Knox's on Ceylon. He had been taken captive by natives on the east coast of Africa where he had worked as a trader. Then he was passed from 'landlord' to 'landlord', or tribe to tribe, within Africa until he found himself in the middle of the continent. Though he was prevented from escaping, he was treated kindly and generously by his captors, just as Knox was by the Sinhalese. Despite his wild appearance, he is a gentleman from London who speaks Latin, French and Italian but not Portuguese (which Knox learned on Ceylon).

After they have plundered rivers for gold in the interior, crossed a vast desert and collected huge amounts of ivory, Singleton and his men, together with the Englishman, come out at a Dutch settlement on the east coast of Africa, just as Knox and Rutland completed their escape from Kandy when they arrived at the Dutch fort at Mannar. From here they all sail back to England – except for the wild Englishman who is no longer needed for the plot, so Defoe dispenses with him. The Englishman sends his wealth home before his own departure and then dies of grief when he learns that it has all been lost at sea.

With Singleton's return to England, the first half of *Captain Singleton* comes to an end. Bob soon squanders all his riches in London and then takes to the sea again and turns pirate. The second half of the novel is devoted to an episodic relation of his criminal adventures at sea. Unlike Knox's post-Ceylon voyage as a privateer, Singleton's pirate career is largely successful. However, it is striking how closely Knox's voyages on the *Tonqueen Merchant* and the *Mary* coincide with Singleton's piratical journeys. It's as if Defoe lifted the map of Knox's travels and used it as his fictional hero's route from Madagascar to the East Indies, the Spice Islands and China.

Not only does Singleton turn pirate, he is soon involved – as Knox was on two of his voyages – in slave trading as well. But first another important character – one of the few in the novel to have a name

– is introduced into the narrative. This is a genial, rational, good-natured Quaker surgeon named William Walters who has no compunction about joining the pirates when his own ship is captured. But he does ask Singleton to provide him with a document stating that he was forced to become a member of their company, so that if they are caught he will be pardoned. William is crafty but he is also a good-hearted, humane man who soon becomes Singleton's spiritual and moral mentor.

He first assumes this role when they capture a slave ship with '600 Negroes, Men and Women, Boys and Girls, and not one Christian or White Man on board'. To Singleton's horror, they soon realise that 'these black Devils had got loose, had murthered all the white Men and thrown them into the Sea'. The thought of this so enrages Singleton's crew that he has 'much ado to keep my Men from cutting them [the Negroes] in pieces'. But William calmly intervenes and 'with many Perswasions' prevails upon the crew 'by telling them that it [the murder of the slave traders] was nothing but what, if they were in the Negroes Condition, they would do . . . and that the Negroes had really the highest Injustice done them to be sold for Slaves without their Consent; and that the Law of Nature dictated it [killing the slave traders] to them'.

Instead of murdering the slaves, Singleton takes custody of all six hundred of them, and William makes a diversionary trip to Batavia where he sells all the slaves 'in less than five weeks . . . and sold the Ship' as well, and all 'at a very good Price too'.[19] Astonishingly, Defoe is either oblivious to or untroubled by the contradiction of having William defend the slaves' right to rise against their masters and then having him blithely sell the slaves himself.*

More borrowings from Knox follow. At the Cape of Good Hope, Singleton and his men come upon eighteen sailors who have run away from their 'severe' Captain who had 'starved' them and 'used them like Dogs'. This is so similar to the testimony given against Knox at the inquiry into the mutiny of his men on St Helena that it's hard not to think that Defoe had this affair in mind. When Singleton returns to Madagascar, he encounters a pirate named Captain Wilmot and also the legendary pirate Captain Avery, who

---

* In his non-fiction writing on slavery, Defoe called for the humane treatment of slaves, but he never denounced the slave trade itself.

have taken the Great Mogul's ship (as Knox was given orders to do on his privateering voyage) and its treasure of 200,000 pieces of eight.

After a series of further adventures, Singleton and his pirates finally arrive at Ceylon. Here they engage in a pitched battle with a 'Savage Army' of natives, and then run aground. An old Dutchman (formerly a captive but now an employee of the native King) and the native King's General try to decoy them ashore. Defoe here lifts the crucial 'captivation' episode from Knox's *Historical Relation*, but William has heard of Knox's story and how the men from the *Anne* were lured onshore at Trincomolee and 'beguiled by the Barbarians, and inticed to come on Shore, just as we were invited to do . . . and they surrounded [them] . . . and never suffered them to return, but kept them Prisoners . . . [and they were] never heard of afterwards, except the Captain's Son, who miraculously made his Escape after twenty Years'.[20]

Another pitched battle with the natives follows when Singleton's men resist entrapment, and firing into the thick of them 'six or seven times, five Guns at a time . . . with Iron, Musquet Bullets Etc', they make 'Havock of them and killed and Wounded Abundance of them', and then sail off.

Singleton then introduces the long passage Defoe plagiarised from Knox's *Historical Relation* with the following paragraph:

> This Passage [recounting Singleton's adventures on Ceylon], when I related it to a Friend of mine, after my Return from those Rambles, agreed so well with his Relation of what happened to one Mr Knox, an English Captain, who some time ago was decoyed on Shore by those People, that it could not but be very much to my Satisfaction to think what Mischief we had all escaped; and I think it cannot but be very profitable to record the other [ie, Knox's] Story . . . with my own, to shew, whoever reads this, what it was I avoided, and prevent their falling into the like, if they have to do with the perfidous People of Ceylon.[21]

Defoe then quotes, or more accurately plagiarises, directly from the 1681 edition of Knox's *Historical Relation*. He copies, almost word for word, large chunks of Knox's narrative between pages 117 and 165, inserting, here and there, brief linking passages to stitch the long extracts together. Eight pages of *Captain Singleton* come straight out of Knox's book.

But Defoe makes two important modifications to Knox's text. He changes the narrative voice from first to third person with the effect that his condensed version seems less personal and immediate. Even more importantly, although he describes the death of Knox's father and how Knox was forced to bury him with his own hands, Defoe entirely omits the dying promise that Captain Knox exacts from his son: the pledge that he will return to England, tell his brother and sister of their father's fate and take care of them in his father's stead. In other words, Defoe deleted what became Knox's primary motivation during all the years of his captivity. This is a crucial omission, and if Defoe left it out because he failed to grasp the significance of Knox's promise, he missed the key element of his story. Defoe borrowed Knox's plot but remained oblivious or indifferent to its underlying motivation and meaning. Knox's pledge to his dying father seals his fate: his life on Ceylon henceforth will be dedicated to returning to England and caring for his brother and sister.

Singleton, in contrast, seems entirely lacking in motivation: he goes, literally, where the winds and chance and fate take him. He has no purpose or mission in life other than to live it to the full. Despite all his borrowings in *Captain Singleton*, Defoe created a hero who couldn't have been less like the serious, dedicated Robert Knox.

The novel ends with Singleton and Quaker William's overland caravan journey back to England, disguised as Armenian merchants. By now they are very rich and William persuades Singleton to give up piracy and indeed even honest trading to retire and do good with their ill-gotten wealth. In what would become a stock feature of most of Defoe's fiction, the hero repents and settles down to a contented and happy old age.

These end-of-novel repentances rarely seem convincing to modern readers and Singleton, perhaps the most rootless and amoral of all of Defoe's heroes, is also the least convincing of his penitents. But subjected as he is to William's persuasive exhortations, Bob eventually embraces his mentor's message of redemption — to such an extent that he becomes, for a time (and somewhat unconvincingly), guilt-ridden and even suicidal. But William persuades him that though he may not be able to make restitution to those he has wronged, he can yet do good in the world and help others. Upon returning to London, Singleton marries William's destitute widowed sister and cares for her and her four children, among other unspecified good works. And thus the novel concludes with Singleton and William living together as brothers with William's sister (now Singleton's wife) and her children in a fine house outside London.

Any reader of Knox's autobiography will be struck by the fact that when William and Singleton return to London, they don't cut their hair or beards, nor do they ever shed their disguise as Armenian merchants. On Knox's escape from Kandy and long journey back to England, he gradually transformed himself back into an Englishman. First the Dutch gave him European clothing at Colombo, then he cut off his long hair and beard in Batavia. When he finally reached London he shaved off his remaining 'old fashioned' whiskers. By increments, then, Knox converted himself from a 'wild man' back into a civilised Englishman.

Singleton and Quaker William, in contrast, make no attempt to resume their old identities. When they decide to return to England they are disguised as Armenian merchants, and when they finally reach London, they continue to wear the traditional garb of such traders, including their long silk vests. The two men don't even speak to each other in English in the presence of others. Ostensibly they maintain their disguise because of their criminal pasts as pirates. But they are also creating a new life for themselves rather than taking up an old one. Singleton, indeed, explains to William how he had never really been an Englishman in the first place:

> I speak English; but I came out of England as a Child, and never was in it but once since I was a Man, and then I was cheated and imposed upon, and used so ill I care not if I ever see it more.
>
> Why hast thou no relations or Friends there, says he [William], no Acquaintance, none that thou hast any Kindness for, or any remains of Respect for?
>
> Not I William, said I, not one, no more than I have in the Court of the Great Mogul.

Nor any Kindness for the Countrey, where thou wast born, says William.

Not I, any more than for the Island of Madagascar, not so much neither, for that has been a fortunate Island to me more than once.[22]

In contrast to William and Singleton's new identities in London, when Knox first came back from Ceylon he expected to recover his family, his old life and his home. But the world had moved on during his long absence. His sister 'starts from' him; his brother soon dies. He makes new friends such as Robert Hooke and finds a patron in Sir Josiah Child, but as Knox's 1698 letter to his friends in Ceylon shows, he never really settled, much less recovered his pre-captive English existence. Instead, he returns to the sea for the next twenty years. During this time, if Knox had any sense of belonging to a particular place — of a home — it was probably to the ship he commanded, the *Tonqueen Merchant*, and to the sea. The ship was his house and his men were his family which is why the mutiny at St Helena felt like such a betrayal to him.

Defoe seems to have understood the impossibility of recovering a lost home but not to have felt or grasped the loss and sadness of this impossibility. Defoe's heroes are forward-looking, action men. They don't ruminate or write long reflective letters to old friends. Where Knox saw loss, Defoe glimpsed a new beckoning life ahead. Defoe's heroes and heroines, for the most part, 'have it all' at the end, and this complete success and their 'happily ever after' lives are crucial elements of the survivor myth. For Crusoe and his later incarnations, there is no isolation or abiding sense of loss late in life, no looking back on what they had and lost in the course of their 'lives of wonder'.[23]

For all their similarity, then, Defoe's books depart fundamentally from Knox's. He missed the point of Knox's story. He stuck closely to its events and facts — the storms and shipwrecks, the geography and islands — but not to its lessons, moral, or meaning. There is no sad undertow in Crusoe's story or in Bob Singleton's, no 'idle and dronish life' in London upon returning from voyages, no yearning for a lost land, time and people. There isn't the bachelor solitude, the eclipse of the author, the forgetfulness of a once admiring world.

For Knox, all these are what lie ahead of him when, in 1700, he retires from the sea after his last voyage on the interloper *Mary*: a kind of posthumous life. When Defoe published his three Crusoe books and *Captain Singleton* he was not yet midway through his startling career as a novelist – a career all the more astonishing because it occurred during the seventh decade of his life.

And yet there is a striking similarity between these two men when they reach their sixties. Although Knox retires from his long career as a sea captain while Defoe is just getting into the swing of his as a novelist, they both spend their sixties writing books about 'strange surprising adventures'. And Crusoe and Singleton are approximately Defoe's own age when they write their stories in retirement. Knox, too, is in his sixties when he retires and devotes his days to writing and rewriting his *Historical Relation* and autobiography. Dissimilar as Defoe's heroes are from Knox, they, too, prolong and perpetuate their past lives by recording them in their books. In the end, it is these books which are the only real survivors.

CHAPTER TWELVE

Ancient Mariners

2 March 1703, 'about 11 or 12 of the Clocke'.[1] Robert Knox was asleep when the loud knock at the door roused the household. The servant and Mrs Bartlett hurried down the corridor to her lodger's rooms, followed by the girl who'd come to fetch him. It was Mr Hooke's maidservant. Her master was dying. Captain Knox was to come quickly.

Robert Hooke, fully clothed, his hair hanging lank on either side of his long, bony face, lay cold and grey on his bed by the time Knox and the girl got to his rooms at Gresham College. They'd arrived too late. Hooke, aged '67 Years, 7 Months and 13 Days' – but looking much older and more shrivelled than his years – was stone dead.[2] It was past midnight; the fire had gone out and the room where he lay was dark and chill. Only when they had lit candles could Knox take in the disorder and squalor of the chamber. Hooke had been bedridden for months, during which time he'd rarely washed or changed his clothes. A compulsive hoarder until the end, the room where he lay contained a chaotic jumble of books and papers, scientific instruments and personal effects (clothing, the remains of meals, bottles of physic). At the foot of his bed stood a large iron chest, heavily padlocked, which contained all his wealth, some £8,000. Rumours had long circulated about the vast amount of Hooke's hoard. Terrified that he would outlive his means, for many years he had begrudged every last penny and practised all manner of absurd economies, noting in his diary exactly how much he spent on a cup of chocolate or dish of coffee at Garraway's or Jonathan's; reluctantly parting with the paltry wage he paid his one maidservant 'who to judge from the way colleagues referred to her was far from being a suitable servant for a man of his standing'.[3]

Knox sent the girl to fetch Hooke's long-time assistant Harry Hunt, and when he came, the two men 'layed out [Hooke's] body in his Cloaths, Goune & Shooes as he Died, & [then] sealed up all the Doores of his apartment with my Seale & so left them'.[4] Sealing the rooms was a precaution against theft when word of Hooke's death got out, for it was no secret that the eccentric old man would leave, in Knox's words, 'a very Considerable Estate all in Mony besides some Lands, yet notwithstanding he lived Miserably as if he had not sufficient to afford him foode and Rayment'.[5]

Three days later Hooke was buried at the medieval church of St Helen's in London. It was, according to Knox, 'a Noble funeral giving Rings and gloves and Wine to all his friends thare, which ware a great Number'.[6] Hooke's friend and first biographer, Richard Waller, concurred that it was an occasion worthy of the man: 'all the Members of the Royal Society then in Town attending his Body to the Grave, paying the Respect due to his Extraordinary Merit'.[7]

Despite the crowd at his funeral and the fine words said of the deceased, in his last years Hooke had driven away nearly all his old friends and associates. He had been querulous and crotchety even in his prime and long dependent on a variety of stimulants and sedatives that made his temper volatile and unpredictable. In his later years, Hooke had managed to antagonise almost everyone, objecting, whenever a new scientific observation, discovery or invention was made, that he himself had already revealed or devised it years earlier. In old age, he'd also become paranoid, suspicious, argumentative and excessively mean. Robert Knox was one of the few who could abide his presence and thus it was fitting that, when he knew he was dying, Hooke sent for his old friend to be by his side as he made his way out of the world.[8] In the end, though, he had died alone.

Knox had returned from his last sea voyage and retired for good nearly three years earlier, in May 1700, when he had taken rooms with the Bartlett family in the London parish of St Peter le Poer. Susannah Bartlett was widowed shortly after the new lodger moved in, and with her husband gone, the household consisted of the forty-five-year-old widow, her four children and the sixty-year-old Knox. Under the circumstances, it was an advantageous arrangement for everyone concerned. Knox had a small plot of his own in the back garden, and he dined with the Bartletts who became a kind of surrogate family. Knox, in turn, provided Susannah with much needed income to raise her children.

He had no immediate family of his own remaining. His brother had died shortly after Knox returned from Ceylon, and he'd learned of his sister's death some seven years earlier when he was at sea. While away on his last voyage on the interloper *Mary*, Knox's one-time patron and director of the East India Company, Josiah Child, had died and so too had Knox's first cousin James Bonnell. The only members of his mother's family still alive were Knox's elderly aunt Ann Colman and her brother Toby Bonnell. And the only one left of his own generation was his cousin John Strype, who, along with Hooke, had encouraged and edited Knox's book.

Even before he retired, then, Knox's world had begun to shrink as his family and friends died one by one. Hooke's death, in particular, was for him the end of an era. Josiah Child had made Knox a sea captain and it had pained Knox acutely to fall out with him and leave the East India Company in the mid-1790s. But Hooke had been an even greater presence in his life after he returned from Ceylon, for it was Hooke who had edited, overseen and arranged the publication of Knox's *Historical Relation of Ceylon* and then encouraged and promoted Knox's careful collection of specimens from, and information about, the remote places he visited. Hooke was the only person who had fully appreciated both Knox's experience as a captive on Ceylon and the material that he gathered on his later voyages.

After he retired Knox needn't have been without a family. He had the opportunity, in fact, to settle down with a wife of his own. His cousin James Bonnell's widow, Jane, when she had word of Knox's return from his last voyage, wrote with more than cursory interest to John Strype for news of him. Knox had scarcely arrived back in London, in fact, when Jane Bonnell told Strype: 'I would be glad to here [sic] of Capt Knoxes safe arrivell or what account [you have] of him.' Jane had not met Knox herself but she professed herself 'concerned' for this relation of her late husband, who she said, 'methinks I partly know [because] I have read his history' and seen 'his picter' – presumably the 1695 Robert White portrait.[9]

Jane Bonnell was stranded in Dublin where her husband had been accountant-general and collector of customs. They had been married only seven years when James Bonnell died in 1699, leaving Jane with two young children to bring up on her own. Captain Knox of course was a well-to-do, newly retired bachelor. He had a reputation for piety approaching that of her devout late husband, who Jane always refers to in her letters as her 'Departed Saint'. Thus Jane Bonnell's interest in Knox had an ulterior motive, as her next letter to Strype makes clear. She had been greatly alarmed by the news of robbers in her Dublin neighbourhood. These apparently were adept London criminals who, she told Strype, had 'a dextrous art of going down chimneys with so little noyse that even those in the roome cannot here [sic] them'. The robbers had broken into several of her neighbours' homes and Jane, who lived with just her children and a servant, was being 'much presst by . . . friends to get a man to ly [stay] in the house'.[10] Like any other relatively young widow of her day, Jane was in need of a husband – to help raise her children, enhance her financial position and give her the protection of a safe home. From what she had heard of him from her husband and what she knew herself from reading his Ceylon book, Knox must have seemed an ideal candidate.

Jane, however, was soon disappointed in her hopes, and jumped to her own conclusions when she heard that Knox had settled with the Bartlett family in St Peter le Poer. In January 1701, she wrote to Strype: 'I admire [am surprised] Capt Knox has never bin to see you. I doubt [guess] he is soe taken up with his Land Lady that he cares for noe body else.' Jane had taken it into her head that Knox had formed an attachment to Susannah Bartlett, which in fact he had, though not of the sort Jane insinuates. But Jane also had another grievance against Knox; James Bonnell had come to the aid of their impoverished elderly relatives, Ann Colman and Toby Bonnell, and this was one burden of her widowhood that Jane was keen to turn over entirely to Knox. 'If he comes to see you,' she wrote to Strype, 'it would be charactably [sic] done of you to say something to induce him to be kind in giving some addition to old uncle Bonnell and Aunt Coleman, they have had from me in a year & three quarters beside their twenty pounds a year promast, above £31 which . . . really is more than I am able to continue doing, but while the Capt was away I thought I would streaten [sic] myself to supply their necessities.'[11]

Knox, however, was already sending money to both Ann Colman and Toby Bonnell and he faithfully continued to do so. Nevertheless, Jane Bonnell kept up her complaints in her next letter to Strype: 'what is our good natured complaisant Cosen Knox doing,' she sarcastically enquired. 'I here poor old Aunt Coleman is dead & I hope he will be kinder to our Uncle . . . I have had considerable losses in my portion this year by the fall of our money in this Kingdom [Ireland].' Knox, in fact, took care of both his uncle and aunt in their old age and arranged and paid for their funerals after they died. His earliest entries in his autobiography after he returned from his last voyage are:

June the 14, 1701. This day Ann Colman, my owne Mothers sister Died, being about 86 yeares old. Her husband left her a poore widow [so] that Cosen James Bonnell & I were faint to Maintaine her several yeares. I buried her where she had desired of me by her husband in Algate Churchyard. The whole charges came to £3.4.

December the 22 Anno 1701. Toby Bonnell, my mothers owne Brother died; he was 83 yeares. He was in low Circumstances [so] that I & Cousen James Bonnell ware faint to maintaine him many yeares . . . He was the last of my Mothers family.'[12]

Jane Bonnell didn't just seek news of Knox through John Strype. She also wrote to Knox directly, and she was far from pleased by the reply he sent back. We don't have their exchange of letters but Jane waspishly referred to them in her communications to Strype, writing in late March 1702 that 'indeed Capt Knoxes Rudeness in his letter did not at all move my resentment. I rather pittied his ill manners & unjust aspersion of me . . . I have suffered too much to let such trifles ruffle me, but I thought it was necessary to let him know bulling and abusive treatment should not provoke my charity, & indeed I had given so much to that poor old cupple in his absence that I could not continue an addition to wt [what] was promast without suffering for it.'[13] Seven months later, in another letter to Strype, who had conveyed news of Knox to Jane, she is still aggrieved: 'I thank you for yur account of Capt Knox. I assure you I am very glad to here of his wellfear [welfare], for such trifles as his rude letter never sticks with me. If he be naturally rude & unpolish'd it would be unreasonable in me to expect that he should change his nature on my account.'[14]

Knox wasn't rude, but he was straight-talking and he had rejected Jane Bonnell's romantic overtures and also firmly informed her of his own generous charity to Aunt Colman and Uncle Toby. But there is nothing like a woman scorned. In her disappointment, Jane devoted herself to commissioning a biography of her late husband and when it was published in 1703 she sent copies of it to London for both Strype and Knox and wrote to Strype, 'pray enquire if it [the biography] be delivered & when you see him [Knox], ask how he likes it. I wish he were like that dear Saint [her late husband] & surely thats the best wish I can wish.'[15]

It wasn't only elderly relatives such as Aunt Colman and Uncle Bonnell that Knox helped when he retired. He also paid for the education of several young boys and sponsored their careers at sea, including Susannah Bartlett's son Benjamin. Knox saw as well to the education of John Harrison, a nephew of John Strype, who Knox sent to study with his old navigation teacher Mr Colson. Knox was clearly fond of this boy and looked upon him as an adopted son, writing to Strype that he was 'witty & sharp; & although somewhat wild, not ye worse to make a saylour, his mother hath bin with me to thanke me, I told her if I live he is at my Care & should not be any more chargeable to her'. In other words, Knox was taking over all financial responsibility for the boy.[16] And when young Harrison completed his studies, Knox placed him with a 'very good Master' or ship's captain so that he could follow in Knox's footsteps and go to sea. On the eve of his first voyage Harrison wrote to his benefactor:

I am now onboard her Majs [Majesty's] Ship the *Severn* in the Downs bound for Verginia [sic], my Capt has made me a midshipman and I hope by gods goodness to improve my selfe so as to Qualify me for better Busines having all [the] Instruments fitting for that Purpose ... I doe not know how to Retaliat [return] the many favors you Dayly heap upon my poore Mother, and hoping Sr, by my constant Zeal for your person and Long Life I may at my Returne Pay you a hartfelt acknowledgmt of These great Favours.[17]

This letter also indicates that Knox was helping John Harrison's widowed mother, Rebecca Harrison. Sadly, the young man never returned. Two years later Knox had the melancholy task of writing to Strype with the news that young Harrison had died in America. Knox was continuing to provide his poor widowed mother 'with subsistence' but Knox didn't have the heart to tell her of her son's death and he asked Strype to speak to her as he was in a better position to commiserate, Strype having himself recently lost one of his children.

Other than his allusions to friends and family Knox says very little of his retired life in his autobiography. He continued to make regular, diary-like entries, but these were usually about extreme weather conditions and the public events of the day. Some eight months after Robert Hooke's death, on 27 November 1703, Knox wrote of the great storm that engulfed south-west England that day:

> At aboute one this morning began a very violent Storme of wind aboute WS.W. & SW. It so frighted many people that they durst not lay in theire beds . . . and many Chumnies were blown downe which . . . Broake through . . . roofes & killed . . . people; it blew the tiles off from many houses . . . & nere 20 sailes of the Queenes Marchant Ships were lost, 4 on the Goodwind Sands besides many Marchants Ships and thousands of men.[18]

Daniel Defoe, newly released from Newgate Prison, immediately began investigating the devastation and ruin left in the storm's wake for his documentary book *The Great Storm*. Defoe prowled the streets of London, surveying the ruined houses, piles of roof tiles strewn on the roads, and the smashed wherries and boats on the Thames. Then he got on his horse and went to Kent, counting felled trees and drowned cattle, toppled chimneys and collapsed buildings. This was history in the making and Defoe's book captured with detailed immediacy the storm's tremendous visitation, not just in London but throughout the whole region it battered.

Knox, in contrast, sat tight in the Bartletts' house in St Peter le Poer, but he read all the contemporary news accounts of the great storm, and in his mind's eye he imagined and recorded the terrific havoc it wrought at sea — the ships that foundered in the tempest and all the lives lost. Landlocked in London, over the next seventeen years Knox carefully recorded every major storm that occurred in England and the destruction these brought to those at sea. Two years later, he described how in 'August 1705 on Saturday 11th at aboute one in the Morning began a violent Storme between S & SW the extremity lasted . . . tell [sic] daylight in which about 30 saile of ships were lost at Portsmouth [where] . . . just arrived a large fleete from Barbados . . . of which 8 ware lost & many others Cut theire Masts; Likewise at Newcastle many Ships were lost'. In 1706, he noted how the naval fleet under Admiral Sir Cloudsley Shovell 'met with a violent storme . . . and Contrary winds that scattered and separated' the fleet's ships on the way to Lisbon.[19] But far worse befell the great naval hero the following year. Knox recorded in his autobiography how Shovell, returning from Gibraltar on his ship HMS *Association,* 'on the 22 October Anno 1707 aboute 8 at night . . . fell in on the Rocks of Silly where' Shovell and the 'whole ships Company ware drownded & not one man escaped'.[20]

In his retirement Knox was marooned in St Peter le Poer but he closely followed and wrote of the terrific force of these and other storms at sea. His diary-like entries in his *Autobiography* concern all sorts of extreme weather conditions, including the great freeze of the winter of 1708–9 when the Thames was turned into a thoroughfare of ice. Knox also logged public events such as Marlborough's victory at Ramilies in 1710, the death of the Dauphin in France of smallpox in 1711, Sir Hovendon Walker's expedition to Canada, and the explosion of the seventy-tonne ship *Edgar* at Portsmouth 'with 500 men and women one board & not one escaped'.

Knox rarely wrote, however, of his own life in London or what he did to fill his days. He omits all mention, for example, of sitting for his oil portrait by the artist P. Trampon in 1708. Knox was approaching seventy: the biblical three score and ten. He knew his end could come at any time. The imposing portrait of Knox, surrounded by the paraphernalia of the sea captain he had been, was — like his autobiography — done for posterity. Knox was preparing for that time. This helps to explain the pervasive and curious impersonality of the later sections of his autobiography. The truth was that his retirement had turned into a kind of afterlife. He helped indigent relatives, sponsored young men who went to sea, took daily walks on Hackney Marsh, read the newspapers and carefully documented the weather; if it was good, he pottered in his garden at the Bartletts'.

The infrequent glimpses we get of Knox's retired life in London come from his letters to John Strype in which he writes of his various ailments and asks after Strype's health. He also writes repeatedly that he would like to see Strype more often. Knox knew that his cousin came to London regularly to meet with his antiquarian friends, but Strype was either too busy, or found Knox's company too tiresome, to drop in on him often at the Bartletts'. On one occasion when he did call, Knox was out and this missed visit provoked Knox to write him a sharp reprimanding note:

> I am sorry I was not at home when you came since you spared so much time as to come to my Lodging; when I goe to see you I sett a whole day apart for that purpose & I am at ye charge of dubble Coach hire, for now I am past walking so far whare as one peny post letter would have found me at home, if you had thought it worth yor while, we two being the onely old Relations living of yt generation. Should my occasions call me so often to come to your towne (as yours doe you to come to mine) & not call in to see you I should think my selfe very unkind to you; we being both so well stricken in age yt we cannot long expect to be in this World. God grant us a happie meeting whare time will be everlasting.[21]

But Knox wanted a visit in this world before their reunion in Eternity, so he was both chagrined and keenly disappointed to have missed Strype on this occasion.

In his letters to John Strype we can see too that Knox spent much of his retirement working on his two books – the long-deferred second edition of his *Historical Relation of Ceylon* and his autobiography. His publisher no longer offered encouragement for, or even interest in, another edition of the Ceylon book, which over the years had grown into a vast compendium of information and recollection – all of it fascinating but, as Knox himself admitted, repetitive and arranged 'without method'. Daniel Midwinter, who had replaced Richard Chiswell as publisher upon the latter's death, informed Knox that republication at present was impossible because of the prohibitively high price of paper. The first 1681 edition was long out of print, and now there was no mistaking that plans for a second edition had been suspended indefinitely. Even when Knox asked Strype to speak to Midwinter on his behalf – Midwinter also published several of Strype's ecclesiastical works – there was no indication that the second edition of his Ceylon book would ever be published. But Knox took the long view. Though there was no prospect of a reprint of the *Historical Relation* coming out any time soon, he continued to believe that his book on Ceylon and his autobiography were, as he said in one letter to Strype, 'ye onely thing [which] will keepe my name in memory in ye world'.[22]

Deferred publication, then, didn't discourage Knox from adding more material to his 'bookes'. He still possessed two separate interleaved copies of the *Historical Relation*: the 'second edition' copy that had been submitted and resubmitted to his publisher – and periodically sent to Strype – with its vast number of revisions and additions, and the other interleaved copy in which he wrote his autobiography on the blank leaves before and after the printed text. But after Knox retired, the distinction between these two volumes blurred as he indiscriminately added more and more passages in both copies.

This curious muddle of what had originally been two separate writing projects reflected how the present and the past had merged in Knox's mind. It also showed that the uneventfulness of his retired life was overshadowed, even overtaken, by his vivid memories of and reflections on his past. The personal passages of Knox's autobiography, written after he retired in 1700, dwell on his long-ago experiences on Ceylon, not his current life in London. Throughout the first decade of his retirement from the sea, he inserted a great deal of new material about Ceylon, including an account of his friend John Loveland's death, general information about how he lived on the island, details of his clothing, hair, beard, diet and sleeping habits. And as Knox reviewed his bygone life on Ceylon, it seemed to become in his eyes, and in his written account, more and more healthy, happy, comfortable and desirable. The Ceylon existence he writes of in the 1700s in his rooms in the Bartletts' house is a sun-filled, idyllic life stripped to essentials. 'I was never better in health and ease of body,' he says, 'than when I went in Indian dresse, barefoot, with a clout wrapt about my body.' Forgetting that on Ceylon he had been a young man in his prime, while he was now a man in his sixties, Knox marvels how he slept so much better on his grass mat on the ground in Ceylon than he ever had since on a feather bed. It was a simple but profound life he'd lived there: 'Worldly affaires I had none nor worldly estate neither.'

These reflections in turn reawakened more memories and in his rambling autobiography Knox retells much of what he had already related in the fourth part of the published *Historical Relation*. He speaks again of the various villages he lived in, of the 1664 rebellion against the King which quashed the captives' hope of escape, of how he then settled down and built a house at Eladetta, how he distilled his own arrack, knitted caps and peddled them and other goods, of his habit of reading the Bible while walking in the fields in the cool of the evenings.

At various points in his autobiography Knox inserted the current date as if he were finishing and signing a completed document. But invariably he came back to his manuscript and added yet more. Thus he dates his account 1706 after adding fifteen folio pages of Ceylon material and then 1708 after he writes that all the printed copies of his book had long ago sold out. Following this, he added another sixteen folio pages on Ceylon, much of which concern the various products of the coconut tree which Knox considered the most extraordinary and versatile plant he had ever encountered, providing as it did flesh or food to eat, milk to drink, the material for rope, huge leaves that could be used as mats and much more.

By 1711, Knox had added nearly all his additional material on Ceylon and after this point the autobiography becomes a kind of extended meditation, as he ruminates on his life. The date is significant because 1711 was also the year that Knox made out his will. The will he had made previously on the eve of his last voyage had been returned to him by John Strype, and the new 1711 will now nullified and superseded it. Knox's circumstances had changed. His nieces and nephews were now adults with children of their own — his grand-nieces and grand-nephews — and he also felt a great affection for all of the Bartlett family with whom he had lived for more than ten years. Knox not only had a large amount of money but also various personal possessions that he bequeathed with care in his will. To his grand-niece Abigail Lessingham Smith he left £300. To his other grand-niece Rebecca Ward he left a silver punch bowl, tea pot and chocolate pot, an engraved silver platter and sconces, 'a Red silk flowred quilt', a 'Repeating Clock in an ebony frame' and 'my picture [by Robert White] ingraven on a Copper plate . . . More my affections would have given her had her circumstances required it.'[23] Knox named his sister's son, Edward Lascelles, as his executor and left to him 'all my books and papers, boath written & printed', with the exception of his 'Booke of Ceylon with Maniscripts of my owne Life', which Knox left to his niece Rebecca Ward's son, 'Knox Ward, who beareth my Name'. To his namesake, indeed, Knox bequeathed all of his most treasured possessions:

> my Ceylon knife & a Picture . . . with 3 Ships, and 2 Silver hilted Swords, And two pair of Pistols & 2 silver-headed Caines & 4 ebony Chaires, with 4 blew Cushens, and my Cedar Chests of Draw[er]s, ye Cedar I brought from Barbados, & ye ebony I cut my Selfe at ye Island of Maurishus and my Steele Seale with ye Knox Coate of Arms I had from Scotland & my Sea bedstead with a flocke bed & 2 feather pillows & a bolster & a small painted quilt & a Carpet & also Water pott with a Silver cover & my Ring dyall & Sea quardon [quadrant] & my Load Stone & Anchor which was ye Honle [Honorable] Robert Boyles & after Dr Rob Hooke['s] & my Commition [as a Captain] under ye great Seale of England all to Keepe in Remembrance of me.

The name of this grand-nephew, Knox Ward, appears only in Knox's will. He is not mentioned in any of the other surviving letters or papers. Without additional evidence, there is no way of knowing whether he had a close relationship with his grand-nephew or why he entrusted his most valuable possessions – including his 'booke of Ceylon and maniscripts of my owne life' to him. Knox Ward was born in 1704 and was only seven years old at the time that Knox made out his will. He clearly hoped that his grand-nephew would live up to his name and when he became an adult accept and carry out the burden and privilege of publishing his great-uncle's book and keeping his name alive. Knox's nephew Edward Lascelles was a full generation older than Knox Ward, already a young man when Knox named him as his executor in 1711. Knox knew that Lascelles could be relied on. Why then entrust his Ceylon book and autobiography – which is to say the record of his life and all that it had meant – to a seven-year-old child? There is no way of answering this question and, in the event, it was a poor choice, though Knox's book – but not his knife, quadrant and lodestone, cedar chest and other possessions associated with his remarkable life – did eventually survive.

Knox left his most valuable personal effects to his relatives but he left the bulk of his money to the Bartlett family, who had most need of it. He bequeathed £200 to Susannah Bartlett and £200 to each of her three daughters. Her son Benjamin 'being away beyond the Sea' was bequeathed £100 'when he shall either come home or send to demand ye same'. Susannah Bartlett was also left 'all ye Remainder' of Knox's 'goods or household stuff . . . for her owne use'. This included bedding, chinaware, plate and 'lumber of any sort whatsoever' and also 'all such money as may be in my hand at ye time of my Death'. At the end of his will Knox also stipulated that £100 should be set aside for his funeral charges and funeral rings, 'strictly forbidding all vaine gaudy Cerimonies', and whatever remained after paying these expenses should be given to 'ye Poore'. Finally, he directed that he should be buried next to his mother at Wimbledon Church.[24]

Knox did not include his will or even mention it in his autobiography, but there is a marked change of tone in his recollections after he made it. In the entries made after 1711, factual narrative gives way to reflective contemplation. Knox was now waiting for the end. He had reached the final phase of life when one ceases *planning* and *doing* and instead looks back on what has been and tries to fathom what it has all meant.

'Being now come to the evening of my Age,' he writes, '& free from all manner of business & tired with fruitlesse Conversation, which seldom leads to edification or to any purpose . . . I began to spend my time in reading & my owne Solitary Contemplations for all worldly pleasures are now to me very insipid and vaine.'[25]

Settled though he was in the midst of the Bartlett family, Knox in old age is like a castaway: alone with his thoughts. Life now is stripped bare, shorn of the inessential. He reads and rereads the Bible and his favourite devotional work, *The Practice of Piety*. He asks the age-old important questions, the same questions, in fact, that Crusoe asks on his island. What is the purpose of life? Where do we come from and where do we go? How should we live and what do our lives add up to in the end? Knox reflects how he was both enriched and impoverished at different times in his life and he concludes that prosperity is meaningless and no indicator of God's favour. He celebrates charity for the sake of relieving the poor, not for any ulterior motive, and he recalls how charitable the Sinhalese were, so that Indians and other 'outlandish' people came from afar to Ceylon to beg alms.

Knox then imagines how the world would look to a man perched up high in the sky on a moon or a star: one half of the earth bathed in sunlight with people active and busy, 'turmoiling themselves', in Knox's phrase, and the other half dark and motionless as people lie immobilised in sleep or death. Despite the marked contrast between these two sides of the world, Knox feels the futility of both. 'Death snatcheth them [both] away, as we see dayly & at length none escapes; neither doth Death make any difference or exception between the degrees of quality and dignity that men make, from the King on the Throne to the Beggar that layeth at his doore, but as they were made of the same Dust of the earth to the same they shall returne.'[26]

It is a dark vision Knox conjures up in the closing pages of his autobiography – he describes a meaningless, futile world, but it is redeemed, in part at least, by his faith in what lies beyond it. He is a devout Christian and believes in a Christian afterlife, but he also expresses a kind of cosmic vision that verges on indifference: we die but the world and universe and life itself go on. We are mere specks of ephemeral matter in the grand scheme of things. 'My time heere can be but short,' Knox writes towards the end, '& this world so vaine that all the time I have spent heere when I review it is but like a yesternights dreame, & the rest hereafter can be no better, for the soule came from God & must goe to God & nothing can satisfy but God.' He sees now as through a glass darkly, and it seems to his 'poore and darke understanding' that God 'hath given us small Crumbs of breathing dust & Ashes of himself', that this is a clear 'manifestation of his goodnesse' – this is a 'holy Mistery rather to be Adored by faith than Curiously searched by reason'.[27]

Then in the midst of these reflections, Knox suddenly brings us up short. Despite the fact that he repeatedly revised his book – and said explicitly that it was the only thing for which he would be remembered and left it to his namesake Knox Ward in his will – despite all this, he claims at the very end of his autobiography that it makes no difference to him if we ever read it.

> These Notions and Contemplations I have scribbled one my owne paper, for my owne use & to please myself and wheather hereafter they are ever or never read by anyone is equally the same to me as to a dead beast what use his skine is put to wheather to make a Muffe or a Ruffle for Ladyes necks or made into shoes or a pare of Bellows or a cover for a Bible; for when the Soule is departed hence into the everlasting state, what matters it what the inhabitants of the earth, who are but small Crumbs of breathing dust, say or thinke of him.[28]

Did Knox really mean it when he said he didn't care what became of his book and autobiography? That it was all one to him what use we make of it, just as it doesn't matter to a dead animal what becomes of its skin? Knox seems to be saying that he has reached a state beyond caring. Soon he shall be safely and eternally beyond all cares. What survives of him in this world is of no consequence at all.

But what of us – his readers – who are still alive, still stranded, still asking the same fundamental questions? Knox's story has moved us profoundly because it shows that life itself is to be taken hostage, to be 'captivated', and imprisoned, with death the only liberation. Why did Knox write and rewrite his story over and over again if he doesn't care what use we make of it or if we even read it at all? The evidence of his will and his letters to Strype contradicts this emphatically stated indifference.

So it is chilling to come across this paragraph at the end of his manuscript. We feel that he has been speaking to us, personally, over the gulf of nearly three hundred years; we have lived his life as he retold it and pondered with him its meanings and legacy. And then suddenly he turns round and tells us that he doesn't care whether we read and comprehend his story. Knox's words in this paragraph seem to sever a lifeline – he has let go of us, cast us adrift – and this marks the true end of his book, though two folio pages of text and a list of dates follow before he signs the book for the last time and writes his name, 'Robt Knox', followed by 'FINIS'.

On 18 April 1720, when he heard that John Strype had suffered a near-fatal stroke while preaching his Sunday sermon, Knox wrote his last letter to his cousin:

> Lo[ving] Deere Cousen
>
> I was much surprised to heare of ye strange Providence of God on you whilst you were attending on Divine Service, & as much Rejoyced to heare his wonderful mercy in so soon Restoring you againe to your former worke. Mr Aynsworth tells me you wondered yt I [who am] so neere related [to you] should not come to visit you at such a time wch indeede I would have done; but Gods providence prevented me by laying on me an itching disposition of body . . . that hath put me into a course of Physick . . . [which made it impossible that] I could sett [sit] . . . longe in a Coach. I thank God I am not sick but feare it will require time if ever Cured. I remember our old Uncle Bonnell had ye same Disease, however I have great Cause to admire the wonderful goodnesse of God towards me in Removing two greate diseases yt have afflicted almost [me] from my youth: viz the Head Ake (a disease incident to our family) & ye Gravell yt used to be very violent in frequent fits boath of which I blesse his name I have not felt lately: to my great Wonder.
>
> Cousen: we are both now become wonderfull old; and I take these things as messengers sent of God to warne us to prepare for a sudden departure hence where we are but Straingers as were our fathers all, if God Continue us heere a few dayes, it is but as a reprieve tell he shall call us hence to our everlasting Rest.
>
> I hope when you come to London you will make a visett to
> Sr yor very Lo[ving] Cousen
> Robt Knox[29]

His 'reprieve' didn't last long, nor did he ever see his cousin again. On 19 June 1720, Robert Knox died at the Bartlett home in St Peter le Poer, eight months short of his eightieth birthday. Thus the symmetry of his life which Knox himself found remarkable – the way in which his life had fallen into twenty-year epochs or chapters – held to the end, because he died twenty years after he retired from the sea in 1700. We don't know the cause of his death and can only speculate that it came suddenly, as the ailments he complained of to his cousin weren't serious ones. According to the parish burial records, Knox was buried, as he wished, beside his mother at Wimbledon Church on 24 June 1720, less than three weeks after Daniel Defoe's novel *Captain Singleton* was published.

• Thus Knox slipped out of the world a year after the first two parts of *Robinson Crusoe* were launched in 1719 and less than a month after his real-life story was recounted (in parts word for word) in *Captain Singleton*. A month and a half after Knox's death, on 4 August 1720, Defoe brought out the third part of his Crusoe trilogy, *Serious Reflections during the Life and Surprising Adventures of Robinson Crusoe* – a repetitive, long-winded collection of meditations that bear an uncanny resemblance to the late, rambling 'contemplations' of Knox's autobiography.

Defoe recognised a good story when he came across it and proceeded to mine it for all it was worth – with the result that Knox needn't have worried about his name being kept alive, though it would be nearly three hundred years before his story was told as he himself had experienced and written it.

As Knox was fading away in St Peter le Poer, Defoe, now sixty, was working frenetically in his house three miles north in Stoke Newington. One of Defoe's most recent (and exhaustive) biographers, Maximillian Novak, describes the period between 1715 and 1724 as the 'great creative period' of Defoe's life when he 'produced a literal explosion of fiction'. Since Novak's starting date is 1715, he includes in this phase Defoe's two-volume conduct book, *The Family Instructor*, his historical survey, *Memoirs of the Church of Scotland*, the fictitious *Minutes of Negotiations of Monsr Mesnager*, and the satirical *A Continuation of Letters by a Turkish Spy*. These works, however, are seldom read today by anyone other than Defoe scholars.

Defoe's major novels were written, in fact, in the space of just five years, between 1719 and 1724. *Robinson Crusoe* and its two sequels,

The Farther Adventures and *Serious Reflections*, along with *Memoirs of a Cavalier* and *Captain Singleton*, were all published between 1719 and 1720. Then, after a relatively barren 1721 (when he published several pamphlets), came Defoe's *annus mirabilis*. He began 1722 with *Moll Flanders* in January, followed by a conduct book, *Religious Courtship*, the next month. In March, his documentary novel *A Journal of the Plague Year* – a historical fiction about the Great Plague of 1665 – came out. After a brief lull, *Colonel Jacque* appeared in December 1722. The following year yielded almost nothing, but Defoe came back with a vengeance in 1724 when *Roxana* was published in April, swiftly followed by the first volume of Defoe's brilliant state-of-Britain travel book, *A Tour Thro' the Whole Island of Great Britain*, and in November, his last novel (but by no means last book), *A New Voyage Round the World*. During these same five years when Defoe wrote his great fiction, he also launched and produced three separate periodicals: the twice-weekly and then weekly *Manufacturer or the British Trade Truly Stated*; the *Commentator*, a twice-weekly Whig journal which ran from January to September 1720; and the *Director*, a bi-weekly periodical concerning the South Sea Bubble, which appeared from October 1720 to January 1721.

As Novak observed, this was an unparalleled explosion of work even by Defoe's industrious standards. Between 1719 and 1724 Defoe wrote incessantly, producing much journalism, a conduct book and a handful of minor novels; but, most importantly, it was during these years that he brought out all the great works which form the basis of his enduring literary reputation. Defoe's extraordinary productivity in the early 1720s was living proof of the Crusoe survivor myth: industry, perseverance and ingenuity create success and, in Defoe's particular case, enduring literary renown.

It is important to stress, too, that unlike his hero, Defoe was far from young and energetic when he demonstrated the validity of Crusoe's story. He was a man in his sixties in failing health. But gout, kidney stones, arthritis and other infirmities did not slow him down. There was no question of Daniel Defoe putting his feet up, taking it easy and looking back at, and moralising on, his long 'life of wonders in continu'd storms'. Rather, in the seventh decade of his life, Defoe was going full speed ahead and writing relentlessly. Notwithstanding unmistakable signs of old age, he was a writer at his peak and in his prime. His advancing years in fact probably added urgency to his task. Defoe was now writing against the clock; he knew he had to make haste. As Michael Wood puts it in his introduction to Edward Said's *On Late Style*, 'death doesn't make appointments ... but death does sometimes wait for us and it is possible to become deeply aware of its waiting'. Said himself made a distinction between two kinds of 'late style': 'late works that crown a lifetime of aesthetic endeavour' and an entirely different sort of 'lateness, not as harmony and resolution, but as intransigence, difficulty and unresolved contradiction'. This second kind of 'late style' 'involves a nonharmonious, nonserene tension, and above all, a sort of deliberately unproductive productiveness'.[30] Defoe's productiveness was unproductive only in the sense of its variable quality – the uneven range of pedestrian or at least undistinguished work with masterpieces like *Robinson Crusoe, Moll Flanders* and *A Journal of the Plague Year*. But it is Said's phrase, 'nonharmonious, nonserene tension', that seems best to describe Defoe's frenetic creative production in the 1720s.

Meanwhile, at the same time that he churned out this astonishing surfeit of written work, Defoe continued to engage in various complicated and time-consuming business ventures which were financed, in part at least, by the money he was now earning by his pen. According to Paula Backscheider, another authoritative modern Defoe biographer, in August 1722 he took out a £1,000 ninety-nine-year lease on hundreds of acres of land in Colchester, including timber rights, and also leased a farm in Earlscolne parish on the Colne River which contained rich brick and tile clay soil. Defoe bred cattle and raised corn, traded in butter, cheese, veal, beef, honey and oysters. 'He even began to sell metal buttons, tanned leather, cloth and imported anchovies in London, Lichfield and Coventry ... So intent was Defoe on a second chance [as a successful businessman] that he began to plan a tile factory on the Colchester land.'[31]

In a word (to use one of Defoe's own favourite phrases), he was an extraordinarily busy man as well as a prolific author in the 1720s. It is surprising that none of his biographers has suggested a retroactive psychiatric diagnosis of manic depression or bipolar disorder as it's now called. We have Defoe's own testimony as evidence of depressive and manic episodes during his life, but it is the frenzied productivity of the 1720s that is most striking.³² When, we wonder, did the man sleep? Defoe now was not just unremittingly industrious, he appears almost superhumanly productive, especially when we take into account the fact that during these years he published a number of pamphlets as well as novels, was at loggerheads with one of his sons and engaged in protracted negotiations to marry off his youngest daughter, Sophia. If Defoe had done nothing other than write all the words he published during the 1720s he would seem amazingly prolific, but there is abundant evidence to show that he had a time-consuming business life and family affairs to see to as well.

The writing of *Robinson Crusoe* seems to have unleashed this astonishing productivity. In his final Crusoe book, Defoe declared in his 'Preface' that his Crusoe story was neither an 'invention' nor a 'romance', but instead an allegory of his own life: 'I . . . hereby declare . . . the Story though Allegorical is also Historical; and that it is the . . . Representation of a Life of unexampled Misfortunes and of a Variety not to be met with in the world . . . there is a Man alive [i.e. Defoe the author] and well known too, the Actions of whose Life are the just Subject of these volumes, and to whom all or most Part of the Story . . . directly alludes.' The Crusoe books, Defoe confesses, are an allegory of 'my real Solitudes and Disasters . . . a Life of Wonders in Continu'd Storms . . . there's not a Circumstance in the imaginary Story, but has its just Allusion to a real Story'. Defoe then goes on to defend his 'allegorical' method in the statement "tis as reasonable to represent one kind of Imprisonment by another, as it is to represent any Thing that really exists by that which exists not'.³³

These words have proved a gift – and licence – to generations of Defoe biographers who have invoked them to defend their interpretations of *Robinson Crusoe* as Defoe's allegorical account of his own life during which he was 'Shipwreck'd often, tho' more by Land than by Sea'.³⁴ In these biographies which decode Defoe's life in terms of Crusoe's adventures, specific episodes represent real events that Defoe endured: Crusoe's shipwreck, for example, represents Defoe's bankruptcy, and Crusoe's imprisonment on the island parallels Defoe's incarceration in debtors' prison and Newgate. These autobiographical readings of *Robinson Crusoe* have produced some ingenious versions of Defoe's life, but in the end, they remain speculative and unverifiable interpretations.[35]

It makes more sense to see *Robinson Crusoe* not so much as an allegory of Defoe's past life but instead as a kind of script or plan for his future. What lay ahead of Defoe in the 1720s was not an era of retirement, but months and years of unremitting creative activity. Between 1719 and 1729 Defoe *became* Robinson Crusoe in his 'indefatigable Application and undaunted Resolution' and the prodigious, even heroic, amount of writing he produced. During this period, even Defoe's most conservative bibliographers calculate that he published forty-eight works, more than half of which were full-length books.[36] Paula Backscheider calculates that between 1724 and 1730 alone, Defoe wrote a staggering two and a half million words.[37] Some of this massive output was ephemeral, some of it esoteric and eccentric (such as *A System of Magick, The History of the Devil* and a conduct book on marriage entitled *Conjugal Lewdness*), but Defoe also wrote interesting works that still deserve to be read such as *The Complete English Tradesman* – perhaps the first how-to-succeed-in-business guide. Also worth remembering is *A General History of Discoveries and Improvements in Useful Arts, Particularly in the Great Branches of Commerce, Navigation, and Plantation in all Parts of the World*. Here Defoe ambitiously recounts the whole history of human progress, knowledge, technology and trade from 'the first ages after the Flood', to the Carthaginians, Phoenicians and Romans, through the Middle Ages and on to the rise of the English wool trade, the discovery of America and the development of overseas colonies; the book then concludes with Defoe's proposals for a colonial settlement in Chile.

What is most important, however, is that buried in the huge corpus of printed words are all Defoe's great works: *Robinson Crusoe, Moll Flanders, Journal of the Plague Year, Roxana* and the three-volume *Tour Thro' the Whole Island of Great Britain*. It is *Robinson Crusoe*, above all, that continues to enchant and enthral. As Ian Watt has observed, the figure of Crusoe has 'attained a universal and international status'. His story has become a myth because it 'is exceptionally widely known throughout the culture, [and] . . . is credited with a historical or quasi-historical belief that embodies and symbolizes some of the most basic values of a society'.[38] Crusoe, the archetypal survivor, is everyman and everywoman; he speaks to the lonely, disheartened castaway that we all are at some point in our lives. And generations of readers have embraced his myth of struggle, survival and triumph against all odds and despite, too, all the contrary evidence of history and our own experience that defeat and death are just as likely to be our fate.

Crusoe, of course, not only survives, he transforms his island into a replica of Great Britain; he civilises its wilderness and then with the arrival of 'savages', pirates and mutineers he establishes a colony. As with Crusoe, so too with Defoe. Even in old age, he didn't give up trying to redesign and improve the world. Old people are often critical of modern ways and yearn for the virtues of the past. But not Defoe. After he had written his great novels, instead of looking back to the good old days, in the mid and late 1720s, he turned again to restructuring and improving as he had done in his first important work, *An Essay Upon Projects*. At the age of sixty-five, he puts his mind to creating a better world even though he knows that he himself will not be around very long to enjoy it.

In the late 1720s, Defoe posited various plans and schemes for social and moral improvement in the fictional persona of one Andrew Moreton, who is aptly described by Defoe's editor, W. R. Owens, as 'a public-spirited, but irritable old bachelor with a pawky sense of humour, unpractised in the use of the pen . . . who lives in a modest way with his sister in Highgate'.[39] Between 1725 and 1728 'Squire Moreton' produced five pamphlets which caught on immediately with the reading public of the day.[40] He continues to delight us still, in part because of the incongruity of his character: a lovable, long-winded old bachelor who spends his twilight years commenting on and proffering remedies for all manner of social ills. Andrew Moreton is both hard-headed and utopian, a pragmatist and a dreamer, without a hint of the weariness and indifference that the elderly sometimes fall victim to. Superficially he bears a resemblance to Robert Knox: both are elderly bachelors with a prolix, rambling style. Moreton refers to himself as the 'most immethodical writer imaginable', and says, 'pardon, therefore Kind Reader my digressive way of writing . . . I write this under many bodily Infirmities and am so impatient to have done, that I forget half I have to say'.[41] Knox describes his own writing in similar terms, but in his last years, he was detached from contemporary issues and problems which he found 'insipid and vaine'. Squire Moreton is still very much engaged and he industriously attacks a wide variety of social ills and proposes practical solutions for them.

One of his most popular pamphlets was an entertaining diatribe against refractory servants and other menial workers. The pamphlet's full title summarises its contents: *Everybody's Business is Nobody's Business; or, Private Abuses, Publick Grievances; Exemplified in the Pride, Insolence and Exorbitant Wages of our Women-Servants, Footmen, etc with a Proposal for Amendment of the Same; as also for Clearing the Streets of those Vermin call'd Shoe-Cleaners and substituting in their Stead many Thousands of Industrious Poor, now Ready to Starve. Everybody's Business is Nobody's Business* lacks the savage bite of Jonathan Swift's *Directions to Servants* but Defoe isn't writing satire in his pamphlet. He is addressing what was considered a major social problem of the day: wayward, careless servants who allegedly pilfered and cheated, neglected callers, took on airs and didn't know their place. Defoe suggests a number of schemes to control them: employment contracts so that they couldn't leave their masters on a whim; mandatory uniforms for women servants so that they didn't ape their betters in their dress; legislation fixing their wages. As for street shoe-cleaners — referred to as a 'race of caterpillars' by Defoe — they picked more pockets than they blacked shoes and should be rounded up and sent down to work in the mines or employed clearing the sandbanks on the Thames. In their place 'ancient persons' and 'poor widows' should be authorised to clean shoes on the streets at a particular 'walk or stand' assigned to them. This would provide them with a useful activity and relieve the parish of the expense of maintaining them.

Defoe's pamphlet on insubordinate servants may seem antiquated today but it aroused a storm of controversy when it came out, and aggrieved servants, among others, attacked its dictatorial strictures. Within months a slew of pamphlets were published, including *Everybody's Business is Nobody's Business: Answered Paragraph by Paragraph By a Committee of Women-Servants and Footmen; The Maid Servants Modest Defense; Every Man Mind his Own Business* and the footman-poet Robert Dodsley's poem *Servitude* which concluded with a postscript 'Occasion'd by a late Trifling Pamphlet entitl'd, *Everybody's Business is Nobody's*'.[42]

Far more ambitious than his programme for reforming servants was Andrew Moreton's pamphlet *Augusta Triumphans or the Way to Make London the most Flourishing City in the Universe*, published in 1728. Here Defoe, in the persona of Moreton, undertakes nothing less than the recreation of a thoroughly modern city – the greatest metropolis not only in the world but the whole universe. The pamphlet puts forth plans for a London university with various colleges located in different parts of the metropolis; a foundling hospital for illegitimate infants; a music academy to train musicians for legitimate entertainment; a crackdown on 'shameless and impudent Strumpets'; suppression of 'Gaming-Tables'; an end to drunkenness, especially the 'Abuse of that Nauseous Liquor call'd GENEVA [gin] among our lower sort'; and the suppression of all 'Sunday Debauches' [profane activities that break the Sabbath]. Andrew Moreton, a lifelong bachelor, also speaks out eloquently against wife-beating and the reprehensible practice of men who send their wives to private madhouses when they want to be rid of them. He calls, in fact, for the abolition of all private madhouses and their replacement with licensed asylums subject to regular inspection.

Moreton is also concerned about the soaring crime rate in London and makes a strong case for a complete reformation of the 'watch', the city's rudimentary law-enforcement system. Current watchmen were too old and feeble; they should be replaced by young, able-bodied men equipped with weapons and a 'bugle-horn' to sound the alarm. Their number should be increased threefold so that there is one watchman to cover every forty houses. In all these schemes and plans, Defoe shows himself a prescient social critic in *Augusta Triumphans* and many of the ills he attacked were later addressed and the proposals he suggested for remedying them, in time, implemented.

Perhaps the most intriguing of Andrew Moreton's pamphlets, especially in the light of Defoe's own life, is *The Protestant Monastery*, published in 1726, because it addressed a problem that Defoe undoubtedly feared he would soon have to face himself: the

dilemma of how the elderly should live and be cared for. He begins
by attacking the general 'Abhorrence of Age' among the young in
contemporary society and lamenting the poverty and neglect suffered
by so many of the elderly:

> There is nothing on Earth more shocking, and withal more common,
> in but too many Families, than to see Age and Grey Hairs derided,
> and ill-used. The OLD MAN or the OLD WOMAN, can do nothing
> to please: their Words are perverted, their Actions misrepresented,
> and themselves look'd upon as a Burthen to their Issue, and a Rent
> Charge upon those who came from their Loins.[43]

Moreton then gives us a dramatic vignette of the plight of the
elderly. He tells us of a recent visit to an old friend who had given
his fortune of £1,200 to his daughter and married her to 'an eminent
Merchant' and then moved in with the couple, believing they would
care for him in his old age. 'During the Honey-Moon and till the
Portion [the £1,200 dowry] was paid, the Old Gentleman liv'd in
Clover,' but when Moreton calls on him some time later he finds
the man lodged in a dingy garret of his daughter's house and they
dine on a paltry meal of 'some Cold Roast-Beef, a few Herrings . . .
a Plate of Fritters' and home-brewed ale rather than wine. 'Never
in my Life,' Moreton says, 'made I a worse Dinner.' When he and
his old friend go out later to a tavern, he learns more about the
'impertinence and ingratitude of the Young Couple'. They have
banned the old man from smoking because the daughter claims it
made her nauseous and 'the house stink and damaged the Furniture'.
The old man cannot express an opinion without his daughter and
son-in-law treating him like 'an Idiot or underling'. As he unbur-
dens himself at the tavern, 'his poor Heart was so full, he could not
contain himself from lodging his Sorrows in the Bosom of his old
Friend. With Tears in his Eyes he recounted all the Indignities he
daily met with, not only from his own Children, but from the very
Servants.'[44] Moreton is deeply affected by this visit to his friend but
'before I could find Opportunity to visit him' again, he receives news
that the old man has died, no doubt of neglect and a broken heart.

After relating the sad fate of his old friend, Moreton goes on to
propose 'A Project for erecting a Protestant Monastery' – a communal

establishment for old people which would enable them to live independently and retain their dignity. A house or hall would be rented in which each resident would be allotted an apartment. This 'college' would involve 'a Joint Stock of Twenty Thousand Pounds . . . raised between 50 Persons, by an equal Deposite of four hundred pounds each . . . for this being no Charity but rather a Co-partnership, there is no need of having a Governor, Treasurer, Director or other commanding Officer'. Instead, the old residents would 'chuse among themselves one Treasurer, two Wardens, and . . . other Officers'. An egalitarian, classless policy would be the basis of the Protestant Monastery. 'As all the Members of the College are to be upon an equal Footing, 'tis highly necessary there should not be the least Distinction among them in Diet, Lodging etc, And if one Person dresses or furnishes better than another, there will be no need of Complaint because they do it at their own Charge: Tho' to speak my Mind, it would look most lovely, to have a decent Equality and Uniformity in Dress.'[45]

This utopian and socialist vision of a communal retirement 'college' is ingenious and persuasive. Defoe even goes into the details of the necessary employees and their annual salaries: a physician, a chaplain, a cook, a laundry maid, a housemaid and two nurses for the infirmary. This 'elder hostel' harks back to Defoe in his projecting prime in his *Essay Upon Projects*. It is a far-sighted plan he draws up even though certain details, like the 'decent Equality and Uniformity in Dress' – presumably the inmates would wear uniforms – may seem far-fetched.

The Protestant Monastery undoubtedly reflected Defoe's anxieties about growing old. In the 1720s, he had come into his own as a successful writer and produced all the work for which he would be remembered, but this didn't bring him either financial security or peace in his personal life. Three things precluded any possibility of serenity in his last years. He became embroiled in protracted and distressing negotiations over his youngest daughter's marriage settlement; descendants and associates of his old creditors came back to haunt him; and then, when Defoe attempted to secure his assets by signing them over to his younger son, Daniel, who was to provide for Mrs Defoe and her unmarried daughters, Daniel allegedly withheld funds from his mother and sisters while himself living in 'a profusion of Plenty'.[46] We have only Defoe's word for these accusations and it's impossible, now, to tell if his son, who was a respected merchant in Cornhill, was guilty of them. Defoe's wife, Mary, in any event, wasn't reduced to destitution because she had been left a handsome legacy by her brother, Samuel Tuffley, who specified in his will that Mary's husband, Defoe, be excluded from her inheritance.

In 1724, an aspiring poet who had been a bookseller's apprentice but now earned his living teaching the deaf a sign language of his own devising came to teach in a Stoke Newington family who were neighbours of the Defoes. This was twenty-six-year-old Henry Baker. He was soon introduced to the Defoe family, which now consisted of Defoe himself, his wife and his three grown daughters, Hannah, Henrietta and Sophia. Baker began to visit the Defoes regularly and he particularly enjoyed conversing with the famous head of the household. When Baker published two volumes of verse in 1725 he no doubt gave copies to Defoe. By this time he had fallen in love with Defoe's youngest and most cherished daughter, twenty-three-year-old Sophia. We know a great deal about this courtship because Baker went to the trouble of recording its progress in a document headed 'Autobiographical Memoranda', and he also preserved all the correspondence it later entailed.[47] In his letters to Sophia, Baker fulsomely declared his passion:

> My Sophy, ah, how I languish for thee! What soft sensations seize me! What fondness inexpressible possesses me whene'er I think of thee! This very moment my soul is stretching after thee with ardent longings. Methinks I hold thee in my eager arms and bask and pant and wanton in thy smiles; and now I hold thee off and gaze upon thy charms with infinite delight, and now all ecstasy I snatch thee to me, and devour thy lips, strain thee with breathless raptures to my bosom . . . unable to endure bliss so excessive and . . . joys celestial . . . To be in love, is a state of madness, a madness, however, not incurable; there is a drug called marriage which is a sure specific in this disease.[48]

Despite his passion for Sophia, Baker did not rush to 'cure' himself. He had been calling on the Defoes and wooing Sophia for three years before he asked her, in 1727, if she had any sort of prior engagement, to which Sophia replied, 'Yes, Sir − [I am] engaged − to God and to my Father, but none besides.'[49] Whereupon Baker formally asked her to marry him and Sophia accepted. On the basis of Defoe's fame as a man of letters and to judge from his fine house and grounds in Stoke Newington, Baker assumed that Defoe would give a handsome dowry to the man his youngest, favourite daughter chose to marry. It was a great blow, then, when Defoe responded to Baker's request for Sophia's hand with the information that he could not provide a dowry, but instead would leave Sophia and her husband a generous bequest when he died in lieu of a settlement at the time of their marriage. Defoe also refused to disclose the details of his financial affairs when Baker requested them.

The younger man was at first shocked and then infuriated by what he considered Defoe's secrecy and miserliness. A lengthy and increasingly acrimonious correspondence ensued between Baker and Defoe as they haggled over the terms of the proposed marriage agreement. Baker wanted Defoe to sign over the lease on his Stoke Newington house to him and also to pay interest on the money that would eventually come to Sophia on her father's death.* At one point they were arguing heatedly over whether this interest should be 4 or 5 per cent per annum. Sophia wrote to Baker that the quarrel had made her father ill: he was suffering from 'a violent, sudden pain, which spreads itself all over him' and which she feared 'is a messenger from that grand tyrant [death] which will at last destroy the (to me) so-much-valued structure [of her father]'.[50] The quarrel also greatly distressed Sophia herself, and she wrote to her fiancé on 7 January 1728, 'Your letter, sir, to my father seems to have much of the air of barter and sale. My fortune, though not great, fully answers yours which is less than I need accept of, and which I think does not justify such nice demands.'[51]

But Baker was intransigent in his demands and months dragged on with the situation still unresolved. In August 1728, Defoe sent an ultimatum to Baker. His affairs, he said, 'do not permit me to advance the money presently, but I offer this as Equivalent. 1. That I pay [scratched out word, presumably the specified amount of

---

* Defoe had bought the lease of the Stoke Newington house in 1727 but then assigned it to George Virgoe, a London merchant, perhaps to protect himself from creditors. Defoe, however, repurchased the lease on 3 April 1729 and two days later gave Henry Baker a bond for £500 and engaged the lease as security (Healey, p. 468, n. 1).

money] at a certain Term . . . 2. That till it be paid I will pay the Interest annually at £4 per cent . . . 3. That in case of Mortality [Defoe's death] Hannah [Defoe's unmarried daughter] will oblige herself to pay the [scratched out amount of money] out of [Defoe's] Essex Estate [property] which shall be legally vested in her . . . and to come immediately upon my Decease into her Hands.'[52]

Defoe's ultimatum enraged Baker and he wrote to Sophia, 'You are my good genius and your father is my evil one. He, like a curst infernal, continually torments, betrays and overturns my quiet . . . Ruin and wild destruction sport around him and exercise their fury on all he has to do with.' In subsequent letters, Baker was even more vituperative: Defoe, he said, is 'all deceit and baseness . . . his purposes are . . . dark and hideous . . . Him I abhor as much as I love you.' In vain did Sophia protest, 'Your suspicions of my father I think wholly unjust and groundless.'[53]

By this time, Baker had become completely deranged and on 1 February 1729 he tried to persuade Sophia that they should take poison together and die in each other's arms: 'The world telling with wonder our amazing story, pitying our youth and our too cruel fate. It might be, some brother bard with monumental verse would celebrate our memory and . . . praise [us] to future generations.'[54] Sophia, however, had, as one Defoe biographer put it, 'no intention of becoming the raw material of poetry'.[55] She refused to cooperate with Baker's proposed suicide pact, but she herself at this point suffered what seems to have been a complete nervous breakdown, during which she also contracted a life-threatening fever.

Sophia's mental collapse and grave illness finally effected a resolution of Baker and Defoe's long, drawn-out dispute over the marriage settlement. Both men seem to have backed down. They reached an agreement and the marriage articles were drawn up and signed. Sophia soon recovered and she and Henry Baker were finally married on 30 April 1729.[56]

Defoe had even more alarming concerns than Sophia's marriage settlement to worry about at this time. After some years of comparative financial security, his early bankruptcies came back to haunt him. Descendants of his original creditors claimed that he had never fully paid the terms of the compositions that had been agreed after he went bankrupt in 1692 and again in 1703 when he came out of Newgate to find himself ruined. Now, in the late 1720s, Defoe was faced with a highly complicated situation that is difficult at this distance to fathom completely. What is clear, though, is that he was once again being pursued for debts in the courts.[57]

Despite all this turmoil in his personal affairs, in the summer of 1729 Defoe was hard at work on another conduct book, the *Compleat English Gentleman*, in which he made the memorable distinction between 'a man of polite learning' and a 'mere scholar'. 'The former,' he says, 'is a gentleman and the latter a mere bookcase.' In this last book, Defoe sought to differentiate between a 'born gentleman' and a 'bred gentleman', and in his unfinished manuscript he argued for the necessity of a comprehensive education in the true or 'compleat English Gentleman'.

As usual, as he wrote the book, Defoe sent batches of manuscript to his printer, John Watts. In late August 1729, when Watts's messenger boy called at Defoe's house for the next instalment, there was no material to collect, a lapse that Defoe explained to him in a letter of 10 September: 'I am to ask your pardon for keeping the Enclosed [a proof sheet] so long ... But I have been Exceeding ill.' He goes on to say that he has now revised and condensed the text 'to bring it within the Bulk you Desire or as Near it as Possible ... I will Endeavour to send the Rest of the Coppy So Well Corrected as to give you Very little Trouble.'[58] But after this letter no further copy was forthcoming, and the next time Watts sent his messenger to Stoke Newington, he was informed that Defoe had left home and there was no information regarding his return.

Defoe, in fact, had become a fugitive again and gone into hiding, just as he had in 1703 when he went on the run after publishing *The Shortest Way with Dissenters*. Now it was a woman named Mary Brooke who was pursuing him – the widow of a descendant of one of Defoe's long-ago creditors. In October 1729, a month after Defoe wrote to John Watts, Mary Brooke lodged a suit against Defoe in the Court of the Exchequer. The jury ruled in her favour with the upshot that Defoe – who did not appear in court and whose whereabouts were unknown – owed Mary Brooke £800 plus £16.10.5 for damages and £14.9.11 for costs.[59]

Defoe's next surviving letter was written ten months later, on

12 August 1730, at an undisclosed location, 'About two Miles from Greenwich, Kent'. This long letter to Henry Baker contains the last words we have from Defoe's pen. Histrionic, aggrieved and anguished, by turns, the letter contains some of the most revealing words Defoe ever wrote. It is addressed to Baker, but it was, of course, also written for Defoe's cherished daughter, Sophia, who had recently become the mother of a baby boy, David Erskine Baker, born 30 January 1730. The discord between Defoe and Baker had by now healed and Defoe begins by thanking his son-in-law for his 'very kind and affectionate letter' which for some reason had taken ten full days to reach him – a delay, as Defoe says, that 'depriv'd me of that Cordial [which] . . . I stood in need of . . . to support a Mind sinking under the Weight of Affliction too heavy for my Strength, and looking on myself as Abandon'd of every Comfort, every Friend, and every Relative' who might give him help. He is, he says, 'under a weight of very heavy Illness, which I think will be a Fever'.

The letter then goes on to explode the Crusoe survivor myth. A time of life has finally arrived for Defoe which no amount of hard work, ingenuity and perseverance can overcome. His situation is hopeless and irremediable. Now seventy, he not only expresses pain, sorrow and regret, he also admits defeat. He describes himself as '*in tenebris*', and sinking 'under the Load of insupportable Sorrows'. It is not 'the Blow I rec'd from a wicked, perjur'd and contemptible Enemy [Mary Brooke]' that has 'broken in upon my Spirit . . . which has carryed me on thro' greater Disasters than these. But it has been the injustice, unkindness, and I must say, inhuman dealings of my own Son [Daniel] which has both ruin'd my Family and, in a word, has broken my Heart.' Defoe clearly felt that his *Protestant Monastery* had proved prophetic, and that he, like Andrew Moreton's old friend, has been traduced and ruined by his own child. He then goes on to detail the inequity of the younger Daniel Defoe:

I take this Occasion to vent my Grief . . . and tell you, that nothing but this has conquered or could conquer me. *Et tu! Brute* I depended upon him, I trusted him, I gave up my two deare unprovided Children [the unmarried Hannah and Henrietta Defoe] into his Hands; but he has no Compassion, but suffers them and their poor, dying mother* to beg their Bread at his Door, and to crave, as if it were an Alms, what he is bound under Hand and Seal besides the most sacred promises, to supply them with; himself at the same Time, living in a profusion of Plenty. It is too much for me. Excuse my Infirmity, I can say no more; my Heart is too full. I ask one Thing of you as a dying request. Stand by them when I am gone, and let them not be wrong'd, while he is able to do them right. Stand by them as a Brother; and if you have anything within you owing to my Memory, who have bestow'd on you the best Gift I had to give [his daughter Sophia], let them not be injured and trampled on . . . It adds to my Grief that it is so difficult to see you. I am at a distance from London in Kent; nor have I lodging in London . . . At present I am weak, having had some fits of Fever that have left me low . . . I have not seen Son† or Daughter, Wife or Child, many Weeks and kno' not which Way to see them. They dare not come by Water and by Land there is no Coach, and I kno' not what to do.

Defoe then continues his heart-rending letter with: 'I am so near my Journey's end, and am hastening to the Place where the Weary are at Rest, and where the Wicked cease to trouble; be it that the Passage is rough and the Day Stormy, by what Way soever He please to bring me to the End of it, I desire to finish Life with this temper of Soul in all Cases: *Te Deum Laudamus*.' He closes with a kind of benediction for Baker, Sophia and their child: 'May you sail the dangerous Voyage of Life with a forcing wind, and make the Port of Heaven without a Storm.'[60]

There was no forcing wind, no Port of Heaven now for Defoe. He was in the midst of his life's last and greatest storm and he was going under. He clung on for some months more, though, and made his way back to London where, still a fugitive, he took rented lodgings in Ropemaker's Alley, not far from Fore Street where he had come into the world some seventy years earlier. Though his end was near, Defoe didn't make a will because he had no need to: he had already signed over everything, as he laments in his last letter, to his younger son Daniel. There was nothing else left to bequeath.

* Mary Tuffley Defoe died two years later in 1732.
† Defoe's older son, Benjamin Defoe, who had followed in his father's footsteps and was a struggling journalist and hack writer.

It was here, in his rented lodgings in Ropemaker's Alley, 'almost as completely alone as his own Robinson Crusoe', that Defoe finally died on 24 April 1731.[61] The entry in the St Giles, Cripplegate parish register recorded: 'Daniel Defoe, gentleman. To Tindall's (Lethargy) April 26.' The official cause of death, 'a lethargy', was a common one given then for the decease of the elderly. Defoe, who of course had been relentlessly productive and anything but lethargic during his long, eventful life, most likely died of a stroke. He was buried two days later in the Dissenters' cemetery, Tindall's Fields (later called Bunhill Fields). The simple stone marking the spot was engraved with the inscription:

DANIEL DE FOE
Author of
ROBINSON CRUSOE
Who Died April 24, 1731
In his 70th year

Defoe's original tombstone

The two Ancient Mariners – Robert Knox and Daniel Defoe – were both now gone. But their stories, which over the course of many years they had compulsively told and retold like Coleridge's ancient mariner, remained. And ever since that long-ago time when Knox and Defoe experienced and wrote about their 'strange surprising adventures', we, their readers, 'cannot choose but hear' their tales of calamity, despair, struggle, endurance, hope and survival. Here, at the end of my story of the lives and books of Robert Knox and Daniel Defoe and the myth they created, it is Crusoe who is the only real Survivor. For Crusoe, in fact, it is just the beginning.

Epilogue

In 1858, when a self-described 'inexperienced and untried writer' in Doncaster named William Chadwick embarked on a new biography of Daniel Defoe,[1] he made a pilgrimage to his hero's grave in the famous London Dissenters' cemetery, Bunhill Fields.* Here he was shocked to discover the derelict and neglected condition of Defoe's tombstone: 'broken, and the inscriptions, two or three, obliterated by neglect and the corrosive influence of the atmosphere'. Chadwick sought out the cemetery caretaker and expressed his concern about the grave's sorry state, only to be told by the man, 'yes sir, the lightning did it'. Apparently, just months earlier, in the midst of a furious thunderstorm, a bolt of lightning had struck Defoe's plain oblong tombstone and nearly cracked it in two. As Chadwick relates in the closing paragraphs of his *Life of Daniel Defoe*, published in 1859, it was clear to him that only an act of Nature or God could have wreaked such damage, 'on that sacred

---

* The name Bunhill Fields probably derives from 'bone hill fields'. In the sixteenth century loads of human bones were brought here from St Paul's overcrowded charnel house for new interment. In 1665, it was decided that the area should be used as a burial ground for victims of the London plague. But before this happened, a Mr Tindall took over the lease of the grounds. Tindall allowed use of the land, which was unconsecrated, for burials of Non-conformists and it became known as Tindall's Burial Ground. Between 1665 and 1853 some 123,000 Dissenters were buried within its small confines. When Chadwick visited Defoe's grave in 1858 the graveyard had been closed for five years and had fallen into a general state of disrepair. The Bunhill Fields Burial Ground Act of 1867 provided for its restoration for public use, though it was closed to further burials. Today Bunhill Fields is an oasis of greenery in the middle of the city, and office workers and shoppers stroll through it. The day I visited, someone had recently put fresh flowers at Defoe's grave.

spot of departed patriotism – the last solemn resting place of Daniel Defoe'.[2]

But what God or Nature had nearly destroyed, the editor of a popular children's magazine and 'the boys and girls of England' hastened to repair. When news got abroad of the condition of the grave, Mr James Clarke, editor of the *Christian World*, placed a prominent announcement in his magazine that subscriptions were sought 'from the children of the realm' of sixpence each for the erection of a national monument to Defoe at Bunhill Fields. 'The response was prompt and hearty . . . two lists were opened, and the boys and girls ran a fair race for the honour of giving most.'[3] Hundreds of adults also sent in even larger contributions and some 1,700 subscriptions in all raised £200 for 'the mortuary memorial'. The sculptor chosen to design and build it was Mr Samuel Horner of Bournemouth, who swiftly drew up plans for an impressive, white marble obelisk to be raised over Defoe's derelict grave.

In order to begin construction of the monument, a solid foundation had to be laid at the grave site, and this in turn involved disinterring the grave. When the work began on a warm but overcast summer's day in 1869, Horner and his assistants and workmen soon found themselves surrounded by a crowd of curious onlookers. According to the London *Daily News*, 'in excavating for the foundation, two or three coffins in various stages of decay were found, presumably being those of members of Defoe's family.* Some ancient coins were also picked out of the earth.' Then, at a depth of twelve feet, the workmen reached the bottom of the grave where they 'came upon a coffin much decayed' attached to which was a brass plate with 'Foe' engraved on it. While attempting to extricate the coffin from the hard-packed earth surrounding it, one of its sides was jarred and fell open, disclosing the remains inside. The crowd of spectators now pressed in on the workmen and peered down at what lay below: the 'skeleton in complete preservation . . . [of] a man about five feet four inches high, with a peculiarly massive under-jaw'. This sight caused a sensation and word quickly spread

---

* Defoe's wife Mary was buried beside her husband in 1732 and his daughter-in-law, the wife of his older son Benjamin, was buried in the family grave five years later in 1737.

among the crowd that these were the bones of Daniel Defoe, author of *Robinson Crusoe*. Uproar then ensued. Samuel Horner and his workmen were far outnumbered by the mob, some of whom now clambered down into the grave to snatch a bony relic of the late great Defoe. Several men emerged triumphantly holding bones aloft. According to the *Daily News*, 'Mr Horner was only able to prevent' a complete ransacking of the grave 'by calling in the aid of the police'. Eventually order was restored, the crowd driven back and then 'the coffin and its contents . . . finally re-buried in the concrete foundation'.[4]

Such is the ludicrous last appearance of Daniel Defoe in this world, and it is difficult to say whether he would have been horrified or gratified by the near riot this first stage of his memorialisation provoked. A year later, on 16 September 1870, another very different event was held in Bunhill Fields: the decorous but equally crowded occasion of the official ceremony to unveil and dedicate the Defoe monument. It too was widely reported in the press: a gathering of many of the leading men of the day, an assembly of the great and the good that would have delighted Defoe, who gentrified his original surname Foe with the prefix De and whose last, unfinished book was entitled *The Compleat Englishman*.

The sculptor Samuel Horner, in honour of the occasion, wrote an account of 'the interesting proceedings connected with its public unveiling', appended to which he included a number of the news stories that appeared in the press. All the encomiums heaped on Defoe at the ceremony by those who presided over it and the monument to Defoe himself stressed they were honouring him because he was the author of *Robinson Crusoe*. It is this book of all the many that he wrote which had summoned 1,700 'boys and girls of England' and their parents to contribute to this monument to Defoe's heroic achievement. As Horner himself said, 'the story of the Shipwrecked mariner is in higher repute than ever, and now calls forth the highest skill of artist, printer and binder, to render it worthy a place on the tables of the wealthy, and make it a cherished treasure in the cottages of the sons of toil'.[5]

The proceedings opened with a speech by 'the grand mover' behind the Defoe monument: James Clarke, editor of the *Christian World*, who in the course of his speech read out a letter from John

Forster, the leading Victorian man of letters and biographer of
Dickens, among others. Forster, who was originally supposed to
be the main speaker at the ceremony, had been 'expected to be
present, but professional duties in Warwickshire prevented his
attendance'. So Clarke read out his written message to the congregation: 'no memory more than Defoe's deserved to be honoured
for the sake of the great principles it represented, though besides
and beyond the services rendered by him in matters still vitally
affecting the welfare of us all, he had himself erected a memorial [*Robinson Crusoe*] which was pretty sure to last as long as a
boy remained in the world'.[6] After Clarke read out Forster's fulsome
praise of Defoe, Mr C. Reed, a prominent Member of Parliament,
took over at the podium and addressed the assembly at considerable length, concluding with his own lavish praise of Defoe's inim-
itable novel:

> *Robinson Crusoe* lives in all lands, and it is a book for all time. How
> romantic the desert island! How charmingly rude the cavern home!
> How picturesque and self-complacent the Man Friday! There are
> some here, perhaps, who, like myself, believed it all to be true . . .
> [Samuel] Johnson thought the story only too short, and we doubt-
> less were of the same opinion. It is his greatest work, and as such it
> stands associated with his name on this monument now . . . unveiled
> for the view of future generations.

According to the *Daily News*, at this juncture in his speech, Reed
paused and 'cut loose the drapery which enshrouded the pillar,
amidst continual cheering [from the crowd]' and said, 'Thus it is
we write history and honour the name of one of England's noblest
sons.'

When the 'drapery' slid off, it revealed a huge, startling white
marble obelisk rising up seventeen feet from a rectangular base eight
feet by four. The inscription on the side of the monument looks as
clear and unblemished today as it must have done 140 years ago.

DANIEL DE-FOE
BORN 1661
DIED 1731
AUTHOR OF 'ROBINSON CRUSOE'
THIS MONUMENT IS THE RESULT OF AN APPEAL
IN THE 'CHRISTIAN WORLD' NEWSPAPER
TO THE BOYS AND GIRLS OF ENGLAND FOR FUNDS
TO PLACE A SUITABLE MEMORIAL UPON THE GRAVE
OF
DANIEL DE-FOE
IT REPRESENTS THE UNITED CONTRIBUTIONS
OF SEVENTEEN HUNDRED PERSONS
SEPT.ᴿ 1870

How pleased Defoe would have been with this memorial. And how accurate – despite the Victorian hyperbole of its unveiling – it truly is. The gleaming white obelisk pointing upwards to the sky identifies the quintessential Defoe, the man who survived all the storms of his life: the creator of *Robinson Crusoe*.

But what of Knox's afterlife? He was buried at Wimbledon Church next to his mother, but his grave vanished when the church was rebuilt in the late eighteenth and nineteenth centuries. As for his literary remains, when Knox died, his only book, the *Historical Relation of Ceylon*, had been out of print forty years and surviving copies were well worn and hard to come by. The book was forgotten. The bulging manuscript of his second edition of the *Historical Relation of Ceylon* disappeared and so did the other copy in which he had written his manuscript autobiography. When Knox died, the second-edition manuscript was probably still in the hands of his reluctant publisher Daniel Midwinter. Knox left the other interleaved copy of his Ceylon book, together with his autobiography, to his grand-nephew Knox Ward.

Knox Ward was born in 1704 and died in 1741. We know a few other facts about his life. As a child he had stood in the pillory with his 'notorious' father John Ward and he seems to have been a wayward character as an adult as well. In 1729, Knox Ward married Elizabeth Nettleton, a marriage which provoked a suit against him the same year by a 'Miss Holt of Hackney for breach of promise'. Presumably Ward had agreed to marry both ladies and then defaulted on Miss Holt. Initially, her case was dismissed on a technicality, but a woman scorned is a persistent woman. Miss Holt sued Knox Ward again in 1732 and this time she was awarded damages of £2,000.[7] Nine years later, when Knox Ward died at the age of thirty-seven, he left no will. His possessions, including his grand-uncle's 'Booke of Ceylon and Maniscripts', disappeared and there is no word of them for nearly two hundred years.

In 1817, the 1681 first edition of Knox's book was republished under the editorship of the Reverend Robert Fellowes and printed by Joseph Mawman in London. This was a slipshod production with modernised spelling and errors of transcription and it was little noticed. After this, the book sank once again until a British journalist and avid amateur historian who lived and worked in Ceylon, Donald Ferguson, read Knox's *Historical Relation* and became fascinated with the man and his life. Ferguson proceeded to go to every place in Ceylon where Knox had lived or visited and then, when Ferguson returned to England in the 1890s, he tracked down all of Knox's letters and also ransacked the East India Company records for every reference they contained of his career. From all these sources Ferguson was able to reconstruct Knox's life in considerable detail. Even more importantly, when Ferguson read Knox's letters to John Strype, he learned of the existence of the (now lost) autobiography which Knox refers to several times. Ferguson published the results of his research in a detailed, seventy-one-page, privately printed monograph, *Captain Robert Knox: Contributions towards a Biography*, published in 1897. He rightly believed that a full biography of Knox could not be written until the lost second edition and autobiography were found and, to this end, in 1898 he sent a letter to *Notes and Queries* enquiring, 'Can any . . . reader of *N&Q* tell me if any of Knox Ward's descendants still live?'[8]

No one responded to Ferguson's letter, but unbeknown to him, the 'second edition' of the *Historical Relation* was almost literally under his nose. Because of failing health, Ferguson had retired from his job as a journalist in Ceylon to live back in England in Croydon, and during his retirement he often came up to London to pursue research in the British Museum. It was here – behind the scenes, not in the Reading Room where Ferguson was toiling – in the late 1890s, that the bulging 'second edition' copy of the *Historical Relation of Ceylon* with all of Knox's handwritten revisions and additions was acquired by Sir A. W. Franks, the distinguished keeper of the British Museum's Ethnography Department. This acquisition, however, was for many years unread and uncatalogued. It was only in 1925, in fact, that Franks's successor, J. H. Braunholtz, and a retired Ceylon government archivist, J. H. O. Paulusz, identified it as Knox's long-lost, revised second edition of his *Historical Relation of Ceylon*.

• Some fifteen years before this, however, the other interleaved copy of Knox's book – the one containing his autobiography – had been located at the Bodleian Library where it had lain, also uncatalogued and unidentified, since 1755. How did it reach the Bodleian and why was it ignored for more than 150 years? Eight years after the death of Knox Ward in 1741, his library was sold at auction and lot 451, 'Knox's history of Ceylon with MSS additions', was acquired by 'that omnivorous collector Dr Richard Rawlinson, who later bequeathed it to the Bodleian. It came to the Library in 1755, along with the rest of the vast and multifarious Rawlinson collection.' This indeed was 'a collection so extensive that it swamped the meagre staff, and ... for more than a century ... large parts of it lay unsorted in cupboards and obscure hiding-holes'.9

In October 1900, Knox's second interleaved volume, containing his manuscript autobiography, was finally unearthed by a young don named Cuthbert Shields of Corpus Christi College. This was a momentous discovery but Shields was apparently unaware of just how important it was. He did, however, mention it in a footnote to an article he wrote on 'The First Century of the East India Company' published in the *Quarterly Review* in January 1901. The bulging interleaved copy of the *Historical Relation* containing Knox's manuscript autobiography wasn't catalogued or generally available to scholars until 1912. Before this, however, someone spotted Cuthbert Shield's footnote in 1910 and tracked down Knox's volume to the Bodleian Library. The following year it was published for the first time, edited by a former Ceylon civil servant, named James Ryan.* But the book was

---

* Donald Ferguson died in 1910, the year before Ryan's edition of Knox's *Historical Relation* with his autobiography came out, so poor Ferguson, who had spent some thirty years searching for the autobiography, never read it.

not readily available. Published in Glasgow by James MacLehose and Sons, the Ryan edition was limited to a hundred signed and numbered copies. These were neither cheap nor easy to obtain and they are still hard to come by and worth a great deal today.

After Braunholtz and Paulusz identified the interleaved copy of Knox's book in the British Library in 1925, they decided to collaborate on editing the long-delayed second edition and publish the book with all its revisions and additions as Knox had wished it to be. They planned as well to include Knox's manuscript autobiography in the Bodleian Library to produce the first complete edition of what Knox had long ago referred to as 'my Booke of Ceylon and Maniscripts of my Life'. Both Braunholtz and Paulusz were busy men, however, and then the Second World War intervened. It was only in 1955, when they received sponsorship for their edition from the Hakluyt Society, that the new, full edition of Knox got properly under way. Braunholtz, however, died several years later, leaving Paulusz to bring it out on his own. Periodically over the next twenty years, when enquiries were made to the Hakluyt Society about the edition of Knox, people were reassuringly told that it was 'forthcoming'.

But it never appeared, and at some point the Hakluyt Society dropped the project, probably because it became dismayed by the extent and scope of what Paulusz was submitting to them. In any event, they withdrew their sponsorship, though as late as 1975, they informed a keen Sri Lankan Knox scholar named Ian Goonetileke that the footnotes were being typed and the book was imminent.[10]* Five years later, however, in 1980, when an Australian researcher named James Crouch enquired about the Knox project, he was told by the Hakluyt Society that 'We regret that the Society's edition of Knox's Ceylon has been abandoned'.[11]

It wasn't until 1989 — by which time eighty-nine-year-old J. H. O. Paulusz had been labouring on Knox for more than sixty years — that the definitive, full edition of Robert Knox's *An Historical Relation of the Island of Ceylon Together with his Autobiography*

* Goonetileke wrote to the Hakluyt Society about the edition in May 1975 and received the following reply from the Secretary: 'It is to be hoped that *An Historical Relation of the Island of Ceylon* by Captain Robert Knox edited by H. J. [sic] Paulusz will be published within the next two years. The footnotes are at present being typed which fills me with optimism, although years of experience warns me not to be too optimistic!'

and All the New Chapters, [and] *Marginal Notes added by the Author of the Two Interleaved Copies of the Original Text of 1681* finally appeared. It was published, in fact, in two volumes, the first of which comprises Paulusz's mammoth 500-page introduction; the second 688-page volume is Knox's book, including all his revisions and additions and his autobiography. In the end, Paulusz's edition was brought out by a Sri Lankan publisher and it remains hard to come by elsewhere. An erudite former government archivist in Ceylon, Paulusz edited, annotated and wrote footnotes for Knox's text and expanded his own introduction over the course of more than three decades and in the process, in his retirement in rural Wales, he grew old and prolix, not unlike Knox himself in his last years in St Peter le Poer, as he worked on and added to his 'Booke of Ceylon and maniscripts of my own Life'.

Paulusz's book-length introduction has been criticised by scholars for being inaccurate and pro-Dutch.[12] Despite such criticisms and despite, too, its inordinate length, Paulusz's edition of Knox can be a delight to read and its comprehensive but prolix character actually captures the haphazard, rambling style of Knox's originals. In order to differentiate between the 1681 edition and Knox's manuscript additions and revisions and his autobiography, Paulusz employs different typefaces which make for a rather dizzying read, but somehow I think Knox himself would have approved. Jumping from one typeface to the next is a bit like turning the interleaved manuscript volumes sideways, this way and that, in order to read all of Knox's marginal notations and additions.

Thus Knox's long-delayed second edition and autobiography were finally published some 269 years after his death. Knox today is well remembered in Ceylon. A reprint of the original 1681 edition is readily available in paperback and there is also a paperback Sinhalese edition of his *Historical Relation.* Knox has left an oral tradition all over the island as well, especially in Trincomalee where he first landed and in Eledatta and Laggendenny where he lived. All three places have Robert Knox roads and memorial stones and when I stayed at a smart seaside hotel in Trincomalee, I was allotted (quite by chance) the 'Robert Knox Cottage' with a hanging name sign in the front and a sliding glass door opening directly onto the beach and sea at the back.

*

Outside Ceylon, however, Knox is little known and even less read. Defoe, in contrast, is alive and well, and Crusoe – well, Crusoe seems to be everywhere. Crusoe hasn't just survived, he has thrived, flourished and proliferated. Translations and adaptations of the novel flooded the market in the eighteenth century. In the nineteenth century, a number of classics in their own right were rightly considered Crusoe's progeny: most notably, *Swiss Family Robinson*, *Coral Island* and *Treasure Island*. The twentieth century has continued this line of Crusoe-inspired books (or perhaps more accurately anti-Crusoes) with William Golding's *Lord of the Flies*, Michel Tournier's *Vendredi*, Jane Gardam's *Crusoe's Daughter*, Derek Walcott's 'Crusoe's Journal' in *The Castaway and Other Poems* and J. M. Coetzee's *Foe*. In the 1930s, Al Jolson wrote and sang the song 'Where Did Robinson Crusoe Go With Friday on a Saturday Night?' and this was followed by a full-blown musical, *Robinson Crusoe Jr.*[13] Inevitably, Crusoe also then came to the screen. The earliest film version, *Mr Robinson Crusoe*, directed by Edward Sutherland, came out in 1932. This was followed twenty years later by Luis Buñuel's masterful and surprisingly faithful colour film, *The Adventures of Robinson Crusoe. Cast Away* (2000), with Tom Hanks, in which Friday is reduced to a volley ball, is the most recent film version of the book. *Robinson Crusoe* was also made into a thirteen-part television series in the 1960s. Nor should we fail to mention animated cartoons of the novel and the sci-fi version *Robinson Crusoe on Mars*.

Crusoe today is ubiquitous, and there are both highbrow and lowbrow Crusoespheres. There is a thriving Defoe Society, a Defoe academic industry (including the peer-reviewed online journal *Digitalised Defoe*), Defoe symposiums and Defoe conferences. Like many institutions, the Defoe industry has different divisions – the most notable being the divide between academics and devotees and fans or enthusiasts. Defoe studies can also be a contentious place. But everyone who reads Defoe, and *Robinson Crusoe* in particular, is hugely indebted to the scrupulous and copious amount of Defoe scholarship and criticism that has been produced in the last century alone.[14] For one thing, at long last, we finally have a clear idea of what Defoe actually wrote (the man himself complained that every anonymous work, especially if it was controversial or scurrilous, was always attributed to him), and there are now carefully edited and annotated texts that enable us to read Defoe's words as closely as possible to the way he actually wrote them, with all their idiosyncratic grammar, capital letters, erratic spelling and punctuation.[15]

And then there is the Crusoe of popular culture: of television series like *Lost, Survivor* and *I'm a Celebrity . . . Get Me Out of Here*. On the radio there is the long-running favourite, *Desert Island Discs*, in which the guest of the week, in true Crusoe and Knox fashion, is always provided with a Bible on his or her desert island. I even have a coffee mug with a desert island and palm tree pictured on it, beneath which is the legend: 'Only Robinson Crusoe could get everything done by Friday.'

Our lives and world now are remote from and alien to those of Defoe and Robert Knox. But it's almost as if the further removed we are from desert island life – connected as we are at all times by Twitter and Facebook and mobile phone texting, and when we can go anywhere in the world in a few seconds on our computers thanks to Google Earth – the more we seem to crave and need desert island tales. Perhaps the most obvious site of Crusoe resurgence today is to be found in the glut of contemporary self-help books, and best-selling inspirational blockbusters such as Rhona Byrne's *The Secret* and *The Power*. Books that tell you that no matter what your situation, you can survive and succeed.

Never mind. Myths travel. That's their chief virtue and why we need them. But let's also look back to where the Crusoe myth began nearly three hundred years ago with two men separated by a few miles in London writing alone at their desks. Robert Knox and Daniel Defoe: the man who was Crusoe and the man who wrote Crusoe. Together they gave voice to the lone castaway that we all are at some point in our lives, and they capture our yearnings for and dreams to escape, connect and survive.

List of Illustrations and Maps

Integrated illustrations

Defoe's house in Stoke Newington; photograph in author's collection
from Thomas Wright, *The Life of Daniel Defoe*, 1894

Robinson Crusoe's island; photograph in author's collection from *Serious
Reflections During the Life of Robinson Crusoe*, 1720

Raja Sinha, King of Kandy; photograph in author's collection from
Robert Knox, *Historical Relation of Ceylon*, 1681

Fleet debtors' prison © Mary Evans Picture Library

Talipot leaf; photograph in author's collection from Robert Knox,
Historical Relation of Ceylon, 1681

Defoe in the pillory; photograph in author's collection from a chapbook
of Defoe's *Jure Divino*

Newgate prison © Topfoto

Title page of the first edition of *The Storm*, 1704; photograph in
author's collection

Title page of the first edition of Knox's *An Historical Relation of
Ceylon*, 1681; photograph in author's collection

Defoe's original tombstone; photograph in author's collection from
Thomas Wright, *The Life of Daniel Defoe*, 1894

llustration section

Defoe in 1706; frontispiece to *Jure Divino*, engraved by M. Van der
Gucht; photograph in author's collection

Eyre Crowe's Victorian painting of Defoe in the Pillory © National
Portrait Gallery, London

Disputed portrait of Robert Hooke by Mary Beale © National Portrait
Gallery, London

East India Company ships © National Maritime Museum, Greenwich,
London

Knox memorial stone at Lagendenny; photograph in author's collection

Seventeenth-century coffee house © Topfoto

East India Company House © Mary Evans Picture Library

Sir Josiah Child © National Portrait Gallery, London

Robert Harley © National Portrait Gallery, London

Robert Knox in 1695; engraving by Robert White; photograph in
author's collection

Portrait of Robert Knox in 1709 by P. Trampon © National Maritime
Museum, Greenwich, London

First edition title page and frontispiece of *Robinson Crusoe*, 1719; photograph in author's collection

St Helena © Mary Evans Picture Library

The 1703 great storm © Topfoto

Maps

Map of Ceylon showing the places where Knox lived and his escape
route from Robert Knox, *Historical Relation of Ceylon*, 1681

Map of the trading regions of the East India Trading Company
© Reginald Piggott

Select Bibliography

Aitken, George A., 'Defoe's Library', *The Athenaeum*, 1 June 1895, pp. 706–7.

Backscheider, Paula R., *Daniel Defoe: His Life*, Baltimore, 1989.

Baines, Paul, *Daniel Defoe: Robinson Crusoe and Moll Flanders*, Basingstoke, 2007.

Bastian, F., *Defoe's Early Life*, London, 1981.

Bennett, Jim, Michael Cooper, Michael Hunter, Lisa Jardine, *London's Leonardo: The Life and Work of Robert Hooke*, Oxford, 2003.

Birch, Thomas, *A History of the Royal Society*, 4 vols, London, 1756.

Blake, J. R., 'A Brief Notice of Robert Knox and his companions in captivity in Kandy for the space of twenty years, discovered among the Dutch records preserved in the Colonial Secretary's Office, Colombo, and translated into English', *Dutch Records of the Ceylon Government*, vol. IV, no. 14, 1867–70, pp. 143–50.

Booth, Martin, *Cannabis: A History*, London, 2003.

Bowrey, Thomas, *A Geographical Account of the Countries Round the Bay of Bengal, 1669–1679*, Cambridge, 1905.

Boyle, Richard, *Knox's Words*, Colombo, 2004.

Brayne, Martin, *The Greatest Storm*, Stroud, 2002.

Brohier, R.L., *Changing face of Colombo*, Colombo, 1984.

Brooke, Thomas H., *A History of the Island of St Helena*, London, 1808.

Brown, Mervyn, *A History of Madagascar*, Cambridge, 1995.

Byrne, Richard, *Prisons and Punishments of London*, London, 1992.

Carpenter, Kevin, *Desert Isles and Pirate Islands*, Frankfurt, 1984.

Chalmers, George, *The Life of Daniel Defoe*, London: Stockdale, 1790.

Codrington, H. W., *A Short History of Ceylon*, London, 1926.

Colley, Linda, *Captives: Britain, Empire and the World 1600–1850*, London, 2002.

Conrad, Peter, *Islands*, London, 2009.

Dampier, William, *A New Voyage Round the World*, London, 1999.

Defoe, Daniel (ed. P. N. Furbank and W. R. Owens), *Works of Daniel Defoe*, 44 vols, London, 2000–8.

—— *A Journal of the Plague Year*, 1722; rpt London, 2003.

—— *Moll Flanders*, 1722; rpt London, 1989.

—— *Robinson Crusoe* (Norton Critical Edition), 1719; rpt New York, 1994.

—— *Roxana*, 1724; rpt London, 1987.

de la Mare, Walter, *Desert Islands and Robinson Crusoe*, London, 1930.

De Silva, K. M., *A History of Sri Lanka*, London, 1981.

Dottin, Paul (trans. Louise Ragan), *The Life and Strange Surprising Adventures of Daniel Defoe*, London, 1928.

Dottin, Paul, *Robinson Crusoe Examin'd and Criticis'd: A New Edition of Charles Gildon's famous pamphlet now published with an Introduction and Explanatory Notes Together With an Essay on Gildon's Life*, London, 1923.

Downie, J. A., *Robert Harley and the Press*, Cambridge, 1979.

Earle, Peter, *Sailors: English Merchant Seamen, 1650–1775*, London, 1998.

—— *The World of Defoe*, London, 1976.

Edwards, Philip, *The Story of the Voyage*, Cambridge, 1994.

Ellis, Markman, *The Coffee House*, London, 2004.

Fausett, David, *The Strange, Surprising Sources of Robinson Crusoe*, Amsterdam, 1994.

Ferguson, Donald W., *Captain Robert Knox: The Twenty Year Captive in Ceylon and Author of An Historical Relation of the Island of Ceylon in the East Indies: Contributions Towards a Biography*, Colombo and Croydon, 1896–97.

Ferguson, D. W., 'Robert Knox's Sinhalese Vocabulary', *Journal of the Ceylon Branch of the Royal Asiatic Society*, vol. XIV (1896), pp. 155–200.

Fisher, Carl, 'The Robinsonade: An Intercultural History of an Idea', in *Approaches to Teaching Robinson Crusoe* (ed. Novak and Fisher), New York, 2005.

Forster, John, *Daniel Defoe*, London, 1855.

Furbank, P. N., and W. R. Owens, *The Canonisation of Daniel Defoe*, London, 1988.

—— *A Critical Bibliography of Daniel Defoe*, London, 1998.

—— *Defoe De-Attributions: A Critique of J. R. Moore's Checklist*, London, 1994.

—— *A Political Biography of Daniel Defoe*, London, 2006.

—— *Works of Daniel Defoe*, 44 vols, London, 2000–2007.

Goonetileke, H.A.I., 'Robert Knox in the Kandyan Kingdom, 1660–1669: A Bio-bibliographical Commentary', *Sri Lankan Journal of the Humanities*, vol. I, part 2 (1975), pp. 81–151.

Goonetileke, H.A.I., 'Robert Knox in the Kandyan Kingdom, 1660–1669: A Bio-bibliographical Commentary', *Sri Lankan Journal of the Humanities*, vols 24 & 25, nos 1 & 2 (1998–99), pp. 248–69.

Goonewardene, K. W., 'Robert Knox: the Interleaved Edition', *Journal of the Royal Asiatic Society of Sri Lanka*, vol. 38, 1992/93 [1994], pp. 117–44.

Goonewardene, K. W., 'Some Comments on Robert Knox and his Writings on Ceylon', *University of Ceylon Review*, 16 (1 & 2), Jan–April 1958, pp. 39–52.

Gosse, Philip, *St Helena: 1502–1938*, London, 1938.

Green, Martin, *The Robinson Crusoe Story*, Pennsylvania, 1990.

Gribbin, John, *The Fellowship*, London, 2005.

Griffiths, John C., *Hostage*, London, 2003.

Grovier, Kelly, *The Gaol: The Story of Newgate*, London, 2008.

Gunther, R.T., *Early Science in Oxford: The Life and Work of Robert Hooke*, vols 6–7, 10 and 13, Oxford, 1930–35.

Hakluyt, Richard, *Voyages and Discoveries*, London, 1985.

Halliday, Stephen, *Newgate: London's Prototype of Hell*, Stroud, 2006.

Hammond, J. R., *A Defoe Companion*, London, 1993.

Hazlitt, William, 'Wilson's *Life and Times of Daniel Defoe*', *Edinburgh Review*, 1 (January 1830), pp. 397–425.

Healey, George Harris (ed), *The Letters of Daniel Defoe*, Oxford, 1955.

Henderson, Felicity, 'Unpublished Material from the Memorandum Book of Robert Hooke, Guildhall Library MS 1758', *Notes and Records of the Royal Society*, 61 (2007), pp. 129–75.

Hill, Brian, *Robert Harley: Speaker, Secretary of State and Premier Minister*, London, 1988.

Holmes, Geoffrey, *British Politics in the Age of Anne*, London, 1987.

Hooke, Robert, *Philosophical Experiments and Observations of Dr Robert Hooke*, ed. W. Derham, London, 1726.

Hoppit, Julian, *A Land of Liberty? England 1689–1727*, Oxford, 2000.

Horner, Samuel, *A Brief Account of the Interesting Ceremony of Unveiling the monument erected by the boys and girls of England to the memory of Daniel Defoe*, Southampton, 1871.

Hutchins, Henry Clinton, *Robinson Crusoe and Its Printing: 1719–1731*, 1925; rpt New York, 1967.

Inwood, Stephen, *The Man Who Knew Too Much: The Strange and Inventive Life of Robert Hooke*, London, 2002.

Irwin, Aisling, and Colum Wilson, *Cape Verde Islands*, Bradt Travel Guide, 2009.

Jardine, Lisa, *The Curious Life of Robert Hooke*, London, 2003.

Jayawickrama, Sarojini, *Writing that Conquers: Re-reading Knox's An Historical Relation of the Island of Ceylon*, Colombo, 2004.

Keay, John, *The Honourable Company: A History of the English East India Company*, London, 1991.

Knox, Robert, *An Historical Relation of the Island Ceylon in the East Indies*, London, 1681.

—— *An Historical Relation of the Island Ceylon in the East Indies together with Somewhat Concerning Severall Remarkable Passages of my Life* (ed. James Ryan), Glasgow, 1911.

—— *An Historical Relation of the Island Ceylon in the East Indies* (ed. S. D. Saparamadu), Ceylon, 1958.

—— *An Historical Relation of the Island Ceylon in the East Indies, Revised, Enlarged & Brought to the verge of Publication as the Second Edition by Robert Knox Together with his Autobiography and all the new chapters, paragraphs, marginal notes added by the author in the two interleaved copies of the original text of 1681* (ed. J. H. O. Paulusz), 2 vols, Dehiwla, Sri Lanka, 1989.

Knox-Shaw, Peter, 'Defoe and the Politics of Representing the African Interior', *Modern Language Review*, 10 January 2001.

—— *The Explorer in English Fiction*, New York, 1986.

Leach, Edmund, 'What Happened to An Historical Relation . . . on the Way to the Printers', *Identity, Consciousness and the Past: The South Asian Scene* (ed. H. L. Seneviratne), Adelaide, 1989.

Lee, William, *Daniel Defoe: His Life and Recently Discovered Writings*, 3 vols, 1869; rpt Hildesheim, 1968.

Lindsay, Jack, *Monster City: Defoe's London*, London, 1978.

Ludowyk, E. F., 'Robert Knox and Robinson Crusoe', *University of Ceylon Review*, July 1953, pp. 243–52.

—— *The Story of Ceylon*, London, 1962.

—— 'Two Englishmen and Ceylon', *Ceylon Observer Annual* (1949), pp. 23–26.

Macaulay, Thomas Babington, *The History of England*, 1848; rpt London, 1979.

Mander, David, *Look Back, Look Forwards! An Illustrated History of Stoke Newington*, London, 1997.

Martin, John, *Beyond Belief: The Real Life of Daniel Defoe*, Pembrokeshire, 2006.

Masefield, John, *A Mainsail Haul*, 1905; rpt London, 1987.

Minto, William, *Daniel Defoe*, London, 1879.

Moore, John Robert, *Daniel Defoe: Citizen of the Modern World*, Chicago, 1958.

—— *Defoe in the Pillory and Other Studies*, Indiana, 1939.

Moore, Lucy, *The Thieves' Opera: The Remarkable Lives of Jonathan Wild and Jack Sheppard*, London, 1997.

Morley, Henry, *The Earlier Life and the Chief Earlier Works of Daniel Defoe*, London, 1889.

Mynshul, Geffray, *Essays and Characters of a Prison and Prisoners*, London, 1638.

Newton, Theodore F. M., 'The Civet-Cats of Newington Green: New Light on Defoe', *Review of English Studies*, XIII (1937), 49, 10–19.

Novak, Maximillian E., *Approaches to Teaching Defoe's Robinson Crusoe*, New York, 2005.

—— *Daniel Defoe: Master of Fictions*, Oxford, 2001.

Parker, G., 'The Allegory of Robinson Crusoe', *History*, vol. X (1925), pp. 11–25.

Paulin, Tom, *Crusoe's Secret*, London, 2005.

Payne, William L., 'Defoe in the Pamphlets', *Philological Quarterly*, vol. LII (1973), pp. 85–96.

Peebles, Patrick, 'Captain Robert Knox and the East India Company', paper delivered at the Tenth International Conference of the World History Association, 1 July 2001.

Peebles, Patrick, 'The Life and Strange, Surprising Adventures of Captain Robert Knox', *Sri Lankan Journal of the Humanities*, vols 29 & 30, nos 1 & 2 (2003–4), pp. 31–51.

Peebles, Patrick, unpublished paper: 'The Royal Absolutism of Rāja Sinha II and Robert Knox'.

Pitt, Moses, *The Cry of the Oppressed*, London, 1691.

Porter, Roy, *London: A Social History*, London, 1994.

Preston, Diana and Michael, *A Pirate of Exquisite Mind: The Life of William Dampier*, London, 2004.

Randrienja, Solofe and Ellis, Stephen, *Madagascar: A Short History*, London, 2009.

Rawlinson, H. G., 'The Adventures of Robert Knox 1640–1720', *Indian Historical Studies*, London, 1913.

Reimers, E., 'Raja Sinha and the British Captives', *Journal of the Ceylon Branch of the Royal Asiatic Society*, vol. 30, no. 78, 1925.

Richetti, John, *The Cambridge Companion to Daniel Defoe*, Cambridge, 2008.

—— *The Life of Daniel Defoe*, Oxford, 2005.

Robinson, Henry W., and Walter Adams, *The Diary of Robert Hooke 1672–1680*, London, 1935.

Rogers, Pat (ed.), *Defoe: The Critical Heritage*, London, 1972.

Rogers, Pat, *Grub Street*, London, 1972.

—— *Robinson Crusoe*, London, 1979.

Royle, Stephen, *The Company's Island: St Helena, Company Colonies and the Colonial Endeavour*, London, 2007.

Said, Edward, *Culture and Imperialism*, New York, 1994.

—— *On Late Style*, London, 2006.

Schonhorn, Manuel, *Defoe's Politics: Parliament, Power, and Robinson Crusoe*, Cambridge, 1991.

Secord, Arthur, 'Defoe in Stoke Newington', *PMLA*, vol. 66 (1951), pp. 211–25.

—— *Studies in the Narrative Method of Defoe*, 1924; rpt New York, 1963.

Seidel, Michael, *Robinson Crusoe: Island Myths and the Novel*, Boston, 1991.

Seligman, Martin, *Learned Optimism: How to Change Your Mind and Your Life*, New York, 2006.

Severin, Tim, *Seeking Robinson Crusoe*, London, 2002.

Souhami, Diana, *Selkirk's Island*, London, 2001.

Spaas, Lieve and Brian Stimpson (eds), *Robinson Crusoe: Myths and Metamorphoses*, Basingstoke, 1996.

Starr, George A., *Defoe and Spiritual Autobiography*, Princeton, 1965.

Steiner, Sue, and Robin Liston, *St Helena, Ascension, Tristan da Cunha,* Bradt Travel Guide, 2007.

Sutherland, James, *Defoe*, London, 1937.

Sutherland, J. R., 'Some Early Troubles of Daniel Defoe', *Review of English Studies*, vol. 9 (1933), pp. 275–90.

Sutton, Jean, *Lords of the East: The East India Company and its Ships,* London, 2000.

Trent, William, *Daniel Defoe: How to Know Him,* 1916; rpt New York, 1971.

Walker, Richard, 'The Life of Robert Hooke', in *The Posthumous Works of Robert Hooke*, London, 1705.

Watt, Ian, *The Rise of the Novel*, London, 1957.

—— *Myths of Modern Individualism*, Cambridge, 1996.

West, Richard, *The Life and Strange, Surprising Adventures of Daniel Defoe,* London, 1997.

White, Herbert, 'Notes on Knox's Ceylon in its Literary Aspect', *Journal of the Royal Asiatic Society (Ceylon Branch)*, vol. 13, no. 44 (1893), pp. 23–34.

Wilson, Walter, *Memoirs of the Life and Times of Daniel Defoe,* 3 vols, London, 1830.

Winterbottom, Anna, 'Producing and Using the *Historical Relation of Ceylon*: Robert Knox, the East India Company and the Royal Society', *British Journal of the History of Science*, vol 42. no. 4. (2009), pp. 515–538.

—— 'Seventeenth Century Records in the St Helena Archives, Appendix 1: East India Company Consultations', *Lives and Letters: A Journal of Early Modern Archival Research*, vol. 1, Spring 2009.

Wright, Thomas, *The Life of Daniel Defoe*, London, 1894; revised bicentenary edn published 1931.

Notes

Endnote Abbreviations

In the endnotes I have used the following abbreviations for frequently cited works. Other references are condensed to the name of the author and sometimes the titles of works cited in full in the Bibliography.

BL	British Library
CUL	Cambridge University Library
EIC	East India Company
HR I and HR II	Volumes one and two of J. H. O. Paulusz' 1989 edition of Robert Knox's *An Historical Relation of the Island of Ceylon*
JS	John Strype
PRO	Public Records Office
RK	Robert Knox

Abbreviations for Defoe's works in the endnotes
WDD *Works of Daniel Defoe*, ed. P. N. Furbank and W. R. Owens, 44 vols. Unless otherwise indicated, references to Defoe's works are to this edition with the exception of the major novels. For these, I have cited more accessible editions:

Robinson Crusoe (Norton Critical Edition)
Moll Flanders (Penguin edition)
The Storm (Penguin edition)
Journal of the Plague Year (Penguin edition)
Roxana (Penguin edition)

Chapter One: *Two Writing Men*

1. We don't know for certain because there are no records of Defoe's birth or baptism. • **2.** *An Appeal to Honour and Justice.* • **3.** Strype's edition of Stow's *Survey of London*, online. • **4.** Abel Boyer, in the *Political State*, June 1717, p. 632. • **5.** Eventually Henry Baker, Defoe's son-in-law, bought the Church Street house from Timothy Sutton in 1741. Secord, 'Defoe in Stoke Newington', p. 216. • **6.** John Strype will chiefly be remembered, however, as an antiquarian and the prolific author of ecclesiastical biographies. • **7.** Strype's edition of Stowe. • **8.** RK to JS, 18 April 1720. CUL. • **9.** Fifteen years earlier, in 1695, Robert White, one of 'the most esteemed and industrious' artists of the day, had done a portrait engraving of Knox that was supposed to serve as the frontispiece for the revised, expanded second edition of the *Historical Relation*. But the second edition and White's engraving weren't published until long after Knox's death. *HR* I, pp. 427–8. • **10.** I have been unable to find any other works by Trampon or indeed any information at all about him. P. Trampon may in fact be the pseudonym of an artist with a completely different name who was unwilling for some reason to acknowledge the Knox portrait, perhaps because he was in the employ of or under contract to a patron and thus moonlighting when he took on the commission to do the Knox portrait. • **11.** Eventually this oil portrait of Knox will end up among the holdings of the National Maritime Museum in Greenwich. But it has never been exhibited. Instead, ever since the museum acquired it in 1932, the portrait has been stored in a warehouse on a backstreet a mile away from the museum. It can only be viewed at the warehouse, as I arranged to see it, by application to and private appointment with the keeper. Like the interleaved manuscript folios of his book, this revealing portrait of Knox has been locked away, out of sight, all but forgotten. • **12.** RK to JS, 8 January 1717. CUL. • **13.** *HR* II, p. 516.

Chapter Two: *Crusoe's Secret*

1. *Robinson Crusoe* was first published in a small octavo-sized volume approximately 7.5 inches tall and 5 inches wide. Octavo books were more portable and cheaper than larger folio or quarto volumes, but they were

bigger than duodecimo-sized and smaller books, tracts and pamphlets.
• **2**. Rogers, *Robinson Crusoe*, p. 4. • **3**. Hutchins, *Robinson Crusoe and Its Printing: 1719–1731*, p. 47. • **4**. Ibid., pp. 67–68, 78. • **5**. Wilson, *Memoirs of the Life and Times of Daniel De Foe*, III, p. 433. • **6**. *WDD*, 'Preface' to *The Farther Adventures of Robinson Crusoe*, p. 3. • **7**. Wilson, p. 434. • **8**. Hutchins, pp. 143–4. • **9**. This is one of the earliest – if not the very first – instances of serialisation of English fiction in the popular press. • **10**. Rogers, p. 12. • **11**. For a history and discussion of the Robinsonade, see Martin Green, *The Robinson Crusoe Story*, Pat Rogers, *Robinson Crusoe*, pp. 12–13, Carl Fisher, 'The Robinsonade: An Intercultural History of an Idea', in Novak and Fisher (eds), *Approaches to Teaching Defoe's Robinson Crusoe*, pp. 129–39, and Paul Baines, *Daniel Defoe: Robinson Crusoe/ Moll Flanders*, pp. 130–3. • **12**. Kevin Carpenter, *Desert Isles and Pirate Islands*, p. 6. • **13**. Rogers, pp. 12–13. • **14**. Fisher, p. 138. • **15**. In the mid-twentieth century, Robinsonades took on a darker, dystopian form and character in books such as William Golding's *Lord of the Flies* and *Pincher Martin*, Michel Tournier's *Friday* and J. M. Coetzee's *Foe*. All of these turned Defoe's uplifting, survival story on its head. They are anti-Crusoes or anti-Robinsonades. • **16**. Watt, '*Robinson Crusoe* as a Myth', reprinted in the Norton Critical Edition of *Robinson Crusoe*, pp. 289–90. Watt, however, goes on to assert that Crusoe's 'ultimate referent' is 'economic man' and that his mythic status derives from his glorification of labour and espousal of the 'gospel of work', p. 304. • **17**. *WDD*, 'A Letter to Mr How'. • **18**. *WDD*, *PEW*, vol. 8, p. 155. • **19**. No one at the time and few since, have remarked on this contradiction of Defoe anonymously calling for an end to authorial anonymity. John Mullan is a rare exception in his excellent study *Anonymity*, pp. 166–7. • **20**. *Lives of the Poets of Great Britain and Ireland in the Time of Dean Swift* (1753). This five-volume work is usually ascribed to Theophilus Cibber but the research for it and most of the text was written by Robert Shiels. A classic of early literary biography, it is available online at Project Gutenberg. • **21**. The history of the dispute over Defoe's canon is a colourful saga in itself which has evolved from the early-eighteenth-century days of hearsay and rumour to twenty-first-century computer-based stylometry and analysis. In the hope of tracking down every word Defoe ever wrote, generations of indefatigable antiquarians, Defoe enthusiasts and scholars have devoted their lives to trawling the morass of anonymous and pseudonymous print that was published between 1688, when Defoe probably wrote his first

pamphlet at the age of twenty-eight, and 1731 when he died. The story of Defoe's expanding canon – and the major literary antiquarians, bibliographers and biographers who created it – is told in fascinating detail in Furbank and Owens's *The Canonisation of Daniel Defoe* published in 1988. This was followed by two further books on the Defoe canon: *Defoe De-Attributions* (published in 1994) in which Furbank and Owens removed – or 'de-attributed' – 252 works from J. R. Moore's standard *Checklist of the Writings of Daniel Defoe* (1971). Furbank and Owens's list of de-attributed works includes their reasons or arguments for expelling each work from the Defoe canon, and the list is preceded by a lengthy introduction on their most recent thinking on Defoe bibliography. Four years later, in 1998, Furbank and Owens produced their own *Critical Bibliography of Daniel Defoe*, which includes another excellent introduction on the history and practice of Defoe bibliography and their own new, downsized list of 276 Defoe works followed by various appendices including one on 'Unresolved Problems in Attribution'. Each of the entries in the *Critical Bibliography* contains detailed bibliographical information, a description and the location of the edition(s), a brief summary of the work and its attribution history. Though the *Critical Bibliography* has met with some critical objections, particularly in America, it far surpasses – and replaces – J. R. Moore's inflated and unreliable *Checklist*. It is unlikely that Furbank and Owens's excellent Defoe bibliography will be superseded any time soon. • **22.** Furbank and Owens, *The Canonisation of Daniel Defoe*, pp. 1–2. • **23.** Abel Boyer, in the *Political State*, June 1717. • **24.** Biographical information on Gildon can be found in Dottin's 'The Life of Charles Gildon', in Dottin's 1923 edition of Gildon's pamphlet and also in the *Dictionary of National Biography*. • **25.** Paul Dottin, *Robinson Crusoe Examin'd and Criticis'd*, p. 72. • **26.** This punishment had, in fact, been perpetrated on another eighteenth-century hack named Edmund Curll after he pirated a work and was punished for this misdemeanour when he was tossed in a blanket by the boys at Westminster School in August 1716. Curll's humiliation was first immortalised by his fellow hack John Dunton in a four-penny pamphlet entitled *Neck, or Nothing, a Consolatory Letter from Mr J. D-nt-n to Mr C-rll Upon his being Tost in a Blanket*. This crude verse satire included a frontispiece showing Curll being tossed in a blanket. Ralph Straus, *The Unspeakable Curll*, pp. 69–71. • **27.** Dottin's edition of Gildon, p. 71. • **28.** Ibid., pp. 71–72. • **29.** Back in 1719 there was no 'English Novel' to speak of. In 1711 Richard Steele wrote in the

Spectator, 'I am afraid thy Brains are a little disordered with Romances and Novels.' But Steele classified novels with frivolous 'romances' that addled the brain, and in 1719 'the Novel' as a distinct species had not yet emerged from the crowded literary sea. Romances and novels were an ephemeral, low kind of writing, and an air of shame clung to them. Clergymen denounced them from the pulpit. Novels were read furtively, late at night, by candlelight, alone. Thirty-six years after *Robinson Crusoe* was published, an unflattering definition of 'the Novel' appeared in Samuel Johnson's *Dictionary* (1755), where the novel is defined as a 'feigned story or tale'. 'Feign', Johnson tells us, means 'to invent, dissemble, relate falsely'. In other words, to lie. A novel is a lie – which is precisely what Charles Gildon had said of *Robinson Crusoe*. Certainly many of Defoe's other enemies, have also branded him a liar. And so have a number of his later admirers including Walter Minto who said of Defoe, 'He was a great, a truly great liar, perhaps the greatest liar that ever lived.' Minto, *Daniel Defoe*, p. 169. Leslie Stephen said Defoe 'had the most amazing talent on record for telling lies'. *Hours in a Library*, p. 3. • **30**. The earliest and in many ways still the best of the books on the real-life sources of *Robinson Crusoe* is Arthur Wellesley Secord's *Studies in the Narrative Method of Defoe* (1924). Later source studies include those written by Rogers, Green and Fausett, and two excellent books written for the general reader: Diana Souhami's *Selkirk's Island* and Tim Severin's *Seeking Robinson Crusoe*. • **31**. Quoted in Baines, p. 32. • **32**. *The Englishman*, no. 26, 3 December 1713. • **33**. *A Cruising Voyage round the World*, in the Norton Critical Edition of *Robinson Crusoe*, pp. 231, 234. • **34**. Colley, *Captives*, p 1. • **35**. Ibid., p 2. • **36**. *Robinson Crusoe* (Norton Critical Edition), p. 95. • **37**. Ibid., p. 83. • **38**. Crusoe can be seen as a prototype of later champions of positive thinking, positive psychology and cognitive behaviour therapy, including Samuel Smiles, Norman Vincent Peale and Aaron T. Beck, and more generally as precursor of the 'self-help' book or manual. • **39**. Seligman, *Learned Optimism*, p. 89. • **40**. *Robinson Crusoe*, p. 49. • **41**. *WDD, Serious Reflections of Robinson Crusoe*, p. 53. • **42**. *Robinson Crusoe*, p. 220. • **43**. *WDD, Farther Adventures of Robinson Crusoe*, p. 3. • **44**. We are never told how exactly this sea captain nephew is related to Crusoe. Crusoe's two elder brothers are quickly dispensed with on the first page of *Robinson Crusoe*: one is killed at the Battle of Dunkirk in 1658 and 'what became of my second Brother', Crusoe says, 'I never knew'. There is no mention of either elder brother leaving children. Nor does

Crusoe mention finding any more brothers or sisters who might have children when he returns from his twenty-eight years on the island. The nephew, however, may be the son of Crusoe's wife's sister or brother. • 45. Hutchins, p. 124. • 46. Lee, I, p. 300. • 47. *WDD* Starr 'Introduction', *Serious Reflections of Robinson Crusoe*, p. 1. • 48. *Serious Reflections*, p. 51.

Chapter Three: *'Captivated'*

1. *HR* II, p. 321. • 2. The Dutch had attacked and taken the fort at Trincomalee from the Portuguese in 1639 but they didn't rebuild and occupy it until 1665. • 3. *HR* II, p. 521. • 4. NS (new style or Gregorian calendar). The Gregorian calendar, in which the new year began on 1 January, wasn't adopted in England until 1752. I have silently adjusted all dates from the Julian (old style) to the Gregorian calendar to avoid confusion. • 5. *HR* II, p. 522. • 6. In February 1660, when the *Anne* arrived, a local Tamil ruler governed the area. • 7. Knox says they were on shore 'some twenty days', but they arrived in February and weren't taken captive until April so it was actually about two months. • 8. Ferguson, p. 7. • 9. This Dissava was Tennekoon who Knox later learned was 'much beloved' by the people, a fact which aroused the King's jealousy. In 1676, Tennekoon, aware of the danger he was in from the King, fled to the Dutch who were always happy to welcome renegades from Raja Sinha who could help them with their insider's knowledge. • 10. Though Knox doesn't mention it, when they went ashore they may have taken the 'black boy' servant they had brought with them from Porto Novo who spoke Tamil and Portuguese as well as English to serve as their interpreter. By the time Knox escaped in 1679, he had learned enough Portuguese to communicate with the Dutch Governor Ryklof van Goens in Colombo. • 11. In 1893, a British colonial servant in Ceylon had a memorial stone erected in front of the tamarind tree or 'White Man's Tree' as it was known, where Captain Knox and his men were taken captive. When the tree showed signs of decay in the 1960s, the Sri Lankan government archivist had it sprayed with insecticide and then propped up with brick columns. But in 1970 a cyclone hit Trincomalee and brought the tree down. The memorial stone was then taken to the National Museum in Colombo. In 1995, a new tamarind tree was planted in Trincomalee in the same spot where the original one had stood. The stone tablet was returned and

installed again in front of this new 'White Man's Tree' where it can still be seen today. • **12**. *HR* II, p. 324. • **13**. Knox's November 1679 statement to Dutch in Colombo. *HR* I, p. 321. • **14**. *HR* II, p. 33. • **15**. Ibid., p. 330. • **16**. Ibid., p. 329. • **17**. Colley, p. 47. • **18**. Griffiths, *Hostage*, chap. 12. Griffiths' observations are borne out by the recent hostage narratives of John McCarthy, Terry Waite, Brian Keenan and Alan Johnston. • **19**. *HR* II, pp. 332–3. • **20**. Ibid. • **21**. Ibid., p. 335. • **22**. Ibid., pp. 336–8. • **23**. Ibid., pp. 339–30. • **24**. Ibid., p. 316. • **25**. Ibid., p. 342. • **26**. Ibid., p. 341. • **27**. Ibid. • **28**. Ibid., p. 343. • **29**. Ibid., pp. 342–5. • **30**. Ibid., p. 351. • **31**. Ibid. • **32**. In Part IV of *HR*, Knox says they were summoned to Kandy in 1664, but in his chapter on the 1664 rebellion in Part II, he says the English captives were brought to the King's court at Nilambe, a town thirteen miles south-east of Kandy. The King had moved from Kandy to Nilambe after civil unrest in 1658. Nilambe was less accessible, because it was encircled even more than Kandy was by mountains and thick forest. There was also a legend that a hare chased a dog in Nilambe which the King took as a good omen for his security there. • **33**. Hendrick Draeck was sent to the King's court in May 1663 to negotiate with the King on behalf of the Dutch on several matters, including the release of the English captives. But the King took Draeck himself captive and refused to allow him to return to Dutch headquarters at Colombo. Instead, Draeck was detained at Diyatilaka where he befriended Knox and the other captives. Draeck died there seven years later in 1670. *HR* II, p. 458, n. 1. • **34**. Ibid., pp 365–6. • **35**. Ibid. • **36**. Bartholomew Bergoncius, the Portuguese priest, was in fact an Italian Jesuit born around 1583. He fell into the hands of the Kandyans around 1651 on his way to assume the post as head of a college in Colombo. He eventually died while still being held in about 1671, aged nearly ninety. • **37**. Knox was aware of Edward Winter's letter to the King and also of the Dutch envoy Draeck's efforts on their behalf. He also told the Dutch authorities many years later that he had received a letter from Madras in 1664 dated 1661 that had somehow been smuggled to him. The narrow roads of the impenetrable forest in the kingdom all had regular watch posts at strategic points with guards who searched every traveller and messenger and seized any goods or letters. Sending clandestine communications was a capital offence and few messengers were willing to risk carrying letters or messages, even if the reward was high. A man from the *Persia Merchant* named William Vassall, however, both sent and received letters from company officials. • **38**. William Foster,

English Factories in India: 1661–64, p. 45. • **39**. Ferguson, p. 13. • **40**. *HR* II, p. 371.

Chapter Four: *Shipwrecked by Land*

1. 'Timothy Cruso', *Dictionary of National Biography*. • **2**. *Review*, vol. 6, p. 341. • **3**. Healey, *Letters*, p. 96, p. 17. • **4**. Biographers are divided on the issue of whether or not Defoe was actually at the Battle of Sedgemoor, but there is no doubt that he was involved in Monmouth's rebellion because his name was later on the list of rebels who were granted a general pardon. For a discussion of Defoe's involvement in the rebellion, see Tom Paulin's *Crusoe's Secret*. • **5**. Frank Bastian, among others, postulates numerous voyages for Defoe, but the bulk of the evidence comes from Defoe's works, including the novels. Defoe mentions numerous foreign places that he has visited in works such as his *Tour thro' the Whole Island of Great Britain*, *The Compleat English Tradesman* and the *Review*. But other than his own word for it, there is no evidence that Defoe travelled abroad. • **6**. *The Compleat English Gentleman*, p. 225. • **7**. George Aitken, 'Defoe's Library', *The Athenaeum*, pp. 706–7. • **8**. James Sutherland, 'Some Early Troubles of Daniel Defoe', *Review of English Studies*, pp. 275–90. Sutherland summarises his findings in his biography *Defoe*, pp. 35–45. • **9**. Sutherland, 'Some Early Troubles', p. 276. • **10**. Ibid., pp. 277–80. • **11**. Ibid., pp. 286–8; Bastian, pp. 144–5; Backscheider, pp. 52, 59. • **12**. Sutherland, 'Some Early Troubles', pp. 281–2, Backscheider, p. 59; Novak, *Defoe: Master of Fictions*, p. 101. Both Bastian and Novak claim Marsh was a friend of Defoe's. • **13**. *Review*, vol. 3, p. 85. • **14**. *Robinson Crusoe*, p. 29. • **15**. Defoe's civet-cat venture is documented at length in Newton, 'The Civet-Cats of Newington Green: New Light on Defoe', *Review of English Studies*, pp. 10–19. • **16**. Ibid., p. 13. • **17**. Ibid., p. 12. • **18**. 'William Phipps', *Dictionary of National Biography*. • **19**. *WDD*, vol. 8, *Social Reform, An Essay Upon Projects*, p. 38. • **20**. Arthur J. Bachrach, 'The History of the Diving Bell', *Historical Diving Times*, 21 (Spring 1998). • **21**. Sutherland, 'Some Early Troubles', p. 284. • **22**. *An Essay Upon Projects*, p. 37. • **23**. *Review*, 23 March 1706. • **24**. Healey, *Letters*, p. 115. Furbank and Owens have questioned this huge amount of Defoe's indebtedness because the only evidence for the amount of £17,000 is Defoe's own account of his bankruptcy in a 1706 letter to John Fransham. Furbank and Owens, 'Defoe's £17,000

Bankruptcy', *Notes and Queries*, September 2002, pp. 363–4. • **25**. Nor did he flee to Bristol, where some of Defoe's early biographers claimed he became known as the 'Sunday gentleman', because he was seen only on the Sabbath, the one day of the week when arrests could not be made. Wilson, I, p. 221; Wright, pp. 38–9; Dottin, p. 59. • **26**. PRO PRIS 1/1A, p. 533; Backscheider, p. 58. Backscheider gives an English translation of the original Latin entry in the commitment book which was discovered by Pat Rogers as described in his 1971 article, 'Defoe in Fleet Prison', *Review of English Studies*, 22 (1971), pp. 451–5. See also Bastian, pp. 173–4. • **27**. Rogers, 'Defoe in Fleet Prison', p. 453; Backscheider, pp. 58–9. • **28**. Strype's edition of Stowe's *Survey of London*, online. • **29**. 'William Wycherley', *Dictionary of National Biography*. • **30**. Pitt, *The Cry of the Oppressed*. • **31**. 'Geffray Mynshul', *Dictionary of National Biography*. • **32**. Geffray Mynshul, *Essays and Characters of a Prison and Prisoners*, pp. 52, 14. • **33**. Ibid., pp 12–13. • **34**. Ibid., p 76. • **35**. It was Leslie Stephen who first pointed this out: 'Defoe tells us very emphatically that in Robinson Crusoe he saw a kind of allegory of his own fate. He had suffered from solitude of soul. Confinement in his prison is represented in the book by confinement in an island . . . Defoe really describes a man in prison, not in solitary confinement.' *Hours in a Library*, p. 37. • **36**. *The Compleat English Tradesman*, p. 31. • **37**. Sutherland, *Defoe*, p 22. • **38**. Mynshul, p. 83. • **39**. Formal discharge of bankrupts only became possible when 'An Act to Prevent Frauds Frequently Committed by Bankrupts' was passed in 1705. Before this, bankrupts could sometimes get released from prison if their creditors agreed to some sort of financial compromise or composition whereby the bankrupt paid off part of his debt, agreed to a plan of instalment payments or some other form of compensation. • **40**. In *The Complete English Tradesman*, Defoe proposes fifteen shillings in the pound as a fair composition settlement, p. 148. Novak says all but four of Defoe's creditors agreed to 15s to the pound, p. 97. Sutherland says that Defoe agreed to 'twenty shillings in the pound', p. 44. The fullest discussion of Defoe's bankruptcy is in Michael Quilter, 'Daniel Defoe: Bankrupt and Bankruptcy Reformer', *The Journal of Legal History*, vol. 25, no. 1, April 2004, pp. 53–73. • **41**. Healey, *Letters*, p. 115. • **42**. Backscheider, p. 61. • **43**. *The Compleat English Tradesman*, p. 81. • **44**. He later claimed that the factory employed a hundred poor families and made an annual profit of £600. Among other contracts, he secured one to supply bricks for the Greenwich Hospital, designed by Christopher Wren. • **45**. Backscheider,

p. 63. • **46**. Pat Rogers, 'Defoe's First Official Post', *Notes & Queries* CCXVI (August 1971), p. 303. PRO T53/13/80. • **47**. In addition to being groom-porter to the King, Thomas Neale was the grandson of Sir Thomas Neale, one of Queen Elizabeth's auditors. Dalby Thomas was a successful colonial merchant, a commissioner for the Million Act Lottery and the author of various tracts and works on colonial ventures and trade. In several years' time he would be knighted before being sent out to the Gold Coast by the Royal African Company. 'Thomas Neale', 'Dalby Thomas', *Dictionary of National Biography*. • **48**. Paulin, p. 87. • **49**. Julian Barnes, *A History of the World in 10½ Chapters*. • **50**. *An Essay Upon Projects*, p. 29. • **51**. *The Compleat English Tradesman*, pp. 59–60. • **52**. *An Essay Upon Projects*, p. 38. • **53**. Ibid., p. 59. • **54**. Ibid., p. 62. • **55**. Ibid., p. 93. • **56**. *Roxana*, p. 298. • **57**. *An Essay Upon Projects*, pp. 98–9. • **58**. Ibid., p. 102. • **59**. Ibid., pp. 102–4. • **60**. Ian Watt discusses Defoe's 'realism of presentation' in *The Rise of the Novel*. • **61**. Leslie Stephen, *Hours in a Library*, pp. 44–5. • **62**. Roxana, the courtesan heroine of Defoe's novel of the same name, is the only one of all his first-person narrator-heroes to come to a bad end. In the final paragraph of the novel, she says, 'here after some few Years of flourishing, and . . . happy circumstances, I fell into a dreadful course of calamities' (p. 379).

Chapter Five: *'Having But Little and Wanting Lesse'*

1. *HR* II, p. 372. • **2**. Ibid., p. 625. • **3**. Ibid., pp. 620–1. • **4**. Betel is still widely used and available in Sri Lanka today and throughout much of South Asia. • **5**. *Robinson Crusoe*, pp. 108–9. • **6**. The four o'clock flower was also called the afternoon flower. Specimens can be seen today at the Peradeniya Botanical Gardens, south-west of Kandy. • **7**. *HR* II, p. 76. • **8**. Ibid., p. 622. • **9**. Ibid., p. 372. • **10**. Ibid., p. 72. • **11**. Ibid., p. 373. • **12**. Ibid. • **13**. Ibid., p. 383. • **14**. In *Selkirk's Island*, Diana Souhami found this aspect of Crusoe's experience unbelievable and speculated that Alexander Selkirk on Juan Fernandez took out his sexual frustrations on the island's goats. • **15**. *HR* II, p. 169. • **16**. Ibid., p 375. • **17**. Ibid., pp. 376–85. • **18**. Ibid., p. 378. • **19**. Ibid., p. 376. • **20**. Ibid., p. 378. • **21**. This memorial stone and the one at Eladetta were both erected by J. P. Lewis, the government agent of the Central Province. Both have the initials JPL engraved on them along with the date 1908. • **22**. Vassall had been the supercargo on the *Persia Merchant* which was shipwrecked on the Maldive Islands in August 1658. Along with other members of the crew, Vassall had escaped to Ceylon in a boat where they were taken captive in September and sent to Kandy. • **23.** *HR* II, p. 361. • **24.** The Buddhist scriptures and ancient works of Pali and Sanskrit literature were written on ola leaves. Horoscopes were also written on them until well into the twentieth century. Ola leaves are durable and hold up well in the island's heat and humidity. They are still widely available today in Sri Lanka as replicas of historical texts or as souvenirs. • **25.** Ferguson, p. 19. • **26.** Pagodas were coins made wholly or partially of gold. They were originally minted by south Indian dynasties. During the colonial period both the Dutch and British issued their own pagodas. The star pagoda, issued by the East India Company at Madras, was worth about eight shillings. The Porto Novo pagoda, issued by the Dutch, was worth about 25 per cent less than the star pagoda. The pagodas sent by the Dutch to the English captives were most probably their own Porto Novo ones. • **27.** Ferguson, p. 21. • **28.** Ibid., p. 23. • **29.** Ibid., p. 16. • **30.** *HR* II, p. 378. • **31.** Ibid., pp. 379–80. • **32.** Ibid., p. 618. • **33.** Ibid., pp. 629–30. • **34.** Ibid., p. 621. • **35.** Ibid., pp. 389–90. • **36.** Ibid., p. 360. • **37.** Ibid., p. 391. • **38.** Ibid., pp. 380–1. • **39.** Ibid., pp. 588–9. • **40.** Nor was it entirely unknown in Europe where it had been used as a folk remedy for a variety of ailments since the eleventh century. In 1621, Robert Burton recommended hemp as a treatment for depression in *The Anatomy of Melancholy*. The seventeenth-century herbalist Nicholas Culpeper also advocated using it in his *Complete Herbal*. Martin Booth, *Cannabis*, p. 91. • **41.** *HR* II, p. 401. • **42.** Thomas Bowrey, *A Geographical Account of the Countries Round the Bay of Bengal, 1669–1679*, pp. 77–8. Bowrey's book was written in 1680 but it remained in manuscript until 1905 when the Hakluyt Society finally published it. • **43.** *HR* II, p. 618. • **44.** Ibid., p. 92. • **45.** Knox is probably referring to the communications from the East India Company to the King on the captives' behalf, which resulted in the summons of the captives to the King's court where they heard they were to be released. This promise was then foiled by the failed rebellion against the King. • **46.** *HR* II, pp. 670–1. • **47.** Ibid., p. 597. • **48.** Ibid., p. 395. • **49.** Ibid., p. 396. • **50.** Ibid., p. 388. • **51.** Ibid. • **52.** Ibid., p. 387. • **53.** Ibid., p. 400. • **54.** Ibid., p. 402. • **55.** Ibid., p. 403. • **56.** Ibid., pp. 404–5.

Chapter Six: *Escape*

1. *HR* II, p. 406. • 2. Ibid., p. 410. • 3. Ibid., p. 415. • 4. Ibid., p. 416, 420–1.
• 5. Ibid., pp. 416–17. • 6. Ibid., p. 418. • 7. Ibid. • 8. Ibid., p. 419. • 9. Ibid.,
pp. 190, 420. • 10. Ibid., p. 426. • 11. Ibid., pp. 429–30. • 12. Ibid., pp. 430–31.
• 13. Ibid., p. 431. • 14. Ibid., p. 463. • 15. Ibid. • 16. Ibid., pp. 432–3. • 17.
Ibid., p. 434. • 18. Among the narrow, crowded streets of the fort area, on
Prince Street, there is a Dutch Period Museum which occupies the Dutch
town hall built in 1780, a hundred years after Knox was in Colombo. The
museum, however, has artefacts from Knox's day, including old coins,
crockery and some dusty European furniture. Several waxworks of Dutch
colonials – looking rather the worse for wear – are dressed in velvet and
lace clothing and there is also a portrait of Gerard Hulft, the commander
of the Dutch forces when they besieged Colombo in 1656. Hulft was killed
during the siege. St Peter's Church, next to the Grand Hotel (built in 1885
by the British), was formerly a Dutch governor's residence though not the
one Knox saw because it was built in 1680, the year after Knox was in
Colombo. • 19. There is a good description and a ground plan of the Dutch
fort in R. L. Brohier, *Changing Face of Colombo*, 1984, pp. 25–41. • 20.
HR II, p. 435. • 21. Ibid., p. 436. • 22. Ibid., pp. 436–7. • 23. Ibid., p. 435.
• 24. Ibid., p. 617. • 25. Ibid., p. 440. • 26. Keay, p. 29. The description of
seventeenth-century Bantam that follows is also drawn from Keay's *The
Honourable Company*. • 27. *HR* II, p. 442. • 28. Knox's indefatigable early
biographer Donald Ferguson was unable to find any mention of Knox and
Rutland's arrival or stay in Bantam in the East India Company correspondence from Bantam or Madras at this time (Ferguson, p. 26). I have
failed to discover any references to their brief stay in Batavia in the current
East India Company records held at the British Library. • 29. *HR* II,
p. 442. • 30. Ibid., p. 515.

Chapter Seven: *Another Escape*

1. Ned Ward, quoted in Wright. p. 85. • 2. Eyre Crowe's painting of Defoe
in the pillory was exhibited at the Royal Academy in 1862. Its current
home is the Salford Museum and Art Gallery where it can be seen in the
Victorian Gallery. • 3. City of London Record Office SF 472; quoted in
Backscheider, p. 104. • 4. *An Enquiry into the Practice of Occasional*

Conformity; in Cases of Preferment (1698). • **5**. Pat Rogers, 'Defoe in Fleet Prison', *Review of English Studies*, 22 (1971), pp. 452, 454. • **6**. Ibid. • **7**. Tutchin had also been apprehended in the wake of the Monmouth rebellion and endured severe punishment. He was imprisoned, fined one hundred marks and ordered to be whipped through all the market towns of Dorset once a year. This prompted Pope to write in *The Dunciad*: 'Earless on high, stood unabash'd Defoe / And Tutchin flagrant from the scourge below.' 'John Tutchin', *Dictionary of National Biography*. • **8**. 'Hack' derives from hackney coach or carriage, a vehicle for hire. The *Oxford English Dictionary* defines a person who is a hack as 'a literary drudge, who hires himself out to do any and every kind of literary work; hence, a poor writer, a mere scribbler'. • **9**. 'John Tutchin', *Dictionary of National Biography*. • **10**. *Observator*, 73 (30 December 1702 – 2 January 1703 [ns]). Just a month after exposing Defoe, Tutchin himself was arrested for 'seditious libel' in connection with another piece he had published in the *Observator*. In January 1704, he and the printer of the *Observator* were 'taken into the custody of the serjeant at arms'. Four years later Tutchin died in Queen's Bench Prison after being beaten up by a London crowd. 'John Tutchin', *Dictionary of National Biography*. • **11**. *London Gazette* (11–14 January 1703). • **12**. Backscheider, pp. 100–3; Novak, *Defoe: Master of Fiction*, pp. 179–80. • **13**. Kingsland was a small village centred on Kingsland High Street on the Old North Road (now the A10) in Middlesex. It is now part of London in the Borough of Hackney. • **14**. Healey, *Letters*, pp. 1–3. • **15**. Ibid., p. 3. • **16**. Ibid., p. 6. • **17**. Ibid., p. 8. • **18**. Corporation of London PRO 475, 5 June 1703. • **19**. Online Proceedings of the Old Bailey. • **20**. Healey, *Letters*, p. 8. • **21**. Moore, *Defoe in the Pillory*, p. 16. • **22**. Ibid., p. 5. • **23**. BL, Add MS 29589, fols 28–9. • **24**. Backscheider, p. 116. • **25**. Adam Smith, *Theory of Moral Sentiments*, I, p. 138. • **26**. BL Add. MS 29589, fol. 46. • **27**. Finch, Letter Book, fol. 318. • **28**. In addition to *A Hymn to the Pillory*, Defoe also wrote other, less ingenious defences of *The Shortest Way with Dissenters*, including *A Brief Explanation of a Late Pamphlet, entituled* [sic] *The Shortest Way with Dissenters* and *A Dialogue Between a Dissenter and the Observator, Concerning the Shortest Way*. Both of these pamphlets were published in January 1703. In the *Dialogue between a Dissenter and the Observator* – ostensibly written by John Tutchin – the real author, Defoe, gets back at Tutchin for revealing his authorship of *The Shortest Way* in the *Observator*. • **29**. Byrne, *Prisons and Punishments of London*, p. 28; Halliday, *Newgate: London's Prototype of Hell*, p. 30.

• **30**. Halliday, p. 32. • **31**. Moore, *The Thieves' Opera*, p. 202; Halliday, pp. 32–3. • **32**. Moore, pp. 202–3; Halliday, p. 34. • **33**. *Moll Flanders*, p. 215. • **34**. Ibid., pp. 216, 218–19. • **35**. Pressing, however, continued in other parts of England. It was last used at the Cambridge Assizes in 1741. • **36**. Halliday, p. 62. • **37**. Ibid. • **38**. Soon this sort of instant criminal biography was given the generic name 'Newgate Calendar' and various compilations, collections and editions of *The Newgate Calendar* became best-sellers. Not all or even most of these works, however, were taken from the original *Ordinary's Accounts*. Rival, 'unauthorised' 'sermons', 'confessions' and 'lives' of famous criminals competed with the Newgate chaplain's pamphlets. The form was also adapted and exploited by Defoe in *Moll Flanders* and by other writers in their fictional or semi-fictional criminal biographies. • **39**. Lorrain wasn't always successful in bringing those he accompanied to their deaths to repentance. In 1701, when the legendary pirate Captain William Kidd was hanged at Execution Dock (where pirates met their ends rather than at Tyburn), Kidd was 'inflamed with drink . . . [and] so discomposed [in] his mind, that he was now in a very ill frame and very [resistant] to the great work [of repentance] now or never to be performe'd on him'. *Ordinary of Newgate, His Account of the Behaviour, and Dying Words of Captain William Kidd, and Other Pirates that Were Executed at the Execution Dock in Wapping, on Friday May 23, 1701.* • **40**. Online *Proceedings of the Old Bailey*. • **41**. *Moll Flanders*, p. 218. • **42**. Ibid., p. 226. • **43**. Ibid., p. 230. • **44**. *Ordinary of Newgate Accounts* online. • **45**. A number of Defoe biographers and bibliographers, including Lee, Trent, Moore and Novak, have argued that Defoe wrote lives of Sheppard and Wild. Richard Holmes had recently edited an edition of them under the title *Defoe on Sheppard and Wild* in a 'classic biographies' series. Furbank and Owens, however, argue that the Sheppard and Wild lives were probably not the work of Defoe. See their *Defoe De-Attributions* pp. 136–7 and 138–9. • **46**. Furbank and Owens, *A Political Biography of Daniel Defoe*, p. 19. • **47**. Healey, *Letters*, pp. 5–6. • **48**. Quoted in J. A. Downie, *Robert Harley and the Press*, p. 60. • **49**. Ibid., p. 62. • **50**. Ibid., p. 63. • **51**. *An Appeal to Honour and Justice*, in Furbank and Owens, *A Political Biography of Daniel Defoe*, pp. 205–6. • **52**. Healey, *Letters of Daniel Defoe*, pp. 10–11. • **53**. Ibid., pp. 16–17. • **54**. *The Storm*, p. 26. • **55**. Ibid., pp. 30–1. • **56**. Ibid., p. 57. • **57**. Ibid., p. 53. • **58**. Ibid., p. 3. • **59**. *London Gazette*, 2–6 December 1703; *Daily Courant*, 2 December 1703. • **60**. *The Storm*, pp. 137–8. • **61**. Ibid., p. 61. • **62**. Ibid., p. 60. • **63**. Ibid.,

p. 59. • **64.** Ibid., p. 91. • **65.** Ibid., pp. 134–6. • **66.** G. M. Trevelyan, *England Under Queen Anne: Blenheim*, pp. 308–10. • **67.** Ibid., pp 310–11; *The Diary of John Evelyn*, vol. 2, p. 373. • **68.** *HR* II, p. 607. • **69.** *The Storm*, pp. 108–9. • **70.** *WDD*, *The Layman's Sermon Upon the Late Storm*, pp. 189, 199. • **71.** *WDD*, *The Storm: An Essay*, p. 290. • **72.** *The Storm*, p. 3. • **73.** *A Journal of the Plague Year*, p. 193.

Chapter Eight: *Stranger, Author, Captain*

1. *HR* II, p. 527. • **2.** Quoted in Roy Porter, *London: A Social History*, p. 117. • **3.** Edward Chamberlayne, *Notatia or the Present State of England*, 1668, quoted in Jack Lindsay, *The Monster City: Defoe's London*, p. 7. • **4.** Quoted in Porter, p. 120. • **5.** Ibid., pp. 120–1. • **6.** *HR* II, p. 527. • **7.** Ibid., p. 528. • **8.** Ibid., pp. 521, 528. • **9.** RK to JS, 16 May 1687, CUL. • **10.** *HR* II, p. 517. • **11.** Ibid., p. 338. • **12.** Ferguson, pp. 10–11. • **13.** The Old East India House (as it became known after it was replaced) was originally the residence of Sir William Craven, Lord Mayor of London in the early seventeenth century. It was rebuilt in 1726 and then replaced by a much larger building in 1800, the 'New East India House' on Leadenhall Street. This building was pulled down in 1862 to make way for the offices of Lloyd's of London. • **14.** EIC papers, Court Book, 15 September 1680, BL. • **15.** Ferguson, p. 26. • **16.** *HR* II, p. 528. • **17.** Earle, *Sailors: English Merchant Seamen 1650–1775*, pp. 57, 36. • **18.** He also declined another post offered to him several months later. On 19 January, a Court Book entry recorded that he was named '4th Mate of yet *Scipio Africanus*' and directed 'to stay at Bantam on ye arrival of ye said Ship there, & to be employed there'. Ferguson, pp. 26–27. • **19.** *HR* II, p. 530. • **20.** 'Josiah Child', *Dictionary of National Biography*. • **21.** *HR* II, p. 530. • **22.** Ibid. • **23.** Ibid. • **24.** Ibid., p. 517. • **25** Ibid., p. 516. • **26.** According to one of Hooke's recent biographers, it was as a schoolboy in his teens, that Hooke first developed curvature of the spine: most likely a condition that was identified in 1921 'as Scheuremann's kyphosis, a severe and inflexible stooping of the thoracic (central) spine . . . brought about by the development of wedge-shaped spaces between the vertebrae'. Inwood, p. 52. • **27.** Ibid., p. 21. • **28.** There is a brief history of the Royal Society on its website. See also Thomas Birch, *The History of the Royal Society* (1757), and John Gribbin, *The Fellowship: The Story of a Revolution* (2005). • **29.** Christopher Wren collaborated with Hooke on designing the monument. • **30**. Members of the Royal Society also planned to conduct various experiments in the monument, but traffic vibrations interfered with these and they were abandoned. The monument unfortunately proved an excellent venue for suicides. A baker who threw himself off in 1788 was the first of these. In 1842, after a servant girl jumped to her death, the gallery at the top of the monument was enclosed in an iron cage. • **31**. The first London coffee house was opened by Pasqua Rosee in 1652, but they didn't really catch on until after the Restoration. Charles II tried unsuccessfully to ban coffee houses because he believed they fomented sedition. But even the King and his proclamations couldn't stamp out the huge popularity of these establishments. By the time Knox returned to England in 1680, there were dozens of coffee houses all over the city. For a history of coffee houses, see Markman Ellis, *The Coffee House: A Cultural History* (2004). • **32**. Hooke's first diary record of a coffee-house meeting with Knox was on Thursday 6 January 1681, but they probably met well before this. • **33**. Gribbin, p. 192. • **34**. *The Diary of Robert Hooke*, pp. 306, 406. • **35**. Ibid., p. 454. • **36**. See Lisa Jardine's discussion of the bond between Hooke and Knox in her biography of Hooke, p. 283. • **37**. John Aubrey claimed that Hooke's father also took his own life by 'suspending himself'. Lisa Jardine more cautiously suggests that he may have been a suicide. Jardine, p. 52. • **38**. Inwood, pp. 150–51. • **39**. Hooke's unpublished diary entries, Henderson, p. 144. • **40**. James Bonnell was the only son of Knox's uncle, Samuel Bonnell, while John Strype was the son of Knox's aunt, Hester Bonnell Strype. A deeply pious, Cambridge-educated young man, Bonnell for some reason failed in his attempt to gain an ecclesiastical appointment from the Crown. When Knox returned to England in 1680, Bonnell held the post of tutor to Ralph Freman, son of a Hertfordshire gentleman. He was later appointed Comptroller and Accountant-General of Ireland where he married his wife Jane. Bonnell suffered from chronic poor health and died in 1699. After Knox's retirement in 1701, Jane Bonnell tried unsuccessfully to make Knox her new husband. • **41**. Thomas Birch, *A History of the Royal Society of London*, vol. 4, p. 64. • **42**. Inwood, pp. 86, 290. • **43**. Knox had left school to go to sea at the age of fourteen, but both Strype and Bonnell were university-educated, like Hooke. • **44**. *HR*, II, pp. xxxvii–viii. • **45**. Ibid., p. 1. • **46**. Jayawickrama, *Writing that Conquers*, pp. v, 2. • **47**. Edmund Leach discusses this and Knox's possible motive for his negative portrayal of monarchy in 'What Happened to an Historical

Relation ... on the Way to the Printers', *Identity, Consciousness and the Past: The South Asian Scene*, 1989, pp. 18–21. Patrick Peebles has also explored Knox's portrayal of the King in his unpublished paper 'The Royal Absolutism of Raja Sinha II and Robert Knox'. • 48. Ferguson, p. 26. • 49. I couldn't find any reference to James Knox's death in the correspondence between Knox and John Strype. • 50. Hooke's unpublished diary entries, Henderson, p. 148. • 51. Anna Winterbottom, 'Producing and Using the *Historical Relation of Ceylon*: Robert Knox, the East India Company and the Royal Society', p. 522. Knox's map duplicates the coastal regions found on Baldaeus' map and he even uses Baldaeus' cartouche. The interior of Ceylon, however, is much more detailed in Knox's map and he shows many more places and features, justifying Knox's claim in the first paragraph of his book that he has 'procured a new one [map] to be drawn' because the Dutch maps of the island are 'very faulty'. *HR* II, p. 1. • 52. Royal Society Archives, Record Book, RBO/1/33. • 53. Ferguson, p. 27. • 54. *HR* II, p. 530. • 55. Ferguson, pp. 27–8. • 56. Hooke's unpublished diary entries, Henderson, p. 148. • 57. *HR* II, pp. xxxii–iii. • 58. Ibid., pp. xxiii–iv. • 59. Ibid., p xix. • 60. Ibid. • 61. Ferguson, p. 28. • 62. Hooke's unpublished diary entries, Henderson, p. 150. • 63. Ferguson, p. 28. • 64. *HR* I, pp. 380–1. • 65. RK to JS, 5 October 1713, CUL.

Chapter Nine: *Captain Knox Recaptivated*

1. RK to JS 13 June 1682, CUL. In his autobiography, Knox devoted only two pages to his first voyage as Captain of the *Tonqueen Merchant*. But this brief sketch is filled out in his letters to his cousin John Strype and also in a fragment of a journal that he kept during this voyage in which he recorded his observations of several of the places he visited. This manuscript fragment is part of a much longer journal which was later lost. The journal probably covered Knox's whole 1681–3 voyage for it is headed 'The Journal of a Voyage to the Kingdom of Tonqueen bordering upon China in the East Indies. By Cap. Robert Knox'. The passages quoted in this chapter are all taken from this four-page journal manuscript in the John Strype Miscellaneous Collections at the British Library. • 2. BL, MSS Lansdowne 1197. • 3. Ibid. • 4. RK to JS 13 June 1682, CUL. • 5. Ibid. • 6. Ibid. • 7. *HR* II, p. 532. • 8. Ibid. • 9. Ibid. • 10. Ferguson, p. 30. • 11. *HR* II, p. 532. • 12. Ferguson, p. 30. • 13. Ibid., pp. 30–1. • 14. Ibid., p. 31.

• **15**. Ibid. • **16**. Unfortunately, none of Knox's artefacts seem to have survived, despite the society's intention to preserve them. • **17**. Ferguson, pp. 31–2. • **18**. *HR* II, pp. 532–3. • **19**. Ferguson, p. 33. • **20**. Ibid., pp. 34–5. • **21**. *HR*, II, p. 534. • **22**. Solofo Randrianja and Stephen Ellis, *Madagascar: A Short History*, pp. 77–80. • **23**. *HR* II, p. 536. • **24**. Ibid., p. 538. • **25**. Ibid., p. 539. • **26**. Ibid., pp. 539–40. • **27**. Ibid., p. 540. • **28**. Ibid., p. 542. • **29**. Ibid., pp. 543–4. • **30**. Ibid., p. 544. • **31**. Ibid. • **32**. Ibid., p. 546. • **33**. Ibid., p. 549. • **34**. Ibid., p. 552. • **35**. Ibid. • **36**. Ibid.

Chapter Ten: *St Helena*

1. Anna Winterbottom, 'Seventeenth Century Records in the St Helena Archives, Appendix 1: East India Company Consultations'. Knox was finally picked up on St Helena by the East Indiaman *Caesar* on its homeward voyage that began in late 1683 and ended with its arrival back in London on 1 January 1686. If the *Caesar* sailed home via the West Indies it probably left St Helena, with Knox on board, sometime in the late summer or autumn of 1685. • **2**. Stephen Royle, *The Company's Island: St Helena, Company Colonies and the Colonial Endeavour*, p. 86. • **3**. Winterbottom, p. 29. • **4**. Thomas H. Brooke, *A History of the Island of St Helena*, chap. 3. • **5**. Philip Gosse, *St Helena*, pp. 76–7. • **6**. Winterbottom, p. 29. • **7**. Royle, pp. 21–3. • **8**. Brooke, chap. 2. • **9**. Royle, pp. 113–14. • **10**. Ibid., pp. 116–17. • **11**. Gosse, p. 89. • **12**. Brooke, chap. 3. • **13**. Ibid. • **14**. Gosse, p. 4. • **15**. Ibid., p. 7. • **16**. Ibid., p. 10. • **17**. Ibid., p. 23. • **18**. Hakluyt, *Voyages and Discoveries*, p. 366. • **19**. *WDD, Robinson Crusoe*, ed. W. R. Owens, pp. 91, 299. • **20**. *The Bradt Travel Guide to St Helena, Ascension, Tristan da Cunha*, p. 11. • **21**. Julia Blackburn has captured beautifully the melancholy history of St Helena in her account of Napoleon's exile there, *The Emperor's Last Island: A Journey to St Helena*. • **22**. William Dampier, *A New Voyage Round the World*, p. 270. • **23**. Royle, *The Company's Island*, pp. 85–8. • **24**. In 2008, British archaeologists uncovered 'the largest slave graveyard in the world' on St Helena when they found the bones of some 10,000 Africans buried on the island. These were the remains of liberated slaves who died on St Helena of disease or malnutrition. All the graves were found in an area where an airport road was to be built. In the words of the lead archaeologist of the dig, Dr Andrew Pearson, this vast slave graveyard brought 'a voice to a forgotten people who died in limbo, in a place physically and conceptually between freedom and slavery'. *The Times*, 10 December 2009. • **25.** The *Caesar* was a 530-tonne frigate with a crew of about a hundred men and up to forty guns. Between 1672 and 1686, it made seven voyages in all. The first three of these were under Captain Thomas Andrews and the next two under Captain Jonathan Andrews, who may have been Thomas Andrews's son. On its seventh and last voyage it was under the command of Captain Edmund Wright. On this voyage, the *Caesar* was attacked and taken by French pirates off Santiago in the Cape Verde Islands. This information comes from documents held in the British Library, Asia, Pacific and Africa Collections. • **26.** *HR* II, p. 552. It is unlikely that Knox only had the 'clothes on his back', as he says when he was picked up on St Helena. (Knox, indeed, several times describes himself in his book as being reduced to the clothes on his back, even when this wasn't strictly true.) He must have had some more clothes made when he was stuck on St Helena, but he still would have greatly appreciated the proper English-made clothes that Captain Andrews gave to him. • **27.** Ibid., p. 553. • **28.** Ibid., p. 556. • **29.** Ibid., pp. 558–9.

Chapter Eleven: *Captain Knox and Captain Singleton*

1. Defoe scholars and biographers disagree over whether Defoe was the author of *The King of the Pirates*, a biography of the legendary Captain John Avery published in 1719, and *A General History of the Pyrates*, a compendium of pirate biographies (1724) that remains the classic account of the 'golden age of piracy' in the seventeenth and early eighteenth centuries. • **2.** *HR* II, p. 559. • **3.** Ibid., p. 560. • **4.** These records are held at the British Library. Ferguson transcribed the most relevant ones in his *Captain Robert Knox: Contributions towards a Biography.* The information which follows recounting Knox's privateering voyage is taken from Ferguson's transcriptions of the East India Company records, pp. 37–41. • **5.** *HR* II, p. 561. • **6.** Ferguson, p. 40. • **7.** Ibid., p. 41. • **8.** R. T. Gunther, *Early Science in Oxford: The Life and Work of Robert Hooke*, vol. 10, p. 360. • **9.** Robert Hooke, *Philosophical Experiments and Observations* (ed. W. Derham), pp. 210–12. Knox's and Hooke's writings on cannabis are the earliest published in English. Another seventeenth-century seaman named Thomas Bowrey also wrote about cannabis in the 1670s but his work wasn't published until the early twentieth century. • **10.** *HR* II, pp. 564–5. • **11.** RK to JS, 22 April 1698, CUL. • **12.** Ibid. • **13.** Ibid. • **14.** *HR* II, pp. 596–7. • **15.** Ibid., p. 601. • **16.** Ibid., p. 603. • **17.** Secord, *Studies in the Narrative Method of Defoe*, p. 127. • **18.** In *The Explorer in English Fiction*, Peter Knox-Shaw devotes a chapter to *Captain Singleton* in which he argues that the wild white man in Africa was based on a real African trader named John Freeman who was taken captive and held in central Africa for many years. Defoe may very well have known about Freeman but he clearly modelled his Englishman-gone-native in Africa on Robert Knox as well. • **19.** *WDD, Captain Singleton*, pp. 135–41. • **20.** Ibid., p. 184. • **21.** Ibid., p. 195. • **22.** Ibid., p. 209. • **23.** Defoe's novel *Roxana* is a striking exception to his standard plot resolution.

Chapter Twelve: *Ancient Mariners*

1. *HR* II, p. 604. • **2.** Richard Waller, in *The Posthumous Works of Robert Hooke*, p. 63. • **3.** Jardine, p. 305. • **4.** *HR* II, p. 604. • **5.** Hooke drafted a will five days before his death in which he left blanks for the names of four friends – one of whom was rumoured to be Robert Knox – who were to inherit his wealth. But Hooke never filled in the names or signed the will and so he died intestate and his entire estate went to a distant relative on the Isle of Wight. Jardine, p. 316; Inwood, p. 438. • **6.** *HR* II, p. 604. • **7.** Jardine, pp. 306–7. • **8.** Hooke's biographer Lisa Jardine states that in his deteriorated state at the end of his life, 'it was no longer appropriate [for Hooke] to send for his gentleman friends, like [Christopher] Wren and [John] Hoskins. A sea-captain,' Jardine argues, 'was less likely to raise an eyebrow at the state of Hooke's living arrangements.' But it's equally likely that instead of worrying about the sorry spectacle he presented, Hooke simply wanted his old friend Knox by his side. • **9.** Jane Bonnell to John Strype, 12 May 1700, CUL. • **10.** Jane Bonnell to John Strype, 15 December 1700, CUL. • **11.** Jane Bonnell to John Strype, 15 January 1701, CUL. • **12.** *HR* II, pp. 63–4. • **13.** Jane Bonnell to John Strype, 31 May 1702, CUL. • **14.** Jane Bonnell to John Strype, 3 October 1702, CUL. • **15.** Jane Bonnell to John Strype, 15 February 1703, CUL. • **16.** Ferguson, p. 51. • **17.** Ibid., p. 53. • **18.** *HR* II, p. 607. • **19.** Ibid., pp. 608–9. • **20.** Ibid., p. 609. • **21.** Robert Knox to John Strype, 5 October 1713, CUL. • **22.** Ibid. • **23.** *HR* I, p. 430. • **24.** Ibid., pp. 430–1. Knox signed his will on 30 November 1711. He reviewed and confirmed it twice after this:

on 13 March 1717 when he was seventy-seven and again on 4 April 1720 two months before his death. • **25.** *HR* II, p. 648. • **26.** Ibid., p. 657. • **27.** Ibid., pp. 657–9. • **28.** Ibid., p. 607. • **29.** Robert Knox to John Strype, 18 April 1720, CUL. • **30.** Edward Said, *On Late Style*, pp. xi, 7. • **31.** Backscheider, p. 470. • **32.** Defoe writes of his personal difficulties and periods of despair in his letters (Healey, *Collected Letters of Daniel Defoe*) and also in his autobiographical account, *An Appeal to Honour and Justice*. • **33.** *WDD*, *Serious Reflections of Robinson Crusoe*, pp. 51–3. • **34.** Ibid., p. 52. • **35.** A number of Defoe's biographers have interpreted *Robinson Crusoe* as an allegory of Defoe's own life; the most sustained and intricate of these allegorical interpretations is Thomas Wright's *The Life of Daniel Defoe*, which Wright originally published in 1894 and republished in an expanded, revised edition more than thirty years later in 1931. • **36.** In *A Critical Bibliography of Daniel Defoe*, Furbank and Owens list some forty-eight works written by Defoe after the publication of *Robinson Crusoe* in 1719. In his earlier *A Checklist of the Writings of Daniel Defoe*, John Robert Moore included considerably more. Moore, however, clearly attributed many works to Defoe that Defoe did not in fact actually write. Anyone interested in the history of the Defoe canon should read Furbank and Owens's persuasive studies, *The Canonisation of Daniel Defoe* and *Defoe De-Attributions: A Critique of J. R. Moore's Checklist*. • **37.** Backscheider, p. 504. • **38.** Watt, *Myths of Modern Individualism*, p. xvi. • **39.** Owens, 'Introduction' to *Political and Economic Writing of Daniel Defoe*, vol. 8, *Social Reform*, pp. 20–1. • **40.** The five Andrew Moreton pamphlets are: *Everybody's Business is Nobody's Business* (1725), *Parochial Tyranny* (1727), *The Protestant Monastery* (1727), *Augusta Triumphans* (1728) and *Second Thoughts are Best* (1728). • **41.** *Political and Economic Writings of Daniel Defoe*, vol. 8, *Social Reform*, pp. 253, 275. • **42.** Owens, 'Introduction', p. 22. • **43.** *Political and Economic Writings of Daniel Defoe*, p. 241. • **44.** Ibid., p. 245. • **45.** Ibid., pp. 251–2. • **46.** Healey, *Letters*, p. 475. • **47.** These papers did not come to light until the 1890s when a Defoe biographer named Thomas Wright was given access to them by one of Baker's descendants in the course of his research. Wright, *The Life of Daniel Defoe*, pp. 355–74. • **48.** Wright, pp. 361–2. • **49.** George Potter, 'Henry Baker, FRS', *Modern Philology*, 29 (1931), p. 310. • **50.** Wright, p. 358. • **51.** Ibid., p. 377. • **52.** Healey, *Letters*, p. 463. • **53.** Wright, pp. 369–70. • **54.** Ibid., p. 369. • **55.** Sutherland, *Defoe*, p. 260. • **56.** Healey, *Letters*, pp. 462, 468. • **57.** The fullest account of these creditors' pursuit of Defoe is in

Backscheider, pp. 503–4, 526. • **58.** Healey, *Letters*, p. 473. • **59.** Backscheider, p. 526. • **60.** Healey, *Letters*, pp. 473–6. • **61.** Sutherland, *Defoe*, p. 273.

Epilogue

1. Chadwick, *The Life of Daniel Defoe*, p. 1. • **2.** Ibid., pp. 463–4. • **3.** Horner, *A Brief Account of the Interesting Ceremony of Unveiling the Monument Erected by the Boys and Girls of England to the Memory of Daniel Defoe*, pp. 7–8. • **4.** Ibid., pp. 6, 22. • **5.** Ibid., p. 4. • **6.** Ibid., p. 11. • **7.** *HR* I, p. 301. • **8.** *Notes and Queries*, 8 January 1898, p. 25. • **9.** Goonetileke, 'Robert Knox in the Kandyan Kingdom, 1660–1669: A Bio-bibliographical Commentary', *Sri Lankan Journal of the Humanities*, vol. 1 part 2, pp. 95–6. • **10.** Goonetileke, 'Robert Knox in the Kandyan Kingdom, 1660–1669: A Bio-bibliographical Commentary (1975; Addendum, 1998), *Sri Lankan Journal of the Humanities*, vols 24 & 25, nos 1 & 2, p. 248. • **11.** Ibid. • **12.** Ibid., pp. 247–69. Goonewardene, 'Robert Knox: The Interleaved Edition', *Journal of the Royal Asiatic Society of Sri Lanka*, pp. 117–44. • **13.** Paul Baines, *Daniel Defoe: Robinson Crusoe and Moll Flanders*, p. 132. • **14.** Pat Rogers's *Robinson Crusoe* remains the definitive account of the novel and covers its genesis, history, critical interpretation and reputation. Rogers gives due credit to Arthur Wellesley Secord's pioneering *Studies in the Narrative Method of Daniel Defoe* (1924). Six years after Secord, Walter de la Mare published *Desert Islands and Robinson Crusoe*. There is a great deal of interesting recent work on Defoe and *Robinson Crusoe*, including Martin Green's *The Robinson Crusoe Story*, Michael Seidel's *Robinson Crusoe: Island Myths and the Novel*, Paul Baines's *Daniel Defoe: Robinson Crusoe and Moll Flanders: A Reader's Guide to Essential Criticism*, and the essays in *Approaches to Teaching Defoe's Robinson Crusoe*, edited by Maxmillian E. Novak and Carl Fisher. Diana Souhami's *Selkirk's Island* and Tim Severin's *Seeking Robinson Crusoe* propose various candidates for the 'original Crusoe', and are highly engaging books in their own right. Neither of them, however, deals with Robert Knox. • **15.** Furbanks and Owens's superbly edited, 44-volume edition of the *Works of Daniel Defoe* is published by Pickering and Chatto. The individual volumes are edited by various Defoe scholars including Furbank and Owens.

Acknowledgements

Robinson Crusoe was the creation of Daniel Defoe and I have mined the work of numerous Defoe biographers, scholars and critics. I owe a special debt to those who discussed the man and his works with me: P. N. Furbank and W. R. Owens, John Richetti and Pat Rogers.

Richard Boyle's work on Robert Knox first convinced me of the vital Defoe-Knox connection and I am grateful to him for his unfailing help and exhaustive knowledge. I owe a large debt as well to Ismeth Raheem, another authority on Knox, who shared his expertise, introduced me to other Sri Lankan scholars and facilitated my own travels on the Knox trail in Sri Lanka. I am also grateful to three other people who have done extensive work on Knox: Sarojini Jayawickrama, Patrick Peebles and Anna Winterbottom.

A Society of Authors grant funded my travels and research in Sri Lanka. Numerous people helped me on the ground: above all, my translator, research assistant and driver, Wasana Perera and a variety of people we spoke to in the course of our travels, including E. D. M. Karunarathna, Prem Kumar, M. M. M. Irfan, K. P. Lalita Saman Ranasingha, and Michael and Nancy Van der Poorten.

I am grateful to the following institutions and their staffs for enabling me to consult manuscripts and books in their archives and collections: the British Library, the Christy Library of the British Museum, the Duke Humfrey's Library, Bodleian Library, Oxford University, and the Cambridge University Library.

For making the book possible, and for their critical acumen and support, many thanks to my agent David Godwin, Will Sulkin, my editor at Bodley Head and also to Kay Peddle.

Lyman Rhoades was my first reader and offered valuable insights and criticism. George Hunt provided excellent photographic images for the illustrations.

Above all, my thanks to Paul Beasley who lived the book with me and contributed in countless ways to the adventure of writing it.

Index